The Politics of Enlightenment

The Politics of Enlightenment

Republicanism, Constitutionalism, and the Rights of Man in Gaetano Filangieri

VINCENZO FERRONE

Translated by
SOPHUS A. REINERT

ANTHEM PRESS
LONDON · NEW YORK · DELHI

Anthem Press
An imprint of Wimbledon Publishing Company
www.anthempress.com

This edition first published in UK and USA 2014
by ANTHEM PRESS
75–76 Blackfriars Road, London SE1 8HA, UK
or PO Box 9779, London SW19 7ZG, UK
and
244 Madison Ave. #116, New York, NY 10016, USA

First published in hardback by Anthem Press in 2012

British Library Cataloguing-in-Publication Data
A catalogue record for this book is available from the British Library.

Library of Congress Cataloging-in-Publication Data
The Library of Congress has catalogued the hardcover edition as follows:
Ferrone, Vincenzo.
[Società giusta ed equa. English]
The politics of enlightenment : Republicanism, constitutionalism, and
the rights of man in Gaetano Filangieri / Vincenzo Ferrone ;
translated by Sophus A. Reinert.
p. cm.
Originally published in Italian as: La società giusta ed equa :
repubblicanesimo e diritti dell'uomo in Gaetano Filangieri.
Includes bibliographical references and index.
ISBN 978-0-85728-970-4 (hardback : alk. paper)
1. Filangieri, Gaetano, 1752-1788. 2.
Republicanism–Italy–History. 3. Civil rights–Italy–History. 4.
Constitutional history–Italy. 5. State, The. 6. Political
science–Italy–History–18th century. I. Reinert, Sophus A. II.
Title.
JC183.F3713 2012
321.8'6–dc23
2012015198

ISBN-13: 978 1 78308 312 1 (Pbk)
ISBN-10: 1 78308 312 3 (Pbk)

This title is also available as an ebook.

CONTENTS

Foreword

POLITICAL ECONOMY
AND THE RIGHTS OF MAN

When Johann Wolfgang von Goethe visited Naples on his Grand Tour of Italy in 1786–1788, he was above all struck by his meetings with the 'remarkable' Gaetano Filangieri, heir of the Princes of Arianello, 'one of those noble-hearted young men to whom the happiness and freedom of mankind is a goal they never lose sight of.' Baffled, he could only admit that he had 'never heard Filangieri say anything commonplace.'[1] From Goethe, this was quite a compliment. At the time, the young Neapolitan he frequented was principally lionized for his massive *Science of Legislation*, one of the most influential works of eighteenth century legal, political, and economic thought, translated into every major language in the European world and published in at least seventy different editions.[2] Luminaries like Benjamin Franklin, who upheld a lengthy epistolary with Filangieri, found the *Science of Legislation* an 'invaluable work,' wishing for more volumes of it in the wake of the 1787 Constitutional Convention, but it also had popular appeal enough to be included in circulating libraries. In 1806, the *Edinburgh Review* called Filangieri's magnum opus 'a work of philosophical excellence, which bears the traces of much learned research, and breathes, in every page, sentiments of the purest virtue, mingled with an undaunted spirit of liberty, and zeal for the improvement of mankind.' Indeed, Filangieri was a man it was 'impossible to venerate too much.'[3] Though largely neglected in contemporary Anglophone scholarship, Filangieri was in effect a titan of his age, hailed, in Franco Venturi's celebrated geography of 'The Enlightenment,' from St. Petersburg to Philadelphia.[4] What follows is the most incisive study to date of his contributions to that complex phenomenon and its legacy.

This book first appeared in 2003 under the title *La società giusta ed equa: Repubblicanesimo e diritti dell'uomo in Gaetano Filangieri*, sparking a major and fruitful debate in the country's leading journals and in academic monographs, and has recently been translated into French.[5] Its author, Vincenzo Ferrone, Professor of History at the University of Turin, ranks among the greatest Italian historians of his generation and is the author of numerous studies on the eighteenth century, among which one of the most magisterial works on the Neapolitan Enlightenment published in any language.[6] An in-depth analysis of Filangieri's seven-volume *Science of Legislation*, the first ever critical edition of which recently was published under the supervision of Ferrone himself, the present study builds on his earlier works to re-draw the map of Enlightenment republicanism, the tenuous relationship between Enlightenment, reform, and revolution, and the early history of human rights and their political economy.[7] For though the book's emphasis is on Naples, and one of its tasks is to widen our geographical understanding of the eighteenth century, it also speaks right to the core of modern historiography on several subjects. Among the major themes with which it engages are Montesquieu's polyvalent influence on the development of Enlightenment political philosophy, the intricate relationship between natural law and natural rights (later human rights), and the emergence of an idiom and a theory of constitutionalism as the only safeguard against absolutist abuses and democratic excesses (whether due to communitarian zeal or the influence of charismatic leaders). What Ferrone offers is an alternative vision of the late Enlightenment, seen from the vantage-point of Naples rather than Paris or Edinburgh, and its bequest to the modern world, as well as a fresh look at the ambiguous and ever vexing relationship between liberal individualism and republicanism at the time. The Enlightenment was a variegated phenomenon, and Ferrone's book reminds us of precisely how rich and polyglot its origins and legacies were.

In his 1969 G. M. Trevelyan Lectures at the University of Cambridge, Venturi warned that the ancient and Renaissance ideals of republicanism had been overcome in the eighteenth century.[8] Picking up on his mentor's work, Ferrone's book re-constructs a long forgotten tradition of Enlightenment constitutional republicanism, and its political economy, in eighteenth century Italy, a tradition which differentiates itself greatly from the better-known republican traditions explored by the likes of J. G. A. Pocock and Quentin Skinner by the fact that it grounds itself, not in a moralistic conception of a virtuous community derived from the experiences of Greece, Rome, or the city-states of Renaissance Italy, but in the *avant-garde* of Enlightenment 'human rights' theory developed by the heirs of the Neapolitan Antonio Genovesi, Italy's first professor of political economy. Filangieri was perhaps the theorist in this tradition who went the furthest in anchoring his political paradigm in a theory of unalienable rights explicitly argued to be shared by all human beings, no matter their creed, their politics, or the colour of their skin.[9] As such, though the origins of this 'democratic' tradition of liberal republicanism are deeply historical and contingent, its appeal was – and, as Ferrone makes clear, indeed still is – intended to be universal.

As a means of elucidating this forgotten tradition, Ferrone's wide-ranging study deeply contextualizes Filangieri's work in terms of the cultural, legal, and political histories of eighteenth-century Naples and, later, early nineteenth-century Paris. In particular, it analyzes one of the most extraordinary receptions of the American Revolution in Europe, highlighting the importance of American independence for the maturation of a Neapolitan tradition of theorizing politics on the foundations of universal human rights and a written constitution, and what they in turn entailed for the very nature of republicanism itself. But this was no monologue. Rather, Ferrone argues it was a transatlantic dialogue in which Filangieri played an inspirational part in the foundation of modern republicanism, not the least by theorizing the possibility, against the influential arguments of Montesquieu and Rousseau, of truly continental political communities. His republicanism was not for the elites of small cities, but for the citizens of vast nations.[10] Ironically, given Filangieri's extraordinary insights into the modern political condition, Naples was also, to a far greater extent than other centres of the European Enlightenment, still thrall to the institutional cluster known as 'Feudalism,' and Ferrone lucidly explains Filangieri's influential polemic with Montesquieu against the background of this particular organizational heritage. Building on the seminal work of Margaret C. Jacob and others, he weaves this account into the rich tapestry of Neapolitan Freemasonry and the means by which new patterns of sociability functioned as a school of political theory and practice. Eminently well read, Filangieri drew on a wide array of canonical sources – Machiavelli, Locke, Grotius, and Pufendorf – but also on an extraordinary local tradition of political and economic thought developed by followers of Giambattista Vico and Genovesi, which allowed him to formalize a transition from doctrines of natural law to a prescriptive analytical framework of human rights, theorizing a form of liberty based on individualism and the 'right to happiness' within an overarching scheme of modern republicanism.[11]

The second part of the book deals with Filangieri's legacy, engaging both with his immediate heirs, like Francesco Mario Pagano, drafter of the short-lived Neapolitan constitution of 1799, and his detractors, like the conservative Vincenzo Cuoco, unveiling a world of themes and authors rarely mentioned in Anglophone scholarship. The book ends with significant chapters on Filangieri's reception in France and in Europe at large up to the time of the 1848 Revolutions, focusing on Benjamin Constant's little understood critique of Filangieri and the tensions between the constitutional republicanism of the late Italian Enlightenment on the one hand and the nascent tradition of liberalism on the other. In doing so, this book not only explains the common roots of these two traditions, but also why they diverged and with what consequences for Italian and European history. This is one of the book's most intriguing aspects, shedding important light on a debate which generally is examined only from the perspective of its ostensible victor, Constant, whose wilful misrepresentation of the *Science of Legislation* was consequential for the development of economic, political, and legal thought in Europe, not to mention for our understanding of Filangieri himself. This brings Ferrone to a lengthy discussion of the tensions between liberalism and poverty, particularly as manifest in the debate over the 'right to work,' as well as between patriotism and cosmopolitanism in the Italian republican tradition, themes all too relevant in today's historiographical landscape. The book ends with an assessment of Filangieri's eventual contribution to these debates and to the institutionalization of the rights of man as a political category and an exigency of political economy in Enlightenment Europe.

I have strived to convey Ferrone's unique voice in translation, and he has personally approved all deviations from the original text. As anyone who knows him might have guessed, he has been an extraordinary presence in the process of translating his book, always eager to discuss the minutest points. I am grateful to Antonella Emmi and Kaitlyn Tuthill for invaluable copyediting, to Robert Fredona for lengthy comments, and to Tej P. S. Sood for editorial support and remarkable flexibility. In her introduction to the English translation of Ferrone's *Scienza natura religione: Mondo newtoniano e cultura italiana nel primo Settecento*, written nearly three decades ago, Margaret C. Jacob thanked him for making her 'think less provincially.'[12] It is a sentiment with which we all, still, can identify.

S. A. R.
Harvard Business School

Preface

A WORLD TO REDISCOVER: THE ENLIGHTENMENT ORIGINS OF MODERN ITALIAN REPUBLICANISM

What did politics mean to the men of the late Enlightenment? Was theirs a singular and independent conception? Did it differ in practices, discourses, representations, and language from what would be developed in the revolutionary period to come? What forms of struggle, what tasks and, above all, what limitations in their way of conceiving politics confronted them in those last, tormented years of the Old Regime? What shape did the newfangled republican and constitutional patriotism take between the American and French Revolutions, between 1776 and 1789, in those enlightened circles which presciently warned of the threat of that despotism which, as the freedoms of antiquity were reasserted for modern times by Rousseau and his many followers, was seen lurking in the eighteenth-century revival of so-called classical republicanism? Through which paths and what struggles were the language of the rights of man, a form of republicanism apt for the modern world, and Enlightenment constitutionalism created, and developed, in Italy? Is there a relationship between the political culture of the late Enlightenment and the genesis of the Italian democratic and republican tradition? This book endeavours to answer these and other questions by formulating some working hypotheses based on the achievements of the new cultural history of the Enlightenment[1] and by developing themes and issues that I have tackled in the past.[2] The entire work, however, centres first and foremost on the analysis and study of a personal history and an important publishing event (together providing the unifying thread guiding this investigation through the labyrinthine politics of the late Enlightenment) which caused a sensation in Europe at the end of the eighteenth century: Gaetano Filangieri's publication of the *Scienza della legislazione* (*The Science of Legislation*) in Naples, in the spring of 1780.[3]

This work, which today is all but forgotten and which still lacks a good critical edition,[4] was, in fact, a resounding bestseller in the decade prior to the French Revolution, talked about with both admiration and surprise by all the scholars of the day.[5] At this crucial moment in European history, it was no accident that translations promptly were undertaken into all major Western languages, and that reprint upon reprint followed in subsequent years.[6] This book on Filangieri attempts to explain the many and diverse reasons for its Italian and international success. A primary reason is, naturally, the ability of the author – who proudly declared himself a 'cosmopolitan' – to address men of every nation without ever losing sight of his own origins in Naples' great juridical, political, and philosophical culture. There, Giovanni Vincenzo Gravina, Giambattista Vico, and

Antonio Genovesi had been the first in Europe to engage with the issue of how to create a just and fair society in light of the rights embodied in the natural law tradition of Hugo Grotius and Samuel von Pufendorf. 'The work,' the French translator Jean-Antoine Gauvin Gallois wrote,

> of which we offer the public a translation, began to appear in Italy in 1780. Five editions, published successively in Naples, Florence, and Milan, attest to the celebrity that it enjoys in that country on earth in which the science of the rights and duties of man is cultivated with greatest ardour and, perhaps, even with the greatest success.[7]

It was the sophistication of this political-cum-juridical investigation into the subversive potential of the language of the rights of man, into the necessity and possibility of embodying them in constitutional form, clearly set forth in the author's new conception of the science of legislation, which fascinated his contemporaries, who were ever more shaken by the events of the revolution.[8] Unlike that other great Italian man of the Enlightenment, Cesare Beccaria, who was more influenced by utilitarian thought than by philosophical reflection, Filangieri took European natural law to its highest degree of theoretical development. His German translators were well aware of this. They presented his works as not only those of a jurist but also, more generally, as those of a political writer ('*politischer Schriftsteller*').[9] They highlighted the original historical framework of natural law propounded by the Neapolitan school, Filangieri's cultural heritage, and compared it to the prevailing rationalism of the interpretations formulated in Northern Europe.[10] The jurists of Göttingen and Nuremberg were most impressed by the publication of the third volume of the *Scienza della Legislazione*. This was entirely devoted to criminal codes and procedures, was grounded in the theory of natural rights, and embodied the first rigorous attempt to develop the right to punish in a republican manner. It reconsidered the very foundations of justice from the basis offered by the principle of equality before the law. In France, Filangieri's work elucidated the republican and fair nature of the accusatorial system, not only to a host of magistrates but also to public opinion in Paris, while simultaneously exposing the violation of the rights of man involved in the ferocious inquisitorial procedures of old. So when Napoleon Bonaparte, then First Consul, solemnly received Filangieri's widow and children at an official ceremony by recalling 'this young man who is a master to all of us,'[11] he was doing nothing more than publicly acknowledging the debt which the French Revolution owed to the *Scienza della legislazione*. As we will see in Chapter Ten, this was evidently an enduring and deeply felt debt if Benjamin Constant, while recognizing the merits of his adversary, still felt compelled to attack the political and constitutional conceptions of the young Neapolitan philosopher in 1822 and again in 1824. In this way, Filangieri became the main target of a sort of generational reckoning between the advocates of the nascent liberal ideology and the direct heirs of the glorious Enlightenment tradition.

The monumental *Scienza della Legislazione* was the culminating treatment of late Enlightenment political thought. By successfully moving beyond both Montesquieu's class-based conceptualization of the Old Regime and his concessions to the legacy of feudalism, as well as the classical republicanism of Rousseau, Filangieri became one of the 'greatest publicists of Europe, the one who has most contributed to shaping the spirit of his century.'[12] The fame of certain pages he wrote spread across the continent: on the necessary connection between morality and politics; against the hereditary conception of nobility; on the arbitrary and anti-economic nature of the feudal system; on the privileges of birth; on the central place of Roman republican law in the new enlightened constitutionalism; on the harm done to individual rights and freedom by an excessive concentration of wealth in the hands of the few. Radicals across the Channel were impressed by that 'political philosopher'[13] who once again dared – after the failed attempt of the 1649 revolution – to demand the abolition of the House of Lords, and who exposed the limitations of a mixed government and the contradictions inherent in British constitutionalism by comparing it to the extraordinary political experiment in representative democracy pursued by the American insurgents.

Nevertheless, despite my realization that a study of the *Scienza della legislazione*'s international success brings to light a fundamental element of the genesis of modern European republican and constitutional thought, my book deals only marginally with that question. My most pressing concern is to present the overall design and the specific content of the work in the light of the context that brought it into being and of the strategic role it ended up playing in the tumultuous history of late eighteenth-century Italy. Filangieri's story is a paradigmatic example of how, under the influence of tenacious political and ideological prejudices, historiography has generally misunderstood or, more often than not, deliberately mystified the *vexata quaestio* of the relationship between Enlightenment and Revolution. In Italy, this question has always been interpreted through an analysis of the so-called Revolutionary Triennial sparked by the French invasion (1796–99). The ostentatious ceremony in Filangieri's honour conducted by the government of the Neapolitan Republic of 1799 produced what we can only call his 'Pantheonization.' While this, on the one hand, made the young philosopher into a legendary hero of Jacobinism and revolution, on the other it condemned his *Scienza della legislazione* to a sort of oblivion and greatly impeded the circulation of his work, which represented the best of the political thought produced by the Italian Enlightenment. The words of Vincenzo Russo, calling upon the members of the provisional government to erect a statue to the eternal memory of Filangieri's works, banish any doubts that the revolutionary experience had its roots in the soil of Enlightenment. Wholly caught up in the propaganda requirements of the moment, Russo proclaimed that Filangieri's volumes should be 'considered one of those banners raised to the revolution before the vast assembly of mankind, under which millions of men would come to swear before the Universe their desire to live freely or die'; 'Let us make a public and solemn vow that a bust of the author of the *Scienza della legislazione* will be placed in the National Chamber and in a temple of immortality whose very existence alone will ensure that it will soon be populated with heroes.'[14] Thus, in short, the same volumes which, in the 1780s, had represented the core of the project drawn up by Italian Enlightenment circles, in harmony with the governments of the peninsula, took on a new life in the changed historical context brought about by the *Grande Nation*'s military invasion, feeding the hopes of those who, in previous decades, had dreamt that gradual reforms could lead to a bloodless transformation of the unjust Old Regime. Nevertheless, the new historical role that Neapolitan republicans now assigned Filangieri's ideas should not have prevented scholars from distinguishing between his actual political thought and the uses made of it in the 1799 Revolution. Similarly, they should never have confused the emancipatory political project of the Enlightenment with the different, autonomous cultural forms that subsequently would evolve in the revolution. Instead, after the cruel Bourbon repression and the changed intellectual climate of the Restoration, this distinction would never be again made. All the men of the late Italian Enlightenment who had played a leading role in the events of the 'Triennial Republic' were automatically dismissed as Jacobins, as foreigners in their own homeland and uncritical followers of French fashions and ideas. In the twentieth century, through a paradoxical convergence of the historiographies of the political left and right, of moderate liberals and Neo-Jacobins of Marxist orientation, the direct linkage and continuity between the Enlightenment and the Revolution continued to represent a kind of impenetrable interpretative paradigm, which allowed the former to condemn both experiences as one and the same, and the latter to lay claim to a noble inheritance.[15]

Though acknowledging the tempestuous events of the Neapolitan Republic as the 'sacred origins of the new Italy,' the celebrated Benedetto Croce had, to some extent, outlined this victorious interpretative model of that decisive stage in Italian history by stating that 'the Neapolitan patriots were great idealists but bad politicians,'[16] generous in their Utopias, but also politically naïve in having relied on a foreign power to realize their plans. From the height of his refined idealistic historicism, aimed at 'understanding' and 'transcending' the era of the Enlightenment, he pointed to Vincenzo Cuoco and the exponents of the budding tradition of liberal 'moderatism' as the real spiritual fathers of modern Italy.[17] In the temple of national glories, among the immortal pillars of Italy's new historical identity as the culmination of the *Risorgimento*, Croce gave pride of place to the great masters of political realism, to men like Machiavelli, Vico, and Cuoco. Despite the efforts of Pasquale Villari to argue for his originality,[18] Filangieri was excluded again, confined to the shadows in which nineteenth-century historians had placed him.[19] Historical honour and respect certainly were paid to that young intellectual, the younger son of Cesare Filangieri, Prince of Arianello, and Marianna Montaldo of the Dukes of Fragnito, who died, without having completed his monumental work, at the young age of 36.[20] Yet, no genuine attention was really given to his political thought, which had been dialectically surpassed by history and by the mysterious workings of the evolutionary phenomenology of the spirit.

By polemically placing the autonomy and supremacy of the so-called Jacobin Triennial at the centre of the national debate, and making it the origin of Italy's democratic tradition, Marxist historiography did nothing, in the wake of World War II, to rediscover the republican and constitutional political thought of Filangieri and of the late Enlightenment.[21] While such research can be credited with bringing to light a world previously ignored by traditional historiography, stressing the events of the revolution as well as the culture and writings of lesser protagonists who in Italy reiterated, with varying degrees of originality, the conflicts, the theoretical developments, and the forms of struggle typical of the Paris of Robespierre or of the Directory, it indirectly succeeded in obscuring even further the unique identity of, and the political programmes pursued by, the men of the Enlightenment. Moreover, this emphasis glossed over the crucial fact that, before becoming dangerous revolutionaries, the followers of Filangieri who led the provisional government of the Neapolitan Republic of 1799 had been enlightened reformers, not given over to abstraction and excess. It was, in fact, the sudden change of context following the French invasion that forced them to make critical choices. And if they were to remain true to their ideals of reform and the overthrow of the Old Regime, these choices had to be made in the face of the violent, despotic reactions of the Bourbon government. So it is not only reductive but also historically inaccurate to see nothing more than the last, convulsive episode of the Italian Revolutionary Triennial in the violent repression carried out by the Bourbons, in the ferocious executions which, week after week, performed the macabre ritual of death in Piazza Mercato in Naples, in the over eight thousand trials, in the innumerable sentences of exile, and in the white terror of the bands of Cardinal Ruffo. Rather than representing the symbolic end of the Republic, the hanging of the great jurist and philosopher Francesco Maria Pagano, faithful pupil of Filangieri, head of the Neapolitan patriots, and author of the first truly modern constitution drawn up in Italy, instead marked the dramatic, bloody conclusion of the peninsula's long Enlightenment.[22] This sequence of events demands an in-depth study covering the last quarter of the century, but especially the crucial ten years from 1789 to 1799, when the original reform project of the Enlightenment slowly was extinguished in the harsh confrontation with revolutionary events taking place in Europe. Only in this way can we avoid making it a mere appendix (in accordance with the classical interpretation developed *a posteriori* by reactionary historians) to the history of the French Revolution. In light of recent studies, we are beginning to realize ever more clearly that those ten years represented something much more akin to a laboratory of Italian modernity, bursting with energy. It was at this time that current forms of communication and political struggle came into being; that the network of lay and Catholic associations rapidly developed, making the emergence of public opinion possible; that the age-old Italian publishing system expanded to a scale and took on tasks never before seen.[23] As we will endeavour to explain, it was precisely in that turbulent period that the intellectual seeds of a great political and constitutional debate were to take root and grow into the republican and democratic traditions of contemporary Italy.

One person who understood the importance of the Enlightenment experience for modern Italian history – and therefore the need to reassert its specific autonomy from models and conceptualizations framed both by liberal and Marxist historiography – was Franco Venturi. He constantly insisted on the need to study the Enlightenment in order to understand 'the rise of the political, economic and social ideas of the last two centuries of our modern era.'[24] Much of his extraordinary work as founding father of Italian democratic historiography was in this way devoted to reconstructing the culture of the Enlightenment in Italy and in Europe, and to investigating its decisive role, to define more clearly the problems that still beset us today.[25] Yet, that imposing work of reconstruction seems at times to have been forgotten, quietly and inexplicably put aside in recent attempts to conduct a comprehensive revision of Italian history. Once again, the experiences of people like Cesare Beccaria, Pietro Verri, and Antonio Genovesi are, if not excluded, seriously underrated in the traditional, time-honoured enumerations of the founding fathers of future national identity.[26] It is true that, like all great historiographic reconstructions, Venturi's is a child of its time. The difficult era of the Cold War and its bitter political and ideological conflicts inevitably conditioned the historiographical debate in which he engaged. But even though the great Turinese historian never directly confronted the delicate question of the linkage between Enlightenment and Revolution, it was always there on the horizon of his work. He referred to it implicitly in his writings and always placed it at the centre of the discussions that played such a great part in my own intellectual formation. He devotes little space to the issue in his *Settecento riformatore*.[27] He probably felt venturing into that minefield meant endangering a good part of the results he had achieved in over half a century of research carried out with the aim of, at long last, conferring the right of citizenship and visibility to the Italian Enlightenment movement. But, more importantly, it would have entailed a definite reckoning with the moderate, liberal tradition on the one hand and, on the other, with those who stressed the importance of the so-called Jacobin Triennial. Today, however, following the collapse of the Berlin Wall, everything seems less confusing and complex. For the new generations of scholars who are critically re-thinking these events in Italy, it will certainly be easier to investigate, alongside the reformist eighteenth century so dear to Franco Venturi, another and no less important eighteenth century: that of the rights of man, of constitutionalism, of republican patriotism, of the creation of the public sphere, of cultural practices and languages of modernity; an eighteenth century that witnessed the direct involvement of the Italian Enlightenment in the birth of Europe's democratic consciousness.

Many colleagues and friends have helped me in the course of my research for this book. My vivid recognition goes to them all. The book is above all the product of fruitful colloquia on the Enlightenment and on the eighteenth century with Raffaele Ajello, Giuseppe Giarrizzo, Daniel Roche, and particularly Giuseppe Ricuperati. The first results of my studies were discussed, with a critical spirit and in the context of old friendship, with John Robertson at St. Hugh's College, Oxford and with Joyce Appleby, Lynn Hunt, Margaret Candee Jacob, Peter H. Reill, and Goeffrey Symcox in Los Angeles at the Department of History at UCLA and during conferences organized by the Clark Memorial Library. For the final revisions of my text, I benefited greatly from the suggestions of Elvira Chiosi, a refined scholar of eighteenth century Naples, and Antonio Trampus, a true scholar of European history. I owe yet another testimonial of fraternal friendship to Massimo Firpo, who patiently and with severity has read every page. Luciano Guerci, from whose scholarly rigour and intellectual freedom I have learned so much ever since my student days, when I eagerly followed his seminars on Mably, did the same. This book is dedicated to Luciano with affection and gratitude.

V. F.

Bonzo, Alpi Graie

August 2002

Part One

THE NEW POLITICS '*EX PARTE CIVIUM*'

Chapter One

THE ENLIGHTENMENT
AND THE POLITICAL CRITIQUE
OF THE *SCIENTIA JURIS*

A law student at the outset of his studies ought first to know the derivation of the word jus. Its derivation is from justitia. For, in terms of Celsus' elegant definition, the law is the art of goodness and fairness. 1. Of that art we [jurists] are deservedly called priests.

Digest, I, 1, I

Why did discussions concerning the right to punish, rather than reflections on different forms of government, imbue and mark large parts of the political debate of the Italian Enlightenment, characterizing it so profoundly in relation to other European milieus? For what reason, for example, did the most original aspects of eighteenth-century discourse on political philosophy – first of all with regards to meditations upon justice and the formulation of a new science of legislation rather than the detailed analysis of governmental institutions or the nature of power – emerge in a historical context like that of the Kingdom of Naples? What lay behind the sudden attention paid by Neapolitan thinkers to the ancient theme of the *Diceosina* and the concept of a just and fair society? We know that the myth of the noble savage, the primitivist utopias of hypothetical states of nature, and of perfect republics never enjoyed great success in Italy. The homeland of Dante and of Machiavelli, of the most refined humanism and of the most ruthless political realism, did not entertain itself with daydreaming when it came to making headway in the art of government.[1] But, nonetheless, the practicality of a utopia simultaneously reasonable and realistic seemed, at the end of the eighteenth century, to find exceptional interpreters in Enlightenment jurists like Filangieri and Pagano. Their texts gave currency, for the first time, to terms which were destined to become key concepts and obligatory points of reference in the modern language of politics: constitution, republicanism, patriotism, civil society, rights of man, citizenship, representative government, popular sovereignty, 'pure' or 'representative' democracy, equality, civil and political liberty. Thanks to their scholarly undertaking, an entire linguistic arsenal, where new words were accompanied by ancient expressions with inflected meanings, succoured the struggle to guarantee a right of existence to the agile yet tormented and subterranean democratic and republican tradition on the peninsula. Though crucial for understanding the history of Italian modernity, this world of Enlightenment reformers has received little attention from political theorists and legal historians.[2] The latter, in particular, have not merely limited themselves to neglecting this historical period and its protagonists in their research, but have gone beyond this to systematically attack its juridical culture itself, contributing to the disregard of that powerful nexus between politics and law which nonetheless represented the real and original cipher of the late Italian Enlightenment.

Only recently have we begun to react against this strategy of oblivion or, more often, of systematic denigration, polemically expressed by those who have not hesitated to proclaim that the philosophers of the Enlightenment suffered from a 'total incomprehension of law, which very often derive[d] from a substantial and almost unbelievable juridical ignorance.'[3] And only recently have we begun to clarify exactly what is at stake and to reveal the invisible linkages between the old and the new *sacerdotes juris*, ever jealous custodians of the power assured them by an undisputed primacy of *interpretatio*, an arcane power held by judges which at the same time guaranteed and was guaranteed by the political and social institutions of medieval and Old Regime society.[4] The authoritative words of a great legal historian, Raffaele Ajello, remain exemplary in this regard for their clarity and effectiveness, and deserve being quoted at length:

> The philosophers of the Enlightenment refuted the humanist-Platonic ideal of a republic governed by wise jurists, called from time to time to represent the *communis opinio*, the common consensus, the people, the sovereignty, the law, the science of things divine and human. Such an ideal had been the ideological presupposition of the entire late medieval and humanist *scientia juris*. The enlightened philosophers rejected the pretension of the jurists to draw on the structures of being, or at least of interpreting and expressing those which already existed. The *sacerdotes juris* were considered incapable of legally representing the entire body politic and accused of being only bearers of special interests, limited to their estate [*status*]… But this was not enough. Reorganizing the theoretical ambitions of legal science, these reformers relocated the responsibilities of legal professionals to a practical-executive level and reduced the polyvalence of their doctrines and their functions to fit within clearer, more precise, defined, and distinct lines: a politico-constitutional program, and not only a myth.[5]

Beyond their differences and the diverse solutions they outlined in its criticisms of the Old Regime, and in particular against the tradition of the so-called '*forensi*,' or the men of the tribunals, works of Enlightenment jurisprudence from Montesquieu to Rousseau and from Beccaria to Filangieri set themselves, in other words, the explicit common objective of finally unmasking the *arcana juris*, or revealing the authentically political, rather than technical, nature of the great theme of justice, at a moment in the history of the West in which past arrangements had begun to fall apart and the question of a comprehensive redefinition of sovereignty, no longer from the top down, but from the bottom up, *ex parte civum*, posed itself with dramatic urgency.

It is therefore not incidental that the young Gaetano Filangieri's first political struggle occurred precisely in 1774, in occasion of Neapolitan Prime Minister Bernardo Tanucci's brave measures to ensure that magistrates were bound to explain the motivation behind their sentences in writing. It was a true act of war between the Monarchy and the courts of justice in the *Mezzogiorno*, or Southern Italy, comparable in terms of emphasis and importance to the conflict begun three years earlier in Paris between chancellor Maupeou and the *messieurs* of the parliament.[6] The responses to Tanucci, originally of Tuscan origin, were generally resentful, in everything worthy of the great arrogance and extraordinary power the so-called *ceto togato*, the ministerial governing class of Naples, had always been known for in the Kingdom.[7] Practically, Tanucci appealed in vain against 'the unlimited *arbitrio* of the judges,' against their arbitrary power, and in vain he invited the *Sacro Regio Consiglio*, a judicial organ, to finally abandon their 'oracular style,' forgetful as they were that 'legislation is all in the hands of the sovereign; and that the *Consiglio* is nothing but a judge and that the judges are executors of the laws and not their authors; that the law must be certain and definite, not arbitrary.'[8]

It was not the first time an attempt at judicial reform ended in a miserable shipwreck on reefs sharpened by the powerful magistrates. Following the arrival of Charles III of Bourbon and the foundation of a national monarchy, the project of giving life to an absolutist phase ran aground the resistance of the *ministero togato*, secular holder of power in the Kingdom alongside the feudal nobility and the clergy. 'At the time of the German government,' an anonymous 1739 report to the sovereign explained with particular reference to the years of the Austrian viceroyalty, 'these ministers were as many kings, or better as many gods on the earth, because far away from their ruler they had supreme dominion, despotic and haughty above all classes of people: they could adulterate justice as they wished.'[9] Charles III had immediately sought to remedy the fragmentation of sovereignty and the particularisms that for centuries dominated public life in the *Mezzogiorno*. He reprimanded abuses, dissolved the *Collaterale*, a high court of justice, founded a new court of law, the *Regia Camera di Santa Chiara*, instituted the new Supreme Magistrate of Commerce – where merchants and bankers sat next to juridical experts – and even launched an attempt at legal codification which, as time would tell, was destined to fail. Little really changed. Financial resources were lacking and one could certainly not promptly substitute the most authoritative representatives of a class that was both decisive and profoundly rooted in the public life of the Kingdom. 'In 1734 and 35,' Tanucci wrote melancholically at the end of his career, 'one thought of reforming the tribunals here by means of a junta, of which I was a member,' but after many confrontations and 'many other disputes one concluded to leave the old system running.'[10] The problem of justice was, in short, already venerable and for a long time at the centre of polemics when Filangieri wrote his thundering *Riflessione* against the *togati*. Elsewhere in Italy, Muratori called, though with a certain insecurity, for codification to remedy the abuses of the judges in his celebrated little 1742 volume *Dei difetti della giurisprudenza*. Stinging articles against the despotism of the courts and the primacy of *interpretatio* and the *scientia juris* also appeared in the *Caffè*.[11] Nearly all the major exponents of the Italian Enlightenment, from Pietro Verri to Giuseppe Gorani, Melchiorre Delfico, and Pagano, competed in the course of the eighteenth century to denounce the anarchic practice of justice and the arrogance of the *sacerdotes juris*.[12] In Naples, for evident historical reasons owing to the extraordinary importance of the tribunal world there, the polemic was of a more bitter and virulent nature. The celebrated arguments of Giuseppe Maria Galanti, who in his *Testamento forense* connected economic underdevelopment and social backwardness to the hegemony of jurists, in this sense represented opinions that were widely shared in reformist circles. 'Our civil law and our political constitution,' he wrote in the 1781 appendix to the *Descrizione dello stato antico ed attuale del Contado di Molise*, 'is a complicated system of ecclesiasticism and feudalism'; 'In Naples all the professions are depressed and disheartened and the voice of the *paglietti* [in the Neapolitan dialect, a lawyer of dubious morality and competence, astute and hairsplitting] form the only reason of State.' 'Everything is uncertainty, contradiction, arbitrariness. Our misery is such that we cannot possess faculties, without depending on the tribunals, nor be citizens, without having need of lawyers... Where in other nations commerce unites people and occupies them in the arts, among us the court divides them and occupies them in odious rivalries... A civil cause is almost an arcanum.'[13]

In his interventions, Galanti publicly denounced a uniquely Neapolitan form of corruption, a reality made of abuses of power in need of remedy, in which the obvious complicity and the close bonds of interests between lawyers and magistrates made them 'a single order with two masks.'[14]

At any rate, in 1774 Filangieri's *Riflessioni* opened a very different season with respect to the traditional canons of the Enlightenment polemic against the *forensi*. The confrontation shifted decisively to the level of politics, beginning with – as the author specified – the most recent 'fundamental principles of politics.' This called on 'public opinion' directly, soliciting respect for the 'civil liberty' of citizens and demonstrating to everyone the unsustainable 'monstrous despotism' of the magistrates which he saw nesting in the very heart of the State. Through the new political language of the late eighteenth century, in which that old diatribe was reformulated, Filangieri sought a definite reckoning with the illegitimately held power of the *ministero togato*. 'The thunder has struck,' he wrote rhetorically and hopefully, 'the sound is communicated; the tremor can be felt everywhere; the *forense* edifice has crumbled; the magistrate has been recalled to the first institution; the sovereign empire of laws has fortunately been re-established, the fate of the citizenry has already been sealed.'[15] The time had come, in other words, to reveal to everyone the 'truth' that hid behind the radiant image of a justice solemnly proclaimed in the name of the ancient *ordo juris*.

The law Tanucci hoped for, which made it a legal requirement to put the motivation for sentences publicly in writing, seriously embarrassed magistrates, who for the first time were required to justify their actions. If it were true that 'men command in despotic governments' while instead 'laws command in moderate governments,' the magistrates of the Kingdom, according to Filangieri, operated as authentic despots, in effect ignoring the limitations set by the law. A sort of 'despotism of the elite' that, by virtue of being exercised by an entire corporation rather than a single individual, was much more odious and dangerous to 'the liberty of the citizens.'[16] Behind this 'arbitrary justice,' permitted by the figurative practice of *interpretatio*, hid the systematic violation of the 'very constitution of moderate governments' which, after John Locke and Montesquieu, required the separation of powers to the point of rendering them 'incommunicable' as a guarantee of civil liberty.[17] Far from exercising only the sole function of 'sacred despot of the laws' and appealing, in their activities as administrators of justice, exclusively to their 'language,' the magistrates had ended up, precisely through the *interpretatio*, politically usurping the same prerogatives of the 'Sovereign as Legislator,' undermining the delicate equilibrium of powers. But not only that: moving from the principle that 'uniformity and equality are the most interesting characteristics of the law...', the right to interpret,'

Filangieri affirmed, 'will eventually destroy this uniformity which is so necessary for social liberty.'[18] The distorted and pretentious use that the *sacerdotes juris* made of the words 'equitable' and 'fair' was the great theoretical error making this situation possible. Understood ethically in an Aristotelian manner as something different from justice, and therefore as an instrument at the disposal of the magistrate to rectify the abstractly universal character of the law with respect to concrete situations, the continual recourse to the equitable mechanism to legitimate the *interpretatio* had permitted the birth of more negative forms of legal despotism by the large courts of justice.[19] Filangieri had no doubts in this regard, 'equity, interpretation, arbitrariness' had become, in the courts of the eighteenth century, 'synonymous terms.'[20] It was not without reason that this suggestive word, so dense with multiple meanings, had been voiced by the 'magistrates of Rome in the fatal era of the decline of liberty,' in which the lack of respect for the 'letter of the law' and absolute 'legal uncertainty' had dominated.[21] The fact is that the idea of a just and fair society, which slowly matured in Filangieri's mind in parallel with his meditation on the political consequences of natural law, foresaw a completely different way of thinking about the relationship between fairness and justice.

As we shall see, the particular interpretation of natural law which delineated itself in Naples emphasized, to an ever greater extent, the inevitable political and moral implications of this critical re-thinking of the idea of justice. This clarified the social and economic presuppositions implicit in a society held to be unfair like that of the Old Regime, and identified the enemies and obstacles that would have to be removed for the Kingdom to be reformed. Piece by piece, Filangieri would construct the gigantic mosaic of the *Scienza della legislazione* around a new interpretation of civil society, founded on the nexus which inextricably linked fairness and justice. In 1774, the fragments of his great design, though partially internalized already for some time, were still far from finding their moment of definite amalgamation in the drafting of the book. The struggle he conducted at Tanucci's side against the despotic power of the magistracies doubtlessly accelerated the process by which he made and, in many ways, clarified his choices. This is certainly suggested by the pages which he dedicated to criticizing the foundations of the *scientia juris*, his call to definitely banish 'from the forums the authority of the doctors [*dottori*]' as the primary sources justifying sentences, and his denunciation of the way in which the judges politically had usurped legislative power. Not to mention his proposal to revolutionize justice to align it with new laws reflecting the equality of the rights of man. With the appearance of the *Riflessioni*, the latent conflict between the party of the new Enlightenment philosophers and the old ministry of the *togati* became a total, irreducible political and cultural confrontation. To contemporary eyes, the two ways of understanding the world were clearly felt to be contrasting and in opposition. For all practical purposes, it was as if a new season in the life of the Kingdom of Naples had opened in the 1770s, a season that would only come to a close with the bloodbaths of the 1799 Republic, with the blazing defeat of the Enlightenment and its condemnation to oblivion by the victors of the struggle.

When Filangieri decided to make the confrontation public, he had the identities of his adversaries very clearly in mind. Furthermore, he knew what hid behind the powerful ideology of the *ministero togato*, which for centuries had nourished itself on the dialectic of the estates, and the power it had usurped, thanks to the patriarchal mediation of class-conflicts in the Old Regime, from the great bureaucratic apparatus. He was certainly not fooled by the symbolic representations of judicial power offered by almost all the greatest jurists of the time. They loved to underline the sacral character of jurisprudence and the sacerdotal nature of the judge, drawing both on Ulpian's celebrated definition, according to which 'jurisprudence is the knowledge of things divine and human,' and on the no less suggestive phrase pronounced by Nicola Toppi in 1665: 'Magistrates are set by God and are themselves called gods.'[22] He knew well that the power and prestige of that ideology had grown appreciably over the course of the eighteenth century. It had done so on the basis of very different arguments compared to the traditional and by then naïve recourse to the *arcana juris*, rather sustaining itself on newer and more insidious political and legal arguments which were hard to counter in the absence of a precise alternative. The tumultuous decades of Louis XIV's authoritarian monarchy had, in fact, transformed not only the institutional history of modern France but changed the very terms of political struggle in continental Europe as well. The furious transalpine conflict between the crown and the parliaments, which had exploded in the second half of the century, was overturning the consolidated equilibrium of powers guaranteed in the Old Regime by the sovereign court's mediation in the dialectic of the *status*. By brutally transforming the 'royal monarchy' into a 'despotic monarchy' – to draw on the language of the era coined by the French tradition of legal politics from Bodin to Montesquieu[23] – the personal government of Louis XIV had broken with old customs and alarmed not only the ancient feudal nobility, which for some time had been hostile towards the crown, but also crucial sectors of the French state bureaucracy. Jealous keepers of a sort of 'theology of administration,' who in exchange for faith in absolutism and in the monarchy received privileges and honours connected to their important political and administrative function, the *messieurs* of parliament felt directly threatened by the new course set by absolutist politics. The revolt of intermediary bodies had begun in France with the diffusion of a polemical and negative reading of the words '*absolu*' and '*despotique*.' If the works of Boulainvilliers[24] expressed the constitutional ideology of the ancient hereditary aristocracy, Montesquieu's 1748 *Esprit des Lois* and then the *Lettres historiques sur les fonctions essentielles des Parlements* by Louis-Adrien Le Paige, which appeared a few years later, rapidly became the canonical texts of the new parliamentary ideology of the *ministero togato*. The first book generally made intermediary bodies an essential component of the monarchical constitutional system, indispensible to guarantee liberty and avoid every form of sovereign degeneration towards despotism. In the second book, however, Le Paige did not hesitate to proclaim the historical continuity between the parliament and the legislative assemblies of the two first dynasties of French kings, claiming, without pause, the representation of the entire '*nation*' on behalf of the *robins*, and transforming the process of registering laws from a simple formal act into a genuine constitutional principle.[25] In the political struggle between the crown and the parliament, the concept of 'legitimate monarchy' was consistently associated with respect for the *consensus gentium*, clearly expressed in the 'fundamental laws of the kingdom.'[26] In this way the exercise of jurisprudence in fact posed limits, in the function of a guarantee, to the exercise of *royauté*,[27] inducing the magistrates to inaugurate a veritable 'parliamentary constitutionalism.' A singular and highly effective rhetoric of liberty was built on the basis of this calling upon fundamental laws, the real meanings of which, however, were only accessible to the holders of the *scientia juris*. Voluntarily neglecting the protagonists' class-based and corporate nature, the rhetoric aimed at stirring great emotion and defining strategies and political formulas to fuel the conflict between powers.

In Naples, this suggestive and organic eighteenth-century version of the ideology of the *ministero togato* found, in the second half of the century, its greatest theorist in the prominent jurist Niccolò Fraggianni, head of the *Sacro Regio Consiglio* and *Delegato della Real Giurisdizione*, all posts which posed him at the apex of the bureaucratic apparatus. In an important, recently published *consulta* to the king, written on and off between 1740 and the mid-1750s to protest against recurring attempts to reform justice in view of the most rigorous absolutism, Fraggianni represented the salient aspects of the new *togato* constitutionalism in Naples. Relying on the works of Montesquieu and Le Paige, and on the legal-political language of the acts promulgated by the French parliament, he warned the sovereign against 'reformers' who, with the establishment of the new national monarchy, had hoped the ancient constitutional equilibrium would be abolished in favour of 'a pure despotism of the prince and his ministers, and of a blind obedience on the part of the subjects.' 'These *novatori* [innovators],' Fraggianni polemicized harshly, 'are the true oppressors of the fatherland.'[28] Following their advice, in other words launching a reform of the justice system so radical as to break the equilibrium between the traditional *ordo juris* and the medieval state of justice, would offend not only liberty, but quickly create the conditions for a dangerous 'general revolution.' 'This new plan [for the reform of justice] could not be executed,' Fraggianni explained in a threatening tone, 'without disgusting the great, the gentlemen, and the people. The violence with which it will shake all social orders cannot but cause a frightening disorder; and without a great revolution the face of the State can never change.' To 'alter our ancient customs…[and] order so many novelties that upset the State' could make sense only in the presence of an illegitimate sovereign forced to impose his empire or of a 'prince that had no other goal but despotism and the use of force': ultimately a new Louis XIV. Naples had no need for a king subversive of the 'fundamental constitution' of the Kingdom. 'The Kingdom has subsisted for two and a half centuries with these laws, defective as they may be, with these customs, unjust as they may seem…, we know, by and large, that its fundamental constitution and all its power lies in the civil arts, that is in the laws and in the forum. This is the basis on which the public peace rests.'[29] Alternating veiled threats and invitations to use 'prudence' with acute reflections originating in the *Esprit des lois*, Fraggianni explained the intellectual frame of reference for his way of conceiving the function of the 'fundamental constitution.' It was the fruit of the *consensus gentium*, and therefore drew legitimacy directly from history, from tradition, from the original customs of every single nation: 'in every nation there is a general spirit on which Power itself [*la Potenza stessa*] is founded.' In the constitutional domain, the practice of jurisprudence exercised by the *sacerdotes juris* and their legal teachings, explicated for centuries through the *scientia juris* and the *interpretatio*, gained a delicate function of guaranteeing and guarding the political equilibriums determined by the separation of powers, impeding despotism and, in this way, representing the interests of the entire nation. According to Fraggianni, the reformers' objective of subtracting the administration of justice from the *togati*, bringing it under the direct control of the king, altered the 'constitution' and threatened the liberty of the 'citizens.' 'The constitution of our government is such that litigants never believe themselves satisfied if their cause is not examined by experts of law [*giusperiti*] and tried in a tribunal [*et in un tribunal colleggiato*]. The King had the authority to give 'grace' but not the administration of justice and the power to punish. 'Justice,' Fraggianni asserted dryly and without fear,

> is an untouchable field for the sovereign will… It is true that the authority of the judges originates in the prince, and by consequence that one is the authority and by necessity inflicts punishments. But it is also true that the public order and the dignity of the crown *demand* that the person of the king does not interfere if not to give clemency, and never to punish. It is a right of the citizenry not to be punished by an arbitrary sovereignty, but rather by the common deliberation of those who have been assigned as judges.[30]

In Naples, in other words, the reform of justice was a political question of extraordinary importance which ended up involving not only the world of the tribunals but every aspect of public life, risking both the social order and the arrangements of power.[31] Filangieri's 1774 intervention and later the draft of the *Scienza della legislazione* result as events devoid of any sense if one ignores this precise historical context and the fact that, in this 'kingdom governed as a republic' as contemporaries loved to call it, the constitutional theses exposed so authoritatively by Fraggianni were not only extremely diffuse, but largely shared by the *togati* of the great Neapolitan courts of justice[32] and by vast segments of public opinion. This determined the objective conditions for a confrontation with the nascent party of enlightened 'philosophers.' Nonetheless, it must immediately be specified that the latter's critiques of common law, of the corporatist conception of a social group which wrongfully assumed, on the basis of the *consensus gentium* and of juridical practice, the representation of the entire nation, perhaps would have been less effective and disruptive if they had limited themselves only to political disclosure and the denunciation of class interests. The force of that criticism was instead also, and above all, in its definite reckoning with the epistemological crisis of the *scientia juris*. This had already begun with the impetuous emergence in the sixteenth century of new ways of thinking about law and traditional knowledge in the wake of the scientific revolution, and the inevitable consequences this had not only in terms of methodology, but also with respect to the social identity and the political function of the new protagonists in the Renaissance Republic of Letters.[33] Next to the humanist jurist of medieval origins, who privileged erudition, rhetoric with its rules of *docendi* and *discendi*, the art of *topica* and of the different dialectics for interpreting texts belonging to the *Corpus Iuris* in accordance with the Aristotelian logic of probability, the modern figure of the 'jurist-philosopher' on the model of Mario Pagano also emerged in Naples.[34] The diffusion of the rational natural law of the moderns, influenced by the research-methods of the natural sciences, profoundly changed the legal vocation from that of interpreter to that of scientific discoverer of the universal laws of human behaviour. The empirical and rational study of the so-called 'nature of things' as a primary source of law, independently of the fetters of the *consensus gentium*, thus ended up placing a subordinate emphasis on the traditional reflection on the consolidated sources of the *Corpus juris*. From the primacy of the *interpretatio* one moved to that of the *demonstratio*, to the idea of a new legal science based on the observation of nature and on deductions from principles. The definite twilight of an aristocratic and sacral conception of cognizance was accentuated in line with the analogous processes imposed on all disciplines by the scientific revolution. Magi and theologians left the field, not without some resistance, to the victorious model of the modern scientist and to renewed forms of democratic, transparent, and secularized knowledge, verifiable by anyone at any time.

God, as Carlo Antonio Pilati explained in polemic with the *arcana juris* claimed by the judges, had in this way given everyone the possibility of knowing the law of nature and the rights of man directly, without interested intermediaries: 'The people and all those who do not find themselves having this capacity must not think themselves obliged to lend faith to the demonstrations and authority of others.'[35] The golden age of the *sacerdotes juris* who dominated public life in the Kingdom waned also in Naples. An entirely new conception was in fact emerging there, which, particularly popular among the younger generations, presented a real alternative to what Antonio Genovesi once presented as the 'true goal of literature and science' (1754): the free and public use of reason (a 'universal art' which 'brings us closer to God,' he called it[36]) by men of letters in all fields, from politics to economics, law, moral philosophy, and religion, always, however, at the service of 'public happiness' and of humanity in its entirety, and not only of the special interests of specific social groups.[37] Against the *togati*, who nonetheless represented the architrave of the *ordo juris* in the Old Regime, and against their conception of legal knowledge as a specialist and arcane instrument of power in the hands of a restricted elite, the new social figure of the enlightened 'philosopher' introduced original values, new cultural practices, and innovative discourses and representations of reality capable of upsetting the ancient relationships of power in the Republic of Letters, as well as those between civil society and the state. Also from the point of view of social identity, however, the new enlightened 'philosopher' seemed to define himself as a radical alternative to the partiality of the *togati*, to the cult that these latter made of personal power, to secrecy, and to reason of state. To the magistrate, in the future destined to occupy an always more circumscribed and limited function of public official and of simple 'executor of the laws,' Antonio Genovesi explicitly opposed the nascent figure of the 'philosopher' as the grand new protagonist in eighteenth-century public life. Born of university reforms, of modern Masonic social patterns, and of the renewal of the academies and the publishing system[38] after the tremendous 1764 famine had bared the worst injustice and structural backwardness of the Old Regime, the party of enlightened philosophers definitely appeared on the scene as a loud and effective force in the Kingdom's political struggle. Genovesi dedicated entire pages of his 1766 *Diceosina* to the movement in an attempt to identify its defining characteristics. Those who 'publicly profess letters and philosophy' had, in his opinion, many more duties with respect to other citizens. 'This word *philosopher*, with regards to the strength and the origin of the term,' Genovesi specified,

incorporates the idea of a great and magnificent person, knowledgeable of both divine and human affairs, and an indifferent observer of worldly matters, which he utilizes to the extent to which they are useful to life; priest and interpreter of the laws of the world, friend of God and of men, reparative of the rights of humanity and liberator of the fatherland.

Of course, the enlightened philosopher should not turn his attention to the 'sects of sophists [*filosofanti*],' but rather 'to the sacred codices of the eternal book of nature,'[39] and above all vindicate the rights of man.

Filangieri retraced the cultural identity and goals of this new party of philosophers once and for all in his 1774 *Riflessioni*. Cosmopolitans, 'lovers of civil liberty,' they no longer limited themselves to addressing the sovereign to auspicate his assistance, but independently individuated their principal interlocutor in 'public opinion.'[40] Unveiling the 'truth' regarding the mechanisms of power to the citizenry, unmasking the enemies of justice and of equality, educating the people, and delineating the salient traits of a future just society through books and pamphlets had by then come to constitute their inalienable objectives. In the *Scienza della legislazione*, Filangieri affirmed that, though it was still true that 'the man of letters is not always admitted to discuss the great interests of the state in the presence of princes,' nonetheless something was changing and one could reasonably begin to 'hope in a century in which the spirit of truth is not incompatible with the spirit of power.'[41] The task of the philosopher to educate the powerful of the earth, pushing them to 'undertake the reform of legislation,' emerged above all from the statement that specialist knowledge and corporatist interests were to be considered things of the past, as the international debate – in every corner of Europe and across the ocean – over the necessity of immediate legislative reforms demonstrated. 'Surprisingly, among all the writers consecrated in the study of law,' Filangieri underlined, 'there are those who have treated the subject only as jurists, others as philologists, some even as politicians, but never taking aim at more than a single part of this immense edifice' [I, 41]. What was needed was instead the work of a philosopher capable of uniting all these competences and of caring for the supreme good of humanity in its entirety. This was the origin of his appeal to all men of letters, to the party of philosophers, to act resolutely and with courage without ever losing sight of their ultimate objectives.

> Sages of the earth, philosophers of every nation; O all ye to whom the sacred deposit of knowledge is intruse, if ye would life, if ye would that your names should remain engraven in the temple of memory, if ye would that immortality should crown labours, employ yourselves on these subjects, which, over two thousand leagues of space, and after twenty centuries, continue to be interesting! Never write for a man, but for mankind; unite your glory with the eternal interests of the human race; …despise the vain applause of the vulgar, and the mercenary gratitude of the great, the threats of persecution, and the derision of ignorance; boldly instruct your brethren and freely defend their rights. Then shall mankind, interested in the hopes of happiness to which you point the road, hear you with transport; then shall posterity, grateful to your labours, in public repositories distinguish your writings; then, neither the impotent rage of tyranny, nor the interested clamours of fanaticism, nor the sophisms of imposture…shall avail to bring them into disrepute, or bury them in oblivion; they will pass from generation to generation with the glory of your name; they will be read, and perhaps washed with the tears of those who would never have otherwise known you; and your genius, always useful, will be the contemporary of every age, and the citizen of every state. [I, 63–4][42]

In light of these short reflections it is not difficult to see how, after years of fruitful collaboration, the rupture between enlightened philosophers and the *togati* had become inevitable in *fin-de-siècle* Naples. There were too many divergences and contrasts between the old and the new actors on the stage of Parthenopean political and civic life. They had fought bitter struggles together for *libertas philosophandi*, against the Inquisition and the Church, in the first half of the eighteenth century; they had shared a common love, first for Cartesian rationalism and then for the critical spirit of Bayle, for Montesquieu, but above all else for the great jurist Pietro Giannone, martyr to the Holy Office. But this could no longer hide their profound differences of interpretation with regards to the nature of the authority of magistrates and, more generally, to the legitimacy and representativeness of the so-called intermediary bodies of the Old Regime.[43] One has rightly spoken of an 'intellectual shock' resulting from the encounter between 'Enlightenment philosophy and the tradition of legal science,'[44] a shock which is all the more evident if one tries to draw together and compare two extraordinary but, and not only in generational terms, distant figures like Niccolò Fraggianni and Gaetano Filangieri. The former, an extremely refined jurist and follower of Bayle and Montesquieu who embodied the prototype of the great magistrate, was conscious of representing a powerful corporation for which, because its values and its points of reference rapidly were failing, the bell was already tolling: 'In Europe [today] there is no longer monarchy, nor democracy, nor despotism. All is commerce, laws, navy. Interest has [become] the principle of all States.'[45] Compared to Filangieri, who set about writing the *Scienza della legislazione* with the intention of indicating 'that which one ought to do' to realize a more just and fair society, the old Fraggianni, stuck on the teachings of his beloved Montesquieu, repeated his fears of the excessive and disquieting reformist fervour of his contemporaries on every occasion, calmly enunciating the philosophy that had always guided the *ministero togato* all over Europe: 'We govern the world like it is and not like it ought to be.'[46] No single phrase could have better expressed the abyss that by that time had come to separate the conservative and corporatist constitutionalism of the Old Regime from the new and subversive constitutionalism of the Enlightenment. The latter, founded on the universality of the rights of man, was arrogantly delineated in the pages of Filangieri's *Scienza della legislazione*, a European masterwork which brought to definite maturation the political and constitutional thought of an entire era. In that text, dominated and simultaneously rendered extremely effective in the eyes of contemporary readers by the dramatic events of the American Revolution, a radical critique of the Old Regime accompanied new analytical conceptions of legislation, of power, and of the very nature of constitutions themselves.

Chapter Two

THE CRITIQUE OF THE BRITISH CONSTITUTIONAL MODEL AND THE POLITICAL LABORATORY OF THE AMERICAN REVOLUTION

After centuries of general oppression, may the revolution which just took place across the oceans, offering all the inhabitants of Europe an asylum against fanaticism and tyranny, instruct those who govern men in the legitimate use of their authority.

D. Diderot, *Essai sur les règnes de Claude et de Néron* (1782), II, § 74

The *Scienza della legislazione* would have been something entirely different without the American Revolution. Less passionate and prophetic, perhaps more traditional and predictable, it would certainly lack those original traits which make it a milestone of Western constitutionalism.

That epochal event gained a 'strong character of exemplarity'[1] for Filangieri that in fact marked his most inspired and durable pages, gave vigour and courage to his most radical political positions, and constituted both a subterranean current in, and the tenacious red thread of, his enormous œuvre. It is well known that the clamorous events across the Atlantic hit the spirit of the young jurist hard also on the human level, seriously influencing the tormented civil and political experience of late eighteenth-century Naples. They were really sincere, in this sense, the words that the young cadet of the ancient house of the Princes of Arianello addressed to Benjamin Franklin on the second of December 1782, asking him to favour his transfer to America:

Philadelphia has attracted my gaze ever since I was a child. I have so gotten used to consider it the only country in which I can be happy that my imagination cannot rid itself of this idea… But how can one leave the service of one's own prince without a cause to justify the decision? Dear and respectable Franklin, who more than you can facilitate this enterprise! Perhaps my works on legislation could persuade you to invite me to contribute to the great code of laws that is being prepared in the United Provinces of America, the laws of which must decide not only their fate, but also that of this new hemisphere? What more reasonable motive could I give to justify my departure? I could also, in principle, ask my court permission to leave for a while, to not exacerbate it with a permanent dimension: but, once in America, who could take me back to Europe! Could I, from the exile of virtue, from the fatherland of heroes, from the cities of brothers, desire a return to a country which is corrupted by vice and degraded to serfdom? Could ever my soul, accustomed to the delight of an emerging liberty, adapt again to the spectacle of an omnipotent despotic authority in the hands of a single man? Could I, after having known and appreciated the society of citizens, desire the company of courtiers and slaves?[2]

Filangieri's escape from the refined Bourbon court to the austere parliamentary halls of the American Republic would never take place. With a pragmatic, completely Anglo-Saxon realism, Franklin discouraged his young friend, whose talent and writings he much appreciated, from confounding dreams with reality; he let him touch as if by hand, in a long and caring letter, the dramatic struggle for survival in the colonies, the hardships of a life very different from that generally conducted by the European nobility.[3] Only come war's end, in 1784, did Franklin return to the topic, encouraging him, unsuccessfully, to have himself nominated representative of the Bourbon government to the new republic. The year before, as a sign of deferral and esteem, he had sent Filangieri the 'code of the American Constitution,' made by the popular assemblies of the thirteen republics, in the hope of having his comments. The latter replied sending him the third volume of his monumental work dedicated to criminal law and reminded him it was written with a cosmopolitan spirit, Filangieri having always had 'before his eyes the legislation of all peoples and of all times,'[4] and therefore perfectly adaptable also to the tribunals of the new American nation which he loved so dearly. Cemented by their common Masonic militancy, the friendship between the two further fuelled – if ever it was thought necessary – Filangieri's constant attention to the events in North America. Only the precocious death of the Neapolitan philosopher at age 36, on the 21st of July 1788, ended that long-distance dialogue of reciprocal admiration. Franklin's last letter, accompanied by a copy of the United States Constitution, had arrived shortly before.[5]

Filangieri lived the American War of Independence intensely, particularly in terms of its intellectual repercussions. For him as for many Enlightenment philosophers of his generation, that dramatic political and social experiment, which opened a new era in Western history posing America against Europe, New World against Old, represented an obligatory paradigm of reference and an inexhaustible source of passionate debate, of unsettling questions, and of daring answers. The political experience of Enlightenment Italy culminated there. Every volume and every page of the *Scienza della legislazione* is deeply marked by the events. Though we will return to this at length, the very political and ideal motif driving the work, that is the critical rethinking of a legislation capable of going beyond the Old Regime, aimed at creating a just society able to 'introduce [the] virtue [of the ancients] to the wealth of the moderns' [I, 55], fusing liberty and fairness, the rights of man with economic development and social justice, becomes forceless and obscure when divorced from the background represented by those turbulent events. For Filangieri (who always loved to think as a 'cosmopolitan philosopher, attentive to the business of all the peoples of the earth), the revolt of the American colonies was in no way a mere marginal episode in the history of eighteenth-century European colonialism. He saw the entire political, social, and economic equilibrium of the world dangerously up in the air as a result of these events. He was acutely aware that the challenge launched against the secular supremacy of Europe by those small colonies united in a great republic was of a peculiar nature, entirely different from all past ones. Filangieri harboured the alarming sense that this represented a complete challenge to civilization, a challenge from which it could not back down without facing definitive decline. In his eyes, the triumph of the American Revolution really could change the history of the world.[6] 'Wealth has therefore become the great instrument of war,' Filangieri wrote in a prophetic passage that merits quotation in its entirety,

and gold and silver the barriers or vehicles of conquest. In accordance with these incontrovertible principles… I say that it is elsewhere that we must turn out fearful gazes. In a corner of America, among a free and commercial people, sons of Europe, but which oppression has made enemies of their mother; among this people, I say, a voice is arising which says: Europeans, if we arrived in the New World as serfs, know that today our wealth and our knowledge of that which we can acquire will no longer suffer an offensive servitude, [but] can be changed into a kind of liberty which will not delay much in placing us in the position to give you laws and which one day will make you repent having been the artificers of our chains. Our independence, fruit of your injustices and our resentment; the advantages of our position; the celerity which our commerce can have; the ease we enjoy in attracting, with a single act of will, the wealth and pleasures of the two hemispheres; the increase of our population, grown both through the multiplicity of marriages produced by public opulence and by the influx of foreigners drawn laughing to our shores by the rays of an emerging liberty; all these advantages, united to the superiority which the vigour of youth gives to states and to men, coupled with the sentiment of prosperity which will make us arbiters of the destiny of America and of the fate of Europe: we will easily snatch the fountains of your riches from you; the immense space which separates us will permit us to prepare our invasions before the rumours of them reach your shores; we will be able to choose our enemies, the field, and the moment of our victories; our treasures and our situation always assure us the felicity of our enterprises; our victorious fleets will always appear around coasts which can be neither guarded nor defended well from distant powers; your reinforcements will arrive slowly; your colonies will, finally, either become our provinces or break their chains with our help, which we will never deny them if asked for by the voice of liberty against tyranny. Thus privy of America, and as a consequence of Asia, which only wants our silver, you will revert to the obscurity and barbarism from which you have emerged, and only your poverty will protect you against our just but not profitable vengeance. This is the melancholy intimation that the English colonies can give Europe, and a people like this, which are not a republic of poor and war-like Romans, can today become the object of its fears. [I, 141][7]

In the face of Europe's *fin-de-siècle* crisis – a conviction diffused in all the intellectual milieus of the continent[8] and on which Filangieri wrote penetratingly in examining the recent history of the great nations – the United States represented the possible future model of Western society: the best legacy of a glorious past and a political laboratory for the future. In this way his numerous pages dedicated to America's economic potential, the virtuous manners of its colonists, and the legislative choices of single republics often came to assume the character of myth. The Pennsylvania of William Penn was defined without hesitation a 'homeland of heroes, the nursery of liberty, and the object of the admiration of the universe.' Among other things, this republic was credited with having understood the necessity of 'entrusting the distribution of charges to the people' with the aim of actualizing the democratic principle [1, 132], seeking, in this way, to combine the individual's inevitable love of power with the general interest. American women were described as 'sweet, modest, compassionate, and charitable.' Families were solid, prolific, and industrious. Vices, libertinism, and prostitution were almost nonexistent there, customs simple and pure: 'what a sad parallel to those of Europe!' The reasons for this were first of all to be found in America's particular climactic conditions, but also in precise political and social choices resulting from its colonial origins: the 'universal wealth wisely divided in the first distribution of lands and by the course of industry,' Filangieri specified, 'multiplies the number of marriages, and all unite to conserve customs and public honesty' [I, 224]. His deep admiration for American history did not falter even in front of things he frankly disagreed with or found wrongheaded, such as the laws on capital punishment for deserters.[9] If anything, a deeper juridical discussion of the case and his open humanitarian criticism of it were accompanied by a call to always remember the paradigmatic value of the American events for the entire West:

> Free citizens of an independent America, you are too virtuous and enlightened to ignore the fact that by conquering the right to govern yourself you have, in the eyes of the universe, taken on the duty of being wiser, more moderate, and happier than all other peoples. At the tribunal of humanity, you will account for all the sophisms that your errors could produce against liberty. Guard yourselves, therefore, against embarrassing its defenders and making its enemies talk. [III, 162]

On one point, however, Filangieri was adamant in distancing himself from the American experience: the presence of slavery in the new homeland of free men. It in fact seemed incredible and unacceptable to him that while in old Europe

> our laws declare themselves in favour of the liberty of man, while mankind everywhere claims its rights, European America is covered by slaves; not only is legislation silent on this abuse, but it protects that foul trade; and in the immense space of this vast continent one finds only a tiny region of heroes who have avoided the regrets of this injustice and the scandal of posterity. Only Pennsylvania does not have slaves.[10]

The dense pages, oozing with disdain, which he dedicated to demolishing 'the iron logic by which a victor supposedly has a right over the vanquished' remain among the most intense and beautiful written by Enlightenment philosophers against the habit by which 'the inviolable rights of humanity and of reason' were bought and sold 'at low cost' [I, 81–4]. But the colonial struggle for liberty and for the construction of a more just and fair model of society nonetheless continued to intrigue him, forcibly drawing him to their side. 'But what can we say of England? I see all of Europe squared off against this republic; I hear all of humanity vote for the independence of its colonies' [I, 285].

Like for Raynal, Condorcet, and Diderot, what was at stake for Filangieri was not only the victory of a handful of men against a giant oppressor, but the possible beginning of an end to British imperialism and the general re-evaluation of Old World colonialism, which for centuries had been conducted, brutally and mercilessly, in the name of an unfair society. The rights of man were either universal or they fell to the cynical political measures of traditional national interests. There could no longer be doubts or uncertainties in this regard. The American case again became the exemplar:

> it was not the excess of wealth and of prosperity which made the American colonies revolt, but the excess of their oppression… Should this example not suffice to bring the other governments of Europe down to earth? Why, instead of seeing the American Revolution as a simple chastising of English pride, should they not rather be considered a terrible lesson to all powers dividing the rich shares of that vast continent? Will they wait for a common cause to make that catastrophe, which forever will divide one world from the other, universal? [I, 300–301]

The revolts of the remaining colonies in the four corners of the world seemed by then imminent and 'inevitable' unless a radical rethinking of the internal and external politics of the great powers took place, a rethinking of their economic and social constitutions in light of the principles of the distributive justice of international wealth and of respect for the rights of man everywhere. The *Scienza della legislazione* emerged, in other words, against the epic backdrop of the crisis of the Old Regime, in the context of a critical reappraisal of the very idea of politics and of global equilibriums in relation to the principles, ideals, and practical implementation of late Enlightenment culture.

When Filangieri published the rich first two volumes in 1780, he certainly did not represent an isolated phenomenon among contemporary intellectuals or in the debates of the dawning European public opinion. Franco Venturi's monumental works on the end of the eighteenth century have definitely clarified the consequences of American history for the development of the late European Enlightenment.[11] If the blinding light generated by the Parisian events of 1789 has veiled these episodes in historiographical darkness, one risks distorting the truth by continuing to underestimate their importance. We know that Vittorio Alfieri was not alone in Italy to write his celebrated ode to *America libera*. Pro-American propaganda in the Masonic circles of the peninsula quickly created a veritable political myth of the transoceanic revolution.[12] Philadelphia became the model of the ideal city to many.[13] The newspapers of Florence, Venice, Milan, Rome, Turin, and Naples were filled with articles describing and analyzing the most important aspects of the war between England and America in their most minute details. Italian readers had available to them richly detailed accounts narrating the Boston Tea Party, the first confrontations at Lexington, the creation of the Continental Army, the arrival of the French fleet, and the siege of Yorktown, all with a delay of only two months. Though outspokenly partial of the colonials, as the publication of Washington's speech before the battle of Trenton or the attention given Adams' discourses in the chamber of representatives testify,[14] the chronicles of the conflict did not hesitate to describe, alongside all the victorious battles, the drama of violence and of the numerous social conflicts in America, as well as the war's devastating financial and human costs. More than the availability of information and the advantages of a system of communication was extended to the newspaper-reading urban and international elites though; what is most important to underline here is the birth of what shortly would become the fundamental nucleus of the modern language of politics.

For evidence of this it is enough to observe the emphasis which newspapers put on English debates as early as the 1770s onwards, from John Wilkes' struggle against the old parties and the crown to the ever clearer fracture in the progressive and reformist front, between radical republicans who looked to the necessity of creating new and original forms of government on the one hand, and the defenders – among whom Wilkes himself – of the traditional British constitutional model of a mixed government, which if possible was to be taken back to its original libertarian interpretation, on the other. That burning confrontation, which for more attentive Italian readers in the end had transformed itself into a sort of 'picturesque course in British constitutional law,'[15] definitely changed its nature and meaning with the *Declaration of Independence* of 4 July 1776. From that moment on, the old and glorious English republican tradition, which thanks to Montesquieu had come to be identified with the model of mixed government and thus an oriflamme for champions of liberty, ceased to be the horizon of reference for many progressives. The new radical republicans denied the authority of the London parliament. Fuelling the polemic with constant references to the rights of man, and, more generally, to the continental ideals of Enlightenment, they finally came to experience institutions and forms of government across the ocean which were more sensitive to the egalitarian and democratic ideals of their age. This clamorous rupture in the political and constitutional history of Europe was immediately received and emphasized by the Italian press. Ample space was devoted to the publication of, and commentary on, the *Declaration of Independence*, which succinctly illustrated the thoughts of an entire era. It appeared in full in the *Gazzetta universale* and in the *Notizie del Mondo*, both published in Florence, immediately diffusing it across the peninsula.

> We hold these truths to be self-evident, that all men are created equal, that they are endowed by their Creator with certain unalienable Rights, that among these are Life, Liberty and the pursuit of Happiness.–That to secure these rights, Governments are instituted among Men, deriving their just powers from the consent of the governed,–that whenever any form of Government becomes destructive of these ends, it is the Right of the People to alter or to abolish it, and to institute new Government, laying its foundation on such principles and organizing its powers in such form, as to them shall seem most likely to effect their Safety and Happiness.[16]

Thus said the text formulated by Thomas Jefferson, the most enlightened of the American revolutionaries. By reflection, it must immediately be said, this short but extraordinary piece came to have a decisive influence in Italy as well. There too, it marked an important step in the rapid politicization of the so-called Republic of Letters and profoundly transformed the vocabulary and language of politics, a fact which we will explore at length in the coming chapters.[17] Newspapers gave a decisive contribution in this direction by letting their Italian readers reach out and touch, almost as if by hand, the dramatic but at the same time exciting condition of the American colonials, who for the first time in history were dealing with a constituent power involving a community of more than 2,500,000 souls. References to the legislative assemblies established by the thirteen republics were innumerable in the newspapers, and the same went for depictions of their intensive political life composed of conflicts, passionate discourses, regulations for identifying those eligible to vote, procedures for selecting representatives to the Philadelphia Convention, federal competences, and institutions guaranteeing the rights of citizens. The comment on article VI of the Delaware Constitution, published by the *Nuove di diverse corti e paesi* in March 1777, affirming that 'liberty is founded on the right which people have to participate in legislation,' clearly revealed to Italian readers how far they had come since the appearance of Montesquieu's *Esprit des lois*. The demand for so-called civil liberty was rapidly being transformed into political liberty, which in the first instance was to be guaranteed by the exercise of popular sovereignty. The story of the construction of democracy in a great republic, day after day, overcoming thousands of difficulties, was generally accompanied in the newspapers by the publication of fundamental documents like the *Articles of Confederation and Perpetual Union of the Thirteen Colonies of the United States*, which appeared on the pages of the Florentine *Notizie del Mondo* in February 1777, or the unabridged constitution of Massachusetts, published in 1780 by the Venetian edition of the same journal,[18] or the 1784 Neapolitan publication in the *Scelta miscellanea* of a long *Extract of the New Constitution of the Thirteen States of North America*.

The appearance of these documents and the commentaries on them clearly demonstrates how American developments in the revolutionary practice of democracy were transforming the foundations of traditional political theory as well. There was no need to call on Thomas Paine's celebrated 1776 bestseller *Common Sense* (immediately reviewed by the *Notizie del Mondo* in April that same year), to realize the great change that was reshaping key concepts like social contract, representation, constitution, democracy, and republic. In the case of representation, in particular, the practical necessity of organizing legislative assemblies in a vast territory had led Americans to consider 'representative government' to be the only way to give concrete shape to popular sovereignty; the only way to bring about that contract between free and equal men which political tracts based on natural law had spoken of only in general terms. Even if still delimited both by property and by gender, representation was transforming itself from a privilege (given, according to a European custom hailing from the Middle Ages, to guilds, classes, cities, counties, and more generally organic communities gifted with a juridical personality) into an individual right conceded to almost all colonists.[19] Contemporaneously with the criticisms against, and the overcoming of, the mixed English model, a modern kind of constitutionalism began to emerge. Made of written texts and deliberated by the congresses of the thirteen republics, it very clearly highlighted the difference between the constitution and the government of a nation, between the 'inalienable rights' announced by the declaration of principles and legislative power.[20] The authors of the 1787–8 *Federalist*, and before that Paine in his *Common Sense*, and then particularly in the 1791 *Rights of Man*,[21] were thus not entirely mistaken in proudly vindicating the great theoretical novelties ushered in by the American experience. James Madison's affirmation that man's history in America could 'claim credit for making the discovery' of representation 'the basis of unmixed and extensive republics' was in many ways sacrosanct. The institutional solutions developed during the Revolution had in fact contributed greatly to clarifying the differences between the ancient and modern conceptions of a republic and of direct and representative democracy: 'In a democracy the people meet and exercise the government in person; in a republic, they assemble and administer it by their representatives and agents. A democracy, consequently, will be confined to a small spot. A republic may be extended over a large region.'[22]

The venerable European debate over the nature of republican government, and in particular over the thesis, made dogma by Montesquieu and Rousseau, that only small communities could give life to forms of democratic government since the only form of democracy known to history had been the direct democracy of the ancients, took an entirely different turn in the United States, at least in linguistic terms. The spectacle of the American legislative assemblies and the forms of government expected by the constitutions gave birth to the expression 'representative democracy' in Europe (an expression which, as we have seen, appeared incomprehensible and downright contradictory on the other side of the Atlantic,[23] whereas it affirmed itself in the continental political lexicon in the course of the subsequent decade). Condorcet was among the first to use this locution. In an 1787 contribution to the debates, denouncing the limitations of the ancient popular republics and commenting with enthusiasm on the 'spectacle of equality which reigns in the United States,' the *philosophe* made precise reference to '*democratie représentative*' as the historical task which the American constitutions had to achieve to guarantee freedom of trade, to remedy social inequalities, and to guarantee the rights of man.[24]

Thanks also to interventions like this, the constitutional debate quickly became the lens through which European protagonists in the Republic of Letters engaged with the American Revolution and its consequences in the 1780s. In France in particular, Raynal and Mably, followed by Turgot, by the marquis de Chastellux, by Honoré de Mirabeau and by others still, began to interrogate themselves on the continuities and differences between the mixed English and representative American governments, between the ancient British political tradition and the innovative constitutional government of the colonists across the Atlantic.[25] The watershed for the argument in favour of a clean break between past and present was certainly 1784, when Thomas Jefferson arrived in France as the United States' representative. Driven by propagandistic motives, a circle of 'friends of America' took shape around him, which counted among its members Du Pont de Nemours, Gauvin Gallois, Condorcet, Morellet, Piattoli, and Mazzei.[26] The most important work to come out of that group was signed by the Tuscan Filippo Mazzei, and summarized their debates and opinions. The *Recherches historiques et politiques sur les Etats-Unis de l'Amériques septentrionale, où l'on traite des établissemens des treize colonies, de leurs rapports et de leurs dissentions avec la Grande-Bretagne, de leurs gouvernemens avant et après la révolution* appeared between 1786 and 1788, inaugurating a new era in the interpretation of recent American history. Polemically liquidating the apologetic but at times inventive reflections of Raynal in the celebrated *Histoire philosophique et politique des établissemens et du commerce des européens dans les deux Indes* and criticizing the worn-out categories employed by Mably in the *Observations sur les lois et le gouvernement des Etats Unis d'Amérique*, which still was stuck on the paradigmatic significance of ancient republican models and of mixed government, Mazzei's volumes instead insisted on the experimental and highly innovative character of the American events. Filangieri was certainly one of the key authors this group drew on. Mazzei knew him well, appreciated his ideas, and did not hesitate to employ them himself.[27] In those very crucial years before the great revolution, Gauvin Gallois completed a fundamental translation of the *Scienza della legislazione* which for a long time would remain central to French political life.[28]

Fuelled by his personal relationship with Franklin, Lalande, Dupaty, Pastoret, and the brothers of the enlightened Masonic lodge of the *Neuf Sœurs* (founded by the *philosophes* gathered around the widow of Helvétius at Auteuil in Paris in 1776), Filangieri's European fame rapidly grew in international republican circles, and his direct involvement in the incensed debate over the political and constitutional consequences of the American Revolution was inevitable. Among the 'political philosophers' of the time (this was how his English translator William Kendall defined him[29]), Filangieri was probably the first to codify the theoretical consequences of the colonial experiments for the art of government.

Filangieri's polemic against the common opinion that republican and democratic government could not exist in a large state had already been delineated in the two inaugural 1780 volumes of the *Scienza della legislazione*. Though admitting that 'a perfect democracy [in the sense which we now define the so-called direct democracy or democracy of the ancients] cannot take place but in a very small state,' the transatlantic experience of popular government seemed to him to reveal an entirely new way of thinking critically about the idea of democracy itself, and thus of republicanism, through the practice of representation. 'If the republic grows,' Filangieri specified,

> if after having been a city, it becomes a nation, then it is necessary to either change its constitution entirely, or to take recourse to representation. Every city, every village must nominate its representatives, which will exercise legislative power in the name of the people, which no longer would be able to unite as before. [I, 101–2]

Previously, while explaining how it finally was possible to bring about 'popular government' in a modern republic in a way that did not repeat the tragic errors of the ancient world, incapable of going beyond direct democracy, Filangieri had added that

> since supreme power in democracies lies in the hands of the entire nation; since sovereignty which elsewhere is enclosed within the walls of a palace does not present itself in those governments but in the public square; since, finally, where the people reign every citizen is nothing on his own, but is everything when united with the others, it does not require much to see that the first object of the laws of this government will be that of regulating and establishing the number and conditions of the citizens which form it. [I, 100]

This was precisely what the American legislative assemblies were doing through the drawing up of their constitutions.[30] It is necessary to emphasize that Filangieri's writings on this subject were not simply superficial concessions influenced by the press. If, on the linguistic level, references to the discourses of great American personalities reported by the newspapers were clear,[31] the idea that it was possible to create a great democratic republic through 'representation' as an alternative to the direct democracy of small city-states (which Filangieri defined 'perfect democracy') emerged from the same theoretical framework as the *Scienza della legislazione*. His tenacious contraposition to Montesquieu's political realism, guilty of never starting from the 'examination of principles' [I, 37], in fact brought him to stigmatize those among the greatest contemporary political theorists who dared to believe 'that domains of great extension are only susceptible to despotic government, [and therefore] that the problem of good legislation can only be resolved in small states' [I, 163].

Another decisive aspect of the immediate success of Filangieri's work in contemporary European political debates was certainly his implacable polemic against British constitutionalism, made of written and traditional laws founded on the principle of mixed government.[32] A widely debated subject in the eighteenth century, it had suddenly been animated by new energies emanating from the turmoil of crisis and revolution in America. Knowing the paradigmatic value of this question to the *novatores* ('this is the government of a nation which for a century attracts the eyes of Europe' [I, 109]), Filangieri had differed greatly from the contestations formulated, at different times, by Diderot, Helvétius, d'Holbach, Rousseau, or Linguet.[33] With respect to Rousseau's myth of direct democracy, or to Linguet's authoritarian conclusions in favour of something all too similar to a dictatorship,[34] which on behalf of the ancients criticized the modern forms of constitutionalism authoritatively prospected by Voltaire and particularly by Montesquieu in his apology of the English model, Filangieri refused to look to the past, instead focusing on the events and constitutional developments in America to the point of becoming the first true interpreter and theoretician of note to grasp the extent to which they diverged from Britain's old legal and political tradition. It was not by chance that these pages hastily were translated by William Kendall in 1792 to fuel the struggle for democratic government reform led by radical Londoners at the time.

Filangieri's analysis of the defects and contradictions of the British constitutional model articulated itself in the precise denunciation of three grave 'vices': 'the independence of he who gives orders to the body politic he commands; the secret and dangerous influence of the prince in the meetings of bodies representing sovereignty; and the inconsistency of the constitution' [I, 111]. For Filangieri, that 'bloated mass [*centone informe*]' of laws, of practices of government and of customs formed over the centuries did not at all guarantee the true liberty of the citizenry, as Montesquieu instead sustained in the *Esprit des lois*.[35] The libertarian vocation of that constitutional system, voluntarily constructed on the uncertainty of the 'distribution' of powers, was all appearances. This was determined by the composite and conflict-ridden nature of its sovereignty, by which

> the prince cannot do anything without the nation, but can betray it at any time; where the public vote is almost always contrary to the plurality of suffrages of those who represent it; where one takes what unhappily are nothing but compensations for oppression to be symptoms of liberty; and where, to the disgrace of its inhabitants, there is more license than liberty. [I, 109]

The first grave defect, in other words the crown's demand for total 'independence' from parliament with regards to the executive, included the absence of a precise, coherent, and coordinated 'distribution' of the three powers to distinct organs in order to ensure proper limits and guarantees. Thus a functioning mixed-government constitutionalism was in effect rendered impossible. In monarchical, aristocratic, and democratic governments, where the identity of sovereignty was clear, 'the different portions of *power* are distributed according to their nature,' Filangieri wrote,

> they are divided up among the diverse hands which are to employ it; but these hands are not independent of each other; and their actions cannot but align with their common direction; one is the fountainhead [sovereignty] from which they spring: one is the principal wheel which gives motion to all the others. If the sovereign makes the law in such a government, he is not the instrument of its execution, if he must leave judicial power in the hands of the magistrates, yet he maintains the public power. [I, 112]

Nothing similar took place in Great Britain, where the logic of mixed government dangerously fractioning sovereignty, simultaneously attributing the title to the king, to the nobility, and to the people, historically had ended up with reserving executive power for the monarchy, thus making it entirely independent and opposed to the legislature. The king thus became treacherously active in all the three 'distributions' of power, creating paradoxical and contradictory situations in terms of constitutional legitimacy if ever it became necessary to revoke his power:

> In this government, where the magistrate is king, and the sovereign is the assembly, in which the king himself is considered one of the three bodies which between them must exercise sovereignty, in this government, I say, where can the right and power to punish him reside? Can the parliament in England dethrone its king? Does it have the right and power to do so? Should not the king himself sign the decree condemning him to legitimate it? Should he not guide its execution? Is it perhaps not a fundamental maxim of this government that the king is infallible, that no earthly jurisdiction can judge him and punish him; that if parliament itself had this right the national constitution itself would have been destroyed, because the legislative faculty would have usurped the rights of the executive, which according to this government is independent by nature? [I, 112–13][36]

With iron legal logic, polemicizing with William Blackstone's *Commentaries on the Laws of England* and the Genevan Jean-Louis de Lolme's *Constitution de l'Angleterre*, Filangieri in the end laid bare the inconsistency of a mixed system and the despotic threat intrinsic to it. In new forms and from a republican angle, he thus reproposed the ancient criticisms against factionalized sovereignty made by absolutists like Jean Bodin, Thomas Hobbes, and, more recently, Jean-Jacques Rousseau.

Actually, the first defect he emphasized could find a reasonable solution – and in part had already done so[37] – in the clear separation of the judiciary and executive tasks of government. Admitting that 'in a well organized mixed government the essence of the constitution is that the king has the executive power of the laws,' Filangieri in no way believed this entailed that the Sovereign exercised 'personally this power in all its extension' [I, 118]. Where granted autonomy of management and respect for their magistrates, tribunals that ensured justice in the name of the king could assure the liberty and security of the citizenry:

> The judicial faculty thus separated from the executive – separated, I say, in effect but not by law – the king, in spite of the invulnerability and independence accorded him by the constitution, cannot evade the law, cannot arbitrarily rule over the life, the honour, and the substance of his citizens. [I, 119][38]

The second 'vice' was both far graver and more difficult to resolve: the capacity of the crown to exercise a sort of 'double influence' on parliament. This influence was apparently entirely legitimate, and in any case foreseen by the delicate equilibriums of the mixed system, in which the monarch, along with the nobility and the people, held sovereignty and thus legislative power,[39] but nonetheless hid a 'secret and dangerous' element able to 'destroy the liberty of the people without altering the constitution.' The sovereign could in fact literally buy the votes of parliament secretly, and with great political ability, using the possibility that the constitution conceded him of being not only titular of the executive and thus 'the only administrator of national incomes,' but also 'the sole distributor of all civil as well as military charges.' English history was full of examples of sovereigns who had manipulated parliament at their leisure without sparking civil wars, limiting themselves, in a Machiavellian manner, to respecting the form of the mixed regime. It was enough for the king, Filangieri wrote ironically, not to destroy 'the appearance of the constitution by his own hand; it is enough that he respects the rights of congress; it is enough that he contents himself with wielding it.' This was what the great Elizabeth and above all Henry VIII intelligently had done. The latter had, with perverse sophistication, brought the art of parliamentary manipulation to its apex:

> What did he not do before the eyes of parliament? Which attempts at the liberty of the people did he not commit…? Was it perhaps not by the hands of the two Chambers that he lit the fires into which the best citizens of the State went to end their days? Was it perhaps not parliament that established that the king's simple will would have the vigour of law? Were, perhaps, not all the blasphemies of tyranny adapted by parliament as principles of jurisprudence during his reign? [I, 115]

The fate of William II would have been very different had he followed the examples of Elizabeth I and of Henry III, practicing 'the art of corrupting the assembly representing sovereignty,' rather than challenging parliament formally like William I and Charles I had done. 'Let us persuade ourselves,' Filangieri noted, signalling a further step in his meticulous project of politically unveiling British constitutionalism, 'that there is no despotism worse than that which is hidden under the veil of liberty' [I, 116].

To remedy this situation required substantial structural interventions, which involved the nature and composition of parliament itself. If the power of the monarchy to nominate other offices of state was beyond discussion, delicate problems were in that sense posed by 'the unjust claims of the crown' in maintaining exclusive control over the nomination of new lords. To Filangieri, this was no less grave a fact than the secret practices of corruption, since it changed the equilibrium between the different titular components of legislative power. 'What remedy,' Filangieri polemically asked himself, 'has Anglican legislation opposed to the prince's influence in the house of peers, which for the permanence of its members and for their condition always plays a greater part in deliberations? Has it not increased rather than decreased this dangerous influence? Has it perhaps not given the prince the right to create as many lords as he wishes? And is not a created lord always a vote more for the king?' Why not consent to commoners nominating new barons directly? 'It is in the nature of this constitution that the assembly representing sovereignty has the right of honouring an individual worthy of being a member of it, that it thus has the exclusive right, before any other authority, to reward those it deems worthy, for great actions and services rendered the fatherland, with the right to sit in the House of *ottimati* [Lords], or of becoming permanent members of that of commons.'[40] Appealing to this internal logic of the mixed British constitution, constructed through the centuries with the objective of furnishing, through the equilibrium of its components, limits and guarantees against the crown's despotic temptations, Filangieri contested the presumed exclusive right of the English sovereign to nominate members of the upper house. 'What is stranger than the King of England's right to create both spiritual [bishops] and temporal lords? Are these not but members of the sovereignty? And, since the King is not sovereign by nature of this constitution, how can he communicate to others that which he does not have?' [I, 122]. The constitution had to be reformed, both so that the House of Commons could resist pressures and so that one finally could substitute 'an assembly of citizens for a congress of courtiers.' This, however, required a specific review of the electoral mechanisms of popular representation. To avoid a pathological increase in corruption and the 'infamous commerce of their votes' countervailing the democratic spirit of George III's London, for example, Filangieri did not hesitate to demand, on England's behalf, an increase in the property-requirements for voting.[41]

And yet, Filangieri's critique of the British constitution certainly touched upon crucial issues, both in terms of recent American history and of the international debate, with regards to the third, most serious 'vice' of them all: 'the inconsistency of the constitution.' The extraordinary constituent power of popular sovereignty in America had, through the different legislative assemblies, consecrated the birth of modern constitutionalism. Filangieri was among the first in Europe to unhesitantly draw the consequences of this for the long and intense debate which had been raging over the nature of 'fundamental laws' and the by then evident limits of Old Regime constitutionalism, which historically had legitimated the dialectic of the estates.

What is a constitution? What relationship exists between a constitution, legislative power, and ordinary laws? To whom is what we call today constituent power due? Can a mixed government give life to a constitution that is clear and consistent in time? These are all important questions which Filangieri did not shy away from, in the process reaching important conclusions that justified the *Scienza della legislazione*'s immediate translation into the most important Western languages. 'In all the governments of the world, the authority to create, abolish, and change the fundamental laws of the nation is its own exclusive right… Or,' Filangieri specified, 'only in popular and mixed governments is the nation itself sovereign; it is thus only in these two governments that the sovereign can change and alter the constitution, if he so wishes' [I, 116]. The American case demonstrated how it was possible for the representatives of a free political community democratically to create a constitution, for the first time in history formulating a concise written document capable of capturing the fundamental principles for regulating the life of an entire people. It was the right path to the future. To create a modern and real constitution in a nation like Great Britain, Filangieri clearly delineated his ideal constitution in 1780, stating 'it would be necessary to create a small code of fundamental laws, which determined the true nature of the constitution, the rights and limits of authority in all of the three bodies, and which neither admitted interpretation nor ambiguity. This code would only include the real fundamental laws, not those which, abusively, have been given this name' [I, 124]. One of the keystones of Filangieri's constitutional thought was precisely the profound difference between the fundamental laws of the constitution on the one hand, and ordinary laws on the other.[42] He in fact neatly distinguished between constitution and government, between constituents and the executive, between the extraordinary phase in which sovereign power was engaged in creating a free political community and the normal legislative production of parliament. 'Legislation, I repeat, must not, nor can it destroy the constitution; it must only repair its defects' [I, 122]. 'It is said that the right to change the fundamental laws determining it cannot be subtracted from congress without destroying the very nature of the constitution. It is therefore necessary to render its use difficult.' Once approved, the 'small code of true fundamental laws' was in fact to be preserved from the manipulations of parliament as its majority interests changed. 'One can obtain this,' Filangieri wrote, 'by determining that, when it comes to changing, or to abolishing, or to creating a fundamental law, a majority of votes is not enough to introduce the proposed novelty in the constitution. Rather, one must require unanimity to render it valid and legitimate. This remedy would not subtract from the assembly that right which it can never lose, but would safeguard the constitution from the continuous events which render it dangerous and inconstant... This is the only case in which the *liberum veto* could become useful in a republic' [I, 124].

It was against the backdrop of this concern that he realized just how different the evolving events in America were from the British political tradition. His first significant preoccupation was with guaranteeing the political and parliamentary life of a rigid constitution, understood as a written, concise, clear, and rational 'small code'; a fundamental text to guarantee not only the orderly political life of a nation, but above all safeguard it against despotism. This was, in other words, something profoundly different from the mixed constitutionalism of the British tradition, which, in Filangieri's eyes, historically had favoured 'the continuous fluctuation of the different bodies dividing authority.' He thus relaunched – if from a democratic and republican angle – the ancient absolutist polemics against the factionalization of sovereignty, the reign of anarchy, of confusion, the inevitable outbreak of civil war, and the dominion of the most powerful. 'The England which has provided the proofs of all my prepositions in this chapter would also offer me abundant evidence for this final truth… I am satisfied with saying simply that the history of this nation is, so to speak, the history of its constitutional vicissitudes; that the character of the king has always dictated the tone of its constitution; that the two chambers have always usurped the royal prerogative under princes weakened by the paucity of their talents, or bound by circumstances, but that under an astute and audacious prince they have always sold large parts of their own.' From Charles I to George III, all social and political disorder had been caused by a constitution that was in 'continuous change,' ready to be cast in doubt by whoever was most powerful at any given time.[43] Filangieri had no doubts that the old British constitutional model, the result of a secular stratification of laws, practices, different interpretations, and perpetual mediations between diverse political subjects, had exhausted its historical function in light of the new democratic and libertarian potential of American republicanism. In spite of it having been the oriflamme of modern liberty for more than a century, the British constitution was unmistakably aligned with the unique logic of the Old Regime. It was necessary that the 'philosophers of Europe,' the 'venerable English,' masters of constitutional thought, finally realized how antiquated and obscure their legislation seemed when compared to the transatlantic 'codes' purposefully crafted to reconcile 'liberty, peace, and reason' in a single written text. Filangieri's suggestion was both clear and definitive in this regard:

> Create new legislation which repairs the vices of your constitution; which fixes all the rights of the crown as well as of parliament; which abolishes all the ancient usages which are compatible no longer with the state of things; which has that unity which cannot be found in legislation made over so many centuries, in so many different circumstances, in so many different periods of your ever changed, ever reformed, but never perfected constitution... By rewarding zeal, punishing fraud and *courtierism*, and finally rendering members of parliament incorruptible because of their virtue and their interests, the constitution will exchange a solid and durable liberty for a dangerous and precarious license, herald of anarchy and despotism. Your enthusiasm for the public good, united to the profundity of your talents, will even make this easy. Seek, I say, to reconcile liberty, peace, and reason in a single code. [I, 125–6]

Chapter Three

AGAINST MONTESQUIEU AND CLASS CONSTITUTIONALISM: THE DENUNCIATIONS OF THE 'FEUDAL MONSTER' AND THE 'TEMPERED MONARCHY'

As one of the most suggestive and important elements in the construction of a new enlightened constitutionalism, the polemic against British legal, political, and institutional thought inspired by the lessons of the American Revolution was certainly no isolated current in the rhetorical structure of the *Scienza della legislazione*. The work was in fact consciously constructed though a scheme that, on the one hand, planned a punctilious and caustic critique of Old Regime Europe, of its unfair social and political order, and of its traditional corporative constitutionalism. On the other, it formulated precise proposals for constructing a new society on the basis of legislation re-founded on the values and principles of the *fin-de-siècle* Enlightenment. In this sense, Montesquieu, always careful to reason 'rather about what has been done than about what should be done' [I, 41], remained a central interlocutor. Similarly, a confrontation with the *Esprit des lois* was inevitable in terms of the historical function of liberty and the guarantee offered by so-called intermediary powers against the despotic temptations of monarchies after Louis XIV, a fundamental issue for the juridical and political debates of eighteenth-century Europe. It represents the veritable keystone of that which recent literature has defined 'Old Regime constitutionalism.' Especially in Naples, where sensibilities to the legal and institutional dimensions of politics were strong, one of the highest magistrates of the kingdom, the *Delegato della Real Giurisdizione* Niccolò Fraggianni, developed an effective constitutional ideology for the *ministero togato*, the ministry of the robe, capable of defending magistrate class interests against the crown's project of constructing a great national monarchy. The feudal nobility too had taken recourse to the pages of the *Esprit des lois* to vindicate the legitimacy of its privileges. This gave birth to a curious republican variant – according to contemporary interpretations – which agitated the banner of 'feudal liberty' against monarchical absolutism and the despotic tendencies of the Bourbons.[1] Already in 1751, a surprised prime minister Bernardo Tanucci wrote to Bartolemeo Corsini about the recourse the Neapolitan barons took to Montesquieu's great book to defend the secular, natural constitution of the kingdom, through which they enjoyed a dominant position, saying '[the *Esprit des lois*] is preached and read from the noble squares for the republican and British [britanno] spirit which triumphs in it [*che vi trionfa*].'[2] Following the Seven Years' War, the feudal question nonetheless seemed to have taken a path which did not limit itself only to legal and political questions, openly tackling social and economic problems as well. The works of Mably, Adam Ferguson, Simon-Nicholas Henri Linguet, and William Robertson, all of which had appeared between 1765 and 1769, and in particular Adam Smith's famous 1776 work on the *Nature and Causes of the Wealth of Nations*, had closely correlated the increasingly evident underdevelopment of continental agriculture compared to that of England and the American colonies with the persistence of feudalism. Filangieri, who probably had read Smith directly or through extracts published in Italian gazettes, made great use of him in the first volume of the *Scienza della legislazione*, dedicated to political and economic law. He loudly called for 'the number of small property-owners to be multiplied' [I, 196] to finally create a free market of land, and, among other things, for the 'exorbitant and inalienable wealth of the ecclesiastics'[3] to be made available and feudal serfs transformed into proprietors. This would empower the 'middle class' capable of producing wealth, feeding commerce and the arts without renouncing the practice of virtue and the search for public happiness. A necessary condition to begin such a process of social and economic transformation, which *de facto* subverted the Old Regime, was, however, the suppression of the cardinal institutions of feudalism. 'Abolish primogeniture before anything else,' Filangieri wrote,

> abolish the fidei-commissum. These are the causes of the exorbitant wealth of the few and the misery of the majority. Primogenitures sacrifice many children to the first-born of a family; substitutions sacrifice many families to a single one. Both reduce infinitely the number of proprietors in the nations of Europe, and both are today the ruin of populations. [I, 196]

Filangieri's public blaming of the feudal barons for the misery and backwardness of Europe, and in particular that of the Kingdom of Naples, only a few years after his 1774 attack on the corporate interests of the *ceto togato* in the *Riflessioni politiche su l'ultima legge del sovrano che riguarda l'amministrazione della giustizia*, triggered an inevitable and immediate reaction.[4] Filangieri replied with serene dignity, affirming 'When I embarked on this work, I promised to overcome all those vile fears which could hinder its course… I will always remember that persecutions and calamities are honourable when they are accompanied by the sighs and tears of the weak, to whom one has tried to lend a brave if impotent hand' [II, 133]. Reproposing Montesquieu's constitutional theories, the obscure provincial *literato* Giuseppe Grippa thundered publicly against Filangieri's disturbing 'political projects,' which aimed at the 'absolute dismissal even of the feudal institutions of majorat, fidei-commissum, and substitution' in aiming for 'the equitable diffusion of the wealth of a nation.'[5] The egalitarian and democratic demon that seemed to possess the author of the *Scienza della legislazione* was in fact unveiled and denounced primarily in the name of the monarchies and fundamental laws of the Old Regime, guarantors of Europe's liberty. If the 'constitution of the governments of Europe's principalities is better than that of the principalities of Asia,' the credit, as Montesquieu had explained, lay in the strong presence of intermediary bodies, in particular the feudal nobility;

'the principalities of Europe do not fall into the despotism of Asian governments because of the system of fiefs and the order of barons.' 'I say the same,' Grippa specified, explicitly quoting the *Esprit des lois*, 'of those mixed governments which need the order of nobles to maintain their constitution.'[6] To destroy the economic foundations of feudalism, in other words, was to assault liberty and favour despotism. If the 'nobility becomes a spectre,' bereft of the wealth and privileges securing its material existence, the monarchy too would be destined to disappear in short order, leaving room for the violence and anarchy of popular governments and the no less dangerous democratic republicanism of small landowners so dear to Filangieri, the young cadet of the princes of Arianello.

The feudal barons of *fin-de-siècle* Naples could perhaps not have defended themselves better. The challenge to reformers inspired by the American Revolution was yet again proposed, on Montesquieu's authoritative shoulders, in political, juridical, and finally economic terms. Grippa's pamphlet had sought to widen the discourse, while seeking to refute, facts in hand, the thesis that feudalism impeded economic and demographic growth. In any case, the absolute centrality of the constitutional vindication of 'feudal liberties' in the defence of baronial privileges was not lost to anyone. The time had come for enlightened thinkers to take the bull by the horns and discuss the feudal question in more properly legal and political terms, to seek finally to reflect simultaneously on the nexus of liberty and equality on the one hand, and on the legitimacy of baronial power on the other. Filangieri did it courageously, and was among the first in Europe to do so, with the 1783 publication of the third volume of his opus, dedicated to penal law. The result was one of the most famous pieces in that innovative constitutional mosaic of Enlightenment culture that was the *Scienza della legislazione*. A merit of this work is also that of identifying the historical and political processes of an era of profound transformations, an era in which it was no longer up to 'feudal liberty' to 'guarantee *equality, liberty, and security*' – according to the opinion of many authoritative contemporary scholars – 'but to the legal authority of the monarch: the government *by law* which must succeed the government *by will*.'[7]

In the terrible 'feudal monster,' Filangieri denounced not only an obstacle to economic development but also a cause of grave problems in liberty and justice, which was destined to trigger a precise political reflection on the nature of monarchical government in the Old Regime. He had no doubt about the fact that the 'skeleton of this ancient monster which has devastated Europe for so long' had to be 'entirely incinerated' because, throughout the centuries, it had given life to an unjust government based 'on the ruins of the people's civil liberties and of the crown's sacred rights'; a government where quotidian violence, the practice of inequality before the law, and the most insolent arbitrariness of the tribunals dominated. It is 'an unjust government,' Filangieri wrote, which 'familiarizes the souls of subjects with injustice so that, step by step, they come closer to considering it without horror.' If it was true that 'nature has not made us the playthings of a few powerful men, but has equipped us with all the means necessary for being free and happy' [I, 132], then 'the absurd way in which justice is administered in most nations today' seemed purposefully designed to deny any hope of having a better society in the future. Only a diabolical mind could, for example, have organized the persistent dominion of feudal jurisdiction in the Kingdom of Naples over more than 70%

of the population, excluding the capital.[8] 'The administration of justice,' Filangieri explained, considering his fatherland paradigmatic of many other states,

> is here divided between the feudal land-owners and the magistrates. The survival of the feudal government still leaves criminal jurisdiction in the hands of the barons. This prerogative, of which they are extremely jealous, forms the first ring in the chain of disorder that entirely destroys our civil society. [II, 134]

Feudal justice was based on a series of privileges that began to seem ever more unacceptable and odious. Barons were entitled to nominate the magistrates expected to investigate and arbitrate on the crimes taking place in their fiefs. That judge, however, ended up in effect becoming 'the baron's vile and miserable mercenary,' perennially blackmailed economically by his employer, subjected 'blindly to the caprices' of his lord through the threat of his power to revoke his appointment, and entirely incapable of guaranteeing real, autonomous justice. 'Without honour, without riches, without enlightenment, without the people's confidence, and incapable of getting it, they [the feudal judges],' Filangieri wrote indignantly, 'have no talent but that required to perturb, to oppress and to rob, to favour whoever is powerful and trample whoever is weak underfoot.' Their tragic task of administering justice on behalf of the feudal lord at times went only so far as a search for proof of the offender's culpability by all means, from prison to torture. At that point, the baron took over directly to agree on an economic recompense in place of punishment. In this way, Filangieri ironized bitterly, 'the public's vengeance becomes a feudal revenue. The feudal master and his judge deal with the delinquent; and in exchange for the payment of an arbitrary sum, they free him from the punishment he deserves' [II, 136]. But it did not end there. Not only was the baron allowed to capitalize on justice, voiding the law for those disposed to pay, but his privilege to concede grace was no less scandalous. 'This right which scarcely is compatible with sovereignty,' Filangieri underlined ever more indignantly,

> this right, which the king himself hardly makes use of in order not to multiply crimes by hope of impunity; this same right is exercised with the greatest indifference by the barons. The feudal lord's favourite, his companion in crime, the instrument of his attacks, is certain of remaining unpunished because he knows that his condemnation surely will be followed by a pardon; while an honest man, who has resisted the caprices of his lord, knows he certainly will be punished if he were to find himself wrapped in the web of the law and in the machinations of a violent and arbitrary procedure. [II, 137]

It was true that various degrees of appeal existed against a sentence considered unjust. But the first two were nonetheless before other judges who, paid by the baron, were no less sensitive to his caprices. And the final appeal to the provincial tribunals of the king seemed invented purposefully to discourage any intent to subtract oneself from the 'injustice of the baron's ministers.' 'Very poorly paid by the government,' which in effect condemned them to 'choose between injustice and poverty,' the judges nominated by the sovereign were forced anyway to evaluate cases on the basis of documents collected earlier in the process. If then, in a spurt of dignity, the first procedure were formally to be declared irregular, Filangieri believed the foreseen remedy was 'worse than the disease.' In fact, the public prosecutor, the king's inquisitor, entered the scene at this point to set the stage for a new trial, which was destined shortly to become a sort of incredible earthly inferno for all those who hoped to escape feudal justice. 'I beg the reader not to think this saddening description an exaggeration,' he wrote. 'I call the entire nation to testify; I call as testimony all the unhappy victims of this shameful system' [II, 139].

First of all, there was the figure of the 'inquisitor,' acting for the prosecution:

[the] most vile and thieving man in the province… a subaltern who not only is not paid by the government, but who pays it to be able to serve it; who ignominiously exercises a ministry which requires great honourableness, but which among us has become infamous for the character of the people to whom it is entrusted; who, in a few words, insensitive to all sentiments of mercy, of honour, and of justice, sees nothing in his charge but the hope and the means of safely stealing under the very auspices of the law.

As a preliminary act, he generally ordered the preventive 'incarceration of numerous witnesses, of the culprits, of accomplices, of suspects.' Immediately afterwards, he began to search for evidence by every means at his disposal, to involve the largest possible number of people to which to propose the way of the 'market [*mercato*],' in other words a cash exchange for absolution. When the baron's direct interest was in play, and the need to hide 'his own or his mercenary ministers' perfidy,' no 'advocate of the poor' would be able to achieve justice. Only in vain could one hope for recourse to free and objective testimonies, for 'the perfidious inquisitor' always got to them in advance of any deliberation, 'scaring them enough to not fear their naïve depositions. His bought witnesses are the only ones who present themselves to the judges' [II, 141]. How could Grippa and the many others who thought like him continue to sustain the privilege and arbitrary nature of feudal justice in the face of these bitter truths? Could the liberty of the powerful few last long in the presence of an 'unjust government' for the many? Did not a just and fair society presuppose equality before the law for all citizens?

The tragic scenario of justice in the Old Regime which emerged from the indignant and resentful pages of the *Scienza della legislazione* allowed Filangieri finally to confront all the aspects of the political and constitutional problem of just and legitimate government. With an impeccable logic, he linked the achievement of the primary objective, that of the 'most sacred rights of civil liberty' in a monarchical regime, to the by now necessary reforms of justice, the overcoming of class privileges which attributed fundamental fragments of sovereignty to intermediary bodies, masking corporate interests in the name of the defence of constitutional liberties.

How, one will ask, to remove the feudal lords from criminal jurisdiction without infringing upon justice? Does not an ancient possession, added to a just title, perhaps render inviolable any right, like it would render any property sacred? Has this jurisdiction that one would like to attack perhaps not been conceded through their investments and their merits, or with their money? Was this not part of the public authority put in the hands of the barons by the kings themselves? If the prince cannot change the constitution of a State; if he cannot destroy the fundamental laws of government, if he cannot violate the pacts with which he ascended the throne, how could he all of a sudden give this blow to the feudal prerogatives which form a part of the government's constitution? Would the destruction of feudal jurisdiction perhaps not facilitate the progress of despotism, removing this intermediary body between the prince and the people? This is what the apology of feudalism reduces itself to. [II, 143]

To Filangieri, the arguments brought to the defence of the presumed constitutional prerogatives of intermediary bodies seemed false and contrary to the 'true principles of politics.' It sufficed to reflect on the nature of sovereignty in the modern world to confirm this. After Bodin, Hobbes, and Rousseau, nobody doubted any longer that sovereignty had to be one and indivisible. As explained by Locke, Bolingbroke, and Montesquieu, the distribution of power as a guarantee was something else entirely: 'In every species of government, authority must be balanced, but not divided; the different parts of power must be distributed, but not distracted. One must be the source of power; every exercise of authority must begin from this point, and must always return to it.' The exemplary case for him was that of the typical democratic government in which the people 'themselves administered their sovereignty' through a precise constitution capable of fixing the limits and the forms of legislative and executive power, as well as the tasks and the prerogatives of magistrates and public functionaries. 'This act,' Filangieri specified, 'by which the constitution of this republic would take on a fixed form, would only distribute the exercise of the different parts of power, not divide sovereignty, which would always remain solely in the hands of the people' [II, 146]. Very different things were happening in Old Regime Europe, where the historical anachronism of the so-called 'feudal monarchy' reigned. This appeared, in the eyes of contemporaries, as a

> kind of government which divides the State into many small States, sovereignty into many small sovereignties; which splits those prerogatives which are not communicable from the crown, dividing rather than repartitioning the exercise of authority, distracting and alienating the power itself, cutting social bonds rather than reinforcing them, giving the people many tyrants in the place of a single king, putting numerous obstacles in the place of the king's efforts to do good, rather than impediments against his evil, giving the nation a domineering body, situated between the king and the people, which usurps the rights of the former with one hand to oppress the latter with the other; which, in short, mixing a tumultuous aristocracy with a divided despotism into a single government, leaves us with all the dependency of a monarchy, without the activity of its constitution, and all the turbulence of a republic, without its liberty. [II, 147]

The era in which feudalism represented a legitimate and universally acknowledged institution of civil law was lost in time. The persistence of investitures had assumed a new sense and historical significance in the political debates of those years, its essence configured as an odious private fact and an evident attack on the modern conception of sovereignty. 'The investiture of a fief,' Filangieri argued,

> is nothing but a solemn stipulation with which the sovereign gives and sells to a private citizen large parts of his authority over another part of the citizenry, who, without their *consensus*, are degraded from their political condition, condemned to a new servitude; obliged to new duties; denied parts of their dearest prerogatives; wrenched from the immediate jurisdiction of the monarch and transferred to that of a man who they rightfully could consider their equal. [II, 148]

The traditional baronial defence, according to which the legitimacy of feudal jurisdiction descended directly from the sovereign power of the king who freely had bestowed the benefits on the baron and his heirs, was entirely devoid of sense in Filangieri's eyes and even repugnant. Posed in these terms, the question could not but intersect the late Enlightenment definitions of sovereignty.[9] 'I ask,' he affirmed, 'if the king is the absolute proprietor, or the simple administrator of sovereignty?' Where was the sovereignty of a legitimate government located? What was the function and what were the limits of a monarch in a mixed government? Was it possible to rebel against a power held to be despotic by the citizenry? He found the answers mainly in the political theories of the author most present in the decisive passages of the *Scienza della legislazione*, 'Europe's greatest thinker, the immortal Locke' [II, 216]. From the second *Essay Concerning the True Original Extent, and End of Civil Government*, which he often cited,[10] Filangieri drew the arguments against the famous right of conquest posed at the foundations of both royal absolutism and of the baronial pretensions. In particular, he found reaffirmed in Locke that principle of popular sovereignty, and the contractual and consensual nature of political power between free and equal men, which seemed to him able to cast doubt upon the hypothesis of those who considered the monarch the 'absolute proprietor' of sovereignty. 'Who has ever dared suppose such rights in the head of a nation?,' Filangieri asked rhetorically.

> Although he ascended the throne by force, and although his titles derive from conquest, he will never be the State's sovereign without subsequent popular consent; he will be its enemy. The state of the nation will be one of war against this usurper, and all his sovereign acts will be illegitimate, violent blows. Only the people, in the hands of which sovereignty rests inalienable, can legitimate its exercise in the person of the administrator we call king or monarch. Whether mute or outspoken, this consensus is without doubt the only foundation of all his rights. If the monarch thus is a simple usufructuary of the crown, if he is an entrusted administrator of sovereignty, how can he alienate parts of it to the detriment either of the people themself or of his successors? What right can a monarch have to make heirs of his assistants? What right could he have to decree that parts of public authority be exercised *in perpetuum* by certain families, that the descendents of these, without having neither the talent nor the rectitude required, be admitted this to the exclusion of all others; and that the reward for services rendered the crown by some, or the fruit of a venal contract, be the prerogative of bequeathing his descendents the

absurd right of dominating part of their fellow citizens and of being powerful before being born? Any concession of this nature, whatever its title is, whatever its motive is, is thus by nature illegitimate and consequently void. [II, 152–3]

The conception of the king as simple 'administrator' of public sovereignty was further developed in his daring treatment of the so-called crimes of lese-majesty in the Old Regime.[11] If a citizen's sacred duty was never to attack sovereignty, understood abstractly as the final result of the 'most precious pact, which has the greatest influence, or, rather, that one cannot violate it without destroying society,' the personal attack on the king or on the dominant political power was something else. 'I have said *sovereignty* and not *sovereign*,' Filangieri specified, 'because whoever throws himself against the man, or against the members of the body which exercises and represents sovereignty, without seeking to usurp this sovereignty, is less guilty than one who would commit the same evil with a worse design' [II, 355]. In republican Rome, where the sovereignty of the people was clear, the crimes of lese-majesty were strictly circumscribed to the subversion of fundamental laws and the consequent violation of 'civil liberty.' The seed of despotism emerged only with Augustus and the empire, which saw an 'arbitrary extension' of the number and nature of the crimes designated lese-majesty and, among other things, confounding the right to criticize with the defence of sovereignty, subversive intentions with real subversive actions. In the Old Regime, all crimes against the king were deemed high treason. Distinction was no longer made between crimes of opinion, knowledge of a conspiracy, and direct participation in subversive activities. The political use of the crime of lese-majesty had rapidly transformed the rightful defence of sovereignty into a decisive instrument of despotism. How could one, for example, consider high treason, punishable by death, the 'simple intention of killing and deposing the king' – established, for example, by English law after Richard II – or all kinds of 'crimes which one commits in the castle'? Why privilege the court, of all things? 'Are perhaps not all the spaces of the monarchy or the republic seats of sovereignty?... Is a thief who, in the castle, steals a jewel from a rich courtier perhaps guiltier than he who steals the instrument of subsistence from a settler in his cabin? Is the pact which he violates perhaps more precious to the State? Is his influence on public order perhaps greater?... How many laws are found to be absurd when one consults reason!' Why assimilate crimes of opinion to high treason? 'I do not call the works of a philosopher who highlights the evils of his homeland to speed up their correction an insult,' Filangieri wrote resentfully. 'I do not call a word, an imprecision, or a malediction said in indignation an insult. I do not even use this word for a free and private debate about the conduct of the head of the nation. If we want to turn words into crimes, society will find itself full of informers and criminals' [II, 358].

Contrary to what one might suppose, this interpretation of the royal figure as public 'administrator' of popular sovereignty was not at all rare in Europe, and particularly not in Naples after the first attempts, at the beginning of the century, to proceed expediently with the creation of an absolute monarchy.[12] If anything seemed new and original it was the project, fully delineated in the *Scienza della legislazione*, of creating a new 'well constituted monarchy' in the future [II, 149] to oppose the prevailing and much criticized 'feudal monarchy,' where the crown's will to power, the despotism of the barons, and the arbitrariness of the magistrates ruled uncontested. Filangieri finally brought widely diffused suggestions and desires to bear with this project, which would be re-launched by all the protagonists of the late Italian Enlightenment.[13] It is in fact well known that the theme of civil liberty, understood as the rule of law, a state of rights and of guarantees for all citizens destined to express itself in the demand for equality before the law, represented the primary objective and true political myth of the Enlightenment on the peninsula.[14] When citizens live 'tranquil under the protection of the law… this *tranquillity* is what is called *civil liberty*; the true and only liberty which can be reconciled with the social state' [II, 2], Filangieri wrote, as he prepared to trace the contours of what we can define the first draft of constitutional monarchy.

Monarchy is the name of that government where only one rules, but with certain fundamental laws. These fundamental laws necessarily presuppose certain channels through which power is communicated and some repressive forces that conserve its moderation and splendour. Thus, the monarchy's nature requires that there be a body, depository of the laws, mediating between subjects and the prince. Nobles compose this intermediary rank, and the magistrates this body depositary of the laws. The laws must thus fix the privileges and rights of the former and the functions of the latter; they must fix the limits of all authorities in the State; they must declare what unhappily is ignored in almost all the monarchies of Europe: they must declare, I say, what the real rights of the crown are, and what the ministry of the individual which bears it is; they must determine up to which point legislative power must extend, and where the executive must begin and end; the subdivisions of this, the different orders of the magistrature, their dependencies, the order of appeals, their respective incumbencies, all must be determined and established by the law. If the security of monarchical citizens depends on this order, on this repartition, if every acquisition, every usurpation by one of its parts always results in a loss for the State; if, as soon as the king wants to be the judge or the judge acts as a legislator, there is no more liberty, no more security in the nation; if, finally, despotism appears in the magistrature, or among the nobles, or in the head of the nation, it is always despotism… [II, 107]

In this type of constitutional monarchy, programmatically constructed to evade despotism and guarantee civil liberty to all citizens, the only acceptable hereditary charge was that of the king, but only 'to avoid the disorders of an election and the disasters of an interregnum.' No privilege of blood or birth was, however, acceptable in the case of the so-called intermediary bodies. Magistrates and nobles were personally responsible for their political power. 'Recompenses,' Filangieri explained, 'are due for actions, charges for talent and merit in exercising them. A son may have the right to inherit the recompenses attained by his father, but could he have a right to inherit his charges?' To recognize the existence of economic and moral elites justifying themselves by their social function as intermediary body between sovereign and the people was one thing; admitting the specific hereditary political characteristics of which Montesquieu spoke was something entirely different.[15] Additionally, Filangieri took care to highlight that in democracies, 'where political equality is in the nature of the constitution, there is always a nobility of opinion' generally based on merit and talent. In a 'constituted monarchy,' this was historically the task – and it could not be otherwise in the eyes of a man who lived immersed in the concrete reality of the Old Regime – of the nobility.[16] The latter, however, had to transform itself, changing profoundly and with time becoming 'a luminous body, but not powerful; it must have certain prerogatives of honour, but not of empire [*d'imperio*]; it must be considered an effect of the laws of the opinions favoured by the government's constitution, rather than a necessary part of the body politic' [II, 144]. Continuing in this direction, after having unmasked, in polemic with Montesquieu, 'the cloak of patriotism and of liberty with which the most absurd system [that of feudal jurisdiction], which unites the vices of anarchy with the errors of tyranny, covers itself,' Filangieri called on the Barons fearlessly to accept the transformations of their fiefs into free private properties. This would contribute to the development of national agriculture, to the accumulation of wealth, and to the creation of a real land market, thus finally rendering them a real and natural elite respected by all.[17]

Compared to this, the purely political and constitutional task held by the *ceto togato*, the class of robed functionaries, was something different. Aware, however, that in 'such a delicate matter, everything is uncertain, equivocal, indefinite,' Filangieri did not hesitate to recognize that his ancient adversaries, ferociously criticized in his 1774 *Riflessioni politiche*, had the delicate task of being both executors of the law, willed by the sovereign, *and* the autonomous administrators of justice. Filangieri in any case hoped 'That these magistrates do not arbitrarily apply the laws, that they do not interpret them capriciously, that they do not distance themselves from their expressed prescriptions in the pretence of fairness; that the citizen does not see a judge in his legislator, nor a legislator in his judge' [I, 108]. In this way, the magistrature would simultaneously guarantee the constitution and the balance of powers, without eroding the necessarily unitary nature of sovereignty:

> The authority of the magistrates is not an alienation of sovereign authority; the power that they exercise is not a dismemberment of sovereignty. Applying the general laws dictated by the monarch to particular cases, they impede the abuse of authority that the monarch could commit, were the exercise of *executive power* united to the exercise of *legislative power*. They therefore balance this authority, but do not diminish its value. The unitary nature of power is maintained in all its extension in this distribution, since who executes without commanding, cannot be said to have a part of the power, but is rather an instrument of it, an organ of authority. [II, 147]

Filangieri has always been presented as a traditional and reassuringly stereotypical exponent of enlightened absolutism, according to a framework common to many other Italian and European thinkers of the age. Nothing could be more reductive and inexact. As we will see in detail, the great Neapolitan political philosopher always meditated on the nature of power, its limits, and its prerogatives, *ex parte civium*, never *ex parte principis*. The legitimacy of power always stemmed from below, never from above. Throughout his life, Filangieri remained a radical and republican thinker condemned to operate in a historical context dominated by the final crisis of the Old Regime, in a Naples in which reforms met opposition everywhere.[18] His eulogies of Frederick II and of Catherine the Great, for the important legislative reforms they had launched, should not lead us astray. Goethe's personal testimony in his *Italienische Reise* had, to those who would understand, already revealed the horror instilled in the young Filangieri by icons of despotism such as Joseph II, though their political actions aspired to Enlightenment.[19] Despotism, generally understood as the expression of a power positioning itself above the laws freely accepted by a political community, always remained the real negative pole of the *Scienza della legislazione*, the great evil to exorcise. Filangieri was probably the greatest Italian representative of the so-called new republicanism of the late Enlightenment, above all sensible to defending the rights of man and affirming a specific and highly original constitutional project. More than the form of government, or the institutional analysis of the mechanisms of popular participation in sovereignty, or the precise identification of *who* commanded, what mattered in Filangieri's eyes was *how* authority was exercised and the decisive respect shown in guaranteeing the law – the lifeguard, above all else, of civil liberties and of the rights of individual citizens. Though his sympathies for the American democratic experiment never diminished and his goodwill towards 'the inestimable good of the republic's political liberty' was confirmed constantly, he realistically realized that he lived in the Naples of Ferdinand IV, at a tormented time for the Old Regime, and that upon close scrutiny, 'every form of government has its particular advantages and some disadvantages which are unique to it.' A democratic republic, for example, would not always secure the rights of man, citizenship, and the rule of law better than a constitutional monarchy. 'In every society,' Filangieri wrote,

> there are two forces: one physical, the other moral. The first is in man, the second in the government… The particular advantage of a well-constituted monarchy is that the moral force finds itself combined with the lesser physical force. In a democracy, the moral force is united with the greatest physical force, and, as a result, civil liberty is immolated in favour of political liberty in this form of government. The furore of a free people, fired up by the eloquence of an orator, has nothing which it fears to hold it back. The decree of a popular assembly [*concione*] is the decree of a sovereign who unites all physical and all moral forces. An unjust law dictated by a meeting is guaranteed by the individual forces of all those who have gathered to approve it. The same does not happen in a well-constituted monarchy. [II, 149]

Also with respect to the mixed system and the traditional kind of constitutionalism of the so-called English 'republican monarchy,' the 'well-constituted' monarchy had the advantage of a greater certainty in the rule of law and the civil liberties of the citizens, if, and only if, it had arrived at a written and 'constant' constitution like the American one: a point explicitly demanded, as we have seen, by Filangieri in his critique of the British system. Nonetheless, in an Old Regime constitutional monarchy, where 'the king is sovereign because he is the legislator,' the great problem of popular participation in legislative power and the formation of political will, inevitable after Rousseau and the events in America, remained unresolved. The American experiment, however fascinating, still remained a hope for a future in need of verification; nor did the bitter political struggle across the Channel, between the crown, the people, and the aristocracy, seem able to furnish solutions for the future, since it was circumscribed to that mixed system which was impracticable on the continent, where absolutism historically had prevailed. How, then, awaiting the maturity that time would bring, to guarantee the exercise of some form of popular sovereignty also for other parts of *fin-de-siècle* European civil society? Alongside other important protagonists of late Enlightenment political culture, Filangieri trusted that task above all to nascent public opinion, to that strange tribunal of invisible and irresistible reason which all of a sudden seemed to have become one of the most interesting political institutions in the European monarchies of the time.

> There is a tribunal which exists in all nations, which is indivisible because it has none of the signs which could manifest it, but which acts continuously and which is stronger than the magistrates and the laws, of the ministers and of the king, which can be perverted by bad laws, directed, corrected, rendered just and virtuous by good ones, but which cannot be hindered and dominated by any of them. This tribunal, which demonstrates that sovereignty really does always lie with the people, and that this in some sense never ceases to represent it, despite it having deposited sovereignty in the hands of many or only one, in a senate or in a king; this tribunal, I say, is that of public opinion. [III, 292]

For this tribunal to function efficiently under all forms of government, but particularly in a constitutional monarchy in which legislative power remained tightly tied to the crown, at least two conditions had to be fulfilled: the people had to be educated at public expense, and the press had to be free. As we shall see, Filangieri dedicated, with a republican spirit, the entire fourth volume of the *Scienza della legislazione* to the first point. His belief was that what we today call the formation of a political public sphere necessitated the government's direct commitment and had to involve the greatest possible number of individuals, progressively enlarging itself to include all social strata, in the forms and manners most appropriate to the starting conditions of the subjects. His second point, the militant defence of the freedom of the press, was instead based on the Enlightenment presupposition, lionized by Kant in his 1784 response to the question *Was ist Aufklärung?*, that the public and critical use of reason in every sphere represented a precious and indispensable instrument for humanity's progress and emancipation. In this sense, every form of repression of press freedom seemed useless and counterproductive to Filangieri. To safeguard against abuses, it was enough to require authors by law to sign their works, at first entrusting the mechanism of personal responsibility in the face of public opinion to the Republic of Letters. 'Public disapproval is both the punishment and the remedy… The publication of the error is itself the best remedy against the seduction of error' [III, 292]. The full freedom of the press would, among other things, allow for the autonomous and authoritative unfolding of important new political powers in the hands of Enlightenment philosophers, and thus the possibility of appealing to public opinion directly. In collaboration with those sovereigns generously committed to achieving public happiness, 'the former would rule,' Filangieri explained 'while the latter directed opinion and philosophized to obtain suffrage for it' [III, 112].

The fact that the *Scienza della legislazione* enjoyed such extraordinary publishing success in the late eighteenth century, in Italy and abroad, is certainly a fundamental point from which to start analyzing it. That arrogant text, fermenting with civic passion, written by an able and penetrating pen, came across as a happy synthesis for many, a veritable manifesto for the political philosophy of the late European Enlightenment. In light of the preliminary results of a promising ongoing study, we know that the book became one of the greatest bestsellers of the *fin-de-siècle*. In Italy alone it went through numerous editions in only a few years, and translations into the most important Western languages followed in rapid succession – into English, French, Spanish, Polish, German, Swedish, Russian, and Danish.[20] Filangieri, 'the young Montesquieu of Italy,'[21] as they began to call him in France, immediately became one of the most luminous stars in the firmament of Europe's Republic of Letters. A veritable myth was soon born about the exemplary young philanthropic philosopher, fuelled by the most celebrated travellers racing to colloquize with him.[22] His unexpected death in July of 1788, at the age of 36, before completing the entirety of his project,[23] increased his celebrity everywhere, above all during the first years of the French Revolution. Beyond the author's personal charm, and the intrinsic value of his monumental work, what most struck his readers was his powerful and explicit polemic with Montesquieu, one of the key characters of the legal and political debates of eighteenth-century Europe. In this regard, however, it must immediately be said that Filangieri never held back, next to his criticisms, public and sincere recognition for the great Frenchman, almost as if he wanted to excuse himself for his ideological contraposition: 'I do not, however, want to neglect confessing my immense debt to this great man's toils,' he wrote respectfully, 'this tract of gratitude is a tribute which I offer a man who has thought before me and who with his own errors instructed me, and showed me the way to rediscover the truth' [I, 45].

The fact remains, however, that the *Scienza della legislazione* effectively was written – and above all immediately received as such by its contemporaries – to polemicize with Montesquieu head on, to definitively overcome the theses expressed in the *Esprit des lois*. Filangieri intended to cast doubt upon the very theoretical foundations and inspirational principles of that great book, frankly denouncing its strong conservative and corporatist character, and in its stead supplying a radically different way of thinking about legislation and about the relationship between politics and the law. 'The task which I propose to undertake,' he proudly affirmed in the introduction, 'is entirely different from this author's.'

> Montesquieu searches for the spirit of the law in these relationships [between law and climate, customs, modes of production, the character and history of people, etc.], I search for their rules. He tries to find in them the reasons for *what has been done*, I try to deduce in them the rules *for what must be done*. My very *principles* will largely differ from his. [I, 44]

He would remain true to his words. In a candid contrast with the sympathy demonstrated by the *philosophes* towards mixed regimes and the idea of a sovereignty divided between crown, people, and aristocracy, Filangieri maintained, for example, unshakable faith in a unitary thesis of sovereignty as the necessary horizon of reference for modern constitutions. He indignantly refuted, as we have seen, the very idea of hereditary nobility as well as the legitimacy of fiefs and feudal jurisdiction, even if understood as instruments of liberty and bulwarks against the despotism of the crown. He denied that the principles and 'motive forces' at the foundations of monarchy, republic and despotism were honour, virtue, and fear respectively, instead dedicating pages and pages to demonstrating the centrality and the different functions of the human 'love of power' in the three forms of government. Finally, to the famous thesis according to which large empires could have no government apart from despotism, the Neapolitan jurist did not hesitate to counter with the reasons for his political volunteerism: 'Is it perhaps true that the greatest bodies in nature are the most imperfect ones, and that art cannot perfect a colossus like it perfects a small statue?' [I, 163]. One could continue to quote many other issues, great and small, to show the depth and amplitude of the increasingly lively and insuperable contrast between the two authors; a contrast born not only from the distance between their respective theoretical frameworks, but also, and above all, from differences in their underlying political objectives. The Frenchman's interest lay primarily in investigating the guarantees of liberty in the modern world, while the Italian was driven to identify a new juridical order capable of ushering in a fairer and more just society that finally would put the rights of man first.

Truth is the two authors were symbolic representatives of two great and distinct stages of the Enlightenment; two moments occupying respectively a large swath of the eighteenth century and its final quarter, the peculiarities of which, in light of recent research, are finally becoming clearer. In the context of conceptualizing nature and scientific knowledge, for example, the first half of the eighteenth century saw a mechanistic, Cartesian and Newtonian kind of rationality dominate, which drew its model for understanding the political and social order from a fixed and immobile order of nature. The clockwork universe, with its iron laws of mathematics, seemed, in fact, to pave the way for the rational comprehension of the immutable laws of society and of social science. The way of perceiving and describing nature that emerged with the late Enlightenment was, in contrast, very different. The crisis of the physical and mathematical mechanistic worldview of Galileo and Newton, the transformism of animal species, the discovery of nature's historical dimension and the great debates at the end of the century over the very definition of what could be understood by 'science' had dangerously cracked the natural determinism of old and opened a doorway to a universe of possibilities. Faced with a natural order which new scientific discoveries revealed to have a far more ancient history than expected, and which perennially was in the processes of mutation, even the political and social order seemed susceptible to change. As though by a spell, human will rediscovered ample space for social and political action. Filangieri rightfully belonged to this new way of reflecting upon reality. The 'ought to be,' the optimistic and prophetic voluntarism, saturated by religiosity, vindicated in the *Scienza della legislazione* would have been entirely unthinkable in a cultural context different from that of the late Enlightenment.[24] Vice versa, the Cartesian and Newtonian Montesquieu perceived reality as a given definitive subject, the eternal and rational laws of which were to be investigated and understood in sociological and historical terms. They were nothing but the 'necessary relations deriving from the nature of things.'

Everything had its own laws. 'The divinity has its laws, the material world has its laws, the intelligences superior to man have their laws, the beasts have their laws, man has his laws.'[25] Like all thinkers largely extraneous to natural law theory, Montesquieu too saw little use in interrogating oneself on the concept of a just society, on the importance of elaborating legislation which assumed as its foundational and ultimate values justice and, in particular, the rights of man, an expression which was foreign to him.[26] These were not his primary objectives and they were not the questions that interested him. History and nature had *necessarily* produced certain relations of power and created situations of dominion that left out human inclinations. These situations ultimately were to be studied and rationally understood for what they were, not for what one would have liked them to be. On the contrary, Filangieri did not conceive of the law as a necessary relation to investigate, a peculiar juridical construction to interpret only on the level of history and philology, but first of all as an eminently political fact, a human act of will and reason: 'The laws are formulas which express the pacts of society' [II, 203]. His idea for a new science of the laws was first and foremost operative before immediately cognitive, the product of a militant intellectual who aimed at individuating the rules and principles of a future universal and cosmopolitan legislation, rather than studying the spirit and the nature of laws as such. In this sense, he developed, in the first volume of the *Scienza della legislazione*, the key concept of the 'absolute goodness of the law,' a point of reference and necessary horizon for all 'cosmopolitan' legislators, beginning with his American friends like Franklin, to whom he trustingly continued to send the volumes of his work as they were published. 'I call the *absolute goodness* of the laws,' Filangieri wrote,

> their harmony with the universal principles of morality, common to all nations, to all governments, and adaptable to all climates. The law of nature contains the immutable principles of what is *just and fair* in all cases. It is easy to show how fertile this spring is for legislation. No man can ignore its laws. [I, 76–7]

A precious integrative function of the principles of natural law was represented by the history of nations, by the teachings of Revelation, and by all those Evangelical and Christian maxims which 'developing the natural principles of reciprocal affection, and equalizing the conditions of men at the foot of the altar, put another seal on the liberty of man' [I, 81]. The insistence, derived from the matrix of natural law, with which Filangieri loved to stress the necessity of always referring to these 'fixed, determined, and immutable principles' every time he indicated an ideal law of 'absolute goodness' must, however, not be misunderstood. It is inexact and misleading to speak, as often has been done, of a 'Masonic hypostasis of the law'[27] in his theories and of his mythification of legislation as something abstract, something transcendent. If anything, he sanctifies and mythifies principles, never laws in themselves. It is enough to think of his vibrant writings against slavery in the name of the 'imprescriptible right of the liberty of man' and against 'the supposed right of the victor' [I, 82]. For Filangieri, one thing was the rights of man, another thing was their implementation, and yet another thing the law in its simultaneously rational and historical dimension. The first were the ends, the law represented the means. It was primarily conceived of as an excellent instrument, a formidable and indispensable weapon, for guaranteeing civil liberty and the rights of man in a just and fair society. But it nonetheless remained an instrument heavily conditioned by its historical context, the form of which was anyway changeable and revocable over time in adherence with man's political wishes. 'I write neither for loners nor for dark misanthropists' [I, 127], Filangieri liked to emphasize to underline the historical, concretely realist and reasonable nature of his utopia. A future enlightened and cosmopolitan legislation derived from principles needed, in this sense, to base itself on 'distinguishing the absolute from the relative goodness of the law.' One thing was in fact the ideal framework of reference, another, instead, the concrete history of peoples. Having pondered over Vico's *Scienza nuova* at length with brothers like Francescantonio Grimaldi and Mario Pagano in the Masonic lodges of Naples, and having thoroughly analyzed his complex and mysterious philosophy of humanity, centred on the suggestive hypothesis of an ideal and eternal history on which ran the course of nations, Filangieri knew well that 'nations do not resemble each other, governments do not resemble each other… the customs of a century are never those of the preceding century, nor of the subsequent one.'[28] Perfect legislation, a mythical political and social order of absolute justice and equity, had never existed, and would probably never exist. Nevertheless, his constant return to the rights of man and to the principles of natural law remained an important anchor from which to construct laws favouring man's emancipation. 'The best legislation,' he specified defining what was to be understood by 'relative goodness,'

> is that which is best adapted to the state of the nation from which it emanates… Two opposed legislations can both be useful to two different nations… who can ever doubt that the best legislation in this world can become the worst one, and that the most useful for a people at one time can become the most pernicious one for the same people at another time… the best codes can thus change… no one has understood this truth better than Locke. He was so persuaded by this that, set to be the legislator of *Carolina*, he wanted its legislation to be changed after a hundred years. This is how philosophical legislators think. [I, 89]

It was not, in other words, about doing violence to history and imposing an improbable ideal and definitive constitution on people of different developments and geographies. Rather, it was about reflecting on the historical conditions of a nation and of a political community in light of the great principles of natural law.

Beyond his evident republican sympathies in favour of the widest possible participation of the citizenry in the political life of a community, it is necessary to again underline that Filangieri by no means was a theoretician of a specific form of government, or the obsessive architect of an omnipresent and bureaucratic state, as some maliciously have argued by recourse to historical categories which, for a thinker of the eighteenth century, are anachronistic.[29] His points of reference were always civil society, justice, and the rights of man. His declared objective remained, above all, the elaboration of a science (entirely different from the ancient *scientia juris*) made of principles and rules to technically construct a new enlightened and cosmopolitan legislation able to change historical contexts and, in a Vichian manner, even the course of nations. This explains his sensibility to arguments which generally were neglected by the great authors of the era, such as the 'changing of a people's legislation,' the nature of constituent power, the complex relationship between popular sovereignty and constitution, the necessity of arriving at a concise written constitution of principles and fundamental laws on the American model, and even his interest in questions very near what we today call the law's test of constitutionality.

Unlike other great protagonists of the European juridical and political debates at the time – Blackstone, Bolingbroke, Vattel, De Lolme, but above all Montesquieu – who had shown little interest in analysing the mechanisms by which constitutions and constituent powers changed, Filangieri instead dedicated them an entire chapter. The study of the modalities through which the 'decline of codes' could occur was in fact a decisive point of his new science. Suffered, defined, and studied as a 'political revolution,' constitutional changes could occur violently, by the hand of 'an entire people enamoured of liberty and unhappy with the government' or through 'a slow revolution which moves silently, and which needs centuries to arrive at its goal' [I, 95]. This was, in Montesquieu's account, the English model and more generally that of the Old Regime. Referring to the necessity of considering the historical moment in which he lived, Filangieri dismissed both hypotheses, proposing a sort of new enlightened constituent power, capable of finally producing what he called the imminent 'peaceful revolution' so longed for in *fin-de-siècle* Europe, by then prey to the first symptoms of the final crisis of the Old Regime. Through strategic alliances with sovereigns responsive to reformist demands, the 'best pens' of the continent would have to denounce the injustices, the arbitrariness, and the contradictions of the old legislation, illustrating the principles and necessary foundations for building modern forms of constitutional monarchy sensitive to civil liberties and the rights of man.

> This is one of the cases in which the government must take recourse to genius. Then the pens of the administration's writers will pave the way for the new legislation. It will instruct the public in the errors of the old laws and the evils which resulted from them. It will show the citizenry the necessity of abolishing them. Then, finally, the voice of education, aligned with the aims of government, will dissipate one of the greatest obstacles, which is the multitude's blind passion for the old legislation. In the present state of things this preparation is already done. [I, 91]

The *Scienza della legislazione* was, moroever, a shining example of this. To Filangieri, the times seemed largely mature for a definitive change of the old social and political system.

Once the political space for such a new legislation (clearly to be founded on the principles of natural law) had been conquered, the successive steps lay in its preservation and its constant updating in relation to the challenges of time. In confronting this thorny question, which also involved the delicate relationship between the exercise of sovereignty and respect for the new constitution, Filangieri did not propose a possible definitive solution. Rather, he limited himself to focusing – and was among the very first to do so – on the multiple aspects of that crucial problem, in the end formulating a proposal resorting to the creation of a new magistracy: 'the censor of the laws.' Consisting of the 'wisest and most Enlightenment citizens in the State,' this magistracy was given the task of warning the legislator when a law began to 'contradict the customs, genius, religion, opulence, etc. of the nation.' Particularly, Filangieri insisted on the need for the new magistracy to guarantee the homogeneity, the rational unity, the comprehensively organic nature, and the effectiveness of the entire legislative *corpus*. The censors would have had to signal the dangerous accumulation, often most useless and repetitive, of the 'immense number of laws which oppress the tribunals and which render the study of jurisprudence similar to that of Chinese characters [*cifre de' cinesi*].' Theirs was the difficult, but decisive task of indicating the correct interpretation of every kind of legislative measure with respect to the fundamental laws, and, if necessary, to propose their elimination.

> The legislation thus continually repaired, reformed, and replaced in its parts, could acquire a certain degree of perfection apt to guarantee it against the insults of time and from the torrent of events which agitate political bodies, and which continually change a society's appearance. Thus, one would no longer see so many laws of exception for a single law of principle, so many interpretative laws for a single fundamental one, nor so many new laws which contradict the ancient ones. Thus, finally, the codes of law that today are the book of disorder and of confusion could become the monument of good order and the aggregate of multiple uniform principles, interlinked and directed towards a common goal. [I, 98]

One must immediately specify that we are still far from the theoretical and institutional achievement of something akin to the so-called modern constitutional test. The real powers of the censors were voluntarily limited. They could not concretely abrogate any laws. 'One must note,' Filangieri emphasized with his usual contrariety towards any hypothesis regarding the fractionalization of sovereignty, 'that the magistrature which I propose could only be consultative, else it would infringe upon the principal prerogative of the legislative faculty' [I, 96]. These pages, however, began to clearly delineate the great historical problem present in the dialectic between constitutionalism and popular sovereignty, a problem that would obsess generations of scholars in the tormented decades that followed. In fact, not only did Filangieri's *opus* clearly indicate the strategic function of the rights of man as a principle of reference for the cosmopolitan legislator, and particularly so in the first volume, but also the differences between ordinary laws and the constitution (defined as a 'small code, kept apart, of real fundamental laws'), and between the respect of the latter and the exercise of popular sovereignty. As we will see below, those precious seeds would germinate quickly, precisely in Naples, where his friend and student Mario Pagano a few years later would pick up and develop these thoughts in his 1787 *Saggi politici*, and then when drafting the *Costituzione* of the Neapolitan Republic in 1799.

Chapter Four

CONSTRUCTING A NEW CONSTITUTIONALISM: MASONIC SOCIABILITY AND EQUALITY

Why, beyond the reasons we rapidly sketched out in the previous chapter, did the *Scienza della legislazione* enjoy such great international success, not only at the end of the eighteenth century, but also in the years of the continent's widespread liberal and democratic struggles, fuelling hopes and simultaneously attracting sharp criticisms? What are the constitutive and characterizing elements, from a political, philosophical, and legal point of view, of the new constitutionalism delineated in Filangieri's work? What dangerous innovation, in other words, lurked in the Neapolitan jurist's framework that was able to generate such durable interest as well as heated diatribes? In answering these questions, one must never forget that those volumes were written in a very particular period in the history of western constitutionalism: between two revolutions, the American and the French, in an era of crisis, of transition, and of rapid changes. Those pages, to which the author, due to his precocious death, would never return, remain precious to this day, the equivalent of a sensitive seismograph, able to register tiny governmental changes, every innovation in the reigning conceptions of law and politics. And, importantly, Filangieri registered the minutest oscillations in the significance of the key term 'constitution,' destined, as it was, to dominate the political battles of the nineteenth century. Compared to most European dictionaries, which on the eve of 1789 fully revealed the uncertain and polyvalent character of the term, Filangieri's reflections contributed considerably to clarifying once and for all the modern sense of a constitution as a 'small code, kept apart, of real fundamental laws.' His contemporaries in Naples and London loved to speak of the Kingdom's 'fundamental constitution,' of the 'natural constitution of the people of England,' referring to a sort of Aristotelian material constitution, made up of laws stratified through the centuries and of ancient forms of government legitimated by the *consensus gentium*.[1] Instead, like Rousseau in the *Contrat Social* and the American revolutionaries, Filangieri preferred to underline the artificial and voluntary character of creating a constitution, an act that was political rather than historical and juridical in nature. He sensed that recourses like those taken by followers of the so-called constitutionalism of the Old Regime – whether corporations of magistrates or the aristocrats of birth – to medicinal metaphors in order to explain the political existence of a nation, representing communities like bodies drawing legitimacy from the natural order of things and from the slow sedimentation of historical processes, devoid of traumas and discontinuities, undermined his entire idea of a new science of legislation to be instituted *ex novo* on the foundation laid by the theory of the rights of man and the new principles of the Enlightenment. To the more inclusive use of the word constitution to mean the regulation and form of government of a political body naturally developed over time, he preferred the so-called legal use of the term, understood as a written law in opposition to the primacy of custom and habit. This use had been affirmed since the mid-sixteenth century in the context of canonical law to indicate the laws of the Church, of the religious orders, and, before that, for drafting medieval communal statutes.[2] In the Old Regime the two uses often seemed to mix in generic definitions like that formulated by Bolingbroke in 1727, in his celebrated *The British Constitution: or, the Fundamental Form of Government in Britain*, which so influenced Montesquieu: 'By Constitution we mean, whenever we speak with propriety and exactness, that assemblage of laws, institutions and customs, derived from certain principles of reason, directed to certain fixed objects of public good, that compose the general system, according to which the community hath agreed to be governed.'[3] Something similar can be said about the concise definition offered by Vattel, according to which 'what constitutes the constitution of the state' was nothing else but 'the fundamental regulation that determines the manner in which the public authority is to be executed.'[4] Only the events in America seemed able to impose a decisive impulse to specify the forms and content of modern constitutional thought, posing a first strong limit to the continuous oscillations in the significance of the word constitution. And, nonetheless, if it is true that what took place across the ocean quickly taught Filangieri to delineate the decisive traits of his *Scienza della legislazione*, his long militancy in the Masonic order was of no lesser influence. He in fact drew points and suggestions of great importance from the intellectual debates and above all from the cultural practices of Freemasonry, which deserve to be examined more closely.

All the greatest exponents of the Republic of Letters, and a large part of the ruling class of the capital's urban elites, were part of the Masonic lodges of Naples at the end of the eighteenth century. As we now know well, the phenomenon was not limited to Italy: more than 250,000 brothers gave life to analogous phenomena in every corner of Europe.[5] Through the Masonic form of sociability, in its role of catalyzing a specific Enlightenment culture only recently analyzed in its autonomous forms and contents, ancient ideals of natural law, the exuberant Enlightenment will to reform politics and society, and the high point of the scientific movement's ideology of progress intermixed, renewing themselves, giving life also to a new religious sensibility reflecting on the nexus of morality and politics in novel ways. Filangieri (the new 'Philander,' as his instructor monsignor Luca Nicola de Luca caringly had decided to call him in order to underline his disciple's instinctual love of humanity[6]) personally practiced, through his Masonic experience, a sort of religion of humanity, Gnostic and prophetic in tone, which made emancipation its horizon of reference. The lodges probably appeared to Filangieri, as they did to other brothers, as a unique world apart, an extraordinary political laboratory which foreshadowed, in the secrecy of its practices, formally open to any who wanted to participate, a new social order with respect to the traditional class and corporate logic of the Old Regime, transforming subjects into free and equal citizens. Since the time of James Anderson's *Constitutions of the Freemasons*, published in London in 1727, brothers in fact imbued their regulations, by virtue of their vows, with a sacral meaning of law through which their private societies, contractually and freely founded, rested and were governed constitutionally.[7] Fuelled by the memory of revolutionary events, and present since the beginning in the English rites, the so-called 'republican spirit' which permeated those communities entered an entirely new phase in the second half of the century, through the circulation of the political writings of John Locke, translated into French by David Mazel and spread through the Amsterdam lodge *Bien Aimée*.[8] That translation, which deliberately exaggerated the radical elements of Locke's thoughts, contributed, alongside other factors, to launching a general critical rethinking of the old classical republicanism reworked in Machiavelli's Italy. In the 1770s, the politicization of European Freemasonry, on which much has recently been written and about which we will say more in the following chapters, was accompanied by public reflections on the consequences of the Seven Years' War, which had shifted the balance in Europe and brought attention to the institutional and cultural models of emerging powers like Prussia and Russia, and by meditations on the growing crisis of the British constitutional model. During his 1765 sojourn in London, Franklin had not hesitated to confront his English brothers with the American question, with all its general implications, founding the 'Grand Lodge of England of the Constitutional Whigs and Friends of the People.'[9] On the continent, in the circles of the Templar Masonry of *Strict Observance*, the vast literature criticizing despotism, of which Vittorio Alfieri's celebrated *Della tirannide* was only one of many examples, had fuelled a desire finally to found a Masonic state, 'now on the Turkish border with Hungary, now on Lampedusa, now on Majorca.'[10] A state, a free land, constitutionally governed by written laws like those of the Masonic codes, where brothers, oppressed by despotism, finally could find refuge and search for that happiness denied them by the unjust and tyrannical governments of Old Regime Europe. The American question certainly triggered a chain reaction, exploding contradictions accumulated over years of tenuous conviviality between the sclerotic secular structures of the Old Regime on the one hand, and the republican and constitutionalist logic theorized and quotidianly practiced in the lodges on the other. Reading Thomas Paine's call to arms *Common Sense*, urging the literati of Europe to come to the aid of the Americans, it is for example difficult not to be reminded of the utopian projects of establishing Masonic states prospected in the early 1770s:

> Europe, and not England, is the parent country of America. This new world hath been the asylum for the persecuted lovers of civil and religious liberty from *every part of Europe...* Freedom hath been hunted round the globe. Asia, and Africa, have long expelled her. Europe regards her like a stranger, and England hath given her warning to depart. O! receive the fugitive, and prepare in time an asylum for mankind.[11]

The *Libertas Americae*, in other words, could and would have to become the ideal battlefield in the war against Europe's spreading despotism. Many both thought and said this openly in the lodges of the Old World. Only the great Lessing, in his famous 1778 *Dialogues* on the historical tasks of Freemasonry, had the courage to ironize those brothers who 'fight for the Americans in Europe,' fuelling 'the fantastic idea that congress is a lodge, and that over there, in America, armed Masons are founding their realm.'[12]

Yet, the authority of these reservations notwithstanding, it is beyond doubt that the new American myth was circulated everywhere, unleashing passions and social reveries. Alongside Richard Price and many other English radicals in the first Parisian lodge of the *Neuf Sœurs* we again find Paine busy recruiting the Masons of the world in service of the American Revolution.[13] That lodge would always maintain close ties with Filangieri, not only through Franklin and the French translator of the *Scienza della legislazione*, Antoine Gauvin Gallois, but also thanks to personal relations with Charles Dupaty and Claude Pastoret, two of the most prestigious Venerables, who authoritatively directed it in the decisive years leading up to the 1789 revolution. Both wanted to meet the young Neapolitan philosopher during their travels and did everything in their power to spread his thought in Paris during the Revolutionary and Napoleonic eras. One must nonetheless resist the fascinating idea of considering Filangieri's masterpiece as something similar to a constitutional project purposefully commissioned by the Masons of Europe. The work's diffusion certainly benefited greatly from the publishing circuits controlled by the brotherhood, and neither is it difficult – as we will see – to find points of contact, coincidental problems and solutions, which seem to validate such a hypothesis. Actually though, as all scholars of the obscure and complex history of Freemasonry know well, it is difficult to prove the existence of a specific, clearly defined and distinct Masonic ideology. It is better, much better, to content oneself with what verifiable influences one can find – and there were many between the culture of Enlightenment and the mysterious world of the lodges in the 1770s and 80s.

The unique fusion of these two worlds, which not only had different origins but for a long time had ignored each other mutually, brought many of the fundamental themes of the *Scienza della legislazione* to maturity, and particularly so in Naples. Take, for example, the great ancient question of equality. It was the Freemasons who galvanized the eighteenth-century debate on the issue. Documents and testimonies both internal and foreign to the world of the lodges testify to this unequivocally. It was common practice in ceremonies of initiation, as well as in meetings, to remind apprentices that all brothers were equal. The only accepted distinctions depended on virtue and talent, certainly not on birth:

'Gathered for a common goal, filled with the same zeal, we are all brothers, and are proud of it,' went a solemn oration recited in a Neapolitan lodge around mid-century, 'similar works of a common providence, we are equal; birth, rank, and fortune do not make us leave this right level, which should, I think, reduce all men to their intrinsic worth. We are distinguished only by virtue and talent.'[14]

The reports prepared by the ecclesiastical authorities to denounce and try the secret activities of the Freemasons were no less precise on this point. First among 'their empty maxims' was the thesis according to which 'God has created man in full natural liberty, in which we are all equal. This natural liberty cannot be restricted in men without intolerable injury.' 'This infamous idea,' the Reverend Provost of the Inquisition in Turin explained in 1751, 'is entirely [related to] the allegory of Solomon's Temple.' Its destruction signified the end of the original 'natural liberty of man' by hand of the 'tyranny of the clergy, of rulers, and of the laws,' while its reconstruction would represent the restoration of the original condition of liberty and equality.[15]

Alongside what we could define the egalitarian practices of the lodges, Naples saw the inevitable development of a first theoretical reflection upon these issues, a reflection that did not limit itself to summarizing the traditional positions of Plato, Aristotle, and Cicero, of Stoicism and of primitive Christianity, to the more recent interpretations of the Renaissance and the Reformation.[16] In the *Diceosina o sia della filosofia del giusto e dell'onesto*, Antonio Genovesi (holder of the chair of ethics at the University of Naples in 1745 and Filangieri's beloved master in the subsequent decades) drew the conclusions of that intricate and secular debate over the nature and form of equality, reproposing the Aristotelian reflections formulated in book V of the *Politics* and, above all, the conception of justice in the *Nicomachean Ethics*. 'Equality between two things,' he summarized for Neapolitan students, 'can occur in terms of numbers, of weights, of measures, or esteem.' The first three cases, also called arithmetic equality, privileged the principle of identity, which consisted in giving everyone the same. Given his sensibilities, respectful as he was of the principle of justice as fairness, the so-called 'equality of esteem,' 'ισοναναλογον' in Greek, was far more important for Filangieri. It was a form of equitable equality between different people which gave the same only to those who had the same merits, 'the equality of proportion, as Aristotle calls it, which means that what you give me relates to my needs like what I give you relates to yours.'[17] An *equitable*, a *fair* way of thinking about equality that, furthermore, was far more representative of social realities and of objective differences between individuals. Even if arithmetic equality was fundamental in specific instances, there could be no doubt that 'the first natural law which regulates every permutational contract' between humans remained, for Genovesi, 'the perfect equality between what one gives and what one receives. This equality, therefore, makes justice known as *equity*, and among the Greeks as ισον, *the equal*.'[18]

The so-called equality of esteem had been the guiding principle of life in English lodges since their beginning, in fact redefining traditional social hierarchies through a constant reference to the ancient rhetoric of civic republicanism. Nobles, wealthy bourgeois, professionals, and merchants learned to live together and practice, in the secret world of the lodges, the principles of egalitarian citizenship guaranteed by constitutions. It thus remains difficult to confute the affirmation according to which a decisive part of 'masonic identity was the belief that merit and not birth constitutes the foundation of social and political order.'[19] In Naples, in a historical context that for the first time saw the advent of a great national monarchy intent on recasting the old social order through absolutism, many exponents of the older hereditary nobility entered the lodges, often taking on roles of administrative and intellectual leadership with the hopes of relaunching their lost political primacy. Promoters of an original 'true nobility,' of a 'virtuous nobility'[20] reinforcing and accompanying traditional decorum with the practice of civic virtue, they openly adopted the principles of competence, of professionalism, and of talent. In so doing, however, these nobles seemed not to notice the very high price paid for the egalitarian logic of Freemasonry, which foreshadowed new and crushing concessions. If in the middle of the century, when the Prince of Sansevero guided the entire Masonic movement in the *Mezzogiorno*,[21] the *Costituzioni* still put noble birth on par with fame derived from virtue and knowledge for the designation of the Grand Master, within a few decades talent, merit, and virtue would decidedly overturn the primacy of birth. At the end of the century, and certainly not by accident, the final struggle against birthrights would emerge from these very same lodges. Led by aristocrats of ancient lineages like Filangieri, by then undeniably converted to the primacy of egalitarian principles based on meritocratic esteem, this struggle sought an end to the hereditary structures and feudal privileges of the old order.

As seen from the extraordinary vantage point represented by the Masonic lodges, the history of equality in the eighteenth century probably saw its most decisive moment in the publication of the works of Jean-Jacques Rousseau. Those short treatises, twinkling with paradox and capable of speaking directly to the hearts and minds of the century with terrifying efficacy, constituted, upon closer scrutiny, a head-on and decisive challenge to the innermost identity of Freemasonry as well. Rousseau's famous reflections on the history of inequality as a symptom of a modern evil, which historically had been expressed through the unstoppable interconnection between the original division of labour, the birth of *mine* and *yours*, the development of arts and sciences, of commerce, riches, and therefore of luxury, inevitable harbinger of corruption, the growing unease with a civilization based on appearances in which rulers and subjects demonstrated that they forever had lost the primitive humanity of free, autonomous and equal men, sounded like a loud condemnation of Western civilization. The great Genevan's caustic and fascinating criticism of modernity mercilessly revealed the contradictions and the dark side of the economic and material progress which was changing man's original essence, from the noble savage to the unhappy and alienated bourgeois of the great urban clusters of Europe. A mysterious force seemed set on negating man's political nature from the foundations, his essence, as Aristotle explained it, which above all was *zóon politikón*, an individual naturally gifted with free will and ability to make choices. With Rousseau, the republicanism of the ancients reappeared on the scene of history armed with new and more powerful philosophical arguments. Where Montesquieu seemed to have closed the question of the ancients once and for all in the *Esprit des lois*, finding in the mixed English government and its constitution the only form of republicanism possible in the modern world, Rousseau arrogantly re-opened the question. This gave renewed currency to traditional themes like direct democracy, revisited in light of the general will and legitimate government; the attack on talent as a source of inequality and obstacle to the spread of civic virtues; and the critique of political representation and of luxury as a corrupting influence on civic institutions. This was enough to arouse alarm and unease in all sectors of political and intellectual life on the continent, and particularly among the *philosophes*, who banished both the debate on the arts and sciences and that on inequality for having given in to primitivism and having outlined, as Voltaire wrote perfidiously, 'the philosophy of an idiot who would like the rich to be robbed by the poor'; 'reading your book makes me want to walk on all fours.'[22]

Rousseau's 'venomous' words, which cast doubt on decades of work by leading thinkers in the Republic of Letters to promote economic and social development through the diffusion of arts, sciences, and commerce, were met with a veritable wall of scorn all across Italy. From Antonio Genovesi to Isidoro Bianchi, from Gianrinaldo Carli to

Pietro Verri, the Italian Enlightenment blocked those critiques of modernity that had fallen immediately on receptive ears in the Catholic world.[23] But it was above all in the lodges that a powerful reaction took shape. And it could not have been otherwise if one considers the philosophy of history enunciated since Anderson's *Constitutions* more closely. Knowledge, in all its forms, from geometry to architecture, from old alchemy to new chemistry, the development of new natural sciences and the modern professions, constituted an integral part of man's regeneration and of the so-called Masonic science.[24] This was the direction taken by authoritative brothers and grand masters like the Newtonian John Theophilius Desaguliers, the eighteenth-century promoter of encyclopaedism Andrew Michael Ramsay, the father of electricity Franklin, and many others. Even the egalitarian logic of Freemasonry, redefined in part by esteem, by merit, and by talent, had been questioned by Rousseau's paradoxes. The new hierarchy which legitimated itself in Masonic lodges on the basis of talent and virtue, those numerous *frères à talens*[25] working in theatre, music, literature, and painting certainly did not love the coarse primitivism theorized by the Genevan's followers, who were distrustful of all kinds of genius and possible social differences.

The most organic and penetrating replies to the egalitarianism and republicanism of the ancients resurrected by Rousseau emerged in the Neapolitan lodges particularly in the last quarter of the century, and developed against the backdrop of the American Revolution and the inevitable divide in the English rite of Freemasonry between those who looked upon the events with hope and those who instead feared their possible dramatic consequences. Francescantonio Grimaldi was certainly among the latter. A refined scholar and Venerable Master of the lodge *L'humanité*, Grimaldi published three volumes under the title *Riflessioni sopra l'ineguaglianza tra gli uomini* in 1779. Had they appeared in the form of an easily read and reasonably sized pamphlet they could, given the intelligence of their argument and the culture they embodied, have become a key text not only of Italian but of European political thought. The protracted result, as farraginous as it was learned and rich with insights, posed the question of the origins and causes of inequality in entirely original terms, overturning Rousseau's thesis completely with an end result that was no less worrisome than what it sought to confute. One of Grimaldi's objectives was to recast, for the first time in Italy, the theoretical foundations of contemporary political thought on solid scientific foundations and in light of the new 'science of man.' Hume's *Treatise on Human Nature* and the crude realism of Machiavelli's *Principe* constituted the guiding lights of his empirical science of politics set on engaging with concrete facts, 'observing' and 'comparing,' on the basis of contributions from disciplines such as medicine, comparative anatomy, physiology, chemistry, ethnology, statistics, and climatology, 'the physical, moral, and political essence of the human species.' Realistically, however, and certainly not 'arranging' things as certain more utopian modern philosophers had, 'we do not want to consider men as they *could* or *ought to* be, but as they in effect *are*.'[26] With this rigorously scientific spirit, Grimaldi proceeded to that which today we would define the 'falsification' of Rousseau's hypothesis regarding 'the equality nature established among men and the inequality they have instituted' with the birth of modern civil society.[27] First of all, he confuted the idea of a clean chronological discontinuity between the natural and social worlds, in other words the very possibility that a fundamentally different primitive man could have existed in the past, as if a different person. Rousseau had hypothesized the existence of a state of nature in which isolated individuals, free, equal, and happy as only men without needs and without contact with others could be, lived without anxieties about time and thus about death. These had been introduced by 'external causes' due to the discovery of metallurgy and agriculture, the division of labour and the appropriation of the soil, inaugurating a new age characterized by moral inequality. This last problem was the negative consequence of conventions, of a civil society governed by laws of appearances and deceit, by the dominion of the few over the many. If physical inequalities between individuals were 'scarcely perceptible' and in any case absolutely uninfluential in the state of nature,[28] the appearance of moral inequality had changed everything in the form of modern society brought about by economic development. This inequality led to unhappiness and alienation in a perverse evolutionary logic, progressively bringing about a final, dramatic phase of despotism at which point, paradoxically, humanity would have returned to its point of departure. The savage, described positively in the travel literature and identified as living testimony of an intermediate evolutionary stage between primitive and social man, was one of the few proofs harnessed by Rousseau to confirm his conjectures.[29]

Polemicizing with this representation of inequality, Grimaldi could rejoice in the fact that the hypothesis of the 'state of nature' had recently been disproven by Voltaire and the authors of the Scottish Enlightenment ('over the past few years it seems that the philosophical mania of searching for natural man and for the state of nature is ceasing'[30]). It was, however, necessary to go further, to prove scientifically that the 'natural state of man is society,' and that the 'most cultivated, most scientific, most distinct' man 'in civil society is nothing but an entity which hears, thinks, and wants like the most stupid and brutal savage.' Unlike what Rousseau had argued, man's intimate 'constitution' had not changed minimally over time. The only things to change had been his history, his context, and his challenges. Since time immemorial, the physical inequality between men, evident to all and proven by innumerable scientific works which Grimaldi obsessively presented and commented upon, had brought with it moral inequality. The new neo-naturalist conceptions of the late Enlightenment left no room for doubt. They insisted on the evident materialist and deterministic connection between the 'physical' and the 'moral,' documenting, in a myriad of studies, an image of man in which 'all the mechanics of internal and external sensibilities are attached to man's physique, and are as varied as it is.' The true history of inequality was to be rewritten from start to finish, so that moral inequality more realistically could be shown to result, not from the conventions of society, but from a complex mixture of an individual's physiological potential and the conditioning it received from the climate, environment, history, and culture of the nations to which it belonged. In other words, there was no 'before' characterized by nature and equality and an 'after' of history and inequality. Man, the real man and not the 'hypothetical' and 'metaphysical' man of Rousseau, had always been the same, a mixture of nature and a history in which diversity reigned sovereign. Man was destined to inequality and its true 'source [lay] in the immutable order of things.'[31] A society without hierarchies had never existed, and, seemingly, could never exist.

Grimaldi boldly became a leading voice in the great European *fin-de-siècle* debate on the nature of civil society, on the relationship between wealth and corruption, between the sciences of man and politics, with his own unique history of inequality in which the great questions posed by the philosophers of the Scottish and French Enlightenments were revisited in light of the works of important scientists, but above all of the teachings of Machiavelli and Vico. The result was a sort of unexpected conservative radicalization of Enlightenment arguments in favour of modern civil society. Discarding the primitive state of nature as a fantasy, Grimaldi's cold and ruthless scientific analysis focused on societies of savages and on what one could draw from travel accounts. Suddenly, the noble savage became an abject being, evil, violent, and sanguine, like he appeared to many explorers. In that initial stage, in fact, the physical inequality, strength, and violence of individuals prevailed over moral inequality, giving free rein to the 'instincts of the species,' to the need of 'subsistence,' to the most beastly and repugnant aspects of humanity. The testimonies brought back by Cook, Colden, Raynal, Forster, and De Pauw were clear on this. Man's 'moral character,' though present at the origins, slowly began to emerge only in the stage of barbarism. The religious ritualization of war, of the collective practices of justice, the birth of the feudal order itself, all represented important signs of a step towards that civil society in which, however, moral inequality reached its zenith. And it could not be otherwise, since this determined the necessary conditions for the advent of what we define modernity.

With respect to the analyses of Robertson, Ferguson, Millar, Linguet, and Smith (all authors which he discussed extensively), Grimaldi argued that the genesis of civil society largely reflected the gradual, positively evaluated eclipse of physical inequality by moral inequality. The overthrowing of Rousseau was in this sense as complete as it was shocking. Beyond his statement, drawn from Ferguson, regarding the irreversibility of the process which connected the division of labour, specialization, and the development of new hierarchies, it had been the emergence of moral inequality, of the mechanisms of honour, of ethical and spiritual differentiation between individuals that according to Grimaldi gave birth to responsible elites and virtuous men; that guaranteed security, civil liberties, and moderate government; that circumscribed individual violence; and that created wealth, art, and progress. Who would prefer a world dominated only by the physical inequality of savage men to a civil society based on moral inequality? The civilization of good manners certainly had its defects, its tragedies and its hardships, its hypocrisy and wretchedness, but nothing that in any way was comparable to the miserable life of savages. A realistic political discourse had to analyse advantages and disadvantages without losing itself in the pursuit of mythical golden ages. Yet Grimaldi's words betrayed a strong sense of pride, both that echoing the Italian aristocracy, defending a millennial history of direct contributions to civilization, and that of a nobleman who dreaded the deviant consequences of Rousseau's reasoning. This is the origin of his need to underline the connection between moral and political inequality, for the latter was also not merely the result of conventions and some original social contract, but reflected a natural fact confirmed by the history of nations.

Why then be obstinate and want to overthrow the world, as utopians and revolutionaries everywhere had sought to do for centuries? Why fool people, inventing the possibility of returning to something similar to a primitive world of free and equal men that had never existed? The absurd pretences of political equality, generally advanced 'by the most miserable and most unhappy in civil society,'[32] had resulted only in bloody 'political revolutions' and new despotisms. Had the inglorious end of the English 'Levellers,' the pain of Masaniello, and the savage ferocity of the 'Lazzaroni' in Naples taught the dreaming utopians nothing about improbable republics founded on communal ownership and on the myth of natural equality between men? The American Revolution, with the hope of social renewal it excited everywhere, was thus not to Grimaldi's tastes. He observed its development through the newspapers with increasing concern. Jefferson's vindication, in the *Declaration of Independence*, of the so-called 'right to happiness,' equal for all men, seemed to him a sign of alarm. That singular request, posed sensationally among the natural rights of man, seemed void of sense and indeed very dangerous; a condition it shared with the entire rhetoric of human rights, derived from natural jurisprudence, embraced by Genovesi's other students, his brothers in the English Rite of Freemasonry. 'Were it true that nature gave us a right to happiness, it would have had to give us a physical or moral force corresponding to the desire to acquire it.'[33] Instead, Grimaldi argued, some men demonstrated having this physical and moral power: others did not:

I leave the useless lamenting over the nature of men to others… It is not that I am stupid for not feeling the evils which afflict myself and those similar, and I would be all too sensitive to the remedies which could cure them; but its impossibility, demonstrated by fact and confirmed by the experience of many, many centuries makes me reasonably lose any hope of success. Nor do I see a more effective remedy against inequality than forcing patience as far as possible. An evil known to have no remedy is immediately less hurtful. This might be the use of my *Riflessioni*.[34]

Grimaldi's *Riflessioni* represent a significant and seductive conservative contribution to the Italian Enlightenment. Their argument was capable of integrating the legal and juridical reasons for Montesquieu's estate constitutionalism with a frank and proud vindication of the moral and political inequality of the elites, those true fathers of civil society in the modern West.

Beyond certain specific questions, Filangieri disagreed with almost all of Rousseau's theses. But neither did he much appreciate Grimaldi and his ideas, no matter his great prestige and their common Masonic militancy in the English Rite lodges of Naples. The provocative intelligence and doctrine of the *Riflessioni*, which appeared in 1779, at a time when Filangieri was writing the first volume of his *Scienza della legislazione*, forced him to confront it directly point by point. Apart from this, the theme of equality represented one of the guiding threads of his work. Without that idea, which he revised and represented in different forms, his beloved constitutional project made little sense. Like Grimaldi and all Italian Enlightenment thinkers, Filangieri openly contested Rousseau's paradoxes against modernity in favour of the myth of the noble savage. Analysing the 'origins of civil society,' he confuted the hypothesis that a state of nature had existed before the advent of civil society in which the first men lived happy, free, and independent, 'as certain misanthropic sophists pretend.' In his opinion, the savage could be considered a 'degenerate man, [a] man who lives against his instinct, against his goal; in a few words, the ruin and degradation of the human species rather than the simulacrum of its infancy' [I, 66]. 'I am thus the first to believe that society is born with man. But this primitive society, this society of which I speak was everything but a civil society' as Grimaldi, for instance, seemed to think in his polemic with Rousseau. 'This would have had to be,' Filangieri specified,

> a purely natural society, a society in which the words noble and plebeian, lord and servant were unknown, where magistrates were unknown, where laws, punishments, and social obligations were unknown. This was a society in which one did not know of other inequality but that which was born from the power and robustness of the body, no other law was known but that of nature, no other bonds but those of friendship, need and kinship. The members of this society had not yet renounced their natural independence, not yet deposited their power in the hands of one or more men, not yet entrusted these with the custody of their rights, not yet put under their protection their lives, their belongings, their honour. This was a society, I say, in which everyone was sovereign because independent; everyone a magistrate because caretaker and interpreter of the laws he carried chiselled in his heart; everyone a judge, finally, because arbiter of the disputes born between himself and others and vindicator of wrongs which were done to him. [I, 67]

Filangieri took care to underline the absence of any form of moral inequality in this phase in the life of man. Quite the opposite in fact, and, in open conflict with Grimaldi, he vigorously presented the ethical postulate that moral equality had endured through all stages in the evolution of the human species, making this the very keystone of his interpretation of the social contract. Referring to the passage from the state of nature to civil society, he elucidated the principle:

> That inequality of power and robustness of which has been spoken, that sole inequality that could not be extirpated in these primitive societies, with time and with the development of the passions, would have produced the greatest disorder. Not being able to resist in the face of physical inequality, moral equality necessarily had to succumb to the preponderance of force. The weaker man necessarily had to be exposed to the caprices of the more powerful... It was necessary to find a remedy for this. Only one was found. It was seen that physical inequality could not be destroyed without renouncing moral equality. It was seen that to preserve oneself and preserve oneself in tranquillity one needed to be independent. It was seen that it was necessary to create a public force that was superior to every private force. It was seen that this public force could not be composed but by the aggregate of all private forces. It was seen that there was a need for a moral person to represent all the wills that had all these forces in their hands. It was seen, finally, that this public force could be united into a public reason, which, interpreting and developing the law of nature, established rights, regulated duties, prescribed the obligations of every individual towards the whole of society and towards the members of which it was composed; which established a norm that, if the citizen adhered to it,

he would have nothing to fear; which created and safeguarded an order apt to maintain equilibrium between the needs of every citizen with the means of satisfying them; and finally, which compensated the sacrifice of independence and of natural liberty with the acquisition of the appropriate instruments for obtaining the *preservation* and the *tranquillity* which were the only reason for which they gave something up. This is the origin and aim of civil society, this is the aim of the laws, and this, by consequence, is the only and universal aim of legislation. [I, 68]

Civil society emerged, in other words, first of all to guarantee the very existence of so-called moral equality. The overthrowing of Grimaldi's ideas was complete, but the distance Filangieri took from Rousseau, who considered modernity evil and saw in it the source of the progressive growth of moral inequality, was also notable. On the basis of the tradition of natural law, and in particular on a careful reading of Locke's *Second Treatise of Civil Government*, Filangieri pursued the question of inequality, adapting the language, vision, and solutions of the British philosopher to the continental and Italian debate. The representation of a state of nature, where free, equal, and independent men gave life to a political community through a free contract was polemically opposed to Grimaldi's crude history of inequality. The maintenance, in civil society, of the fundamental character of Locke's 'natural equality' took the place of Rousseau's assertion of moral inequality. These were, however, not merely lexical mutations, variations of judgment or emphasis, but a radical change in the very contents of the great polemic over what was to be understood by the expression 'equality' in the Old Regime. Filangieri clearly wrote in frank dissent towards the way in which Rousseau and Grimaldi, as well as other European intellectuals, had posed the problem. 'What is to be understood by natural equality, I wonder? It is nothing but the equality of rights. Men are thus equal in the state of nature because they have the same rights' [II, 219]. All the rest seemed superfluous and confusing to him. And, again, to reflect properly on the political and social nature of equality, it was necessary to refer 'not [to] that metaphysical equality wished for in the dreams of philosophers, but [to] that equality which animates popular governments, the aim of which is not the *faculties* of men, but their *rights*' [I, 133]. The analysis thus shifted completely from the privileged vantage point of the new 'science of man,' of the scientific, psychological, physiological and historical study of man and his faculties, towards a point of reference given entirely by history and politics, founded on the moral and juridical hypothesis of a natural equality of rights. Finally, one had to ask oneself what this meant for the vertices of power in the Old Regime, for the individuation of a legitimate government able to reconcile modernity and virtue, the original equality of rights and the concrete historical forms of political, social, and economic inequality.

At the University of Naples, Filangieri had learned to reason about politics and law using the logic of the rights of man. He had been taught what we today call the rhetoric and language of rights by one of the spiritual fathers of the Italian Enlightenment, Antonio Genovesi, author of a manual, *Della Diceosina o sia della filosofia del giusto e dell'onesto per gli giovinetti*, first published in 1766, that at the time represented the best overview of the international debate over natural law available on the peninsula. Genovesi had distinguished himself for giving life to a bitter polemic against Rousseau as an enemy of science, the arts, and promoter of the myth of the noble savage,[35] proposing, against the revival of political and social models drawn from the ancient world, a different path which engaged with Mandeville, Hume, Locke, and the representatives of European natural law. Set on clarifying the possible nature of modern republicanism, Genovesi's young disciple Filangieri also embarked upon this narrow and difficult path with his *Scienza della legislazione* and with his attempt to think about the Old Regime, and the controversial aspects of modernity more generally, in light of a conception of equality conditioned by the rights of man. In the first instance, the confirmation and increased intensity of the confrontation with primitivism and with the indisputable primacy of the general will over the rights of man in Rousseau's work was inevitable.[36] As previously argued, the great Genevan philosopher had loudly relaunched the classical conception of republicanism with regard to the apparently inseparable nexus between wealth and corruption, between commerce, the arts, luxury, and the affirmation of new inequalities. The immediate effect of this was a progressive decrease in civic virtue in the modern world, an argument that greatly troubled contemporary reformers of a more enlightened mould, who had pointed towards precisely the same kind of economic development as a vehicle for resolving ancient social injustices. It was certainly no coincidence that the first two replies in favour of modernity, both of which would instigate important debates in which key questions had their roots in distant eras, had appeared in economically backward but intellectually lively contexts such as Scotland and the Kingdom of Naples.[37] Filangieri fully understood that he was contributing to a great international confrontation with multiple political and philosophical consequences when, in a forthright illustration of the problem, he presented his own early solutions to Rousseau's challenge.

> One thinks that virtue cannot take root in the middle of a nation's opulence. A dangerous opinion, to which we perhaps owe the despondent state of the present legislation. Is humanity then so miserable as to have to choose between being poor or vicious? Now that today that wealth is necessary for the conservation and prosperity of States, must virtue be excluded from civil societies? Can agriculture, the arts, and commerce perhaps not be exercised by virtuous hands? Is perhaps Luxury itself, which today is necessary for the diffusion of wealth, incompatible with good manners? Must the ancients' ferocious spirit of war, because united with a spirit of frugality, perhaps be more analogous to virtue than the pacific and laborious spirit of the moderns, because united to the spirit of luxury? This is really the common opinion of moralists, but we will risk demonstrating that this is rather their common error… We will show how wise legislation, harnessing the great motion of the human heart… harnessing, I say, the *amor proprio*, will be able to introduce virtue among the riches of the moderns, with the same means by which ancient legislation introduced it among the legions of the ancients. [I, 55]

According to Filangieri, the question was to be posed and resolved within an interpretative pattern present in large parts of the *Scienza della legislazione*, namely the recourse to the parallel between ancients and moderns, underlining similarities and differences, denouncing anachronisms and the persistence of political myths. Plato, Phocion, Lycurgus, and Solon had been the first to pose the question and to 'attribute the decline of nations to riches,' connecting luxury and tyranny, opulence and corruption. They were responsible for the fact that 'the system of Greek and Roman politics… was to preserve frugality through poverty, and through frugality preserve power and courage, tolerance of toil, and the rigidity of customs' [I, 141]. In the modern world, however, none of that made sense any longer. 'What would happen to a republic today, were it to banish, like in Sparta, gold and silver, prohibiting navigation and commerce, depressing agriculture and the arts, and branding trade with a certain kind of infamy?' 'What would these laws do to England and to Holland?' [I, 139]. The nature, history, and very mechanism of wealth creation had changed profoundly. 'Does the history of antiquity show the rich receiving laws from the poor?,' Filangieri argued,

> do not the modern annals of Europe perhaps show us the opposite? Would there perhaps be nothing to fear in the present state of things from a republic that had the same principle, the same aims, and the same institutions as Rome? I have said it: the nature of things has changed. It is no longer the strong that lays down the law to the weak, but the rich who dominate the poor. The time is gone when one brought war to an entire nation with two legions. Today one needs armies to fight, and armies need treasure.

Polemicizing with those in Naples, Paris, or London still daydreaming of a future reappearance of something similar to a new virtuous 'republic of poor Roman warriors' so dear to Machiavelli, capable of arresting the modern world's march towards corruption, Filangieri resolutely argued that the real hope for a better future lay in the republican model offered by the American colonies. 'That free and commercial people, sons of Europe' [I, 142] were, in fact, attempting to unite wealth and virtue through the formulation of a new constitution for moderns, respectful of those rights of man which he held so dear. Wealth was by itself no longer an absolute evil laying in ambush, and it was not to be exorcised from civil society, also because 'the dominant spirit of the century is that of acquiring riches,' and all governments were rightly devoted to that aim. According to Filangieri, the error of Rousseau's and Mably's followers, and more generally of those who obsessively insisted, in all corners of Europe, on returning to ancient models of republicanism, resulted from their failure to understand that the change in the mode of producing wealth brought with it a profound reconsideration of the entire question. The principal sources of rapid enrichment for people in the ancient world had been war and conquest. Every time a small, poor, and virtuous republic conquered a richer one, the arrival of immense riches, slaves, and luxury changed its economic and social structures, triggering a spread of corruption and the disappearance of civic virtues. 'Procured not through the sweat of agricultural workers, through the industry of the artificer, through the speculations of the merchant, but through the violence of arms,' the sudden increase in goods determined 'the alienation of occupation and of work, the embrace of inaction and of sloth, the vane quest for all pleasures' [III, 264]. As the Scottish Enlightenment thinkers and Grimaldi had explained so lucidly, the production of wealth in the eighteenth century instead depended above all on quotidian labour and the growth of national economies. Scientific and technological progress, the division and specialization of techniques of production, and the intensification of international trade greatly expanded the potential for national enrichment without necessarily turning to violence. This had changed the fundamental variables of the problem. Finally, one could consider the connection between wealth, public happiness, and civic virtue in a new light, among other things returning to the meditation on certain precious indications already present in the most famous 'political thinkers of the ancient world.'

Two points in particular weighed on Filangieri's shoulders: 1) the principle that wealth corrupted people only when it was unjustly and unequally distributed; 2) the existing nexus between the eighteenth-century concept of public happiness, guaranteed in the first instance by economic development, and the classical one of virtue. Not only could a wealthy people more easily embark upon the path to happiness, satisfying their material needs, but they could rediscover, in the very practice of virtue, one of the privileged ways of tasting the most profound aspects of civic life, achieving public happiness, civic passion, patriotism, and glory. The virtuous life rendered happy, in other words, and wealth consented easier access to happiness and thus to virtue. The English example of so many rich and virtuous men was extremely pertinent in this regard. Across the Channel, a great number of affluent people lived virtuously through the practice of philanthropy, feeding public happiness with voluntary donations to hospitals, scientific academies, and university structures. 'These subscriptions, which distinguish wealthy Englishmen from the wealthy of other peoples, clearly demonstrate,' Filangieri argued, 'that wealth nurtures virtue, when virtue is nurtured by the passions' [III, 272]. Studying analytically the 'real causes by which wealth has, is, and may corrupt people,' he did not hesitate to maintain that the principal cause of corruption in the modern world was not wealth in itself, as Rousseau's followers and the promoters of an improbable return to republican forms of communist agrarianism maintained, in open contrast to the development of manufactures and of commerce, but rather 'the excessive opulence of the few and excessive misery of the many.' His description of the corruption, misery, and moral decline brought about by the poverty of the many in relation to the wealth of the few spared nothing in foreseeing an inevitable and proximate social confrontation between 'the class' of the rich and that of the poor. Faced with the rapid economic development of the West in the eighteenth century and the delay of reforms in European states, Filangieri asked himself bitterly

Does not poverty, which is sufferable in equality, become unbearable in sight of opulence? Do privations, which are indifferent when one ignores enjoyments, perhaps continue to be so once these are known? Does not misery double in unhappiness when added to humiliation?... Can civil liberty, which cannot be weakened without destroying public happiness, conserve its vigour between excesses of opulence and of poverty? Is the happiness of the wealthy in this population perhaps increased if that of the poor multitude is diminished? Is not the disproportion between needs and the means of satisfying them perhaps equally contrary to happiness when the excess is in one and in the other?... When wealth is in few hands, to what good is the toil and industry of acquiring it? Will lowliness, vileness, intrigue [*cabala*], and fraud be the only ways of passing from misery to wealth and from oppression to violence? Must, then, the poor man who wants to become rich not pass through all the points of abjection and consequently through all the vices that this requires? [III, 265]

The response to this dramatic vision was, however, not a return to the communist kind of egalitarian politics in Plato's *Republic*, or a recourse to the agrarian laws of ancient Rome, violently imposing 'the precise equality of fortunes and lands.' Anachronistic and impracticable, such measures were, as we soon will see in detail, deeply antithetical to Filangieri's constitutional and legislative propositions. His personal reflection on the vexed question of equality moved in other directions, seriously considering the most significant voices that had been raised in the eighteenth-century debate on the issue. In this sense, he almost held himself to be a sort of official point of arrival for the ancient controversy in the more radical circles of the Italian Enlightenment. From the Aristotelian polemic against Plato's ideal republic, and from Grimaldi's crude and realistic considerations – never quoted explicitly, almost as a way of underlining his fundamental disagreement – Filangieri was convinced that 'an exact distribution of national riches, a precise equality in the faculties of citizens, cannot take place except in the very youth of an emerging republic.' Yet again, the American experience held important lessons. It was, in fact, only at the foundation of a republic that one could give everyone an 'equal portion of land, and at this point all these families can claim to be equally rich.' In time, the order of property was destined to change rapidly. Already in the second generation, economic and social inequality became a fact because different needs, diversity of talent, the fragmentation of families, the division and specialization of labour, and the growth of commerce put in motion an irreversible process at the culmination of which 'money is acquired with money and wealth with wealth,' creating a disturbing polarization between rich and poor. Thus the dry conclusion that it was in no way 'possible to obtain an exact and precise equality between the families of a State' at any advanced stage of the history of modern civil society.

And yet, this did not at all hinder the constitutional and legislative adoption of a politics of equality as fairness, thus achieving an 'equitable diffusion of money, which, avoiding its reunion in few hands, causes a certain common welfare, the necessary instrument for the happiness of men' [I, 359] and for guaranteeing the social conditions necessary for the practice of civic virtues, understood classically as free participation in communal life. It goes without saying that to argue 'it is not necessary for all citizens to be equally wealthy, but that wealth is equitably divided' [I, 351] meant uniting realism and utopia, going beyond the equality of civil and political rights of which Locke spoke in his *Second Treatise*.[38] It meant interpreting the same logic of rights in a novel and extensive way, expanding it to encompass those economic and social themes which gave a new, concrete, and revolutionary sense to words which seemed destined to remain general rhetorical appeals to the ideals of justice. To distinguish, like Filangieri did in his *Scienza della legislazione*, when it was necessary to take recourse to the concept of equality as fairness (in the social and economic sphere) or as so-called arithmetic equality (in the political and civil sphere) meant initiating a complex meditation on the potential implicit in a courageous politics of equality, understood as a reduction of extreme differences, which was neither declamatory nor anachronistic in its appeal to a distant past. Without hiding behind the impossible practice of extreme and sectarian egalitarianism, Filangieri replied to all the points made by Grimaldi, who inexorably linked modernity to inequality, signalling the inevitable appearance of ever new and more powerful sources of the latter.

He was, in fact, entirely aware that men had never been equal and that they would never be so if not by creating situations of obvious injustice through the use of force and violence. The only realistic politics to pursue was that of vigorously fighting the excesses of inequality, reducing its presence and consequences wherever possible. The solid theoretical foundation for such an enterprise remained the preliminary acceptance of the ancient, but ever-valid ethical postulate claiming man's equality of rights and morals. Only that act of faith, which put human beings on the same level with regards to rights, seemed to him able to supply the appropriate arms and plausible political formula to fight the most odious forms of inequality in human history. 'The idea of a perfect equality of ranks,' he wrote only a few months before passing away, sympathetically reproducing a passage from Richard Price's *Observations on the Importance of the American Revolution* with reference to the English context,

> although rejected by people of good sense because of the impossibility of its existence, has never been entirely banished from the human spirit. It is what forms the first principle on which ideas of good, evil, and liberty are founded, it is what restricts power and tells it, at least in England: you can go this far, but no further; it is what makes men abhor what they find unjust; it is, finally, to what we owe the free constitution that we enjoy. [III, 483]

In other words, there existed a sort of third way between the realism of those who, like Grimaldi, preached a resigned acceptance of natural differences in all areas and the radical utopians who, inspired by the theories of Rousseau and Mably, sought a return to the equality of the ancients. This third way aimed for a different and reasonable utopia that, against the background of the American Revolution, entrusted the new politics of Enlightenment, founded on a government of laws and on the constitutionalism of the rights of man, with the task of reducing, by all means possible, the dramatic and dehumanizing consequences of modern inequality, destined to increase with the growth of the economy and the development of the 'arts and sciences.'

Chapter Five

THE NEAPOLITAN SCHOOL OF NATURAL LAW AND THE HISTORICAL ORIGINS OF THE RIGHTS OF MAN

After the general idea of virtue, I know no higher principle than that of right; or rather these two ideas are united in one. The idea of right is simply that of virtue introduced into the political world. It was the idea of right which enabled men to define anarchy and tyranny; and which taught them how to be independent without arrogance and to obey without servility. The man who submits to violence is debased by his compliance; but when he submits to that right of authority which he acknowledges in a fellow-creature, he rises in some measure above the person who gives the command. There are no great men without virtue; and there are no great nations – it may almost be added, there would be no society – without respect for right; for what is a union of rational and intelligent beings who are held together only by the bond of force?

A. de Tocqueville, *Democracy in America* (1835)

The central place occupied by human rights in Filangieri's constitutional and political thought certainly represents a fundamental vantage point from which to approach the *Scienza della legislazione*.[1] Though largely unexplored by scholars, this was the avenue of interpretation Filangieri himself gave, with reference to the American colonists' exercise of their right to resist and thus the legitimacy of their revolution, when explaining his comprehensive thoughts on the matter, underlining the amplitude and absolute importance of the questions involved:

Are colonials perhaps not members of society like the inhabitants of the metropoles are? Are they perhaps not sons of the same mother, brothers of the same family, citizens of the same fatherland, subjects of the same empire? Should they perhaps not have common *rights* and prerogatives, and among these *rights* is perhaps that of property and the liberty of disposing of that which is theirs not the most precious one? These *rights*, which man acquires at birth; which society and the laws must guarantee; which are essential in us, and which form our political existence like the soul and body form our physical existence; these precious *rights* which cannot be removed without dissolving the knot which unites us to the State; these *rights* we can never be deprived of, and their exercise can be suspended only by urgent need, inevitable and universal to the entire body politic. But when this cause no longer exists (like in this case), when this divinity which is called the *public interest* cannot be entirely placated by this violent and frightening sacrifice; when this public interest does not dare to claim it, then merely the suppression, even momentary, of this exercise becomes a frightening injustice, a dangerous attack, a manifest oppression: Could these *rights*, finally, which must be respected in the person of a private citizen, of a simple individual of society, be denied to a large part of the body politic? Could they be banished from the colonies of a nation? [I, 297]

It is difficult to imagine a better summary of the contractual nature of modern natural law and its meaning and importance for the political, juridical, and moral aspects of Filangieri's peculiar version of Enlightenment and of the republican theories of the rights of man. Respect for rights, the violation of which by the English government constituted not only the sufficient reason and principal motive for the revolutionary explosion and the foundation of the new American Republic, but also the mandatory point of reference, the true guiding light in defining relationships between individuals, between individuals and political power, between peoples, and even in the controversies between states. It is by no coincidence that, in indicating the necessary measures for finally creating a just and fair international order of political economy, Filangieri vigorously returned to the ethical postulate of man's natural equality understood as equality of rights also in the thorny sphere of commercial conflicts. In order to avoid wars and confrontations over exclusive forms of economic imperialism, for example, Filangieri rigorously applied the cosmopolitan principle according to which a just idea of 'commerce wants that all nations consider themselves a single society, the members of which have equal rights to the goods in all the others… The general liberty of industry and of commerce is the only treaty which a commercial and industrial nation should establish at home and search for abroad' [I, 289]. Locke's theories of the social contract and the rights of man, read in light of an evident sympathy for the reborn 'republican spirit' of the late eighteenth century, exercised their greatest influence in terms of analytical originality and creativity in the celebrated 1783 third volume of the *Scienza della legislazione*, dedicated entirely to *Leggi criminali*, to criminal law. Literally every page based its reasoning on the ideal compact between free and equal men and on the guarantees supplied by positive laws regarding respect for the natural rights with which every individual, without distinction, was imbued at birth.[2] In this context, Filangieri's specific contribution to the great eighteenth-century debate in Europe over the theoretical foundations of the so-called right to punish is of the greatest interest and deserves closer scrutiny.

Compared to Cesare Beccaria, who first of all insisted on the social and conventional elements of the right to punish – derived from the decision of man in the state of nature to part with some of his original liberties[3] – Filangieri saw things differently. The right to punish was for him a fundamental right in the primitive state preceding civil society; an absolutely central right which not only safeguarded the existence of all other rights but which also was crucial for guaranteeing respect for the laws of nature between individuals as well as between nations.[4] Beccaria's utilitarian contractarianism carelessly and concisely mixed elements drawn from Locke, Rousseau, and Helvétius[5] to give substance and force to his humanitarian proposal for moderate sentences and the abolishment of capital punishment. Filangieri, on the other hand, interpreted the modern paradigm of natural law with rigorous logic, neatly separating the natural and civic stages of social evolution. The first stage saw only the existence of the rights of man, the second, after the social contract, witnessed others: 'As a man I have certain rights, as a citizen I have others. Society assures me the enjoyment of the former and gives me the latter. Both become *social rights* as soon as society gives them or defends them' [II, 211]. The right to punish, definable also as a sort of universal right to justice, had unhesitantly to be considered a natural human right. There could be no other way. 'To what use was it to give men that many obligations without simultaneously giving him a restraint to impede their violation? To what use was it to give them that many rights, and then to deny them that which was absolutely necessary to induce others to respect them? The law of nature would have been absurd had it denied man this right. Hence the logical and categorical conclusion: 'the imperfection of the *state of nature* does thus not derive from the deficiency of the right to punish, but from the deficiency of available means, that is of the necessary force to validate this right and to exercise it at all times.' How, for example, to guarantee justice for the weak, for women, for the helpless? Only civil society could respond positively to such a need. 'In this state[, however,] one has not created a new right,' Filangieri noted, 'but one has rendered the exercise of an ancient right more secure. In this state, it is no longer a private man who arms himself against another individual to punish him for a crime he has committed, but it is society in its entirety; the depository of public force is what exercises this right which individuals gave up to invest it in the whole social body, that is in the sovereign who represents it' [II, 218].

Even the legitimacy of capital punishment was sustained and argued for in the *Scienza della legislazione* largely on the basis of these same considerations. Filangieri dedicates an entire chapter to the question, correcting the arguments of Pufendorf and Rousseau, even though in favor of capital punishment, on the basis of their contradictions. And his polemic with Beccaria's 'sophisms,' derived from a poor understanding of jurisprudence,[6] was evident, though mitigated by their common humanitarian battle to fight the 'deadly venom' of abusive capital punishments in the Old Regime. Yet again, a key to Filangieri's reasoning can be found in the state of nature and the rights of man. 'Do I, in this state of natural independence, have the right to kill an unjust aggressor? Nobody doubts it. If I thus have this right to his death, he has lost his right to life, because it would be *contradictory* if these two opposed rights existed at the same time. In the state, then, of independence, there are cases in which a man can lose the right to life and others can gain that of taking it.' In the case in which a victim succumbs to his injuries, 'does perhaps the right which he had acquired over the aggressor's life extinguish itself with death, or does it spread to the rest of mankind, every member of which is an avenger and a custodian of the law of nature?' Filangieri's reply to this followed Locke's thesis in the *Second Treatise of Civil Government* to the letter:[7] 'If the right to punish crimes exists in the state of nature it is clear that everyone must enjoy this right over all others, because all men are naturally equal' [II, 216].

What strikes the reader, however, in Filangieri's bona fide treatise on penal law is its organic completeness, supported by logic and argued with a rational and deductive method. Beginning with a few 'general principles' drawn from the theory of the rights of man and from a peculiar republican reading of contractarianism, Filangieri explained to his ideal audience, the enlightened and cosmopolitan legislator responsible for the compilation of future penal codes, that punishment was nothing but the 'loss of a right' as a consequence of a crime violating a contract. 'If laws are the formulas which express social contracts, every transgression of the law is thus a violation of the contract,' Filangieri explained. 'If social compacts are nothing but the duties which every citizen contracts in compensation for the rights which he acquires; every violation of a compact must thus be followed by the loss of a right.' The different kinds of rights violated would indicate 'the different species of punishments' that would be inflicted. Punishment, in the end, should aim both at preventing damage to society and at dissuading others from committing crimes.

This is not the place in which to investigate the retributive, utilitarian, or humanitarian aspects of Filangieri's philosophy of punishment, emphasizing his novel insights and his concessions to more traditional contemporary arguments. With greater competence, authoritative legal historians have finally begun to do so, underscoring the interest in Filangieri harboured by great scholars of penal law across Europe, and particularly in Germany, in the subsequent century.[8] If anything, it is necessary here to clarify and specify an aspect of the political rather than legal significance of Filangieri's understanding of natural law which all too often has been ignored, and that is his republican and strongly egalitarian interpretation of the theory of the rights of man. Compared to the widely shared adhesion to so-called enlightened despotism and to the pro-absolutist theories of natural law proposed by Pufendorf and the Austrian school of jurisprudence in the North of the peninsula,[9] the Neapolitan Filangieri did not hesitate to identify, in the right to punish in the state of nature, a particular but at the same time decisive aspect of the more general citizens' right of resistance against sovereign violations of the *pactum subjectionis*.[10] He explicitly criticized Pufendorf and those who defended the conventional nature of sovereign prerogatives and considered the right to punish one of them, affirming that punishment had sense and legitimacy only and always as an 'act of authority by someone superior over someone inferior,' something which, paradoxically, is impossible to bring about in the state of nature, where equality instead reigned among men. Filangieri replied yet again, specifying the theoretical implications of his way of understanding the concept of equality. If one accepted that men were to be considered equal in the state of nature because they had equal rights, then it was possible to affirm that when

> one loses a right while others keep it, he who loses it is no longer naturally equal to those who keep it, for they are superior. Now, in the state of nature, he who attacks the right of another, at the same time loses (as one has seen) the corresponding right which he had; in this case, then, he is no longer equal to other men, and as a consequence all the others, who have not lost this right, are superior to him, and as superiors they can punish him. The crime thus transmits the right to punish as it destroys equality. [II, 219]

There is no doubt that the suggestive pages of the *Scienza della legislazione* stir strongly with the republican spirit of the late Enlightenment, a spirit which identifies the direct participation of citizens in the administration of justice as one of its primary objectives. Filangieri's necessary premise for always confirming equality before the law was the thesis according to which the right to punish was to be considered one of the principal natural rights of man rather than a sovereign prerogative. The purpose of this was in fact to guarantee *civil liberty*, or rather the *security* and *tranquillity* of all members of the political community:

> This kind of political liberty which reassures all the classes, all the conditions, and all the orders of civil society, which restrains the magistracy, which gives the weakest citizen the aggregate of all the forces in the nation; this voice which tells the powerful, *you are a slave of the law*, and which reminds the rich that they are equal to the poor; this force which always balances, in a man's actions, the interest which he could have in violating the law with the interest which he has in observing it, must result from criminal laws. [I, 51]

This opinion was repeated vigorously in the long-distance but ongoing polemic with Montesquieu's concessions to the class-based justice of the Old Regime, to the chaotic simultaneous presence of different legal systems, to the extraordinary monarchical prerogatives regarding the power of 'grace.' Civil equality,[11] uniformity in treatment, and the necessity that 'no crime remains unpunished in the republic' forced Filangieri to criticize the celebrated phrase of the *Esprit des lois* according to which 'the prince must pardon and the law must sentence [people]' as something 'amusing and false.' Indeed it seemed to him a true 'injustice against society' to leave to the Monarch the possibility of pardoning ministers, generals, and courtiers guilty of grave crimes. And he was astutely aware of the fact that, in an absolutist and despotic system where sovereign privilege and social distinctions ruled, 'the principal interest of the citizen will not be to obey the law, but to please the monarch' [II, 466].

This republican idea of the individual as proprietor of the right to punish by virtue of being a man, entwined with the demand to participate directly in the administration of justice by virtue of being a citizen, proved all the more evident in the volume dedicated to criminal procedure. The fundamental points of the long analytical discussion which, as a lawyer and professional jurist, Filangieri conducted in light of the 'torch of reason,' were: the vindication of civil rights and of the principle that people were free until sentenced; the abolition of the inquisitorial process and its substitution by the accusatorial system of republican Rome; the creation of popular juries; the reform of the mechanisms for appeals and for refusing judges; the humanization of detention and of punishment; the abolition of torture. The final objective was that of simultaneously guaranteeing 'the greatest security for the innocent, the greatest fear for the wicked, the least arbitrariness for judges' [II, 201]. Filangieri dedicated pages and pages, worthy of Voltaire's best in the Calas affair, to denouncing the inquisitorial process,[12] an 'absurd and ferocious method which only despotism could think up' and which the medieval Catholic Church had contributed to affirming in the West, legitimating it through the procedures envisaged by canon law, and destroying, forever, in one blow, many of the conquests of civilization in the ancient world.[13] 'Should we suffer,' Filangieri asked indignantly,

> that the system created by an ambitious Pope still prevails over that which Greek and Roman wisdom had instilled in liberty's breast? That the *inquisition* ordered forth from the houses of bishops maintains its seat in the temple of justice [*di Temi*]? Must we be

embarrassed by finding many articles of the criminal procedure to be the same as in barbarian times? [II, 51]

That mysterious and secret procedure, without guarantees for those on trial, which united prosecutor and judge in the same person, deprived citizens 'of all those rights which only violence can take away,' and 'intrepidly sacrificed justice and civil liberty to a false idea of public tranquillity, which under tyranny can only be the security of the despot.' As an alternative, Filangieri proposed a return to the Roman process of prosecution and the restoration of the republican right of every citizen to accuse ('the right to accuse has been one of the prerogatives of citizenship in large numbers of nations and for many centuries' [II, 5]), accompanied at the same time by the creation of a new public magistracy of the so-called 'prosecuting magistrates [*magistrate accusatori*]' to be chosen among the 'most distinguished and honest people in society.' Finally, he fought for the public conduct of debates; the iron respect for the principle of legality; the possibility for the defence to contest the testimonies of the prosecution from the very beginning of an investigation; the judge's role as a separate, impartial part of the process; a decisive role for popular juries; and the respect for the laws of *habeas corpus* which, invented by the Romans, had been renewed in early modern English penal procedures. It was, in other words, necessary to always treat 'the accused as a citizen, until his crime was not entirely proven.' One should, for example, jail the accused separately from the condemned on the model of republican Rome. Only thus could one avoid the human tragedies which forced those on trial to accept the same perverse logic of the inquisition, to declare themselves guilty only to end their own suffering.

Against the inquisitor, and his determination in finding evidence of the presumed guilt by recourse to incarceration, to torture, to violent interrogation, to every kind of humiliation capable of offending human dignity, there was no possible defence without a radical reform of penal procedures. Speaking in the third person and putting himself in the shoes of an innocent victim of an unjust procedural mechanism, Filangieri made palpable the sense of impotence, the dramatic emptiness and the abyss of violence into which a common citizen had fallen, denied every right in the hands of the inquisitor. 'The state in which I find myself,' the poor soul desperately concluded after having narrated the ferocious mistreatments he had been subjected to,

inclines me to believe that the laws directing the judges and the judges that execute them are susceptible to all excesses. I am therefore about to make a false confession which will accelerate a death which I plead for every instant, and which only the perjury that has to anticipate it has impeded me so far from obtaining. [II, 50]

To Monstesquieu, who had denied that it could make sense, in a large modern monarchy, to recover the Roman accusatory model on the grounds that its presence presupposed a strong 'republican spirit' and the diffusion of ancient civic virtues, Filangieri replied drily, 'to believe that the freedom to accuse is useful in a republic and dangerous in a monarchy, because every citizen in a republic must have an unlimited zeal for the common good while in a monarchy this right could be abused to favour the aims of the prince… is the same as deducing the opposite consequence of that which naturally should be derived from a principle' [II, 22]. The citizen's 'freedom to accuse' in fact belonged to the more general and universal right to punish, and had nothing to do with specific forms of government or even with sovereignty itself.

Upon closer scrutiny, however, Filangieri gave a similarly original treatment of the entire issue of the accusatory process and of justice inspired by the republican model, a treatment that differed greatly from the classic humanitarian arguments of Beccaria and the French *philosophes*. Filangieri constantly emphasized the foundational importance of the rights of man for all the specific aspects of law he engaged with. In the case of the polemic against 'the infamous,' who had 'apologized in justification of torture,' and against the ecclesiastical Inquisition, which had introduced the use of torture in canon law, 'adopting it alongside its other tyrannical institutions,' Filangieri did not limit himself to the indignation characteristic of Enlightenment circles. The continual reference to the stoic concept of 'humanity' (a notion that 'always guides my ideas'), definitely seemed to him an insufficient and rhetorical affirmation in the face of those philosophers of criminal law who over the past centuries had attributed a positive value to torture as a legitimate test in the search for truth. On the other hand, the question had to be addressed primarily on the logical and juridical level by demonstrating that torture was contrary to the laws of nature themselves:

> Does the magistrate have the right to claim the culprit's confession for his crimes? Every right presupposes a duty; if the magistrate had this right, the culprit would have the duty to reveal his crime. But can a duty that is contrary to the first law of nature ever be a duty? The first law of nature is that which obliges us to conserve our own existence. [II, 87]

On the basis of what considerations, in other words, could one force a man to defy the order of nature? Finally, on the historical level, Filangieri had no difficulty in demonstrating how torture represented a degeneration born from the 'despotism of the first Caesars,' with the introduction of the infamous '*lex julia*' which considered prisoners of conscience guilty of '*lèse majesté*,' overthrowing the original 'Roman jurisprudence' once and for all. Only serfs could be tortured in the republican period, and this was already a grave fact which seemed to him to define the beginning of a dangerous involution. In that case though, 'if justice was shaken by this attack committed against all its principles, at least civil liberty saw the precious rights of citizenship respected by the same laws which so indifferently had violated the rights of humanity.' Only the barbarians, and then the Church of Rome, however, had definitely transformed torture, a disgrace against man, into a paradoxical instrument of truth and justice.

The *Scienza della legislazione* represented a new and decisive stage for the glorious tradition of European natural law on its centuries-long path of constant and, depending on the context and the historical functions it assumed, at times drastically changing interpretations.[14] Filangieri certainly represented a novel analyst of the so-called natural law of the moderns in the eyes of his contemporaries.[15] The dialectic between natural and positive law had been interpreted by the Stoics and then, differently, by Christians, from Gratian, the monk who founded canon law, to Aquinas. A variant of this had, since the seventeenth century of Grotius, Hobbes, Pufendorf, and Locke, shifted the attention towards a much more subversive theory of the natural rights of man, examined with the rational methods of the scientific revolution.[16] In fact, Filangieri had mastered the entire theoretical arsenal developed by that school of thought, and it was with great nonchalance that he employed concepts and expressions common to the modern theorists of natural law in his complex political and legal arguments. He used terms like nature, civil society, compact, and rights, though without ever dismissing the so-called natural law of the ancients, and particularly the valuable teachings of his beloved Cicero.[17] His substantial adhesion to the paradigm of natural law, however, did not prevent him from freely articulating both consent and dissent with respect to the authorities of the tradition. We have seen with what harshness the republican Filangieri distanced himself from the absolutist readings of the right to punish proposed by Pufendorf and his numerous devotees. Even with respect to Locke, who after all had indicated the master path of constitutionalism to guarantee the rights of man, Filangieri's ideas differed regarding the typology of rights and the truly universal nature of equality and of the human right to citizenship. Furthermore, how could Filangieri accept the former's justification for the slave trade (from which, as is well known, Locke drew substantial financial gain) by recourse to the presumed theoretical validity of the infamous right of conquest? The issue seemed, from all points of view, repulsive and incomprehensible to Filangieri.

Truth is that the century which had passed since the appearance of those first great works of modern natural law had seen much water pass under the bridges of European political and constitutional thought. Filangieri belonged to an entirely new generation of Enlightenment reformers who, though utilizing the language and framework of the natural law paradigm, had no qualms with radically transforming its modalities and objectives, changing important and decisive parts through their cross-contamination with other traditions. This led to the formulation of new and unexpected questions, the answers to which were light-years away from those posed by the enlightened absolutists of the seventeenth and eighteenth centuries. David Hume, an author whom Filangieri appreciated greatly, had, to give just one example, indicated different ways of defining the mechanisms of the social order by examining the positive nature of civil society and of its self-sufficiency, through the recognition and study of human passions, customs, and the history of nations without recourse to the theory of rights and of the social contract, which he found too abstract and artificial. The writings of Montesquieu, Rousseau, Mably, Helvétius, Ferguson, and Smith, all of which ample use was made in the *Scienza della legislazione*, had gone far further than Grotius, Pufendorf, and Locke in exploring the great and thorny question of the relation between the tendentially anarchic rights/powers (to put it in light of Hobbes' conceptual framework) of the subjects and the sovereign's potential capacity for social control and guaranteeing the survival of civil society. The great historical question raised by the modern literature on natural law consisted in defining a new concept of citizenship, different from that offered by the absolutist model of the citizen-subject. This new definition – capable of seamlessly combining the rights of man, through the social contract and participation in the execution of sovereignty, with the exigencies of the social and political community – came to constitute the very core of late Enlightenment political thought, and particularly so in the wake of the American Revolution. In some senses, Filangieri posed himself at the end-station of this long and tormented process of change and development undergone by the paradigm of natural law in its encounter with Enlightenment culture.[18] He consciously drew the definitive consequences of Locke and Montesquieu's fundamental reflections on the decisive bond discovered between positive laws and individual liberty, between a specific model for a republican or monarchical constitution and the organic and immediate correspondence with a peculiar political and social order. From the tradition of thought that historically considered natural law as an absolute criterion of justice to compare with existing legislation, Filangieri, and with him many Enlightenment thinkers of the late eighteenth century, had accepted the challenge and the impulse to radically reform the Old Regime, to create a new political and juridical order through legislative reform. Compared to the perhaps purely rational analysis of *what is*, which seemed to have attracted the fascination of the first Enlightenment thinkers, set on exploring the self-sufficient mechanisms of the social and natural order, Filangieri had never hesitated to privilege the construction of the future, to live that burning drive towards *what ought to be* which instead accompanied all the political protagonists of the late Enlightenment.

Besides, the paradigm of natural law lent itself extremely well to yet another similar interpretation. For lovers of natural law, the law had never represented a mere measure of action. It was also and importantly a moral evaluation, an irrevocable definition of right and wrong. It was not only the source of legality, it also indicated the morality of an event, the existence of a consensus internal to the political community. Privileging this type of exegesis, the Enlightenment culture of the second half of the eighteenth century felt it finally had found the possible theoretical horizon of reference for a political project to overcome the Old Regime; a project that once and for all welded, on the theoretical and practical levels, politics and the law, legislative reforms and the creation of a new order to be achieved through a process of legislative and constitutional change. Denis Diderot had been among the first to invite the *philosophes* to repudiate an entire previous season of optimistic reflections on a possible spontaneous resolution to the conflict between individuals and society, between the rights of man and the duties imposed by sovereignty, in light of naturally harmonious mechanisms of social interaction between private passions and public virtues. Instead, political conflict was now understood to be inevitable, and was if anything relocated to the very centre of the Enlightenment party's actions. The safeguarding of man's natural and inalienable rights had to become the ultimate goal of future political institutions. In that sense, rights were to be resolutely promoted, and before that historically grounded and defined also 'in indignation [and] in resentment, these two passions which nature seems to have placed even in animals to compensate for the lack of social laws and public vengeance.'[19] The next step, indicated almost universally by the greatest exponents of the European Enlightenment, could not be anything but the categorical demand for a 'government of laws.' Therein lay the only possible solution to the political and institutional problems posed by the modern natural law of the rights of man. Only through radical legislative reform of the Old Regime, as Rousseau, Beccaria, and above all Helvétius had augured, could one hope to organize public and private interests, uniting rights and duties, individual and sovereign, and finally recognizing the productive and organic link between politics and law in the modern world.

Who clearly and concisely expressed the necessity of this decisive step in Western political history was, of course, the acute and ingenious Voltaire. 'In what state, under what sort of rule, would you prefer to live?,' he had one of the characters of his *Dictionnaire philosophique* ask a wise Indian Brahmin. 'The one where people obey only the law' was his reply. 'Where is that land?' Another immediate and significant answer: 'We have to search for it.'[20] Filangieri searched and found it through the *Scienza della legislazione*. Its great editorial success can also be explained by the fact that he concretely realized the fundamental political project of the late Enlightenment. That is he formulated the criteria, the modalities, and the technical and juridical blueprint of a new science of legislation which really was cosmopolitan and enlightened, developed on the basis of respect for the rights of man. In so doing, he went far beyond the commonplace moral and political reflections of eighteenth-century scholars trained in the school of natural law, technically transforming rights, on the specifically legal level, from a universal moral principle into a positive right. He gave life to a pioneering and original attempt at creating the conditions to begin, in a very near future, the construction of a solid legislative edifice consisting of clear and concise codes which on the one hand reduced religion to an auxiliary role, and on the other liquidated the old *scientia juris*, putting the legislator face to face with the absolute necessity of legislating around every aspect of civil society, always taking into account the rights of man. 'I call the *absolute goodness* of the laws,' he had warned in the opening of the *Scienza della legislazione*, in a passage we have already looked at in depth,

> their harmony with the universal principles of morality, common to all nations, to all governments, and adaptable in all climates. The law of nature contains the immutable principles of what is *just and fair* in all cases. It is easy to show how fertile this spring is for legislation. No man can ignore its laws.

To appreciate more fully the most innovative aspects of the *Scienza della legislazione*, the aspects which vindicated the purely political passage from natural to positive right, from a generic exoneration of the philosophy and morality of the rights of man to a concrete production of laws and codes necessary for guaranteeing their realization, one should reflect on the fact that the theoretical foundations of Filangieri's natural law were very different from those of other Enlightenment thinkers. Behind him, in fact, stood what Pierre-Louis Ginguené in 1815 defined a 'great school of political philosophy,'[21] a 'noble school' that, if it had found its brilliant herald in Vico and in his penetrating critique of natural law on the rationalistic bases developed by Grotius and Pufendof, also owed much to Gianvincenzo Gravina.

This great jurist in fact deserves credit for having launched a new tradition of political studies based on the historical and more generally philosophical analysis of the existing nexuses of politics and law.[22] The European fame and circulation of his *Originum juris civilis libri tres* (1701–1708) had quickly, over the course of the eighteenth century, imposed the necessity everywhere of finally reconstructing the progressive formation of Roman

Law on a historical and philological level and of critically evaluating the political and philosophical components implicit in the dramatic passage from republic to principate.[23] In *De romano imperio* and above all in *De imperio et jurisdictione*, Gravina, as a famous jurist and historian of law, had drawn the argument for delineating the salient traits of an original juridical order capable of limiting the future power of princes precisely from the model offered by the Roman Republic. Properly understood, this was something very different from the use of that model which Machiavelli had lionized in the *Discorsi sopra la prima deca di Tito Livio*. The great Florentine had taken recourse to Livy's reconstruction to investigate, in paradigmatic terms, the moral nature of civic virtue and the risks of corruption in the republic, the public spirit, religious practices and convictions, the art of war, and the very destiny of the republic in the secular history of humanity. Gravina, in contrast, focused his attention entirely on the law, institutions, legislation, and political constitution of the Roman republic and later, the principate. His learned and sophisticated historical investigations gave force to the contractual argument both for the origin of rights and duties in political communities and for the delimitation of public powers. These arguments would later attract the interest of Europe's best jurists, and particularly of Montesquieu in the *Esprit des lois*.[24] Distinguishing between the *merum imperium* of the prince and the *jurisdiction* reserved to magistrates, insisting on the political and constitutional function of legislation, Gravina had in effect launched the debate over the division and balance of powers in Italy, over the priority of the legal system, as a constitutional guarantee to respect that principle of legality and legitimacy which so profoundly had animated the history of the Roman Republic.[25]

One finds the same centrality of Roman law and of its historicity in rethinking modern political institutions, and more generally the centrality of the idea of law in the eighteenth century, also in Vico.[26] In his case, however, attention towards that decisive phase of the ancient world represented by republican and imperial Rome was driven above all by precise philosophical interest related to the necessity of recasting natural law, which was back in vogue in the second half of the seventeenth century, on entirely new epistemological foundations.[27] This added up to a lively polemic with Grotius, Pufendorf, and with the North European theorists of natural law, who by recourse to the methods of modern science and by the evidence of reason alone had drawn the epistemic criteria for laying a new theoretical basis of natural law. Vico had, in fact, preferred to insist on his original doctrine of *verum ipsum factum*, on the equivalence of knowledge and action, from which he derived the general gnosiological principle that only those who have done something can really understand it, by which man can have a *science* of history because he made it.[28] We know that Vico took his first steps in the direction of a definitive formulation of the celebrated *Principi di scienza nuova d'intorno alla commune natura delle nazioni* by meditating precisely over the existing relationship between 'ideal and eternal' law and the positive law of nations, between law as a general idea, as a universal and rational value, and law as a historical reality resulting from the will of man.[29] The findings of English, Dutch, and German scholars in the seventeenth and eighteenth centuries with regards to the 'maxims of a just government,' conducted on the basis of only rational evidence without considering the history of nations, seemed to him wrongheaded and insufficient 'as a result of a lack of critical method [*arte critica*].' They had confused 'the natural law of nations, coming out of their customs, with the natural law of philosophers, which they had understood as the force of reason.'[30] Against all theorists of natural law, who since Grotius systematically had ignored the paradigmatic significance of Roman Law and the valuable teachings of history, Vico reminded his readers of the principle according to which 'doctrines must begin from when the subjects they treat do.'[31] It was not acceptable to build knowledge only through logical abstractions. All forms of knowledge had to be considered simultaneously products of history and of the mind, and thus of the convergence of the 'certain' and the 'true.' These methodological caveats regarding the historicity of 'universal law' even in the quest for the 'maxims of the eternally just' were picked up by other illustrious exponents of the Neapolitan school engaged in the great debates of the Enlightenment. They were, for example, though with great uncertainty and theoretical fragility, adopted by Antonio Genovesi, always considering Vico one of his masters[32] alongside Cicero and Locke. But Vico was above all followed by Pagano and Filangieri in their great works at the end of the century.

In the *Diceosina*, Genovesi was among the first in Italy to combine the typical language of republicanism with that of individual rights to critically reconsider, through the study of history and philosophy, the nexus between law and politics in the wake of the works of Montesquieu, Mandeville, Hume, and Rousseau. He investigated the 'maxims of the eternally just,' in Vico's famous phrase, by a simultaneous recourse to Roman law, Newtonian science (to imbue the concept of natural law with rational and scientific legitimacy) and the entire arsenal of the rights of man in Grotius, Pufendorf and Locke, to found the modern 'moral science' on a solid basis. Mario Pagano would later confirm this genealogy for the Neapolitan school of natural law, insisting heavily on the centrality and paradigmatic value 'of the Roman laws.' 'That shapeless mass,' he wrote in the introduction to the second edition of his *Saggi politici*, 'where onto monuments of the most terrible despotisms are grafted maxims of the most enlightened philosophy and the human and moderate sentiments of the most docile principles; in that mass, I say, one finds scattered the seeds of the moral sciences.' In early modern jurisprudence, the 'idea of an eternal law and justice, of the immutable and inalienable rights of man' was based on the principles present in the *Institutions* and in the *Digest*, but above all in the universalist inspiration of Roman law.[33] True to Vico's teachings, Pagano took his distinct distance from Pufendorf and Grotius' partiality for the rational foundations of natural law. Though recognizing that Grotius had given 'system and body to the new ideas,' Pagano accused him of neglecting the teachings of history and of Roman law, relying solely on rational models: 'He favored reason over memory, and instead of quoting, he demonstrated.' Grotius' importance would certainly have been greater if, in his research, 'he had not confused facts with law, if he had matched the idea of order and natural co-existence with the principles of utility and strength.' The honour of having founded modern political thought instead fell on John Locke, 'the immortal *Giovanni Lok*,' for having finally conceived of the possible connection 'between political bodies and the rights of man.' Montesquieu had taken the idea of a 'temperate constitutional monarchy' and of a division of powers from Locke, Rousseau 'the first ideas of equality, of the rights of man and of the social contract, the origins of the right of property and the right of inflicting the death penalty.'[34] Only Vico, in Italy, could equal these giants. He was the only one who, with great originality, particularly in terms of method, had engaged with the rebirth of natural law and the new 'political and moral studies' blooming in Europe. Filangieri had been his direct heir, the one to draw the final consequences of his political and philosophical reading of natural law, arriving at the realization of an innovative science of legislation able to unite rational method and historical knowledge, the principles of reason and respect for the customs of nations and their histories, ideal and eternal law on the one hand and positive law on the other.[35]

In his simultaneously rational and historical construction of law, Filangieri dedicated little space to specific philosophical reflections on the foundations of modern natural law, and in particular on the rights of man, as these seemed to him territories which had been largely explored by his predecessors and above all by the great Vico.[36] Filangieri had indeed drawn important insights from Vico and his celebrated distinction between the historical course of nations and their ideal and eternal history. Principally, he used them to formulate his fundamental comparison between the 'absolute goodness' of the laws, which referred to natural law, and the 'relative' goodness of positive law. The foundations of the 'natural law of nature' seemed, to him, beyond dispute. Nobody in the eighteenth century dared doubt that it contained 'immutable principles of what is just and fair in all cases' and that its roots were buried deep in the very hearts of men:

> It is easy to see how fertile this source is for legislation. Nobody can ignore its laws. They are not the ambiguous results of the moralists' maxims, nor the sterile meditations of philosophers. These are the dictates of that principle of universal reason, of that moral sense of the heart which the creator of nature has impressed upon all individuals of our species as a living measure of justice and honesty that speaks the same language to everyone and prescribes the same laws at all times. It, as Cicero says, is older than cities, than peoples, than senates; it has a stronger voice than that of the gods and that is inseparable from the nature of thinking beings; it subsists and will always subsist, notwithstanding the efforts of all passions fighting against it, notwithstanding the tyrants who would like to drown it in blood, and notwithstanding the impostors who would have liked to annihilate it in superstition. The Tahitian savage therefore knows as well as Locke that a beast killed by someone else cannot be his, that the products of the soil cultivated by someone else cannot be his property without their owners' consent, and that defence alone can give a man the right to another man's life. This is what morality decides, this is the right of nature, the first norm of the laws. [I, 76–7]

Like Diderot and Jefferson, just to name two of his many contemporaries, Filangieri too, in the end, considered the rights of man, inscribed in the laws of nature, to be entirely self-evident truths. Yet, the progressive historical recognition of these rights across nations and across the centuries, and their transformation into a wellspring of political energy, an instrument of emancipation, and an oriflamme in the political struggles of the time, was an entirely different issue. Here, Vico's lessons, which separated but at the same time dialectically reconciled philosophy and history, ideal and eternal history with the concrete historical course of nations, had left profound traces in the thinkers of the late Neapolitan Enlightenment. Traces which very soon were cancelled by an Italian political tradition set on criticizing and demonstrating, by all means, the theoretical and philosophical fragility of natural law.[37]

The last quarter of the eighteenth century differed from the time, almost a century earlier, when Grotius and Pufendorf wrote pages upon pages to demonstrate the logical and rational foundations, the philosophical and scientific legitimacy, of the 'sacred rights of humanity,' when they questioned, with admirable passion, the 'holy book of nature.' The goal pursued by late Enlightenment reformers like Filangieri was very different, namely the definitive transformation of natural law from 'universal morality' into a republican 'government of laws.' It was necessary to pass from theory to concrete practice: to go beyond what the French revolutionaries would define the Old Regime. The new *politics*, understood as an instrument for transforming social reality, an act of will, suddenly gained pre-eminence over the old conceptions of reason of state and of the *scientia juris*. For Filangieri too, the appearance of a new conception of politics, attentive to the legislative dimension and set on constitutionalizing rights, emerged as the necessary and auspicious finale to the European Enlightenment's great tradition of natural law.

Chapter Six

BEYOND 'REASON OF STATE': THE MORAL AND RELIGIOUS FOUNDATIONS OF THE NEW POLITICS *EX PARTE CIVIUM*

The time was ripe for a comprehensive reconsideration of the traditional way of conceptualizing the political. The Old Regime was creaking everywhere, clearly revealing the epochal changes that were taking place not only in terms of society, politics, and institutions, but in terms of the very way in which people thought. In the old Europe of the eighteenth century, Filangieri was certain, 'a peaceful revolution is brewing.' He explained its causes and motives in his usual prophetic and optimistically visionary tone in the *Introduzione* to the *Scienza della legislazione*. For centuries, princes had privileged the solution to a single obsessive problem: how to win wars and extend their dominions. '*To find the way to kill the greatest number of men in the shortest time*' was the constant preoccupation of those participating in that veritable 'military mania' which, in the seventeenth and eighteenth centuries, had led the absolutist powers of the continent to favour the creation of huge standing armies, and the construction of formidable arsenals, while neglecting public happiness.[1] Finally, after decades of preaching by philosophers like Grotius, Pufendorf, Locke, and Montesquieu, things seemed to be changing rapidly.

> The scene has changed and the princes have begun to acknowledge that the life and tranquillity of men deserve more respect; that there are other means, independent of strength and arms, to reach greatness; that good laws are the only foundation of national happiness, that the goodness of the laws is inseparable from uniformity, and that this uniformity is not to be found in twenty-two centuries' worth of legislation, emanated by different legislators in different governments to different nations, sharing in all the greatness of the Romans and the barbarity of the Longobards. [I, 36]

The stage, in other words, was set for overcoming the chaos of legal systems and begin the construction of a single, great, and uniform legislative edifice capable of guaranteeing public happiness and the rights of man. The historical conditions seemed ready, as the obstacles to change came crumbling down, one after the other. The feudal nobility was being attacked everywhere, the privileged bodies of the Old Regime openly denounced for their self-interest; the absolute sovereignty of the monarch was called into question;

the collective customs and sensibilities of Europe were ever more oriented towards the maxims taught by the *philosophes* and by those in favour of reforms.

> To reach this end, philosophy has come to the assistance of governments and has produced the most salutary effects… Superstition, I say, which, by perpetuating ignorance and errors among men, always would have impeded all legal reforms, has been proscribed; and religion, which fanaticism had stained with the blood of nations and the misery of peoples for centuries, has become the bond of peace and the foundation of social virtues, as it should be and as it originally was. The priesthood does not infringe upon the government any more. The state is more peaceful and the altar is better served. [I, 38]

But, nonetheless, the great enlightened legislative reform of the Old Regime presupposed the definitive overcoming of a way of thinking and living politics which was traceable back to the theoretical and practical universe of the so-called reason of state, which had dominated Europe in the previous centuries.[2] It should be pointed out that Filangieri did not even take into consideration the celebrated 1589 definition given by the Jesuit Giovanni Botero, who considered reason of state as knowledge of the 'means to establish, conserve, and enlarging' a state, intending by state a prince's 'firm dominion over peoples.'[3] That way of thinking and acting politically, which entrusted the task of governing peoples to the *arcana imperii* and to sovereign will, seemed to him to belong to a distant past with which it was no longer worth crossing swords. 'Everything has changed; the political ideas themselves have lost that character of ferocity and intrigue that made them dangerous instead of useful' [I, 38]. The political struggle in fact began to unfold in broad daylight, involving ever wider groups and social classes. Wherever one looked, modern forms of participation in the political struggle began to delineate themselves. Even the great kings were publicly called to answer for their actions. Citing the episode of 1775, when the Bishop of Tours, Jean de Dieu-Raymond de Boisgelin de Cucè, thundered against Louis XVI the very same day of his coronation at Reims, Filangieri noted how 'this brave subject dared to summon his king before the court of public opinion, and remind him that this tribunal would judge him one day, and found the courage to show him upfront the point at which his rights end and his indispensable duties begin.' The republican spirit was being reborn all over Europe in the late eighteenth century. 'This language, which has not been heard among men since the time when Greece decayed and Rome lost its liberty, has today become the common language of philosophers and writers' [I, 39].

Such language, however, had different and deadlier enemies than the old reason of state. For the first time in Western history, Filangieri articulated a political language founded on the rights of man and public happiness, innovatively reformulating the conception of ideal politics which, from Aristotle to Cicero, had been understood as the pursuit of the common good, as the virtuous education of the citizen, as the creation of a community of free men living together in justice under a government of laws. What now began to emerge was a powerful reaction, inspired directly by the principles of a crude and modern political realism, by an iron respect for the primacy of *is* over *ought*, and thus by a rejection of the ethical postulate that all men are naturally equal. Couched in scientific empiricism and empowered by original historical and social research, the fundamental theses enunciated by Machiavelli in *Il Principe* returned triumphantly to the fore even among enlightened thinkers. Many authors of the second half of the eighteenth century in fact shared, without reservation, the theoretical and epistemological framework clearly formulated in chapter XV, in which the Florentine secretary had explained that

> because I want to write what will be useful to anyone who understands, it seems to me better to concentrate on what really happens rather than on theories and speculations. For many have imagined republics and principalities that have never been seen or known to exist. However, how men live is so different from how they should live that a ruler who does not do what is generally done, but persists in doing what ought to be done, will undermine his power rather than maintain it. If a ruler who wants always to act honourably is surrounded by many unscrupulous men his downfall is inevitable. Therefore, a ruler who wishes to maintain his power must be prepared to act immorally when this becomes necessary.[4]

At the end of the eighteenth century, the annoying question of Machiavelli's morals, or his lack of them, the specific aspects of his statecraft, and the republicanism of his *Discorsi* no longer seemed as important and conclusive for the final verdict of his character, or at least seemed to retreat from the forefront of the international debates as things known and taken for granted.[5] Instead, what grew in relevance was the real and permanent nucleus of Machiavellianism, that is his realist creed and the profession of faith in a radical scientific empiricism evident throughout the great Florentine's political œuvre. His was a political discourse programmatically focused on facts, on the concrete and rational history of humanity, and on the true nature of man, without any concessions to social reveries, eschatological or providential reasonings, or to the resuscitant desire for utopias. In Naples, this contrast, this evident contraposition between two ways of conceptualizing the new politics, symbolically fought around the figure and legacy of Machiavelli, was made clear to all by Filangieri's brusque taking of position. The author of the *Scienza della legislazione* knew all the Florentine's works well. He often cited particular passages favourably and appreciated Machiavelli's republican vein in its entirety, though he always preferred, in this case, to retrace his original sources in Latin and in Greek, privileging the direct teachings of his beloved Cicero, Xenophon, Plato, and Aristotle, while neglecting, like the rest of eighteenth-century Italy, the more recent republican legacy of civic humanism. And yet, in spite of Filangieri's evident admiration for Machiavelli, he did not hesitate for a second in transforming him into the declared nemesis of the rights of man: 'One no longer hears those maxims unless taught, or at least put in an equivocal light, by a politician who has gained the praise of men, even though he has compromised their rights.' History seemed to him to finally and forever have defeated that way of thinking about politics.

> [If] a new Machiavelli today dares to say that a virtuous prince who wants to maintain his position must learn not to be virtuous, unless need requires it; that he must guard his personal goods carefully and squander those of the public… that he must not be

virtuous, but appear that way; that he must appear to be human, loyal, just, and religious, but must learn to be the opposite; that he cannot observe all that which makes other men pass as good, because the needs of the state often forces him to operate against humanity and against religion… [if] this new Machiavelli finally managed to place vice at the thrones, all of humanity would throw itself against him, and public disapproval will be the just prize for his baseness. [I, 39]

The poisons of Machiavellian politics should, in other words, never return to Europe, which began to be ruled by a public opinion and a conception of politics *ex parte civium*. Yet, the teachings of the Florentine secretary suddenly gained a renewed and singular currency precisely in Naples, among the same Enlightenment disciples of Antonio Genovesi, in Masonic lodges which in face of the American Revolution were dangerously torn between moderate and radical brothers, between the supporters of American republicanism and those of traditional English constitutionalism.[6] The principal architect of this turn of events was Francescantonio Grimaldi. His three 1779 volumes on inequality opened – as we previously stressed – a new season in Italian political debate, purposefully and polemically setting Rousseau's conception of politics, based on a positive anthropology utopianly projected on a republican and egalitarian future, against Machiavelli's crude, factual, and entirely empirical political realism. To Grimaldi, it was frankly useless to ask oneself how 'governments ought to be,' it was much better to accept the lessons of the *Il Principe* and 'examine how nature has wanted them to be.'[7] The ferocious and bellicose nature of men, and their hierarchical relationships, seemed to him beyond dispute, scientifically demonstrable *and* demonstrated. In the third volume of 1780, after having polemicized with Jefferson over the presumed universal human right to happiness hailed by the *Declaration of Independence*, he probably referred to none other than Filangieri when affirming the need to always 'accommodate equality to established justice, and not establish justice to the maxims of equality.'[8]

Still in 1779, Giuseppe Maria Galanti, another famous student of Antonio Genovesi, published his *Elogio di Niccolò Machiavelli*. The *Elogio*, published anonymously, was part of an impressive editorial project in which it would precede the reprint of all Machiavelli's works. A project which, in spite of its large number of subscribers, was aborted by the Church's immediate censorial intervention.[9] Galanti's pamphlet exalted the figure of Machiavelli and defended his memory and his republican spirit, drawing on past testimonies and more recent endorsements by Montesquieu, Rousseau, and Linguet, who regarded it 'very evident that *Il Principe* is a satire and not a eulogy of tyranny.' As a moderate Enlightenment thinker, Galanti did not hesitate for a moment in clarifying his substantial adherence to that current of thought which we today sum up as political realism,[10] and which, at least in late eighteenth-century Italy, seemed to have found its modern spiritual father in Grimaldi. 'How many useless books have been written on what men should do! And Machiavelli,' he affirmed polemically, 'enjoyed describing what they really do.'[11] Analyzing the forms taken by states and the political debate of the time, he did not see – as Filangieri instead did – a conflict between the 'rights of the human species' and the maxims proclaimed by the great Florentine. The latter seemed to him timely and still valuable for the government of men. How, for example, could one not disagree with Mably, Rousseau, and his own teacher Genovesi – and, we can add, with all modern theorists of natural law – that Machiavelli was right in asserting that there was a clear 'difference between politics and morality'? The first 'judges what man is in society.' The second indicates 'how they must be, or how it would be desirable that they were.'[12]

Behind this suddenly inflamed debate over the true meaning of Machiavelli's legacy was a century of struggles against the hegemony of reason of state, against that way of governing '*à l'italienne ou à la florentine*,' as the French loved to put it, which, in the wake of the religious and civil wars of the late sixteenth and seventeenth centuries, had asserted itself rapidly with the practice of absolutism in Europe. It was no coincidence that in Italy, in 1749, Ludovico Antonio Muratori still saw it the task of the prince to pave the way forward for a new antimachiavellian politics, destined to privilege the collective good above all, in his celebrated tract *Della pubblica felicità*. 'By public happiness,' wrote the Modenese priest, 'we do not mean anything but that peace and tranquillity which a wise and loving prince or minister works towards for his people to enjoy as far as possible.'[13] In reality, the revolt against the conception of politics primarily as the conquest and maintenance of power had found powerful enemies in Campanella, Grotius, Pufendorf, Gravina, Maffei, and many others.[14] Since the early eighteenth century, it had become clear that there existed at least two different ways of understanding politics: on the one hand by the old *reason of state*; on the other by the new 'true politics' which Pufendorf, even though he was a champion of the theorists of absolute right, argued should be interpreted as a '*doctrina quae modum gubernandae civitatis ad legitimum finem docet*,' a politics the aim of which was only the '*salus popoli*' and the respect of rights.[15]

In Naples, in 1710, it had been Paolo Mattia Doria who led the revolt against the followers of Tacitus and Machiavelli. In his political treatise on *La vita civile*, this singular and fascinating heretical republican, whose courageous proposals for reform triggered violent contemporary reactions from the Bourbon monarchy and from the Church,[16] publicly vindicated what he defined the 'true and right politics' against the 'malicious politics' of the theorists of absolutism. Building on Plato, Aristotle, and Cicero, Doria reproposed the figure of the philosopher counsellor of princes, affirming he wanted to fight those who thought it better to 'consider man in the state in which he is, [rather] than in that in which he ought to be.'[17] That first way of thinking had found that 'virtue, the just, and the honest were entirely lost from sight,' creating grave failures in the government of people and morally diseducating new generations. Tacitus and Machiavelli bore principal responsibility for this. They had, with their works and through their modern followers, 'established the evil system of politics in a guise that renders it impossible to speak of wanting to regulate man according to the norms of a virtuous politics without being considered chimerical and extravagant.' Machiavelli, however, had less direct responsibility for this than Tacitus. Author of both the *Discorsi* and *Il Principe*, Machiavelli seemed to Doria more like a unique 'pharmacopoeia open to all recipes' than a perfidious inspirator of despotic governments. It seemed excessive to accuse the Florentine of having been the first and most authoritative author to have counselled 'the use of the mistaken and malicious reason of state.'[18] And, nonetheless, Doria had no doubts that a conception of politics founded solely on the search for the common good, on virtue, on the government of laws, and on public happiness could be re-established and affirmed though the overcoming of Machiavelli's crude political realism.

Antonio Genovesi had also embarked upon this path, which was destined to reopen, in new ways, the republican discourse in eighteenth-century Italy. His specific contribution was, for the first time in Naples, to place the rights of man at the centre of a new 'science of morality,' to be attained in short order through a scientific and rational analysis of natural law. The postulate of equality before the law constituted, in this sense, the rock-hard foundation on which to construct the new moral edifice. This, furthermore, was the really innovative part of modern natural law, the champions of which, across Europe, turned to examine the existing relationships between law and politics, above all revisiting the history of the different theories of morality and the ethical conceptions of the ancients regarding the natural equality of men, resolutely placing the theme of the rights of man at the centre of political debate.[19] Not by chance, Jean Barbeyrac defined, in his introduction, the contents of Pufendorf's famous 1672 tract *Le droit de la nature et de gens ou système genèrale des principes les plus importants de la morale, de la jurisprudence, et de la politique* as a 'Science of manners [*des mœurs*]… a subject related to morals or natural law.' According to Barbeyrac, for example, Aristotle had not understood the full potential and profound moral and political significance of natural law, because he persistently had denied the principle of equality before the law any validity in his theories: 'He does not seem to have had very clear ideas regarding the natural equality of all men, and expresses himself in a way that leads to the belief that there are men who naturally are slaves.'[20] His *Politics*, which had continued to dominate the thoughts of ruling parties in the West for centuries, thus lacked those solid moral roots which were indispensible to launch a comprehensive reconstitution of political culture.

During his fortunate career as a university lecturer, and in particular in his final years, when his chair attracted people like Longano, Galanti, Filangieri, Pagano and many other future protagonists of the Neapolitan Revolution of 1799, Genovesi concentrated his thought on the foundations of morality and on what should be understood by a just and fair society. He thought he would find the answer in the study of moral sciences, comprehended above all as a 'science of man, his properties, and his rights.' 'The just and honest man' was accountable to a single moral law of universal value at every moment of his life, a law that was 'simple, felt naturally by all'; to all it said 'preserve the rights of everyone, and if you have violated them, work on restoring them to prime condition [*in primo grado*].' Thus, Genovesi concluded, 'this law commands that one upholds the rights of God, our own rights, and the rights of others, who, by nature, are our equals.'[21] These considerations would have to form the moral foundations from which to overcome reason of state and the negative implications of Machiavelli's empirical insistence on respecting the existing social reality in all its harshness, an insistence that seemed to bar any form of reasonable utopia. Genovesi had no doubts on the matter: 'Every politics, every economy which is not based on justice, on virtue, and on honour destroys itself.'[22] Rousseau had clearly explained in the *Contrat Social* that only the general will, as the fruit of a pact of union between men considered preliminarily free and equal, could give birth to the modern conception of morality and legitimacy in political action. The 'transition from the state of nature to the civil state produces a most remarkable change in man by substituting justice for instinct in his conduct, and endowing his actions with the morality they previously lacked.'[23] Genovesi shared the substance of Rousseau's account of the genesis of morality in human history. There is no doubt that the former's analytical and, to a certain extent, also original research on the rights of man in the *Diceosina* had contributed greatly to broadening the debate over these issues among young Enlightenment thinkers in Southern Italy. However, one must not underestimate the contribution of the Masonic lodges to the establishment of a new conception of politics. It was in that world, towards the end of the eighteenth century, that all the contradictions of the old way of thinking came to a violent boil, and in which one began to notice the possible political consequences of insistent moral advocacy.

Next to the recovery, in new forms, of natural law and the emergence of a strong Enlightenment culture privileging reforms as an instrument for overcoming the injustices of the Old Regime, the Masonic world in fact played a role which has been ignored by historians for too long. It played an indirect role, difficult to specify but certainly decisive in the progressive affirmation of a language and a collective mentality of cultural values and practices very close to the modern 'republican spirit,' which saw in the equality of rights the keystone for rethinking the relationship between politics and morality. The Masonic community, acutely defined as 'the strongest social institution of the eighteenth-century moral world,'[24] in some way prefigures the creation of a civil society different from that of the traditional Old Regime. Although strictly separated from the world of the profane by its secrecy and rites of initiation, the outside influence of Freemasonry cannot be discounted. One must never forget that the catechisms of the brotherhood spoke of little but moral laws, virtue, equality, justice, liberty, philanthropy, merit, education, and respect for humanity, always, of course, with precise references to the rights and duties of brothers and to the written guidelines governing life in the lodges. The so-called profane world was something else. In James Anderson's 1723 *Constitutions*, the fundamental collection of all Masonic regulations in the eighteenth century, the most important declaration was the categorical 'the mason is oblig'd, by his tenure, to obey the moral law.'[25] One can find what this meant in practice in the numerous discourses held by Grand Masters and notables of all nationalities in the lodges of Europe. A well known speech of 1737, held in France by the Scotsman Andrew Michael Ramsey, for example explained that the objectives of the 'Order of Freemasons' were 'humanity, pure morals, the inviolable secret, and taste for the fine arts.' The people of the lodges had internally to practice and externally to publicize 'philanthropy,' civic virtues, cosmopolitanism, love of science and of technology. Over time, the Order was to change the community of brothers through respect for 'healthy morals,' denouncing, without hesitation, 'love of fatherland poorly understood' and the aggressive sort of Machiavellian republicanism which appeared to be spreading in English lodges. In response to the latter's dangerous influences, it was necessary to 'shape men, and able men, good citizens, good subjects, who always maintain their promises, faithful adulators of the god of friendship, greater lovers of virtue than of recompenses.'[26] Nearly identical suggestions can be found in the catechisms and discourses presented in the Neapolitan lodges. Also in this case, the 'novices' were invited, with insistence, to live the Masonic experience virtuously, to unite respect for statutes and regulations with an individual morality attentive to the duties of friendship and brotherhood, and more generally to the 'laws prescribed by humanity.' 'Our works are a continued study of virtue, our ranks are nothing but the fruit of a tight and rigorous morality.'[27] Only thus could the brother's moral melioration go hand in hand with the construction of a harmonious society founded on virtue.

Actually, recent studies of the social and cultural history of Freemasonry have documented how different reality was from its noble theoretical enunciations, and how very complex and contradictory the concrete experiences of the brotherhood were over the course of the eighteenth century. The propaganda and diffusion – elements which certainly were relevant in the formation of new collective mentalities – of the value systems of the lodges, along with the constant reference to the universal moral laws of the universe, were rendered less important by quotidian compromises and the individual brothers' calls for privilege.[28] Today, we know that, over the course of the years, contrasting figures and projects alternated rapidly in the internal life of Masonic society, the profile and true character of which, beyond the rituals and the ceremonies, seemed to become ever more vague and imprecise in contemporary eyes, precisely at the moment of its greatest success.[29] In the 1770s and 80s, when Filangieri frequented the brotherhood, the momentary but highly significant confluence of numerous exponents of late Enlightenment culture in the Masonic movement accompanied profound conflicts and contrapositions of every kind between the lodges of English Rite, the national lodges of Strict Observance, and the Great Orient in France. These were decisive years in the history of the Order. From a society which kept secrets, Masonry was developing into a secret society, drawing on sectarian and conspiratorial models, politicizing its adepts and its project of social emancipation.[30] From moral sermoning it moved, more or less consciously for many brothers, to propaganda and political action, to the subversive quest for a republicanism which, no longer limited to the Masonic community, was meant for the world of the profane. It seemed the time was finally nigh for drawing the inevitable political consequences of decades of moral preaching. It is enough to note how, over the course of a decade, the very names of the lodges in Southern Italy changed to realize how the climate was changing. In the 1770s, names like *Les Zèlès*, *La Sécrète*, *La Candeur*, *La Constance*, and *La Fidèle* were still dominant. Twenty years later, the leading lodges were called the likes of *Dell'Eguaglianza*, *Della Pace*, *La Philantropia*, and *L'Humanité*.[31]

In 1786, further confirmation of these ongoing changes appeared anonymously in a treatise (probably published by the Masonic editor Lorenzo Manini of Cremona) which was extremely indicative of the Masonic world's growing need to find, as quickly as possible, a concrete and, above all, operative cultural and political identity with which to substitute the traditional and, more often than not, generic and inoffensive references to universal morality, to civic virtues, and to philanthropy. It was written by the Camaldolese priest Isidoro Bianchi[32] in express response to the grave crisis of European Masonry in the wake of the conflict between radicals and moderates triggered by the American Revolution and the uncovering of the conspiracy of the Bavarian Illuminati, which had taken place two years earlier, and the consequent alarm it raised in governments everywhere. The text was to confront the grave accusation, which had been levied against the brotherhood, of making secrecy an ever new, terrible, and efficient political weapon, fuelling subversion and general protest. The little volume's emblematic title, *Dell'Instituto dei veri liberi muratori*, clarified the author's precise will to furnish public opinion with yet another reassuring interpretation among the many which continued to appear in those years, particularly in Germany (it is enough to think of Lessing's 1778 *Ernst und Falk. Gespräche für Freimaurer*), regarding the substantially apolitical nature and specifically moral tasks of Freemasonry. It was a kind of Enlightenment interpretation of the phenomenon, which sought to justify the sudden alliance established between worlds so different as that of the Enlightenment and that of the lodges, in light of a common search for a civil religion founded on a generic, primitive, and church-less Gnostic Christianity capable of profoundly reforming the Old Regime.

An outcome of the 'laws of sociability animating men,'[33] Bianchi argued that Masonry was born primarily to 'bring man back to his original goodness' and respect for his natural rights. Confronted with the historical development of Western society, ruled by 'false and corrupt education, the excessive inequality of ranks and of fortune's goods, the collision of so many different interests, the pride of power and the ambition of authority,' the goal of the 'Order of Freemasons' was to rekindle 'the providential and consoling laws of nature' in the hearts of men.[34] Apart from rendering him 'humane, reasonable, and virtuous,' Masonry's task was to teach him the truth, and make him 'better' by educating him to attain the 'most perfect morality.' 'The members of this respectable society,' Bianchi explained, relaunching cosmopolitanism,

> are all brothers who do not distinguish themselves by the language that they speak, the clothes that they wear, the opinions that they have, their social roles, the goods that they possess. Equality is their first law, and they therefore consider the entire world a republic in which every nation forms a family, and every individual a son.

The brotherhood's eminently moral task had been rigorously set forth – according to Bianchi – since the earliest constitutions, and continuously reinforced in successive regulations by the fact that, to the brothers, it was 'expressly forbidden not only to discuss any points of religion or politics in the lodges, but even to mention them.'[35] Politics, understood as seventeenth-century reason of state, *arcana imperii*, absolutist types of government, international diplomacy, and court intrigues, had seemed to the early compilers of Masonic constitutions as something neatly distinct and to be kept systematically separate from morality, so as to guarantee the existence and security of the lodge. Morality and politics were conceived as incarnations of two different institutions, as if they were two different worlds devoid of contact. On the one hand there was the state, absolute master of politics and the public sphere, on the other the private lodges, where morality instead ruled supreme.

At the end of the eighteenth century, this radical division, which seemed to guarantee reciprocal tranquillity and the absence of conflict, was rapidly losing its meaning in the collective consciousness, thanks above all to the works of Enlightenment thinkers and the affirmation of the modern natural law of rights. Beyond being an important document of the Italian and European experience of Freemasonry, the *Dell'Instituto dei veri liberi muratori* represents a striking witness to the changes underway and to the deep – to our eyes at least – contradictions resulting in the thought of those Enlightenment Freemasons. In fact, the work was articulated and developed to deny what was impossible to deny: the politicization of Freemasonry through the transformation of the very way in which politics was understood after the lodges also began to experience the rise of the language of rights. Faced with the accusations of those who, identifying subversive political ends in this, openly contested both the legitimacy of Masonic secrecy and the increasingly more evident political consequences of their moral propaganda, Isidoro Bianchi sought in vain to supply plausible answers to reaffirm the persistent pertinence of the ancient distinctions. Besides, what could one reply to those who argued that 'only illicit and evil things must remain occult, not those which are good and useful,' and that even the Church and the State definitively proposed to teach people correct morals like the brotherhood did? What really hid in the powerful and mysterious European web of lodges?

Above all, Bianchi denied the existence of the dangerous politics that had appeared evident to many governments as a result of the support for the American Revolution apparent in many important Masonic circles and, most importantly, of the thorny case of the Bavarian Illuminati,[36] instead sustaining that even princes and sovereigns were among the major members of the brotherhood. Secondly, the same secrecy that now was used to criticize Freemasonry had been employed, historically, by the first Christians to defend the mystery of the Trinity and the incarnation in the advent of better times, and, still in antiquity, by numerous schools of philosophy who sought to protect the truth from the dark era in which they lived. Like the brother Joseph de Maistre, according to whom secrecy was to be considered an integral part of 'natural law, because it is the link of trust, the great basis of human society,'[37] so too Bianchi conceived of its practice as a very real right of humanity. A right, however, which was necessary above all to guarantee the search for, and diffusion of, truth in difficult moments of history, when the 'practice of hiding the arcane' could be decisive in the fight against those who denied the rights of man. To him, Freemasonry was only a simple association of philosophers devoted to the common good: 'Freemasons thus considered a respectable society of philosophers, one will never be able to consider the secrecy of their truth and of their mysteries a crime.' Secrecy, understood as a practice, a useful instrument for civil society, and not only as something mysterious, had in fact multiple functions, all of them legitimate. It served to cement reciprocal trust among brothers, to defend their opinions in the outside world, and, by recurring to specific symbols and languages decipherable only inside the community, to 'recreate and sublimate the spirit' in the struggle to regenerate humanity.

> Consider, for an instant, how ingenious and exact the allegory of society is. Freemasons propose to raise a temple, and it is that of virtue which they want to erect. The instruments of this edifice are equally symbols of the various affections of the human heart. The set square, the triangle, and the compass represent equality, justice, and probity. The light indicates only virtue… The Freemasons do not admit any distinction among them but that of virtue. One puts aside birth, rank, and fortune when one admits a new candidate to the first level.[38]

Their secrecy did not represent a danger for states. If anything, Bianchi thought, the debate should to be pursued regarding its contents, the truths which, from time to time, secrecy hid from the eyes of the profane. The accusation of having transformed the moral truths preached in the lodges into political theory and action seemed to him entirely unfounded if evaluated within the typical cognitive schemes of the Masonic world. 'One will tell me that the *equality* and *liberty* professed by the Freemasons do not conform to the good order of the State'; and thus their diffusion among people constituted an entirely political fact and an objective threat to the social order. One had, however, to agree on the meaning of words. Masons always and only privileged 'the moral sense' of those expressions that suddenly, and by no fault of the brotherhood, had become red hot in the political lexicon of republicanism at the end of the century. They had 'never dreamt' of equality as something similar to 'a perfect equality of ranks, orders, and conditions.' Their conception of equality was rather based on the ethical postulate of equality of rights for all men.

> Men are certainly not equal in terms of power, talents, or figure. Beyond this, everyone has that terrible and natural inclination to dominate others. And if this is the case, who is that man endowed with reason who can persuade himself that it is possible to render all men perfectly equal? Now, all the equality of the Freemasons consists in regarding each other like brothers, in helping each other reciprocally, in sharing all the offices of gentility, of attachment, and of charity in uniformly respecting all the rights of men which the beneficence of nature has conceded equally to all. The humble vassal, without hiding the mediocrity of his condition, approached the affable prince with modest frankness, and he, forgetting his greatness, moves towards him, his face beautifully serene, and with that tender and frank character of goodness which is advisable for the wise man who recognizes a natural equality of relations with his kind. And who does not see that good morals are based precisely on this highly desirable equality?[39]

Did not the first Christians also want something similar?[40] The same discourse was useful for the word liberty. There was nothing subversive or political in the Masonic interpretation of it. In this case too, what mattered was 'the idea of liberty developed by good moralists,' an idea that simultaneously conceived of liberty in terms of the rights of man and of the subsequent laws to be promulgated by a government set on remaining just and legitimate.

> Every just and moderate government is founded on liberty; since its real aim is only to guarantee every citizen the free and peaceful exercise of his faculties; and so liberty is a right which all men have received from nature by their very existence, in such a way that it must be permitted to everyone to freely exercise their rights when one makes it a duty for all to satisfy all the duties of civil society…Now, the system of the Freemasons is entirely contrary to irregularity and to license, and admits only that liberty which is founded on the most solid principles of a healthy morality.[41]

The most disconcerting aspect of Bianchi's work is the fact that he seemed absolutely unaware of the wholly political reading which was emerging of terms such as brotherhood, equality, and liberty compared to then current interpretations. His repeated reassurances that the Masons 'always have devoted themselves to the good of the republic and of their fellow citizens without ever interfering in politics,' and that since their object was solely moral, Freemasonry would never let itself be carried away in 'conspiracies' and in 'projects that are pernicious to the State' today seem like obvious logical absurdities, triggering perplexities and pertinent question-marks regarding what Masons really meant by politics. His text, in reality, is only seemingly contradictory, and must be contextualized and understood in light of the sudden changes undergone by political culture in those years. If it is true that the author's goal was that of negating the politicization of the brotherhood, his arguments nonetheless reveal themselves valuable and acquire meaning not so much because, as we have already underlined, two different conceptions of politics were squaring off publicly in the eighteenth century, but in relation to the contents of this new way of considering politics. A way ever more focused on the rights of man and their as yet unexplored potentials, which was supported with increasing vigour by vast swaths of the Enlightenment establishment in their bitter polemic against the last defenders of reason of state.

The language of rights, which spread through the lodges of English Rites only in the second half of the century in the wake of the Dutch brothers' promotion of Locke's works, directly and contemporaneously permeating the moral and political spheres, easily permitted enlightened Masons like Bianchi to play on the multiple origins of natural rights.[42] By focusing all the attention of public opinion on the moral dimension of rights, Masons denied any direct responsibility for their inevitable political consequences. In this way, the apolitical nature of the ancient Masonic constitutions was safeguarded, and the brotherhood's moral mission relaunched without further fear and need for justification.

Certainly, the chaotic arrangement of different, Machiavellian interpretations of the ostensibly purely moral meaning of Masonic propaganda opened the way to no few suspicions from the Church,[43] not to mention to subsequent misunderstandings as seen in liberal historiography, which always has upheld the apolitical nature of Freemasonry, wholeheartedly accepting the rejection of politics proclaimed in its constitutions. But it is above all the lack of reflection upon the real nature of the complex arguments developed by the most authoritative Freemasons in the 1770s and 80s that has hindered our understanding of two decisive questions in the political history of eighteenth-century Europe: first of all the alarming, but at the same time stimulating and contradictory introduction into the lodges of the language of the rights of man and the passage from morals to politics which it consented; and secondly, the actual significance lurking behind the clamorous convergence of Freemasonry and a large number of Enlightenment thinkers at the end of the century. Voltaire, it is worth recalling, was initiated in a grand ceremony concluded with music by the brother Haydn and a toast to the American insurgents, in the lodge of the *Neuf Sœurs* in Paris in February of 1778, only a few months before passing away.[44]

With regards to this last question, which is as pertinent as it is unexplored, Reinhart Koselleck has arrived at somewhat surprising and debatable conclusions about the so-called 'hypocrisy of the Enlightenment' as the true cipher of its dangerous conception of politics. According to his analysis, permeated by prejudice and subtly reactionary points,

> The political secret of the Enlightenment lay in the fact that its concepts, analogous to the indirect assumption of power, were not seen as being political. The political anonymity of reason, morality, nature, and so on, defined their political character and effectiveness. Their political essence lay in being non-political.[45]

Without ever referring specifically to modern natural law, to republicanism, or to the theory of the rights of man, and purposefully confusing the experiences of Enlightenment thinkers and of Freemasons at the end of the century ('directly non-political, the Mason is indirectly political after all'[46]), Koselleck has placed the Enlightenment 'critique' and its dialectical consequences on the defendant's bench, accusing it of having brought about (with its renunciation of political realism, veined with hypocrisy, and with its abstract utopian moralism) the negative aspects of modernity and the 'crisis' not only of the Old Regime, but also of the Western world of today. In reality, the real conception of politics in the Enlightenment had nothing to do with such fantastic, if suggestive trajectories. Anyone who knows that world well knows that the reformulation of the relationship between politics and morals passed through different channels, and that the claim of *libertas philosophandi*, and of the critical and public use of reason in every field, certainly did not have to await Kant's arguments in his celebrated 1784 *Was ist Aufklärung?* to become one of the declared objectives of the Enlightenment. Had it perhaps not been the young Diderot to maintain that if he had been impeded from speaking publicly about '*religion*' and '*gouvernement*' he would have been left with nothing else to do in life?[47] The obstinate struggle against reason of state and, above all, the simultaneously political and moral reading of the rights of man – the true unifying thread of large parts of the Enlightenment political debate – had begun openly and genuinely in the first half of the eighteenth century. Gaetano Filangieri's own human and intellectual experience represents an emblematic case for understanding the points of contact, but also the necessary and decisive distinctions, which always need to be drawn between Freemasonry and Enlightenment if one really wants to understand the multiple forms taken by the crisis of the Old Regime.

Though friend and brother in arms of Isidoro Bianchi – who took charge of diffusing the *Scienza della legislazione* in Northern Italy – the brother Filangieri would probably neither have subscribed to the Masonic rejection of politics, nor to its systematic separation from morality as called for by its constitutions. It suffices to read the volumes of his work to verify this. Politics, as the search for public and private happiness in a just and fair society, constituted the very core of his entire project. In the eyes of the Neapolitan jurist and philosopher, the 'new principles' which radically were changing the nature and significance of politics emerged from the modern theory of rights interpreted in an openly republican and Enlightenment sense. 'These *rights* which man acquires at birth; which society and the laws must guarantee; which are essential in us... form our political existence like the soul and the body form our physical existence' [I, 297], he repeated on every occasion. The simultaneously moral and political nature of rights, which natural law since the mid-seventeenth century had brought to the attention of scholars, seemed to permit the definite overcoming of the old dichotomies imposed by reason of state. The universal and cosmopolitan nature of rights, their equality for all human beings – as Antonio Genovesi had taught – generated, on the level of reason and common sense, those indispensible presuppositions for defining moral character. Finally, the objective of converting rights from being the foundation of 'universal morals' into a republican 'rule of the laws' fuelled, almost naturally, the birth of a renewed archetype of politics which gave importance to the legitimating function of morality.

The assumption of these horizons of reference nonetheless imposed ulterior and necessary developments along the path of a continual exploration of the potentials implicit in the 'new principles' – for example, the nearly inevitable reflection on what we might define as the universal character of the right to politics. With a republican spirit, Filangieri resolutely embarked on this road, which lead to the recognition of the principle of participation in communal life in the most appropriate and, above all, historically possible forms and means by all men, with no exception, if one wanted to maintain the relationship between politics and morality alive:

> It is a right common to all individuals in all societies; it is a right which cannot be lost, nor renounced, nor transferred, because it depends on a duty which obliges every society which exists, as long as it does, and from which nobody can be freed, without being excluded by society or without this being destroyed. This duty is that of contributing, as far as individually possible, to the good of the society to which one belongs, and the right which depends on it is that of showing society the ideas one thinks conducive to this, or to diminish only its evils or to multiply its goods.

The call for governments to finally proclaim the freedom of the press in Old Regime Europe was founded precisely on this natural right and duty of the individual to participate in political life, which was not, coincidentally, defined as something which 'cannot be lost, nor alienated as long as one belongs to a society, because it depends on that [natural law] which embraces all and precedes all.' To this end, freedom of the press was immediately introduced as an indispensible premise for the formation of a free public opinion in which all could participate. 'The legislator must establish it, the legislator must protect it. The public interest requires it,' Filangieri proclaimed vigorously, 'the length of his legislation and the permanency of the fate of the people demand it, and, furthermore, *justice*, that inflexible divinity which always must be counselled and never disobeyed by the legislator, manifestly forbids its privation' [I, 293]. As for other Enlightenment thinkers of the end of the century, Filangieri also saw in public opinion not only a sort of indirect confirmation of the primacy of popular sovereignty in the control of power, but also a decisive instrument for ensuring the moral assessment of princely action on behalf of civil society; hence, the depth of analysis of it and the questions he formulated regarding the necessary conditions for guaranteeing its existence and correct functioning. Though we will return to its decisive importance for the republican project of the *Scienza della legislazione* later on, book IV was entirely dedicated to the construction of a system of public education, precisely to create the indispensible conditions for the free participation in public debate by all members of the political community.

Fact is that the reflection on the relationship between morals and politics, which, however problematic, was held ever more indispensable, worried and animated the entire Enlightenment world for decades. The celebrated Kantian conclusion according to which politics had to 'kneel before morals' would certainly have been supported without hesitation by Mably, Diderot, Voltaire, Rousseau, Jefferson, Lessing, Filangieri, and many more still. They would probably also have shared Kant's bitter criticisms both of the theorists of the new political realism and those modern government professionals accused of cynically and ruthlessly manipulating morality at will to sustain their suspect dealings with power. 'The political moralist begins where the moral politician rightly leaves off, and by thereby subordinating the principles to the end (that is, putting the cart before the horse), thwarts his own intent to bring politics and morality into agreement with one another.'[48] Beyond the different eighteenth-century theories for constructing a new moral science on a rational foundation, no Enlightenment thinker doubted the universal character it would require to really furnish an efficient response to those who supported the radical autonomy and self-sufficiency of politics. This, in fact, was one of the foundations which put the *ought* of morality on par with the *ought* of politics. Understood as a free and autonomous act of individual will, an essential mechanism in the process of emancipation and realization of human personality, politics had to kneel before morality only if the latter based its choices on truly universal criteria.[49] Ultimately, a truly republican government, and the practices of transparency and publicity in every decisive moment in the life of the community, constituted the essential corollaries for completing the picture, finally – according to the common opinion of many Enlightenment thinkers at the end of the century and not just Kant, who can be credited with the first efficient overview of it – giving politics the solid moral foundations necessary for radically transforming the Old Regime.

One continually finds these concepts repeated throughout the *Scienza della legislazione*. As we have already seen, Filangieri had initiated his politico-philosophical activities denouncing the *arcana juris*, polemicizing against the violence of the inquisitorial process with great civic passion, championing the public showing and transparency of penal law, and even the direct participation, in appropriate ways, of citizens in the practice of justice. He was less partial to the *arcana imperii*, symbol and instrument of every despotism. The use of secrecy in the public sphere and in the art of government deeply contradicted his republican ideal of a free, emancipated individual, living among equals and responsible for his own actions, entitled to rights and duties to be exercised publicly and transparently, unless its inherent moral legitimacies were contradicted. How, then, to reconcile these convictions, clearly expressed in the *Scienza della legislazione*, with his adhesion to the Masonic lodges where, instead, the practice of secrecy reigned supreme? This is a question that one could ask of all the Enlightenment thinkers who in the 1770s and 80s entered the brotherhood in great numbers. What did illustrious characters like Diderot, Lessing, Condorcet, Voltaire, or Filangieri hope to find there? What had European Masonry and, conversely, the late Enlightenment, become in the last quarter of the century?[50]

The 1782 Convent of Wilhelmsbad, in which brothers of different nationalities passionately discussed the origins, the functions, and the very nature of Freemasonry, had done nothing but bring to the fore a grave crisis of identity long in the making, precisely when the lodges' success everywhere was most resounding and unexpected. Princes, kings, nobles of all ranks, ecclesiastics, literati, musicians, artists, merchants, artisans, adventurers, businessmen, and charlatans of all kinds seemed suddenly to have found a sort of ideal space in that suggestive form of sociability, a space in which to express their intense need for ritualism, for the exclusive and secret belonging to a new and seemingly more just and virtuous social order compared to the ancient hierarchies of the Old Regime. They all found what they looked for. Masonry in fact functioned simultaneously as an effective society of mutual assistance and as a meeting place for groups secretly searching for new intellectual experiences of the mystical, occultist, philanthropist, religious and, finally, political kind. While an artist easily could find brothers able to guarantee lucrative commissions or valuable recommendations for his work, Joseph II hoped at length to organize the necessary consensus for his politics of reform within the Order.[51] The American insurgents saw Freemasonry as a privileged place for their anti-English propaganda. In the wake of the suppression of the Society of Jesus, former Jesuits instead discovered in the lodges a possible refuge and a powerful weapon of propaganda to create a new Catholic public sphere capable of giving life and vigour to the politics of religious restoration sought by Pius VI after 1782.[52] The Enlightenment thinkers, finally, were the last to arrive, and did what they could to control that formidable instrument which seemed purposefully constructed to guarantee the international circulation and diffusion of their discourses and cultural practices. Besides, had it not been Voltaire, as of the 1770s, to pave the way for this when he called on the *philosophes* to organize 'like the Masons' to defend the Enlightenment against the attacks of their enemies?[53] The confrontation between *Aufklärung* and *Schwärmerei* in the German lodges represented, in this sense, an important chapter of this incessant struggle between different factions to control the Masonic system for their own ends. Upon closer scrutiny, Filangieri's own experience assumes an almost paradigmatic character in the face of the vexed question of the relationship between Freemasonry and Enlightenment – a relationship which, properly analyzed, can reveal many aspects of the inextricable intersection which developed between morals, politics, and religion in the late eighteenth century.

Younger son of the princes of Arianello (the title had been granted by an imperial diplomat of Carl VI of Habsburg, while the family traced its lineage back to 1045, to the oldest and most prestigious Norman nobility which had followed Robert Guiscard to Southern Italy), nephew of the archbishop of Naples, Filangieri had been educated by a tutor, don Luca Nicola de Luca, known for his Jansenist and royalist leanings, adverse to the temporal claims of the Roman curia. Alongside the classics of religion, politics, and philosophy, he also introduced Filangieri to the books of Pietro Giannone, Antonio Genovesi, the *Entretiens de Phocion sur le rapport de la morale avec la politique* of the 'wise Mably,' but above all to the works of Anthony Ashley Cooper, third Earl of Shaftesbury.[54] His Neoplatonism, in particular, which underlined the harmonious and natural social arrangement of individual and collective interests through its strong appeal to the moral sense intimately and autonomously present in the souls of all men, had contributed considerably to transforming and strengthening Filangieri's spontaneous ethical enthusiasm into social energy, into the categorical will for action and for the political reform of the injustices of the Old Regime. That egalitarian pantheism saturated with powerful and natural religiosity, that moral sentiment instinctively sensed by all humans and justified on the rational and aesthetic levels as the virtuous love of the whole by its parts, like the celebration of a social harmony founded on fairness and justice, probably pushed the young Filangieri to reflect ever more intensely upon the way in which religion linked individual will, politics, and the mechanisms of the social bond. This was a religion to be reformed civically and returned to the centre of European political life like an Augustinian *coagulum populorum*, according to the provocative framework delineated by Rousseau in his 'Creed of the Savoyard Priest' and in the *Contrat Social*, as well as in proposals emerging from the heated debate, launched in the 1760s in many Enlightenment circles ever more hostile to the traditional libertine and materialist readings of the phenomenon of religion, which were quite evidently incapable of accounting for the specific needs of the multitudes.[55]

Filangieri was probably among the first in Italy, but certainly not the only one, to seize the occasion offered by the lodges to confront the delicate question of general religious reform in the West. Freemasonry seemed to him, in this sense, above all a formidable religious society, an institution capable both of satisfying the growing need for religiosity among the elite, disappointed by the traditional faiths, and of introducing indispensable changes in the content and objective of popular religion with its specific necessities and languages. Present everywhere, with their mysterious ceremonies and baroque rites, with their moral preaching and practice of universal brotherhood and philanthropy, the lodges in effect represented the only true alternative to the Churches and Christianity as it had developed historically.[56] Did not, after all, even the great Lessing say much the same things when he compared Freemasons to the first Christians and called for the creation of a new religion of humanity founded on the use of reason in his 1776 *Gespräche für Freimaurer*?

Incomplete and published posthumously, book V of the *Scienza della legislazione*, entitled *Delle leggi che riguardano la religione*, was entirely dedicated to this extraordinary project of reform. Filangieri openly aimed for the creation of a modern civic religion capable of overcoming the ruinous logic of the two authorities introduced by Christianity and in particular by Catholicism, with its obstinate idea of a Church separate and tenaciously opposed the State. The convinced heir of Pietro Giannone and the great royalist tradition, Filangieri had no doubts regarding the primacy of civil over religious government.[57] A good legislator had, first of all, to prevent the two extreme evils he found most dangerous on the social and civil level: 'fanaticism and irreligion.' He would then have to intervene with laws purposefully adapted to limit the temporal power of the Church, imposing tough restrictions on the different forms of immunity, regulating ecclesiastical appointments, reducing the excessive number of priests, taking care of their education, deciding their age and the contents of 'their predications' by law, and, finally, directly attacking the very heart of the Catholic Church, that is striking 'the evil at its root' and reforming 'the very nature of the rents of the priesthood' [I, 59] and drastically secularizing the greater part of ecclesiastical properties.

The violent reaction of the Inquisition and the immediate placing on the Index of the first two volumes of his work, where the general lines of his project for reform were delineated comprehensively, did not stop Filangieri from proposing, in book V, a sort of natural history of religions in the spirit of Vico, Hume, and d'Holbach; a history in light of which he could illustrate the originality of the new civil religion and construct the modalities of a secret reformist process destined to set Freemasonry and the state against revealed religion. Though accused by the theologian Domenico Nicola, in his 1784 opinion to the Congregation of the Index, of having upset 'entirely the most solid principles of religion,'[58] Filangieri did not hesitate for a second in proposing, a few years later, the history of the birth of religion as a phenomenon independent of any concessions to Biblical history and to Revelation. The origin of religion in the earliest societies was explained as the natural fruit of fear, of impotence, and of weakness, which had led to anthropomorphic cults and to polytheism, but was also to be explained in light of that '*contrast* of *finite* and of *infinite* observable in human nature' which in the best minds produced the need to question oneself rationally on that singular 'unknown and universal force' [III, 318] which mysteriously upheld the fate of the universe. In the decisive phase of transition from the barbaric stage of humanity to that of civil society, three forms of religion emerged historically according to Filangieri: that of the 'multitude,' with its fervent popular imagination and the poetic and fantastic theology which gave form to polytheism; that of 'government,' with its civic ceremonialism, 'augurs, auspices, oracles, feasts, sacrifices'; and finally that of the wise, who above all sought to correct the superstitions and excesses of popular religion, secretly questioning the true theological character of nature's mysterious forces. Filangieri's punctilious analysis of this last form of religion, so similar to the initiatory and secretive nature of primitive Christianity and of the masonic and sectarial practices of the original Masonic lodges, allowed him finally to clarify the historical and instrumental quality of the *arcana Dei*. These mysteries originally emerged as a consequence of the social differences which imposed more 'reserved rites' on the patricians compared to the superstitions of popular credence. With time and with social and economic change that 'disgraceful inequality' become unsustainable. A way of overcoming those contrasts and excessive divisions had been found in the invention of the 'mysteries,' useful for widening, in some way, the circle of initiates to the exclusive rites without, however, changing their spiritual and elitist nature.

It was thus necessary to modify their inaccessibility without destroying it; it was necessary to grant access to all orders without granting it to all their individuals… There was only one way of doing this, and circumstances indicated it with such great evidence that it should not be surprising that it was adopted equally by all peoples. Thus *intitiation* was introduced everywhere, and everywhere initiates were prohibited from divulging the mysteries they saw or practiced. No secrets were concealed, nor could they be concealed, in their celebrations, but the ban on divulgation and the difficulty of initiation, prescribed for other reasons, would shortly make people believe that there were… The more perspicacious *adepts* made conjectures, and their conjectures thus became the *grand arcanum*. This is how the mysteries of all peoples were instituted, on which much has been said and written, and on which there has been such a variety of opinions because one has not wanted to investigate the universal and eternal in the course of human things. [III, 346]

The time had come, in other words, to overcome those ancient partitions and reunite the three religions, destroying the superstitious and dangerously fanatical forms of popular polytheism which easily complemented the disproportionate power gradually gathered by the 'priesthood,' always ready to use the weapon of the *arcana Dei* against the state. A tacit agreement between enlightened legislators and those few 'adepts' sensitive to the great religious reform was necessary to achieve this. In brief, Filangieri proposed, between the lines, a precise accord between governments and the Masonic world to introduce a modern kind of civil religion. 'This convention,' he specified, 'should be occult, unknown to the multitude, unknown to the very initiates who should be ignorant of the legislator's hand which conducts them.' By degrees, without sudden accelerations, the 'vulgar religion,' saturated with continuous references to miracles, to superstition, and to the fanatical power of the 'clergy,' was to be put in doubt, discredited, and finally attacked head on. Then, through the introduction of new rites, of new ceremonies 'regulated by the occult hand of the legislator,' one was to proceed to the diffusion of a new civil theology introducing a renewed symbolic language capable of speaking both to the people and to the elites. 'Finally, once the new building, constructed in the silence of the mysteries, has acquired enough extension and sufficient solidity… then the mysterious veil should be removed, then the legislator should publicize the new religion and declare it the religion of the State and of the government' [III, 369]. Filangieri lucidly presented the 'characteristics of the new religion to be substituted for the old,' focusing above all on their primary objective: 'to produce and eternalize the people's virtue and happiness.' Where the legislator did not go so far as imposing virtuous behaviour, religion would have to. 'The dogmas of its faith should not oppose themselves to the precepts of its morality; but there should be a constant midway between what one must believe and what one must do.' A noble and sober idea of divinity, which left no room for fanaticism and superstitious cults, was able to enforce virtuous behaviour and respect for social duties. Even the dogma of the resurrection was to be interpreted opportunely to that end. 'Atonement should not be excluded, hope should not be taken away from those who have sinned; but this must rest upon means determined by the profound will to repair evil and by the complete correction of the heart.' The new civil religion had courageously to challenge the muddled theological system of the Church fathers and the Church's temporal power (never mentioned explicitly, but always obviously intended) by imposing a radical policy of reforms. The solemn temples of the new religion

> should be the shelter of the needy and not the asylum of the wicked. Its solemnity and its feasts should safeguard men from crimes, and not criminals from punishment. The priesthood should form one of the noblest parts of the body politic and not a separate body; it should be the model of citizens and not the object of privileges; it should teach others to carry public burdens in peace and not to be immune from them; it should inculcate subordination to the legitimate authority and not be removed from it. [III, 371]

Filangieri passed away before entirely completing the design of his civil religion. This great challenge to the revealed religion of the late Enlightenment inaugurated an unexplored and fascinating chapter in the history of the West, a chapter that was destined to live on for a very long time indeed. To consider religion no longer a simple lie, but a socially and politically relevant fact to be studied and understood threw open doors which for a long time had seemed the dominion only of the many churches. Filangieri had no doubts that religion ('so intrinsic to human nature, so necessary for the formation, perfection, and conservation of society and so terrible in its degeneration' [III, 311]) represented a decisive historical and political phenomenon in the modern world. One should of course not entirely confound religion with politics. Their rules, objectives, and the very logic through which both phenomena historically had conditioned the development of European societies were different. Though identifying their intimate and profound bond, to the extent that they operated on the same subject – human society and the individual – Filangieri neatly distinguished the tasks of politics, and particularly that of legislation, from those of religion: the so-called '*forum externum*' (the public tribunal) was not to be confused with the '*forum internum*' (conscience), just as crime remained something different from sin.[59]

> Public order, private tranquillity, the security of the citizen require that the law does not seek to know everything, to see everything, requiring rather that its authority stops at the door to his home, that it respects this asylum of his peace and his liberty, that it does not try to investigate his thoughts and intentions, that it leaves the course of his desires free, that it considers him innocent, even though guilty, as long as his crime is not manifest, segregating, in a word, from the inspection of the law all that which is hidden to its eyes; it simultaneously requires that another restraint compensates for this necessary defect, requires that another tribunal, another judge, another code regulates the occult actions of citizens, scares their secret transports, encourages their occult virtues, directs their latent desires towards the common good, and finally forces the citizen to be good, honest, and virtuous, even in those places, in those moments, in those circumstances in which he is far from the eyes of his ministers. This is the work of religion. [I, 57–8]

The *arcana imperii* were something very different from the *arcana Dei*. On the basis of references to the ancient esoteric legacy of Neoplatonic humanism and the tradition of Nicodemism, as well as to the simulation and dissimulation which always had animated religious history,[60] Filangieri considered the use of the latter two legitimate, while he was profoundly convinced in stigmatizing the existence of the first. The brotherhood's instrumental practice of secrecy made sense in his eyes only in its particular religious context. Political conspiracies, plots like that which the Bavarian Illuminati were developing in Germany, were something very different. Had he lived long enough, the umpteenth metamorphosis of Freemasonry, in the wake of the French Revolution, from a religious society to a political sect, with the transformation of many Southern Italian lodges into Jacobin clubs, would probably have surprised him and would have created quite a few problems for the theoretical consistency of his principles. Did the sacrosanct war on despotism, against a ferocious and oppressive power, legitimate recourse to secrecy in the political struggle for liberty? We do not know what Filangieri's answer would have been. His friend and disciple Mario Pagano, to give just one example among many possible, did not hesitate for a moment in saying yes.

What is certain is that, according to the framework proposed in the *Scienza della legislazione*, politics was always to be conducted in plain view. Better still, for politics really to be *politics* in the new and original meaning given to it in the Enlightenment, it intimately and structurally had to coincide with public openness and transparency. It had to involve, in solemn respect for the republican spirit, all citizens. Looking closely, one must not be led astray by centuries of malicious misunderstanding and of historiographical underestimations based on framework created first in the early years of the nineteenth century and then during the Restoration. The persistent confusion with regards to decisive aspects of these themes seems entirely erroneous and veined with prejudice, fuelled by scholars, even famous ones, who insist on a utopian, abstract, generic, moralizing, and ambiguously hypocritical Enlightenment conception of politics. Given the concept of politics (as understood by the so-called followers of political realism) as the permanent effort of human existence to account concretely for and neutralize the endemic and natural conflict between men, Enlightenment thinkers, with their moralistic *ought* aimed at overcoming the rationale of the Old Regime, stand accused of having naively sought to change history, paving the way for the crisis of the contemporary world, to the disquieting stage of the 'modern utopia' and its dangerous social reveries.[61] In reality, the bitter criticisms raised by the Left and from the Right, by the worlds of Catholicism, Liberalism, and Marxism,[62] almost always suffer the consequences of a debatably teleological reading of historical processes which leads them to interpret the events of the Enlightenment always and above all in light of the French Revolution. To comprehend what really should be understood by politics in the world of the Enlightenment, however, it is instead necessary to emphasize its historical autonomy, underlining its original aspects and the spatial and temporal discontinuity that saw its prominent thinkers act against the backdrop of the dramatic crisis of the Old Regime.

Beyond the theoretical originality of the Enlightenment political debate, which for the first time reflected upon the forms of the state *ex parte civium* in light of the rights of man, of the concept of popular sovereignty, of the social contract, and of the division of powers to guarantee individual liberty, what was really innovative and peculiar was, first of all, the way in which the practice of politics was conceptualized empirically and concretely in the second half of the eighteenth century. Today we know that the Enlightenment was not a simple movement of men and ideas, at times conflicting and heterogeneous, but rather the ambitious creation of a veritable alternative cultural system to that which dominated the Old Regime: a complex system which accompanied the birth of modern *civil society*, finally understood to be fully separate from the state conceived as an instrument rather than an end in itself. In that cultural system, with its innovative institutions and urban forms of sociability, new discourses, practices, languages and values associated with new representations of reality in the entire constellation of knowledge interacted dialectically. Enlightenment humanism, with its project to emancipate the individual from ancient organic class-based structures and from the traditional principle of subjection, required a general redefinition of the concepts of public and private, of the relationship between individual and society, beginning from a precise hierarchy of priorities which always put man and his rights centre-stage to reflect on the function of justice, the market, religion, and of new social values to oppose traditional ones.

To achieve all of this, late Enlightenment thinkers invented large parts of the modern form of political struggle. They radically transformed that which today we call the modalities of political communication, giving life – as we will see in detail in the last chapter – to an original reinterpretation of the republican tradition through the use of public opinion and the concept of the public as an entity different from the absolutist state. The celebrated and fundamental article 11 of the 1789 Declaration of Rights, which recited 'the free communication of thoughts and opinions is one of man's most precious rights: every citizen can thus speak, write, and print freely, except to respond to abuses of this liberty in cases determined by the law,'[63] faithfully reflected not only, as we have previously seen, the calls of Filangieri and of so many others for freedom of the press and the republican right to political participation, but it sanctioned, on the juridical level, the birth of the public sphere of modern politics. The thinkers of the Enlightenment had been among the first to realize how, in civil society, changes in the publishing market, the processes of professionalization, and the overcoming of corporatist and class structures in society had given men of letters great power. Politics now had to take account of the emergence of public opinion, the issue of popular consensus, and the creation of cultural hegemonies before it could launch directly political and institutional transformations.[64] Filangieri was aware of the positive importance of, but also the dangers inherent in, the appearance of public opinion. He in fact called for government education programmes for all classes so as to widen, as far as possible, free participation in public debate. But, above all, Filangieri called on philosophers to adopt the greatest possible consistency in respecting an ethic of individual responsibility saturated with civic sense and religious respect for the ideals and values of the common Enlightenment project of emancipation:

What would become of us if in the midst of the depravation of our customs, of the vices of our education and of the imperfection of our laws, if among one million four hundred thousand men who always are armed and ready to defend the attacks of Europe's masters, the free writings of philosophers did not inculcate luminous principles of morality to combat vice, did not make the tyrant's face blush? What would become of us, if public opinion, managing and directing itself, did not cover in infamy the monarch who orders an unjust law, the minister who proposes it, and the magistrate who ensures its execution? What would become of us if the arbitrary blows hurled by omnipotent authority were not met immediately by a thousand brave pens manifesting them to the entire people together alongside the ignominy of their authors? What would become of us if the virtues of our princes did not find eloquent panegyrists and their vices brave accusers? What would become of us, if the voice of liberty was never heard by the people in our monarchies, recalling in them the memory of their precious and inalienable rights? [III, 6]

The strong moral and religious nature of the new way of conceiving of politics *ex parte civium* developed in the late Enlightenment could not have been summarized better. In the *Scienza della legislazione*, through the powerful and creative mind of Filangieri, a political philosopher with a legal background, all the elements we have analyzed in the preceding chapters, from the republican political myth of the government of laws, to the centrality of the theory of the rights of man, to the critical revisitation of the egalitarian principle, precipitated in the Enlightenment project of a renewed constitutional politics. A politics which found its definite horizon of reference in the republicanism of the moderns.

Chapter Seven

NATION OR FATHERLAND?
THE REPUBLICAN AND
CONSTITUTIONAL PATRIOTISM OF
ITALIAN ENLIGHTENMENT THINKERS

What I call *virtue* in a republic is love of the homeland, that is, love of equality. It is not a moral virtue or a Christian virtue; it is *political* virtue, and this is the spring that makes republican government move… It is in republican government that the full power of education is needed.

Montesquieu, L'esprit des lois (1748)

Any state which is ruled by law I call a 'republic,' whatever the form of its constitution; for then, and then alone, does the public interest govern and then alone is the 'public thing' – the *res publica* – a reality. All legitimate government is 'republican'…

Rousseau, Contrat social (1762)

Does one have a fatherland where only
one wants, and all obey?

Alfieri, Virginia, a. III, sc. II

What did it mean to be a republican thinker in the eighteenth century?

Our knowledge of the developments of the republican tradition in the political history of the Enlightenment has not made great advances in recent decades.[1] Paradoxically, the recent explosion of interest in these issues among philosophers and historians of political thought has probably not furthered our understanding of them, for they have ended up privileging a sort of imagined republicanism, divorced from its context, made up of arbitrary metahistorical reconstructions, the paradigmatic nature of which systematically gives ample concessions to anachronism: the true mortal sin of the professional historian. To be frank and straightforward, the great works of John Pocock and Quentin Skinner,[2] the importance of which nonetheless remain beyond dispute, have ended up directing studies in ways that are not always positive, in terms of inspiring both acolytes who are less equipped than their masters and historians of other disciplines perennially short on ideas. First of all, to understand the key directions, the original nature, and the peculiarities of eighteenth-century republicanism, still today we need to return to the *Trevelyan Lectures* held by Franco Venturi in Cambridge in 1969, published under the title *Utopia and Reform in the Enlightenment*. Those pages noted the definite overcoming, in the early years of the eighteenth century, of the republican model as a political and institutional reality in the face of the increasing power of the great absolutist monarchies. After a century of wars and revolutions of every kind, in which the confrontation between the two forms of government had always been resolved, sword in hand, in favour of monarchies, the progressive marginalization within the international context of the United Provinces, of Venice, and of Genoa (bombarded and humiliated by the ships of Louis XIV in 1684) seemed to justify those who, like Montesquieu, considered the solution to the struggle between monarchy and republic to be found definitively in the constitutional monarchy founded in England over the course of the seventeenth century. That solution, which relaunched the institutional formula of mixed government, the division of powers, and solemnly proclaimed the protection of English rights through the *Bill of Rights*, had furthermore given a first concrete and convincing answer to the problem of liberty in the face of absolutism in modern commercial societies. This was the true great political question, so dear to the French *philosophes* and, more generally, to political thinkers of the time. From that moment on, the authentic republicanism of the ancients seemed to have been defeated forever, relegated to the dustbin of history precisely because it had revealed itself inadequate for resolving the decisive problem of liberty.

Referring to the two forms of republican government that had appeared in history, Montesquieu passed judgement saying 'Democracy and aristocracy are not free states by their nature. Political liberty is found only in moderate governments'[3] – the only governments which, practicing the division of power and recognizing the principle of legality, concretely guaranteed personal liberty. In 'most kingdoms in Europe,' monarchies had won the battle against the republics by faithfully following this precise constitutional path. 'The ancients,' Montesquieu specified, delineating an interpretative paradigm that would be developed and lionized by Constant, 'who did not know of the distribution of the three powers in the government of one alone, could not achieve a correct idea of monarchy';[4] just like in more recent times the 'Italian republics, where the three powers are united [in the hands of a few families], there is less liberty.'[5] In France too, after the despotic excesses of Louis XIV, the auspicious renewal of a 'moderate monarchy' based on the natural secular constitution of the 'gothic government' of the German peoples, which invested intermediary bodies, the hereditary nobility, and the feudal lords with the historical task of guaranteeing liberty, thereby limiting the power of the sovereign, rendered recourse to republican institutional forms entirely anachronistic. Politically, in other words, republicanism was no longer useful. In effect, it became an outmoded political project and a loser in the face of the hard lessons of history. Its death certificate was famously drafted in 1748 in the *Esprit des lois*, when Montesquieu declared the decline of virtue, substituted by honour as the principle of government, in modern moderate monarchies called upon to govern societies which by then were conditioned above all by commerce, production, and consumption rather than by war. In these monarchies, he specified,

> politics accomplishes great things with as little virtue as it can… The state continues
> to exist independently of love of the homeland, desire for true glory, self-renunciation,
> sacrifice of one's dearest interests, and all those heroic virtues we can find in the ancients

and know only by hearsay. The laws replace all these virtues, for which there is no need; the state excuses you from them… virtue is not the spring of this government! Certainly, it is not excluded, but it is not the spring.[6]

Though still influential, the politics of republican virtue and the primacy of public spirit were of secondary importance in an era when *l'esprit de commerce* ruled undisputed. Nevertheless, the *Esprit des lois*, like all richly suggestive and rhetorically complex masterpieces, is prone to be understood equivocally and read in different keys. While the book certified the death of ancient republicanism, emphasizing its anachronism as an alternative to monarchy, at the same time it also distinguished republicanism's driving force – the passion for virtue – from republicanism as a form of government, and traced, in its extraordinarily succinct outline, a fascinating ideal type dense with fresh details and never-before-formulated critical reflections on the issues of education, economics, and justice.[7] Identifying the innermost nature, the authentic *esprit* of republicanism in self-government, in the primacy of political virtues as the moral mentality, habit, and commitment of individuals in favour of the collective, Montesquieu more or less consciously gave his contemporaries something very similar to a perfect republican's manual. In collocating what would become the arsenal of eighteenth-century republican thought in the *Esprit des lois*, Montesquieu, however, also chose the fields that would influence successive Enlightenment debates most profoundly. The eulogy of, and admiration for, the Greek *polis* and Ciceronian Rome were, in fact, accompanied by severe criticisms of the archaic aristocratic republics which still survived in early modern Europe. Without ever hinting at the glorious communal experience of self-government and civic humanism of Italy's medieval and Renaissance city-states, derogatory words were reserved to the still existing oligarchies of Venice and Genoa, for their conservatism, for their obvious lack of liberty, and for the corruption that plagued those aging and sclerotic patriciates lacking in vision, prisoners of their own glorious pasts and incapable of renewing themselves or adapting to the new exigencies of the times. The verdicts passed on the so-called federated republics of Holland, of Switzerland, and of the German Empire were certainly less negative. All this did not bridge the distance between the vital and prosperous world of the ancient republics and that of the modern aristocratic republics, condemned, by their intrinsic nature, to immobility in order to survive.

The framework developed by Montesquieu, besides faithfully reflecting the historical reality of the moment, in some way took account of the birth, in England, of the umpteenth metamorphosis of classical republicanism – a metamorphosis yet again founded principally on the myth of Cicero, on the rediscovery of texts by Latin authors such as Livy and Sallust, on examples and influences largely drawn from ancient Rome, used above all, and at the same time, both as a general libertarian and anti-absolutist critique and as a frank denunciation of the progressive disappearance of civic virtues in modern commercial societies, where the primacy of individual interests began to reign supreme over those of the collective. This umpteenth variation of the republican tradition, born, in a sense, with the English revolution in the mid-seventeenth century, took shape first in the form a 'neo-Roman theory of free states' that took particular care to define 'civil liberty' in the face of the monarchy. Then,[8] as a result of the rapid consolidation of the Hanoverian monarchic-constitutional regime, it expanded to effectively criticize the degeneration of morals and the corruption that accompanied English society's transformation into a modern market economy. Direct heirs of Machiavelli, Sidney, and that James Harrington who would have loved to see London as the 'new Rome in the West,'[9] the English *Freethinkers* of the Augustan age developed, in the first decades of the century, a republican culture capable of denouncing every form of despotism, of tyranny, and of concession to absolutism, while championing political along with philosophical liberty, insisting on religious tolerance and on reason's struggle against superstition with a tone and accent already of an enlightened mould. On the composite front of these new *commonwealthmen*, which went from Toland to Shaftesbury, to John Trenchard, to Matthew Tindal and Anthony Collins, some preferred to dedicate their efforts – and with a certain success – to accrediting the suggestive image of England's constitutional monarchy in Europe, which beyond its form of government substantially respected republican principles, having re-launched that mixed form of government which had been so dear to Polybius, Cicero, Machiavelli, and Sidney. Others instead insisted on propagandizing ancient republicanism as a moral philosophy, denouncing corruption, appealing to the practice of civic virtues, of *libertas philosophandi*, of a patriotic government open to wider popular participation. Anthony Collins' celebrated 1714 *A Discourse of Free-Thinking* really represented an efficient overview, and principal manifesto, of the ideas which circulated in this composite and contradictory world, which nonetheless was united by its hatred of royal despotism.

By mid-century – also thanks to Montesquieu who knew that fertile debate against Walpole's ostensible government of corruption well through the works of Swift, his friend Bolingbroke's *The Craftsman*, and, above all, from having sojourned in England in 1729–30 – the need to distinguish between the form of a government and the principles which 'drove' it and characterized it became a common trope in the European debate on republicanism. Certainly, the insistence with which Montesquieu explained the organic and indispensible connection between customs, economy, and political institutions in the ancient republics seemed tailor-made not to leave much space to those who still dreamt of demolishing the monarchies. According to the framework of the *Esprit des lois*, there was no longer any room in the changed economic and social conditions of the time for a return to political communities similar to Sparta, Athens, or Rome. The classical republicanism of direct popular democracy was, in most people's minds, effectively gone forever. In reality, that death knoll, and in particular the overall representation of republicanism that separately analyzed the forms and principles of government, was variously commented upon and used to reflect on what was still left of the republican tradition in the mid-eighteenth century. For example, the theory that excluded the principle of virtue as a spring of monarchy, reserving it only for republics, controversially was rejected in many milieus. In France, it clashed head on with a long-standing artistic and philosophical tradition which attributed the virtues of the ancients first to the *ethos* of the aristocracy and then to the monarch. Had not, perhaps, Corneille and Racine moved in this direction in their tragedies against tyranny? Rollin and Bossuet had written book upon book to render 'ancient public ethics compatible with the monarchical framework and with the Christian horizon [of reference].'[10] The hypothesis that only pagans were capable of living virtuously and that there was no longer any room for virtue in the modern world repulsed too many. Montesquieu's political realism showed itself to be much too excessive. Almost to emphasize the need to diffuse the patriotic and republican spirit of the ancients in modern monarchies, and thus morally transform them from the inside out, Bolingbroke's famous *Idea of a Patriot King* appeared in England in 1749. Across eighteenth-century Europe, and in particular in Italy, the expression 'republican spirit,' understood as an anti-despotic and libertarian mentality and way of life, spread quickly in spite of the power and prestige of absolutism and the diffusion of a model of court society based on luxury and a culture of appearances. The truth is that far from consigning the formidable myth of ancient republicanism to a glorious past, as probably had been the author's intention, the considerations which were developed in the *Esprit des lois* had ended up further fuelling the lively political debate on the issue, definitively paving the way for the birth of modern republicanism.

Modern republicanism first appeared as a new moral philosophy, a libertarian spirit in opposition to the restricted bourgeois and noble elites, only to become, over the course of the eighteenth century, a critical and innovative reflection upon the political and legal aspects of possible republican forms of government. Respectful of popular sovereignty and the rights of man, the baptism of this kind of republicanism found its decisive moment in the culture of Enlightenment, in its capacity to merge different traditions and experiences through an original way of critically and liberally deploying reason in all fields. Franco Venturi described this complex transformation of the meaning of a tradition in the face of its changing historical context succinctly, investigating the 'republican ferment' which in France animated the *philosophes* and parliamentarians in their struggle against absolutism, and identifying its confluence and successive metamorphosis in contact with 'the new worldview which was taking shape in Paris,' above all on the level of morality.[11] This search for an original moral science grounded in solid rational bases, able to give new meaning to law and politics, was, as we have sought to explain in previous chapters, one of the crucial issues addressed in seventeenth and eighteenth-century European intellectual life. After the strong criticism of reason of state and of the *arcana juris*, the language of the rights of man developed by the so-called natural law of the moderns could no longer escape the confrontation with what still remained alive of the republican tradition. If the order and class constitutionalism of moderate Old Regime monarchies and the respect for the principle of legality invoked by Montesquieu pointed, on the one hand, towards a solution to the question of civil liberty, on the other it certainly did not confront the great issue, again put on the order of the day by natural law, of just and legitimate government, of the institutional methods necessary to guarantee the rights of man and above all their equality. At the end of the seventeenth century, John Locke – to take the example of England, which had relaunched republican debate and practice in the years of the revolution – had explained that the legitimacy of political power was not to be found in brute force or the right of conquest, but in the consensus of free and rational men to a founding contract for an independent community, 'which the *Latines* signified by the word Civitas, to which the word which best answers in our Language, is *Commonwealth*.'[12] The principal goal of this community was the respect and protection of the natural rights of individuals. Today we know that ever since 1723, the glorious tradition of Livy's and Cicero's classical republicanism, as revisited by Machiavelli and by Sidney, fruitfully mixed precisely with Locke's natural law in John Trenchard and Thomas Gordon's *Cato's Letters*, inaugurating a season of republicanism grounded on very different theoretical foundations from those of the past. Trenchard and Gordon did in fact not hesitate to let Cato speak the new language of the rights of man and of contractarianism alongside the ancient one of civic virtue (a theme that was entirely absent from Locke's reflections[13]), opening a political discourse which would fuel not only the English political struggle but also that of the American revolutionaries, and principally their autonomous search for a republicanism suitable for the modern age.[14]

On the European continent it was above all Rousseau who reflected on the legitimacy of political power, and thus of just government, in light of a renewed republican spirit; a spirit in which the exigencies, based on Enlightenment natural law, of the rights of man advanced by *philosophes* like Diderot and Voltaire became ever more important. Venturing beyond Locke, who nonetheless bravely had launched the definitive reckoning with absolutist readings of natural law, and wilfully ignoring the second contract of dominion which, ideally stipulated after the first contract of union, traditionally entrusted the care of individual rights to the sovereign, Rousseau polemicized with Grotius and Pufendorf, who had been its greatest interpreters, supplying an alternative, clear and conclusive republican analysis. Through the social contract between free and equal men, destined to redraw the conception of sovereignty in light of the general will, Rousseau constructed a winning republican theory for large parts of the eighteenth century, resolutely positing the no less important and decisive principle of legitimacy next to that of legality. Legitimacy finally supplied the foundations for a morality of political action which for decades had anguished the heterogeneous theorists of natural law in their polemic against the doctrine of reason of state.[15] According to Rousseau, the government of laws no longer sufficed to make a republic. It was first of all necessary to ensure the participation of the people in the formulation of laws. Republic thus meant general will, self-rule, direct popular participation. Then alone, in short, 'does the public interest govern and then alone is the "public thing" – the *res publica* – a reality.' And yet, if it was beyond doubt that 'all legitimate government is republican,' not all republican governments which had appeared historically, were to be considered legitimate, and particularly not those which had been systematically distant from the theoretical horizon of the new conception of popular sovereignty. For Rousseau too the key problem was not what form the government took. The institutions of public administration could change without corroding respect for the legitimacy of political power. Once the doctrine of the simple mandate given to the ruler, and thus to the monarch, by the sovereign people was admitted, the creation of appropriate institutions responded solely to historical exigencies, to the contingent necessities of individual nations.[16] If anything, that rigid and organic theory of sovereignty in the *Contrat Social*, opposed to both the division and the balance of powers, which unmasked the mechanism of representation as a usurpation and invoked an impossible return to the direct democracy of the ancients in its place, was destined not only to attract cruel criticism, but to reveal itself inadequate in practice to assist the birth, or the transformation, of the republican governments still extant in eighteenth-century Europe.

Where Rousseau was daydreaming, preaching the creation of utopian political communities in which people and sovereign were one and the same (all citizens knew and loved one other, thus loving their common fatherland and respecting the liberty and equality of all), the melancholy history of the repeated failures of institutional reform in the small and bellicose aristocratic republics of the second half of the eighteenth century set out to disprove him factually. What would prove exemplary of this was Rousseau's personal participation, in the early 1770s, in one of the most controversial phases of the Genevan republic's long 'civil war,' as Voltaire called it, between patricians and bourgeois to widen participation in power with respect to the strict dominant oligarchies of the earlier communes.[17] Between compromises which gave much reason for hope from the point of view of the democratization of the system in 1768 and the violent reactions which followed, the reform failed entirely in 1782 when neighbouring monarchies began to interfere. The attempts at reform in Genoa, Venice, and Amsterdam fared analogously. Under the weight of their long histories, ancient aristocratic republics were everywhere unable to renew themselves and attain Rousseau's new republican ideal, sensitive to the democratic instances of popular sovereignty. Montesquieu's ironic and irreverent arguments against the old republican patriciate seemed, on the occasion, to be nothing less than sacrosanct.

On the moral and philosophical level, and above all on the political and institutional level, it was certainly not from the streets of Geneva or the canals of Venice or Amsterdam that the principal challenge posed by the modern republicanism of rights and popular sovereignty emerged against an Old Regime which historically had expressed itself through absolutist models and through the principle of heredity, and which had been confirmed by mixed governments and by the more or less moderate great monarchies. Without the American Revolution and the 1776 *Declaration of Independence*, the ideal call to the ancients' practice of virtue and to that republican spirit which was ever more present in the debates animating the European Enlightenment would probably have taken even longer in finding the master-path of constitutional rethinking and of the concrete reform of political institutions necessary to give life to modern republicanism.

If, indeed, it is true that the revolution of the American colonists owed much to the Enlightenment,[18] its epochal influence on the history of republicanism and on the political culture of the late Enlightenment is equally certain. The fascinating spectacle of constituent power enacted in the colonial assemblies across the Atlantic changed everything. The suggestive republicanism reproposed by Rousseau and Mably, inspired by the direct democracies of the ancients and frankly hostile to the corruption of the moderns and the production of riches which seemed to lack a true alternative, found a hardened and above all real opponent, in political and institutional terms, in the definitive affirmation of representative mechanisms of popular sovereignty as developed by the Americans. From the theoretical debate and the rhetorical and generic appeal to civic virtues, one finally moved to practice. The overcoming of the Old Regime seemed within reach to many Enlightenment thinkers. It is hard for anyone today who studies the books and journals published in those years to escape the sensation that 1776 represented an important date, signalling the advent of a long and tormented phase of concrete political experimentation in the field which was destined to profoundly change the republican tradition. One should never forget that those events aroused deep hopes and emotions, unleashing vital energies which quickly triggered chemical reactions, the components of which for a long time had been ready to react together. It was certainly not a coincidence that, in the decade before the taking of the Bastille, the old criticisms of the mixed model of English government, and of the very idea of a customary constitution itself, were radicalized. As we have seen in the previous chapters, the language of the rights of man was adopted in the 1780s, once the strategy of reform based on the support of enlightened absolutism was put aside, by the Masonic lodges of Europe – ever more infiltrated by Enlightenment thinkers – to give new political and constitutional vigour to the republican myth of civic virtue, of philanthropy, and of a new social morality among free and equal men.

As opposed to the work done in recent years in the English context, the history of the birth of modern republicanism in the rest of eighteenth-century Europe remains to be written. The result of such a project would probably be surprising. Just think that the very term 'republic' for a long time remained indeterminate and polysemic everywhere, even in the United States. As late as in 1816, a perplexed Thomas Jefferson, despite having been one of the principal protagonists of those years, felt compelled to write, 'Indeed, it must be acknowledged that the term *republic* is of very vague application in every language.' The issue risked becoming embarrassing, all the more so in face of those who circulated arbitrary interpretations in which Lycurgus' celebrated 'mantle of republicanism' covered 'every government of laws, whether consistent or not with natural right.' Persuaded of the myth of direct democracy and of the self-rule of peripheries in relation to cores, Jefferson did not hesitate to present his personal interpretation of republicanism as 'government by… citizens in mass, acting directly and personally, according to rules established by the majority…; every other government is more or less republican, in proportion as it has in its composition more or less of this ingredient of the direct action of citizens.'[19] Actually, Paine had already begun quite lucidly in 1790 to define what was to be understood by modern republicanism, synthesizing a decade of fiery debate and highlighting, in particular, its differences to, and distance from, the classical interpretations of Machiavelli, of the *Freethinkers*, and above all of Rousseau. 'I do not understand by republicanism that which bears the name in Holland or some Italian State. I mean simply a government by representation; a government founded on the principles of the Declaration of Rights.'[20] Two years later, in the second part of the *Rights of Man*, he returned to the argument, explaining that modern republicanism made no sense if it continued to reject progress and oppose history with naked political will in accordance with the arguments presented by the proponents of direct democracy and the critics who saw in wealth only a source of corruption. With the division of labour and the evolution of Western civilization, representation had become the way in which popular sovereignty and human rights could and should express themselves: '[A] Representative system takes society and civilization for its basis; nature, reason, and experience for its guide.' Of course Paine admitted that a republic 'is not any particular form of government.' Historically, the institutional examples vindicating that expression had been many, from the communes of Poland, with its bizarre 'elective monarchy,' based on a 'hereditary aristocracy,' to a Holland which conserved 'a hereditary stadtholdership.' In reality, the word republic, *res-publica*, simply signified 'public affairs, or the public good; or, literally translated, the *public thing...* In this sense it is naturally opposed to the word *monarchy*, which has a base original signification. It means arbitrary power in an individual person; in the exercise of which, *himself,* and not *res-publica*, is the object.'[21] In that precise historical moment, demolishing every concession to privileges of birth and entrusting the government of the people to representation, the United States best embodied the authentic spirit of republicanism as the '*public business* of a nation.'

The *Scienza della legislazione* was probably read by contemporaries not only as a valuable constitutional text, but primarily as an openly and systematically republican book precisely in light of Paine's considerations, which reflected ideas and convictions which were very common in the Enlightenment circles of the 1780s. Filangieri had also in fact posed the principle of legality, the respect of human rights, and the constant reference to popular sovereignty as the primary objectives of every legitimate, and thus by nature republican government. He had done so while bitterly criticizing the 'moderate monarchy' of Montesquieu, mixed government, and the generic and customary character of the English constitution – and above all while dedicating pages and pages of passionate historical and legal analysis against the famous right of conquest and the concept of politics and of power as based on relations of force, taking sides in favour of the equality of the rights of man in a courageous polemic against the hereditary principle incarnated by the feudal lords and nobility of the Old Regime. Alongside Condorcet, the very same Paine, and many others partaking in the culture of the late Enlightenment, Filangieri must certainly be counted among the spiritual fathers of the new republicanism. A republicanism still to be invented and experimented with, able to reconcile the virtues of the ancients with the wealth and progress of the moderns, and at the same time safeguarding civil liberties and progressively introducing more and more people to political liberty in firm respect for the rights of man. But, above all, and it is thanks to this element of real originality that the work's success is due, this new republicanism was capable of moving from principles and from the enunciation of rights to their concrete exercise through a government of laws and a specific constitutional politics. Little reflection has been dedicated to the fact that, though an immediate expression of the great European Enlightenment debate against the despotism of monarchies and intermediary bodies of the 1770s and 80s, the republican thought contained in the *Scienza della legislazione* simultaneously, and without reverential fear, took account of the venerable history of the Italian republics. Resolutely, it took its distance from that world which, in the deep conscience of the nation, was deemed archaic and anachronistic but still incredibly vital. And it could not have been otherwise. Unlike France and the other nations of the continent, which had never had a specific tradition in this field, Italy could boast of glorious examples of republican self-rule ever since the Middle Ages. The centuries-long presence of free communes and small republics had profoundly marked the character and mentality of the people inhabiting the peninsula. Nearly all travellers sensitive to the contemporary political debate noted this immediately and reflected on the argument. From *Abbé* Coyer, to Mably and Lalande, to the English and German travellers, none were able to escape the fascination and suggestiveness of that glorious tradition which was immortalized in works of art and breathtaking monuments. Still in 1797, the editors of the '*Moniteur*' frankly recognized that 'of all the parts of Europe, Italy is perhaps the country in which liberty has reigned most constantly. It has had, from the most remote times, more republics than kingdoms.'[22] Nonetheless, it should be pointed out that the men of the Enlightenment hardly loved this world, and did not see in it an example or model to propose future generations.[23] Defended by the sword against German emperors and the ambitions of the Papacy, the ancient liberty of the communes had all too quickly deteriorated into political and social anarchy, into violent factionalism between Guelphs and Ghibbelines, between *popolo* and *signori*. In the fifteenth and sixteenth centuries they had definitively degenerated into restricted oligarchies, which were anything but sensitive to civic virtues, to the equality of rights, and to the need of widening the circle of those able to enjoy modern civil and political liberty. Furthermore, Sismondi wrote, in his brilliant and monumental *Histoire des républiques italiennes*, though recognizing that the birth of '*liberté italienne*' can be credited with being the first and decisive chapter in the history of liberty in the modern West (the Italian republics lived off the wealth produced by the work of their citizens and not of slaves), he certainly did not herald it as an auspicious model for the future of European liberalism. Following the collapse of the Roman Empire, Sismondi argued, the peninsula experienced an extraordinary period of liberty determined by two admirably intertwined elements: the conquering people of the north who knew '*liberté sans patrie*' and the Italic peoples which, instead, had arrived at a '*patrie sans liberté*.'[24] In that happy era for the rebirth of liberty, after the then distant experiences of the Roman Republic, wealth and public spirit seemed finally to have found the right equilibrium to coexist. The rapid changing of the historical context however, and the failure to create a great federation to defend the small Italian states against the outside world and to cement necessary social equilibriums internally inevitably had brought individual self-interest, the logic of class and social order, and factional strife to the forefront in institutions of self-government, making particular interests prevail over collective needs. With the Renaissance, and then with the slow agony of the eighteenth century, the republican tradition had entirely consumed its prospects for liberty. Little remained of the old civic spirit, and liberty, reserved for the few, had degenerated ever further into licentiousness and abuse.

During the so-called 'revolutionary and republican triennium,' Sismondi saw with his own eyes how negatively that inheritance weighed upon Italian history. It was an example – extravagantly feared and repudiated by Enlightenment thinkers – of anarchy and of individualistic factional strife without any concern for the general interests of society, destined to result in the despotism of *signori* or restricted oligarchies. The arrival of the French in fact made the old habits of fragmentation, of partisan contraposition between municipalities, and of violent and ferocious hatred between neighbouring cities bloom everywhere. Many revolts rose against sovereigns and the more detestable aspects of Old Regime society, which quickly transformed themselves into bloody reckonings with a past that simply refused to go away. In a reconstruction of those events, interpreting them also as evident signs of a disconcerting 'municipal revolution,' Franco Venturi rightly insisted on the importance, and at the same time on the limits, of the political debate over the future of Italy which developed in those crucial years, maintaining that one 'spoke of federalism where it was localism [*campanilismo*],' and of the reappearance, on the scene, of ancient notables forced on the defensive by the universalizing and centralizing reformism of the Enlightenment. The attempt to establish a great united and federal 'modern republic' on the peninsula, as had been done in France, 'thus found itself faced with the survival of archaic republics.'[25]

Pagano, Filangieri and the Enlightenment thinkers in general, who in the 1780s had reflected on the nature and necessity of giving life, also in Italy, to modern forms of republicanism, had always feared all that. They were fully aware of the necessity of definitively breaking with that past marred by particularisms, and going beyond the medieval tradition of communal liberty which wearily had survived in the governments of Genoa and Venice, where it was dominated by a conception of politics as the mere expression of power relations. Against that conception, and against the reason of state of absolutist theorists, critical reflection had already been launched in Southern Italy in the late seventeenth century which would serve as the foundation of that Neapolitan school of natural law discussed at length previously, precisely because it is there that one must search for what we can call the intellectual origins of the republicanism of the moderns developed by Neapolitan Enlightenment thinkers. At the basis of the theoretical reflections of that 'great school of political philosophy,' as Ginguené defined it, lay indubitably the republican model of Cicero's Rome, and in particular the paradigmatic function of Roman Law to rethink modern political institutions in light of a simultaneously historical and rational conception of natural law and the modern theory of the rights of man.[26] In that sense, the republicanism of large sections of the late Italian Enlightenment preferred to ignore possible references to the previous experiences of the free Italian communes and, though respecting the genius of Machiavelli and his extraordinary function in renewing Italian and European political culture, clearly felt they had other fathers and above all other tasks in facing the thorny problems which animated international debate and Italian events in those years. The language of virtue and corruption, to give just one example, taken directly from the sources of Greek and Roman history and certainly not through the mediation of the *Discorsi* or the most celebrated texts of the tradition of Renaissance civic humanism, was by then no longer perceived merely as a political, philosophical, and moral question, but rather as a legal and institutional one to be examined in light of the theory of the rights of man. Similarly, the very same wealth of the moderns which was so feared by the proponents of classical republicanism was, far from being considered the inevitable source of the corruption of manners, instead experienced by many Enlightenment republicans as an opportunity for development and equality.

What mattered at the end of the eighteenth century was not simply lamenting the loss of the ancient republics, but really constructing a modern one. The Renaissance, with its princely courts, its 'lords of the castle,' the ferocious civic disputes between restricted groups of power within the patriciates, and between nobles and the people, was by then a distant and detested memory. After the affirmation of absolute monarchies, the political struggle in the Old Regime assumed very different forms. Compared to Machiavelli, who had presented the primary objectives of his republicanism as 'public liberty' and 'free life' without being dominated by anyone, assigning a decisive function above all to crude relations of force and to the free expression of social conflicts as they took place in the institutional mechanisms of mixed government, Enlightenment republicanism developed its libertarian logic entirely within the natural law paradigm of the universal rights of man. A paradigm which, focusing simultaneously and equally upon achieving respect for the principle of equality for all citizens and the concrete exercise of popular sovereignty through a government of laws and constitutional practice, in effect imposed severe limits on the 'political way of life [*vivere politico*]'[27] theorized by the Florentine secretary, on that Aristotelian conception of man as *zóon politikón*, an individual who, in his existential autonomy, enjoyed the full faculties of choice on the level of morals and politics. This is a decisive aspect which should never be forgotten or undervalued when analyzing the differences between the classical republicanism of the humanists and that developed by Enlightenment thinkers such as Condorcet, Filangieri, and Paine, who gave central importance to constitutional thought in its function of limiting political actions and guaranteeing respect for rights. The *Scienza della legislazione*, in particular book four of 1785, represents a precious document for understanding how far the underlying vision, questions and possible solutions had changed over the course of the centuries. Dedicating the entire volume *Delle leggi che riguardano l'educazione, i costume e l'istruzione pubblica* – perhaps the most important and original of his opus and certainly the most explicit in elucidating the republican faith – to the delicate question of education, Filangieri confronted matters that had their roots in the ancient world and in the Renaissance tradition of *studia humanitatis*, in which education was given the task of forging man and citizen, preparing him for the *vita civile*.[28] He did so in full awareness of living in a world very different from that of past republicans. The problem of education was no longer restricted to the elites, but involved ever larger sections of society. The birth of public opinion, the necessity of providing for the emancipation of large parts of what Antonio Genovesi defined the 'middle class' in view of ever wider political participation in the exercise of sovereignty, but principally the complex relationship between upholding rights, acknowledging individual passions and interests, and the need to promote new social bonds, pushed him to dedicate an entire volume to these matters. In the eyes of many exponents of the late Neapolitan Enlightenment, this was indeed the keystone for the possible success of future republics. Montesquieu too – through referring to the republicanism of the ancients – was convinced of this and wrote it clearly, affirming that 'it is in republican government that the full power of education is needed.'[29] Nonetheless, Filangieri did not hide the inherent difficulties, nor did he seek to circumvent the obstacles. Education, he asked, 'must it be public? Can it be so in large nations? Could all the classes of society be part of it? What should its aim be? What should its means be?' [III, 8].

In the same years which witnessed the definitive stranding of democratic reforms in the ancient republics of Genoa and Venice, and which saw the spread of Francescantonio Grimaldi's moderate theses in favour of a renewed 'republican nobility,' capable of wedding civic virtue and privileges of birth,[30] Filangieri replied to these questions by further radicalizing his resolute rejection of Old Regime society. This, however, entailed the burden of critically rethinking and giving foundations to the matter of education in light of the more advanced political reflections which had emerged in the context of European debates over natural law. From the seventeenth century onwards, it was clear for all to see that a thorny problem existed of how to peacefully reconcile the dissolving and anarchic effects of individual rights and duties on the one hand with the need to guarantee effective community membership on the other. After the absolutist interpretations of natural law offered by Hobbes and Pufendorf, which had directly imbued the absolute sovereign with the practices of social disciplining and the task of creating a body politic, while at the same time assuring the stability and organic comprehensiveness of society with the guardianship of rights, the eighteenth century had seen the appearance of other possible readings. In Naples, Genovesi had insisted on the spontaneous and natural character of social harmony. A faithful follower of Locke, it had seemed to him enough to recognize the bond between rights and natural law to achieve the objective of legitimizing a future political and social order based on the principles of justice and fairness. The idea of social harmony as a natural and spontaneous ethical fact, diffused by the early eighteenth-century works of Shaftesbury and relaunched in the Enlightenment by Diderot, had aired a new, renewed republican conception of virtue as love of the fatherland, of the cosmopolitan community of free and equal men, insisting on the naturally social vocation of a subject entitled with rights.

The following years saw a plethora of works on the natural character of philanthropy, on the concepts of humanity, of friendship, of fraternal and republican solidarity between all human beings. But in the 1770s and 80s, that acknowledgment of the innate social nature of man no longer seemed to suffice. With ever greater success, the theories of those who posited passions and interests at the base of political action circulated and spread.[31] Filangieri could not ignore this in his *Scienza della legislazione*, asking himself about the means and objectives of modern public education. Faced with the task of finally overcoming the ancient hierarchies of birth and the strong corporatist bonds which had guaranteed the secular cohesion of Old Regime society, he asked himself how a new political order could be constructed based on natural law, made up of free individuals of equal rights and duties. Helvétius' 1772 *De l'homme* in particular, which seemed written on purpose to resolve many of his doubts, had pushed Filangieri down this path. The traditional ideas of the utilitarian philosophers, among whom the most prominent were the thinkers of the Scottish Enlightenment, who approached social interaction from the standpoint of the dominion of the passions, were enriched with precise indications regarding the perfectibility of man and thus the strategic function of public education and in particular of legislation in creating the conditions for a more just and fair society. Finally, in that part of the œuvre which later would be accused of materialism, the anthropology of self-interest was happily wedded to the myth, reproposed by Enlightenment natural law, of the government of laws. According to Helvétius, it was the task of the legislator to channel personal interests into the virtuous logic of the collective interest. This was the model upon which the Roman Republic was erected, relying on appropriate legislation in the field of customs and education to modify behaviour and transform selfish love into passion for a common fatherland.[32]

Filangieri shared the principle, set forth in *De l'homme*, that a political community was not spontaneously united by the public acknowledgment of the rights and duties of individuals, but by passions and interests purposefully directed by the laws. Man must 'be conducted by virtue along the same path of the passions' [III, 5]. Apart from this, he distanced himself yet again from the republicanism of the ancients which had become so influential in France after Rousseau and Mably, refusing to follow the road indicated by Helvétius in favour of the classical and traditional model of small, poor, and warlike republics over rich and commercial ones.[33] In the first half of the 1780s, while the American Revolution was creating a great modern republic which would be able to overcome old prejudices, Filangieri was very clear, as he wrote without hesitation, on the 'difference that must exist between the public system of education of the ancients and the public education of the moderns.' It was one thing to deal with a 'people solely occupied with arms' and work in the fields, with a 'republic of a few thousand citizens'; a modern 'monarchy of more than a million subjects,' a 'nation at the same time warlike and agricultural, devoted to manufacturing and to commerce' [III, 15] was something entirely different. While their goals and objectives largely remained the same as in ancient Rome, the new, vastly different historical context radically changed the means and modalities of educational programmes. To unite the public spirit of the ancients effectively with the wealth of the moderns, education 'in large peoples and in modern nations' had to involve everyone. 'If a sole class of citizens were excluded from my plan,' Filangieri specified, 'it would be imperfect and vicious.' One would be unable to stem the tide of corruption, and fail to bring about that 'public emancipation' through popular education which he held necessary to assure wider, critical participation in the public sphere and the delineation of a republican public opinion. But, above all, one would lose the strong social bond which Filangieri identified precisely in education, considering the apparent solitude – atomization we would say today – of individual holders of rights and duties which Enlightenment thinkers theorized would result from the overcoming of traditional Old Regime ties. 'To instruct a man I prefer domestic education, to instruct a people I prefer the public variety.' After having called loudly for the banishment of hereditary hierarchies and the corporatist model, his principal worry was strengthening 'the social union.' It was necessary to forge quickly the 'national character' of a republican political community of free citizens enjoying equal rights, teaching them to be 'like members of the same body, sons of the same mother, and individuals of the same family' [III, 13]. The good of the republic, respect for the laws and the constitution, were to be inculcated in the young by showing them how personal interests ultimately coincided with those of the collective. 'As the bonds which unite citizens multiply, the social body acquires greater vigour and its liberty is less exposed.' But above all, the development of a strong sense of belonging would limit the terrible consequences of political and social conflict: 'The inequality of conditions and of fortunes will lose a large part of its sad effects; and the powerful voice of nature, which imposes on men and reminds them of their equality, will find the ears of the citizenry disposed and prepared to hear it' [III, 14].

To achieve all this, however, it was necessary to rethink the organization of society and its archaic hierarchies from the bottom up. It was necessary to venture courageously beyond the Old Regime and its unjust distinctions, to hypothesize a new republican and contractual order capable of being considered legitimate, just, and fair by all. A legal order and a society in which differences and inequalities, although recognized as impossible to eradicate, were in any case tolerable, cushioned, reduced, and no longer based on birthright or on simple wealth, but rather on the public acknowledgment of natural talent and individual virtue. It was a priority of the collective to utilize these qualities according to the scheme that would be recognized by the 1789 *Declaration of the Rights of Man*, which affirmed that social distinctions in the new regime could be based only on common utility. The educational reform illustrated in the *Scienza della legislazione* presupposed precise political choices in line with the republican spirit and ideals of the late Enlightenment: 'It requires,' Filangieri underlined, 'that all individuals in society can participate in it, but all according to their circumstances and their destinations.' In that sense education had to be simultaneously 'universal, but not uniform, public, but not communal' [III, 16]. In contrast with considerations based on social order, and on the usual conditionings of a society based on honour and dignity, the Neapolitan philosopher thought of a precise, future 'repartition of the people' into two classes of reference with regards to the nature of their studies and their curricula. A first class for the youth assigned to follow courses which we today would define as vocational: 'All those who serve or could serve society with their arms,' destined to work in agriculture, manufacturing, commerce, and the crafts. A second class would instead prepare those who would dedicate themselves to the practice of the so-called 'liberal arts': doctors, lawyers, magistrates, political men, and the clergy. In pages and pages dense and punctilious in identifying specific modalities and syllabi for every category and group of students, and considering, at times polemically, the pedagogical works of Locke, Rousseau and other great intellectuals of the seventeenth and eighteenth centuries, Filangieri traced the first great and persuasive republican framework for education. The recurring thread uniting all the different educational syllabi was in fact their common teaching of 'the luminous principles of universal morality.' The teachers, elevated to 'an order of magistrates among the most respectable in the State,' were to remind students of the extraordinary function which the political community had attributed to public education. 'You owe the fatherland all these benefits. Which of you will be ungrateful?… Be happy: search for happiness; but do not fool yourself in the choice of the means which must procure it for you' [III, 89]. Filangieri, for example, entrusted the strategic task of initiating the young 'to moral discourses' to so-called 'youth novels.' In that literary genre *à la mode*, which suddenly had become a decisive vehicle of Enlightenment propaganda,[34] 'the writer's art should be that of highlighting the civil as well as the military virtues' [III, 61], providing heroes to imitate in all fields, from the farmer to the magistrate.

Beyond the specific indications provided in terms of syllabi and teaching methods to which we cannot give the attention they deserve,[35] it is worth stressing that the true key of reform, its systematically republican character of a democratic persuasion, is evident from Filangieri's refusal to copy the existing, to confirm the ancient hierarchies of birth and honour. Filangieri clearly and repeatedly specified his thought on the matter: 'The two classes, into which I have divided all the individuals in society, do not concern their political status, but their destination; not the conditions of their birth, but that to which circumstance, which we soon will expose, will bring them' [III, 18]. The kind of open and dynamic society he was imagining, where social distinctions were the fruit of merit, of talent, and of personal virtues, is evident from the means we have discussed with regards to the mechanisms by which youngsters were selected. Fathers decided in which of the two classes to enroll infants. In the case of the second class, which led to prestigious careers and more remunerative professions, costs fell on the families, while the state took care of the first. The issue was different for young people with talent who, for economic and social motives, were forced to partake in the first class. These cases triggered republican solidarity and the principle of equal opportunities. To respect 'the destination which nature has assigned them' and safeguard the 'liberty of talent' [III, 32], Filangieri thought of something similar to modern state or administrative scholarships. To that end, a 'Supreme Magistrate of Education of the Province' would have had the task of examining the candidate in question and, possibly, moving the talented young person up to the second class. Thus, one would give the son of a farmer the possibility of assuming a post meant for those of high society without regard for his starting conditions.

By the mid-1780s, as a faithful republican and increasingly more attentive and participatory reader of the radical English thinkers, Filangieri no longer hesitated to accompany his subversive proposals in the realm of education with veritable accusations against the bulwark of Old Regime absolutism itself: the standing army. 'Abolish the perpetual troops and educate the people' [III, 93], he exclaimed with a tone worthy of an authentic Plebeian Tribune, calling for a 'healthy change in the destination of the most considerable part of public revenues' [III, 95]. Filangieri argued fierily against Rousseau and his followers, who had downplayed the importance of the arts and sciences as arms in the defence of liberty, civilization, and the well-being of a people. The 'apologists of ignorance' should in fact never 'ignore the multiple and undeniable relations which exist between public education and public opulence, between the state of knowledge and of enlightenment [*dei lumi*] of a people and that of its industry and its wealth' [III, 276]. While education had no relevance for savage or barbarian nations, it was the bastion of liberty against despotism and tyranny in civil society, where 'relations multiply almost to infinity.' It was the very foundation of civic virtue: 'virtue requires public education, because it is necessary to dictate good laws and necessary to ensure they are appreciated and respected' [III, 273].

An absolutely key place in the general republican reform of the system of public education was reserved for customs.[36] History and experience, Filangieri argued, had largely demonstrated 'the impotence of the laws without customs' [III, 5], but also the sometimes suffocating and reactionary effect which secular traditions and institutions, created purposefully to save ancient beliefs, had in impeding the emergence of new legal systems to match the times. Through a reading of Vico and particularly of Hume, he had realized the importance of the delicate equilibrium between these two fundamental aspects of the social and political life of a nation. Wise laws and a good constitution were not enough to guarantee social stability and economic wellbeing. It was necessary to recognize the essential function of customs and think of targeted legislative measures able to reform obsolete aspects gradually, adapting them to the conciliation of individual rights and the need for strong social bonds. It was precisely through the direct legislative intervention on customs that modern republicanism finally would try to resolve the age-old problem of combining '[individual] liberty with [social] dependence,' the love of self and of power with man's social nature, giving life to a 'society where individual interests and passions are combined with the interest of society itself, so that one cannot search for his own happiness without contributing to that of others' [III, 220].

Polemicizing with Montesquieu from the very first volume of the *Scienza della Legislazione*, Filangieri denied the existence of three different driving principles of human action based on the different forms of government: virtue in republics, honour in monarchies, and fear in despotic regimes. He argued that there was always only one driving force: 'the love of power.' This was the immediate expression of that which was the only true and undisputable original, 'universal and constant' passion of man: self-interest. It was the task of law to 'steer this passion to render it useful': 'The same *love of power* which in a free and well ordered republic renders the citizen virtuous and loving of the fatherland, makes him a monster in a despotic government' [I, 128]. In a republican and democratic system, truly assuring, on the level of substance, the equal right to elect and be elected was enough to force all candidates to behave virtuously and on behalf of the public interest if they hoped to 'acquire the people's opinion' [I, 132]. Filangieri was nonetheless conscious of how passions were a dangerous and incandescent issue: 'Let us not abuse the name of *passions*,' he repeatedly warned his readers. Alongside the original and natural passions of man such as self-interest and a vocation to live in society, there were the so-called 'conducive passions,' capable of uniting will with duty and of harnessing great emotional energies towards specific, and not always noble goals. This type of passion was a classic artificial and historical product, a sort of ideological creation as scholars would say today, fruit of the precise cultural and legislative choices of peoples and social groups. Some of these conducive passions had the terrible effect of 'arming a people against another people, generating war and slaughter, sanctifying tyrannies, and mobilizing ferocious masses like the followers of Odin and of Mahomet.' Others pushed more positively towards heroism and martyrdom, towards the exercise of liberty and of republican virtues. In the context of the republican reform of manners, Filangieri focused on what he thought were the two fundamental conducive passions of antiquity, which suddenly had regained currency in late eighteenth-century Europe: love of the fatherland and love of glory; 'The first, mother of all social virtues, renders the second a very fertile source of the prodigies of these same virtues' [III, 237]. On the occasion of this reflection on the nature of modern patriotism developed in the late Neapolitan Enlightenment, Filangieri finally unveiled his definitive choice in favour of a republican and constitutional political community in which, beyond the forms of government, the principles of legality, of legitimacy, and the rights of man were safeguarded by a precise legal system, built directly on the indications of the *Scienza della legislazione*. With exemplary clarity, he delineated a political community which in effect incorporated all the most relevant results of pre-Revolutionary Enlightenment republicanism:

> Let us suppose a body politic instituted in accordance with the legislative system which forms the object of this work. Let us suppose that the political and economic part of the laws have spread property and multiplied the number of proprietors, have destroyed and prevented the causes which produce excessive opulence in one part, and excessive misery in the other… Let us suppose that, abolishing a mercenary troop which impoverishes and scares the people, it has substituted it with a civil troop which reassures the citizen and the fatherland, which guarantees the use rather than the abuse of authority… Let us suppose that a wise criminal legislation has founded the people's civil liberty on the

two pillars of public tranquillity, which are the greatest security of the innocent and the greatest fear in the criminal… Let us suppose that a plan for public education similar to that which we have proposed has been adopted, that all the sons of the fatherland have been, since their infancy, educated by the common mother, that their education, directed by the magistrate and by the laws, has already destroyed and prevented errors, diminished ignorance, prepared the rectification of public opinion, multiplied and fortified the bonds of civil union, brought different conditions closer and prevented a large part of the sad effects of their inevitable inequality… Let us suppose that the laws concerning religion, at the same time as they protect this divine force which can produce so much good in society, have corrected the abuse which has been made of it and which has produced so many evils… Let us suppose that the temple's enclosure, raised within the city-walls, showed the priesthood the principles which depend on this position; that, in a few words, the altar, the temple, the royal castle, and the forum were equally involved in inspiring the same virtues in the citizens, the same love for the fatherland, and the same respect for its laws… Let us suppose that knowledge of the laws, combined with the form of the government, in some way has regulated the repartition of power and the emanation of authority, so that no individual in the State is excluded from the possibility of participating in it by the nature of his condition.

Only through the concrete construction of a similarly free and republican political community, open, in other words, to the participation of all, and directed towards the common good, would the patriotism of the moderns have resurrected the public spirit of the ancients and the practice of civic virtues. Only under such conditions, and not others, would '*the love of fatherland* be introduced everywhere, sustained, diffused, invigorated' [III, 240–41]. Still, independently from its specific and original contents, this part of the *Scienza della legislazione* merits being analyzed and evaluated also as an important and significant document in the fiery confrontation that broke out at the end of the eighteenth century between different ways of interpreting patriotism and the republican legacy of the previous centuries.

What does it mean to be a good patriot? What is a fatherland? What must be understood by republic? Such questions were posed by journalists, politicians, and literati everywhere in France, Germany, and Great Britain, particularly after the Seven Years' War which had upset the international balance of power and changed many categories of the political debate.[37] The problem posed by the sudden reappearance of patriotism, precisely in the century of Enlightenment and cosmopolitanism, has been debated heavily in recent Italian historiography. The social, political, and cultural origins of what Franco Venturi defined the 'nascent patriotic ferment' which abruptly emerged at the centre of intellectual life on the peninsula in the last quarter of the eighteenth century have been explored, with surprising results.[38] Awareness is finally growing of the existence of multiple and different readings of all those, and there really were very many, who appealed increasingly to love of the fatherland and to a militant patriotism, cloaking concrete partisan political interests in noble words. In this way it has been easy, for example, to reveal that the growing interest in municipal history and in the events shaping the late medieval municipalities, as documented by the publication of a large number of town histories fermenting with

patriotism, actually hid strong hopes of revolt and frank opposition towards the final
attempts of the absolutist monarchies, supported by the reformism of important parts
of the Enlightenment world, to impose central control over the provinces. Behind the
publication of these texts, which invoked the historical and political causes of these small
fatherlands, of the traditional representative bodies of the municipal patriciates, and of
the medieval civic statutes lay an increasing resentment against a top-down reformism
understood to be despotic and authoritarian, a veritable attack on ancient local liberties.
There is, in other words, no doubt that the brusque acceleration in the process of reforms
on the peninsula, put into play in the 1780s by Joseph II, Victor Amadeus III, Ferdinand
IV and Leopold II with the objective of modernizing, rationalizing, centralizing, and
standardizing the state apparatus also in the provinces, demolishing what still remained
of the particularism of the ancient communal privileges and thus reducing the power
and prestige of the notables, precisely at a time of strong economic and civic growth in
the provinces and of bitter polemic with the capitals, easily fuelled the rediscovery of the
fatherland as a 'land of the fathers' to be defended at all costs. It suffices to read a work by a
then well-known Italian polygrapher like Giambattista Roberti, *Dell'amore verso la patria*, to
find summarized all the salient points of patriotism. Severe-faced and resolutely opposed
to the Enlightenment ('admonish the sect of the cosmopolitans and of the egoists,' the
former Jesuit repeated), its nimble rhetoric united republican opposition to absolutist
despotism with the cult of the small fatherland, understood as respect for the traditions,
manners, lineage, and venerable memory of the fathers, all – fortuitously – indicated as
the 'founders of those patrician assemblies'[39] at the origins of the legitimate local nobility.
The crisis of the Old Regime manifested itself, also and above all, as a piercing crisis of
identity among old social groupings, a rupture of communitarian and corporatist bonds,
the substitution of ruling factions, and the denunciation and rejection of a past where
the liberty of the few had meant the oppression of the many. Faced with this, men like
Agostino Paradisi, Giambattista Giovio, and Roberi willingly revisited the patriotic and
republican myth of the small aristocratic communes of medieval Italy. Often adding fuel
to the fire, purposefully inspiring the more conservative forms of this patriotism in its
denunciation of the cosmopolitanism and the universalism of Enlightenment reformers
in name and on behalf of particularism and tradition, were the survivors of the Society
of Jesus, the authority of which had been revoked by Pope Clement XIV under pressure
from sovereigns, and which had been among the first victims of Europe's great absolute
monarchies. Count Gherardo d'Arco was in this sense right when, questioning the true
nature of the new patriotism which ever more openly attacked reforms from above in
1786, affirmed that 'the phenomenon derives in a straight line from *Jesuitism*, propagator
of *patriotism*, that is the spirit of *insubordination*, of *ambition*, and of *interest*, masked under
the name *patriotism*. I have firm evidence of this truth. The Jesuit party is the origin of
this so-called *patriotism*.'[40]

In reality, patriotism was a very old phenomenon which certainly was not ascribable
to one of the many conspiracies attributed, at the end of the eighteenth century, to the
fervid and restless political imagination of former Jesuits in search of revenge and new
patronage. As is well known, there existed an old contraposition between the conception
of *patria* as fatherland, the 'place where one is born,'[41] a profound sense of belonging,

a social bond founded on love and respect for the traditions and customs of a community, and the conception of those – particularly Enlightenment thinkers like Filangieri – who imagined it above all as a political institution, a republican community of free men with equal rights, subject only to laws which they gave themselves. The distant roots of this latter interpretation dug straight into the myth of the Roman Republic, into Cicero's *De officiis* and works of Sallust, which had been given new life by Renaissance civic humanism. Compared to this, the first conception of fatherland was certainly more recent, dangerously closing in on that of nation in its primitive significance of ethnic community, of *gens*, laying the foundations for their definitive overlapping in the nineteenth century.[42] Robert Filmer's *Patriarcha, or the Natural Power of Kings*, posthumously published in 1680, can be considered among the most authoritative sources of these first modern attempts to clarify the significance of the word fatherland.[43] That celebrated text, against which Sidney and Locke polemicized, confirmed the centrality of the hereditary principle and the thesis that the true patriot could not be anything but monarchical, as the correct interpretation of fatherland as land of the fathers naturally and legitimately attributed patriarchs the power to rule, to the king first of all as *pater patriae*, as took place just as naturally in familial relations of power between fathers and sons.

In Naples, this neat contraposition arrived precociously in the first decade of the eighteenth century as a consequence of Shaftesbury's sojourn and the relationships he built with local scholars.[44] Through the rapid diffusion of his major works, the author of the *Characteristicks* had sown important seeds for the appearance of the modern cosmopolitan and republican patriotism which would find its classic theorization in book IV of the *Scienza della legislazione*. As a faithful student of Locke, Shaftesbury denounced the errors of Filmer's followers, defined 'patriots of the soil,' insisting on the ambiguities of the English language, which lacked the word *patria*, but above all on the fact that absolute power destroyed the love of fatherland itself.

> Absolute power annuls the publick and where there is no publick, or constitution, there is in reality no mother country or nation… A multitude held together by force, tho' under one and the same head, is not properly united, nor does such a body make a people. 'Tis the social ligue, confederacy and mutual consent, founded in some common good or interest, which joins the members of a community and makes a people one.[45]

Traces of this argument are visible in Paolo Mattia Doria's *Vita civile*, which attributed ancient patriotism an important function in launching a new politics against absolutism and the doctrine of reason of state.[46] Conversely, the position emerging from Vico's *The New Science* was very different. Here, the mythical republican love of the fatherland, the civic virtues of the ancients – and particularly of the Romans – were rejected and unmasked in light of a raw and realistic historical reconstruction of the ferocious battle between patricians and plebeians; a struggle which seemed to confirm Filmer's intuitions, revealing that the 'true fatherland' in archaic Rome always had been 'the interest of a few fathers.'[47]

By moving the concept of fatherland closer to that of nation through a problematic and polysemic reading, Antonio Genovesi raised the quality of theoretical reflection on the issue. Already in the late 1760s, he clearly knew that the question of the nature of patriotism was becoming increasingly an incandescent political battlefield: 'A question is born here,' he wrote, 'which is much disputed among politicians, and it is "Does man have a *fatherland* except for the republic?"' If, in the *Esprit des lois*, Montesquieu neatly had declared that love of the fatherland could be nothing but love of the republic, of political virtue, and of equality, thus annoying defenders of the monarchy, Genovesi was more doubtful when teaching his loyal students at the University of Naples, taking his distance from those who denied the possibility of patriotism in a community without liberty.

> Because whoever has no right to rule has no fatherland, and one only has this right in republics and mixed governments. I think they are wrong. The idea of a fatherland is a very complex one. It embraces all the rights which men have within the body politic and the many affections contracted through birth, climate, place, friendships, and kinship, through the tombs of their ancestors, through religion, and through the form of government.[48]

It was, in other words, undeniable that patriotism continued to ferment and act upon the souls of men even under a tyrannical government. Genovesi convinced himself of this above all while meditating on the 'right of citizenship.' Pondering the dual essence of that right, he was forced to recognize it not only in those who accepted their subjection to the laws of a republican political community, but principally in the first founding fathers, in other words in that ethnic community which historically had the 'primitive right to citizenship, that is to say the right of the indigenous.'[49] Both these conceptions of fatherland remained at the centre of the dispute throughout the 1780s. On the one hand, there was the political and rational conception dear to Enlightenment reformers, which emphasized its connection with the libertarian and constitutional form of republican government; on the other there was the historical, effectively conservative conception, attractive to promoters of local elites, which was dangerously close to the concept of nation and rather underlined the decisive and legitimizing function of custom, tradition, and lineage.[50] An analysis of the discourses and languages which fuelled the hard political struggle in the Naples of Ferdinand IV and Maria Carolina, however, shows it could not have been otherwise. It is enough to mention the violent reactions triggered by the costly and imposing military reforms which finally would provide the kingdom with a great 'national army'[51] able to compete with the best forces in Europe. Reintroducing measures dating from the 1760s, the year 1782 saw, in accordance with a precise scheme promoting the presence of 'national' troops over mercenary ones, the reform of the provincial militias. A few years later, all national and foreign regiments were finally brought under a single centralized body responsible for military affairs, the *Intendenza generale dell'esercito*. With an impressive financial effort, which saw the investment of at least 4 million ducats, no less than two thirds of the kingdom's revenue, the effects were felt by 57,587 men in peacetime and by 61,543 in wartime, including some 15,000 men from the provincial militias.[52] The navy was given particular attention and great resources.[53] The entire process, which obeyed the logic of constructing a modern absolutist state in Naples inaugurated by Charles III in 1734,[54] met with violent reaction. That part of the nobility of the sword which felt its prerogatives directly affected and which found the possibility of handing over military command to bourgeois officials unacceptable, rose up in the name of the 'nation.' What offended them the most had been the intentions and choices of the secretary of war, the Irishman John Acton, and by Queen Maria Carolina of Austria, who had imposed the order to 'reconstruct the army on a German footing,' on the model of Frederick II, inviting foreign instructors to the provincial battalions, calling on technicians from every corner of the continent, and centralizing the mechanisms of recruitment to the provincial militias. The number of 'disconcerted generals,' the 'disgust' at the imposition of iron discipline, the demand for strong professionalization, and the attention to merit and competence which was preached obsessively in the new military academies built in Naples in the years of Tanucci's period in office, spread rapidly, weakening the process of reform from within. Despite the invitation of many reformist-minded nobles to push ahead along the path of military education, since 'military education greatly influences that of the whole nation, because if these, who often are the most licentious, are dutifully disciplined, it serves as a good example and deterrent to others,'[55] the reaction continued to gain ground. While in the mid-eighteenth century, following the model of political struggle of the Parisian parliamentarians, it was the great leader of the Neapolitan *togati* Fraggianni who had appealed to the 'nation' and called for respect for the ancient 'natural constitution of the Kingdom' to contest the absolutist process of creating a modern bureaucratic apparatus controlled by the monarchy, in the late 1790s that same appeal was made against military reforms by the nobility of the sword. Publications against the reforms mounted. Authoritative functionaries proselytized against the government, rhetorically asking how one could treat the Kingdom of Naples in the same way as Peter the Great's Russia, and the provincial battalions of Apulia, Lucania, and Sicily as if they were 'troops of savages' to civilize in the barracks and training grounds built for that purpose.[56] For centuries accustomed to plurality and to conflicts of power between *togati*, barons, and the monarchy, to the rejection of excessively direct government controls over the provinces, the politics of centralization and the forced discipline imposed by the 'foreigners' who had usurped the crown were denounced above all through appeals to the nation, to its secular history, to its habits, its customs, and particularly its natural hierarchies.[57] The Neapolitan people, the Neapolitan nation, Neapolitan public opinion, and the Neapolitan fatherland began to conflate in the denunciation of reforms that threatened centuries-old habits and privileges.

Upon closer scrutiny, Vincenzo Cuoco's virulent polemic against the cosmopolitan patriotism of the late Neapolitan Enlightenment in the *Saggio storico sulla rivoluzione di Napoli*, and particularly against Mario Pagano, represents little more than the dramatic culmination of a long and tormented dispute. As we will see in subsequent chapters, Cuoco publicly accused Filangieri's followers of having separated arbitrarily, in the decades leading up to the Neapolitan Revolution, the concept of fatherland from that of nation, inventing a false and abstract republican and constitutional patriotism showing no regard for the history of Naples: 'Did we perhaps want to make the republic independent by scorning the nation?... One can never do good for the fatherland unless one loves it, and one can never love the fatherland if one does not esteem the nation.'[58] In his impeccable bill of indictment, Cuoco often and willingly spoke of 'national pride' ('that sentiment which only inspires the public spirit and love of the fatherland'), of the 'disheartening of the nation,' hurt and betrayed by the cosmopolitanism of Enlightenment thinkers accused of having favoured 'a frivolous mania for foreign fashions' and above all of having supported the centralizing reforms of the crown against what remained of the old system of autonomous municipal 'liberties.' Referring to the customary concept of nation as a natural entity, a concrete form of historical individuality, a community that is simultaneously spiritual, cultural and political, imperiously hurled into the political debate by revolutionary events in France,[59] he distinguished between a genuine and positive patriotism, focusing on a concept of nation[60] that was respectful of history, of popular traditions and of the characteristics of small, federated communities in the Neapolitan nation, and a patriotism that was completely political, constitutional, artificial, false, meaningless, imposed from above, coldly invented in the debates of those popular societies that he despised, holding them to be lairs of opportunists and loafers: 'whoever is really a patriot doesn't waste time chattering in halls.'[61]

In reality, the *Scienza della legislazione*, like Mario Pagano's *Saggi politici*, had treated the question of how finally to give a common body and identity to the Neapolitan nation as the crisis of the Old Regime wore on, despite the very evident differences between regions (Pagano never tired of repeating that 'an inhabitant of the mountains of Abruzzo differs from an Apulian like a German from a Sicilian'[62]) in far more complex and problematic terms than what Cuoco purposefully and polemically wanted it to seem like. Filangieri had dedicated an entire chapter to the so-called 'genius and temperament of peoples,' explaining that it was one thing to respect the peculiarities of nations shaped by history, geography, and climate, but altogether different was the necessary search for common elements in the human species, like the natural law of peoples, or the 'universal spirit which in every age animates the majority of nations' [I, 137]. Real patriotism in the modern world could not be anything but passion and love for a republican and constitutional fatherland of free and equal men with regard to universal rights; otherwise it risked degenerating into a negative passion, into a dangerous source of war and injustice. Addressing the issue of patriotism in a separate chapter entitled *Dell'amor della patria e della sua necessaria dipendenza dalla sapienza delle leggi e del governo*, Filangieri urged for the greatest clarity on this delicate argument: 'Let us not confuse the most distinct ideas. Let us not abuse the sacred name of *love of the fatherland* to indicate that mere affection for the fatherland which is an appendix of the very evils of civil unions and which one can find both in the most corrupt and in the most perfect society' [III, 238]. His beloved university mentor, Antonio Genovesi, was right to signal the existence of a sense of natural belonging which accompanied community life, something similar to a profound and indestructible historical and ethnic bond. Nevertheless, that mode of conceiving the fatherland, inspired by the constant need to take the mind back to memories of childhood, of the 'cradle' and of the fathers, to the primordial and irrational senses of ethnic belonging which had always hid behind the word nation, had nothing to do with the authentic love of the fatherland disseminated by Enlightenment thinkers, understood solely and clearly as simple love of the republic and its laws. This latter patriotism, which like all 'conducive passions' united reason and will, was an ideological product precisely because it was an act of rationality, and as such it was consciously to be introduced, diffused, and given currency in public opinion. '[T]he love of power,' Filangieri explained by way of example, always and naturally exists in every society, that of the fatherland 'must be introduced… it must first be aroused and then used' [III, 242]. This, however, entailed a conscious reckoning with the changes that had taken place in traditional forms of social communication, the identification of objectives and instruments for intervention different from those of recent past, and above all the development of a new political strategy to face the ever more dramatic crisis of the Old Regime and of its traditional political institutions like the absolutist monarchies and the Roman Church.

As is well known, the sudden appearance on the European scene, in the second half of the eighteenth century, of the historical phenomenon of public opinion shook the very foundations of Western political culture.[63] The *Scienza della legislazione* took it into account in every decisive chapter, seeing in that emergence both risks and opportunities. In fact, the possibility of constructing a renewed republicanism among the moderns, to which all of book IV was dedicated, based itself precisely on the hypothesis of the participatory and emancipative potential offered to increasingly larger groups of citizens by the nascent public opinion: a phenomenon – it must be stressed – which was entirely unknown to the ancients in the forms which the men of the eighteenth century had to deal with.[64] As for the evident novelty and power of the phenomenon, Filangieri would probably have agreed without hesitation with the words of Louis Sébastien Mercier, in popularizing a common trope in the Enlightenment reflection on the argument in his celebrated *Tableau de Paris* in 1782, affirming 'a great and important revolution in our ideas has taken place only over the past thirty years. In Europe today, public opinion has a preponderant force, one which one cannot resist.' 'An invisible power,' Necker would echo shortly after in his writings on financial administration, 'that without treasury, guard, or army, gives its laws to the city, the court, and even the palaces of kings.'[65] It was no coincidence that, repeating word for word the reflections formulated by Diderot in Raynal's *Histoire philosophique et politiques des… deux Indes*, Filangieri had caught on immediately to the political and constitutional function which public opinion was assuming at the end of the century as a form of direct expression of popular sovereignty in the confrontation with despotism.[66] Against the *arcana imperii* and the reason of state characterizing the old politics of the absolutist monarchies, he explored the necessary legal conditions for guaranteeing a correct, free, egalitarian and transparent participation of all citizens in the formation of public opinion. He did this first of all by turning to the theory of the rights of man, identifying the necessary foundations for modern and republican public opinion in the freedom of the press, in the fair distribution of wealth to avoid concentrations of power, and above all in the commitment to public education. The basis of his reflections was certainly the conviction that the birth of public opinion, as well as that of the free market, far from representing sources of new and more odious inequalities and controls, were instead to be considered great occasions for emancipation and for progress. This, at least, if opportunely interpreted and regulated by politics through legislative measures inspired by the idea of constructing a new, more just and fair civil society, definitively autonomous from the absolutist state and its unjust social order. This interventionist approach, of *ought* over *is*, which, as we have often highlighted, marked the underlying identity of the entire political culture of the late Enlightenment, also shaped the meditations of book IV on the existing interconnections between the work of diffusing modern patriotism, the necessity of thus abandoning the ancient strategy of reform from above in favour of a republican conception of reform from below, and the very understanding of the nature and workings of public opinion itself.

Filangieri shared the interpretation which began to appear in Enlightenment circles at the end of the century, according to which public opinion – beyond the rhetoric hailing it as a prestigious new political authority and institution comparable to the monarchy or the Church, to which one could appeal to legitimize demands, almost as if it were an objective and neutral tribunal of universal reason – was above all the fruit of individual initiatives and of the conscious militant action of groups in terms of communication and information. Diderot had explained it clearly to Necker in 1775, writing that public opinion

> Of which we know the full power for good and for evil, in its origins is only the effect of a small number of men who talk after having reflected, and which incessantly form, in different points in the city, centers of instruction from which errors and reasoned truths gradually gain ground out to the very ends of the city, in which they are established as articles of faith.[67]

Many other initiatives, like those in the pages of the *Encyclopédie méthodique*, had served to reinforce these theses, which sought in practice to reveal the hidden mechanisms of communication processes and shed doubt on their presumed neutrality.[68] It was thus necessary to no longer limit oneself to stating the existence of, or eulogizing, this powerful moral and political authority represented by public opinion, but rather to arm oneself to steer it, guide it, 'rectify' it as Filangieri liked to say, by thinking of it as an institution which could be 'managed and directed' [III, 6] by philosophers. Today we know that the *messieurs* of the French parliament were, more or less consciously, among the first openly to utilize public opinion in this way through their appeals to the people and the nation, at every occasion proclaiming themselves the legitimate representatives of popular will in the context of their political protest against absolutism.[69] In 1775, it was the Church's turn to notice definitively the clamorous changes introduced by the appearance of a public sphere in Western politics and the unambiguous overcoming of the ancient and obsolete logics of control and repression of cultural production and consumption. The terrible Inquisition, the talons of which had been honed by absolutism, and the *Index librorum proibitorum* were thus largely left with the task of repressing and disciplining clergymen within the Church, for different logics operated outside. With Pius VI's encyclical *Inscrutabile divinae sapientiae*, which aimed to vehemently unmask and denounce the demoniacal nature of that Enlightenment culture which was poisoning an entire continent, all the ecclesiastical structures and religious orders were mobilized and equipped to guide international public opinion towards the cause of the Holy See.[70] With no holds barred, the modern struggle for hegemony in the intellectual and political life of Europe could be said to have been decisively inaugurated at this point. It was in those same crucial years that many Enlightenment thinkers made the decision to enter the lodges of Masonic society to increase their chances of spreading their own ideas, taking into account the phenomenon of the rapid politicization of the 'literati' and the innovations which had taken place in the world of publishing and urban sociability. The appearance of the 'political public,' which absorbed, 'like a river its tributaries, all other publics literary, philosophical, scientific,'[71] in this sense attributed a strategic function to the abstract authority of public opinion in realizing what Marx would have defined the Enlightenment's historical task of fuelling, on the level of ideology and culture, the process by which civil society was rendered autonomous from the absolutist state of the Old Regime.[72]

The *Scienza della legislazione* rightfully belongs to this stormy and unexpected season in the struggle for the conquest and control of public opinion. There is no doubt that the project of diffusing republican and constitutional patriotism, developed, not by chance, in the book he dedicated to public education in 1785, took account of the radical changes that had taken place in the forms of social communication. How should love of the fatherland and its laws be disseminated? How should individual passion for glory and civic virtue be affirmed? How should the long era of Old Regime subjection be overcome and the citizen of the future forged, not by recourse to violence and revolution but rather gradually, through legislative reforms, in time creating an efficient cultural hegemony of republican and constitutional values in the modern civil society that was emerging? To these questions, which were more common than one might think in the late European Enlightenment of those years between the American and French revolutions,[73] Filangieri responded by appealing to the teachings of the ancients. They had been the undisputed masters in the delicate task of forming the so-called public spirit, by 'invigorat[ing] the social bonds.' What mattered in the eighteenth century was revisiting, and if anything updating, the lessons to be learned from the republican past of Rome, Athens, and Sparta in light of the rights of man and the more recent political theory of the passions, uniting, on the legislative level, self-love, power, and glory with man's social nature, always considering the working mechanisms of public opinion.

Reflecting upon the laws of the ancients as regarded the granting of public honours and recognitions for having served the fatherland well, and in particular with public liturgies ('when, through imposing and terrible ceremonies, the Roman devoted himself to the welfare of the fatherland' [III, 245]), Filangieri dedicated numerous pages to analyzing the 'passion for glory,' to the extent that he held it a key piece in the mosaic of modern republican culture. Before a modern world which had lost the values of civic virtue and the collective interest in favour of individual economic self-interest, he retained that it was necessary to restore, as quickly as possible, adequate space for the republican cult of heroes who had sacrificed themselves for the collective. Governments had to return to organizing public ceremonies and provide for honours and prizes to those who had served the fatherland, who had been inspired and driven to sacrifice by passion for glory and for power, understood solely and exclusively as a service to the community. To spread this passion, it was nonetheless necessary to 'render glory representative; one must give material dressing to this moral being; one must give public opinion signs which express the suffrages, which manifest favourable opinions' [III, 248]. Filangieri was absolutely convinced that the imitative psychological process of social communication functioned perfectly in Ciceronian Rome, in the Naples of Ferdinand IV, and in the Paris of Louis XVI: 'the enthusiasm of the individual communicates itself to the multitude, the energy of one passion is communicated to the other; the people run where the hero calls them; and that which love of glory has produced in only the one, that for the fatherland thus produces in the multitude.' From here, the meticulous revisitation of the ceremonial burials of heroes by their fatherland in the ancient world, of the organization of games prizing merit and talent, the choice of appropriate literary subjects, in novels, in poetry, in music and more generally in the entire 'system of ancient spectacles' [III, 254] purposefully organized to exalt civic virtues and reinforce the public spirit.

The most organic and ambitious proposal was that of radically reforming the laws on theatre. The vexed question of whether theatre was to be considered a school of virtue or of vices was then a burning topical issue and involved Enlightenment thinkers like Lessing, Voltaire, Rousseau, Diderot, and Marmontel. In his 1758 *Apologie du théâtre*, a polemical reply to Rousseau's celebrated *Lettre à d'Alembert*, Marmontel had summarized the positions taken in a venerable debate over the function and nature of theatre, which had always experienced the hostility of the Church above all, and the desperate attempts of experts to vindicate its dignity and social prestige. Against those – and there were still many in the eighteenth century, as evident from Pope Clement XIII's 1759 prohibition on clergymen attending public theatrical performances – who considered all actors as scoundrels, marginal and reproachable figures, Voltaire had insisted since 1746 for a change of attitude and a return to giving them credit and educative functions.[74] In the last quarter of the century, the growing interest in the ancient world, the renewed love for classical tradition in the arts, and the republican legacy revived the dispute everywhere. In Italy, Filangieri resolutely sided with those who openly believed in the theatre's political and pedagogical function. The theatre of the moderns had to return to what it had 'been at its origin, the school of virtue and the grazing-grounds of glory.' It was thus necessary to go beyond the generous and worthy attempts of Corneille, of Racine, of Maffei, and of Voltaire, who, narrating the exploits of Brutus and Cato with talent and great sympathy,[75] had sought to emulate the tragedies of the ancients, showing 'kings and those who counsel them the frightening effects of tyranny and injustice' [III, 257]. Filangieri called for precise laws, for the construction of a network of popular theatres guaranteeing free shows for all citizens at state expense, and radical reforms to transform actors and dramatists from 'disgraces,' rejects at the margins of society, into nothing less than 'priests of glory,' authoritative protagonists in that new civic religion which was to preach the practice of virtue to people.[76] This reform, the Neapolitan philosopher specified, 'should not only render actors citizens, but should also work to render, like in Athens, citizens actors'; 'It should simultaneously place theatre at the service of glory and correct public opinion, making it esteem what really is worthy of esteem, and by celebrating some great action of some meritorious citizen and frequently of some illustrious contemporary' [III, 260].

Through their dramaturgical activities, Francesco Saverio Salfi and Francesco Mario Pagano, two of Filangieri's disciples, immediately turned their beloved mentor's precise indications into reality in Naples, indications aimed at giving life to modern patriotic theatre also in Italy, as a key pillar of republican hegemony in the nascent political public sphere.[77] Salfi, in particular, did not limit himself to writing and staging tragedies following Filangieri's counsel, but also sought to expand further on the theory of political communication and of republican pedagogy independently through approaches to theatre that had already begun to circulate and be discussed among Italian literati.[78] In that sense, in the *Saggio del gusto e delle belle arti* of 1785, he identified two fundamental principles: the social and political nature of the languages of poetry and literature and the neat difference between theatre in monarchical and republican regimes. On the basis of studies by European authors in the field of aesthetics, and in particular Vico's analyses of the poetic conception of the first nations, Pagano distinguished a primitive archaic phase of humanity, in which pleasure and the sensations had dominated poetic discourse, and a second phase belonging to civil society, where reason and philosophy had changed the purpose of poetics. 'When philosophy took charge of it, she [poetry] was directed towards the public good, exciting those passions which most conformed to the common good and inspired horror for wrong and harm. Thus she became minister of civil knowledge and the basis and foundation of society.' Pagano formulated the distinction between monarchical and republican theatre with similar clarity:

> In republics, the theatre must understand the entire people; in monarchies, only those who are cultured and refined. In republics, the *theatre* and the *forum* are the school of a people who must be as erudite and cultivated as one which has to govern itself. But in a monarchy the people can be as ignorant and uncouth as indeed they are. Enlightenment and culture are not useful to them.[79]

Dedicating his first tragedy, *Gli esuli tebani* of 1782, as well as his 1789 *Corradino* to Filangieri, Pagano made it very clear what his chosen form of theatre was: 'tragedy is a political action, great, interesting and national, brought on the scenes usefully to move and pleasurably to instruct the people.'[80]

In his numerous tragedies, Pagano brought together the best of that 'republican spirit' which at that stage openly dominated the Italian political scene of the 1780s, fuelled by the enthusiasm triggered by the American Revolution and the growing disenchantment of contemporary thinkers with enlightened despotism. Though the issues he treated changed significantly with the rapid unfolding of events, the themes of love of the fatherland, understood as love of liberty, love of the republic and love of its laws indelibly remained at the centre of his works. The Theban exiles who secretly returned to their city of origin to 'free the fatherland' from the tyrant Leontidas, shouting 'either death, or liberty we all seek,' were a classic opportunity – according to Pagano's republican dramaturgical paradigm – to educate the public and underline the difference between natural and positive law, between the law of nature which gave solid foundations to the rights of man and the arbitrary and unjust laws willed by a despot. To the tyrant, who before dying resolutely affirmed 'laws have no power over princes / that if they are their authors / they do need not be subjects of their own work,' Pagano had replied that 'yet they are subjects of that eternal law / which noble nature wrote by her own hand.'[81] *Gerbino* and *Agamennone*, both written in 1787, denounced courtiers, the fatal passions of the king and the use of torture, emphasizing the limits which natural law put on

princely power. In his 1789 *Corradino*, a tragedy in which personal love stories are played
out against important events in Italian history, it was the Church's turn, the execrable
'Vatican,' to be tried for having obstructed the national cause by favouring an alliance
with a foreign king against an Italian prince. Compared to this, Pagano's 1792 comedy
Emilia was completely eccentric, but not for that reason any less interesting. Ironizing over
French fashions, which had seemed to flood Naples and all of Italy uncontrollably after
1789, Pagano felt the need to insist on national traditions, associating ever more closely
the terms fatherland and nation, and taking on, with vigour and irony, those 'libertines
by fashion' who argued that Naples had no *'point d'esprit, point de société*. It is all bad…'[82]
That these were not literary quirks but elements of the deeper political project of the
late Italian Enlightenment, partaking in an entirely new and original phase of reformism
directly inspired by a republican spirit which brought it ever further away from the old
model of Enlightenment despotism, is unequivocally demonstrated by the contents of
his 1799 *Progetto di costituzione della Repubblica Napoletana*. In *Titolo X*, dedicated the central
theme of *Educazione ed istruzione pubblica*, in lively polemic with the constitutionalists of
the *Direttorio*, Pagano reiterated, point by point, the arguments of his mentor Filangieri.
Significantly, article 290 included the solemn commitment of the state to establish a
chain of 'republican theatres in which performances are directed towards promoting the
spirit of liberty.'[83]

Finally, in that same constitution, alongside public education, considerable space
was allotted to that other great bulwark of republican reformism present in the *Scienza
della legisalzione*: legal reform. Pagano had already enunciated its principles and essential
outline in 1787, in a fortunate pamphlet entitled *Considerazioni sul processo criminale*.
On the basis of Filangieri's theories of a new penal code founded fully on the rights of
man, and above all on the direct participation of citizens in the exercise of justice, he had
proposed radical reforms aimed at substituting the practice of the inquisitorial process,
which dominated the European tribunals in the Old Regime, in favour of the ancient
accusatorial system of the Roman Republic. The underlying thesis in the *Considerazioni*
was exceedingly clear. 'The true accusatorial system can never take place in a monarchy:
inquisition is necessary here'[84] if the prince wants to save his absolute power. Only in a
republican context could the accusatorial system make sense and exist, since it required
precise historical conditions such as the rigorous respect for the 'rights of the citizen,'
of 'civil liberty,' the principle of the equality of all before the law, a strong 'sentiment
for the public good,' and a solid love of the fatherland and its laws. In a republic, the
law was the business of everyone. Everyone had the right to accuse, just as everyone
was given the possibility to refuse judges for valid reasons. All trials were to take place
publicly, in absolute transparency and fairness. Witnesses, whether for the prosecution
or for the defence, were cross-examined in the presence of the defendant and of the
court composed in part by jurors and in part by *togati*, judges selected by the people.
The very nature of the accusatorial process required the reconciliation of conflicting
needs such as the 'rapid and exact punishment of criminals and civil liberty,' individual
rights and 'public security.'[85] The return to the 'ancient accusatorial system' would in
other words transform hearings into a sort of ideal stage, before the people elevated to
the role of supreme judge, on which the social need for security and individual rights

could battle it out in a fair arena, where every citizen enacted his natural right to justice. Whence Pagano's idea that the forum and the theatre represented the great schools of patriotic virtue. In the republic, he explained, 'every citizen, being a member of the sovereign people, must bear the burden of three sovereign charges, that of the legislation, of the judges, and of the executive. He is born judge, soldier, legislator.'[86] It was thus no accident that the accusatorial system had emerged and was developed in the 'Roman Republic'[87] to then survive, with difficulty, in the modern world solely across the Channel, in the English system, 'which most resembles that of Ancient Rome among all the [legal] systems of Europe,' with its popular juries, 'the famous law of *habeas corpus*, the pillar and foundation of British liberty,' intransigent lifeguard of the rights of the defence. Pagano dedicated pages and pages to explaining the merits of a trial procedure which respected civil rights, applying the norm according to which 'the conditions of the accuser and the accused must be equal,' and that 'the judge is the middle between two litigants; he compares the opposed and contrary arguments, he balances them, and then judges,'[88] and thus cannot represent the prosecution as well, as instead took place in inquisitorial trials.

To strengthen these theses, he gave ample space to reconstructing the historical genesis of the inquisitorial system and to the unmasking of the *arcana juris* which legitimated that terrible legal system, the natural heir of every kind of despotic power to have appeared in history. Like all the major exponents of the Neapolitan school of jurisprudence, Pagano was convinced that a legal system really was the yardstick of how civilized a people were. To write its history meant retracing the development of nations from the most primitive forms of association to modern civil society. In the case of the inquisitorial system, it had all begun back in Ciceronian Rome, at the time of the Catiline conspiracy, when, in departure from custom, a secret procedure for conducting investigations and gathering testimonies to be discussed before the Senate without first informing the defence was applied, though solely for crimes against the state. 'With the fall of the republic' and the establishment of the empire, that procedure then progressively expanded to cover many other crimes. Pagano dedicated only a few pages to trial methods 'in barbaric times' among the Longobards, the Normans, and the Germanic peoples, such as the 'duel, the oath, the boiling water, the burning iron, and other divine experiments [which] were the means then employed, the evidence used in treating cases.'[89] He was far more interested in clarifying philologically and historically how history had arrived at the modern inquisitorial system, 'the criminal mystery.' In contrast with many opinions circulating at the time, he did not blame the canon lawyers but rather Frederick II of Swabia and his inexorable vocation for building a modern absolutist monarchy in which the judge represented the will and the interests of the sovereign and not those of the people. After centuries in which the two procedures had been applied together, depending on the crimes in question and the different procedural phases, the decisive turn of events came about with the Staufen and their despotic laws in the middle of the thirteenth century. 'And already here, the fatal arcanum is introduced,' Pagano explained indignantly with reference to Frederick's criminal legislation, 'the deadly mystery which substituted insidious taciturn secrecy in the place of the public nature of the ancient judgments.' In the following centuries, medieval jurists, 'lacking the light of erudition, and not guided by the torch of philosophy,' undertook to make the inquisitorial system lawful and legitimate and 'formed the monster that is the present system, which is composed of so many formalities and legal acts.'[90] Nonetheless, that procedure would not have come to embody the most insolent injustice and arbitrary abuse without the concurrence of 'that terrible and ferocious [method] introduced by the ecclesiastics' of forcing detainees to testify against themselves by any means whatsoever, including torture. Canon law, born from Roman law to build the 'pontifical monarchy' on a solid foundation, had, in its ferocious battle against heresy, conceived of as the disobedience of an absolute power rather than an attack on the faith and its dogmas, developed a unitary and organic idea of the trial which always favoured the assignment of guilt above the quest for truth. 'The inquisitor,' Pagano explained, 'wanting to accord and combine everything together, is sometimes forced to gaol and pressure witnesses, to the point of becoming a veritable novel, or rather a tragic poem, in which the accused is the unhappy protagonist.'[91] It was time to denounce these atrocities in public and to call for a return to a republican conception of justice, to an accusatorial system that would finally limit the arbitrary power of the *togati* and the despotism of the monarch through a reform of the penal code and the drafting of a new constitution able to guarantee the rights of citizens at all times.

Pagano though, like Filangieri and all the other exponents of the late Italian Enlightenment, was no dreamer or cloud-chasing utopian. His sense of reality was strong. It was no coincidence that the *Considerazioni* were dedicated to Luigi de' Medici, Prince of Ottaviano,[92] then an up-and-coming figure in the context of the new group of bureaucrats which had taken shape in Naples after the dismissal of Tanucci and the creation in 1782 of the *Supremo consiglio delle finanze*. This institution, with which Filangieri had also worked, was the very core of *fin de siècle* Bourbon reformism. Just as for all his brothers in arms, the difference between the difficult situation of Naples under Ferdinand IV and the ideal republican horizon of the proposed reforms was always exceedingly clear to Pagano. The projects were one thing, achieving them was another. He practically wrote two books to that end in the *Considerazioni*. In the first, he illustrated, with participatory enthusiasm, how the essence of the accusatorial system fully had emerged in Ciceronian Rome, delineating the ideal and final objective of reform; in the second, he instead asked for prudent, but significant legislative action by the government to that end, for the introduction of the mechanisms of double recusal, reforms to provincial hearings, public and transparent hearings and the right of appeal to a supreme tribunal of the province, thus limiting the inquisitorial procedure to the severest of crimes. 'Since great reforms encounter great obstacles… we will propose, in this chapter, such a correction of the present system, which, not depending much on the method used, paves the way for the system proposed above.' 'If you ask me,' Pagano concluded realistically, confirming the gradualist, far from politically violent or revolutionary, nature of Italian Enlightenment thinkers, 'if ever this is the best reform, I repeat the words of that book: these are the best laws of which the present circumstances are capable.'[93] But as we all know, circumstances would change radically with the onset of the French Revolution, which swept up, for better and for worse, the very fate of Italian republicanism in its course. In fact, there is no doubt that the surprising victories of Napoleon in 1796, and the arrival of the *Grand*

Armée in Naples a few years later, contributed greatly to precipitating the crisis of the Old Regime and of the Bourbon monarchy. Marvellously, the social and political reveries of many exponents of the late Enlightenment had the chance to become true. The republican legal reforms hoped for in Pagano and Filangieri's books found their full and immediate formulation in the laws of the revolutionary government[94] and in the articles of the 1799 constitution. Yet, precisely this result, as extraordinary as it would prove ephemeral, destined to last only a few months and to end tragically in a bloodbath which brought with it the historical memory of the Enlightenment's contribution to the birth of modern Italian republicanism, again reiterates for scholars the difficult and controversial problem of a balanced evaluation, free from ideological biases, of the positive and negative consequences of the French invasion for the reformist movement, and in particular for the republican and constitutional patriotism of the Italian Enlightenment thinkers which we have sought to reconstruct through the pages of the *Scienza della legislazione*. We know that after 1789 – once initial enthusiasm had died down for a revolution which in Italy too was greeted favourably as something believed capable of accelerating the march of the great monarchies towards their definitive constitutionalization – the rapid turn of events and the alarmed reactions of governments slowed down, and eventually grinded to a halt, the momentum of great structural reforms on the peninsula. In the 1780s, and for a part of the following decade still, Naples, like Turin, Milan, and Florence, saw men of the Enlightenment begin to experiment with a new sort of reformism from below, which no longer aimed solely for a so-called enlightened despotism, but for public opinion, for constitutional politics, for the diffusion of a republican spirit of participation, favoured by the spread of new forms of urban social structures and by the demand for information and education for ever wider segments of civil society. It was a long-term emancipatory programme, detailed and organic like that delineated in the *Scienza della legislazione*, which suddenly was forced to take account of a new historical context determined by what all the newspapers were calling 'news from France.'

Mario Pagano's personal experiences, intrinsically intertwined with those of the Neapolitan Enlightenment, are in this sense emblematic. In July of 1789, the crown nominated him, with all honours, *Avvocato dei poveri presso il Tribunale dell'Ammiragliato e Consolato del Mare*, involving him directly in the reformist process which at that time had reached its zenith. Five years later, we find him defending his Masonic brothers of the *Società patriottica* – Lauberg, Massa, Galdi, and many others – accused of 'conspiracy, of plotting against religion, monarchy, and the state.'[95] The situation had changed dramatically in the meantime. The transformation of the lodges into revolutionary clubs, and the inquisitorial attitude of rigid closure and outright rejection of earlier reformist periods by the Bourbons, had decisively pushed large parts of the late Enlightenment world towards revolutionary and subversive practices. Those months, pressured by the events of the time but also by questions of intimate consistency with past affirmation, witnessed the birth of that patriotic and republican Enlightenment movement which would spur many exponents of the revolutionary elites to action during the Triennial. Whereas, in the preceding years, books like the *Scienza della legislazione* and the *Saggi Politici* were read freely and eulogized at court, in the lodges, in the salons of the capital and in the provincial book clubs, in the changed context after 1795 their significance suddenly changed, and they took on a new life after having been publicly denounced and banished by state inquisitors. Thus they became the primary sources of republican catechisms, the spiritual guides for those intellectual circles which were organized everywhere in response to the reactionary turn of governments. In January 1795, the second edition of the *Saggi politici* was put definitively on the Holy See's *Index*. In February of the following year, Pagano was arrested and gaoled until July 1798, then only to be sent, alongside other patriots, into exile first to Rome, then to Milan. He returned to Naples in 1799 to partake in the republican government and meet his death on the Bourbon scaffold. Throughout his misadventures, which merit being reconstructed in their entirety to understand how circumstances could transform a reformer into a revolutionary, he remained a point of reference in the heated political conflicts that developed in the constitutional circles of the peninsula after Napoleon's victories and the birth of the first republics.

Before the anarchic violence of that chaotic 'municipal revolution'[96] of all against all, which the French invasion and the demolition of the old governments had created – fuelling an extraordinary debate over the federal or unitary structure of the republic to be imposed on Italy[97] – Pagano would certainly and unhesitantly have endorsed the views of Matteo Galdi's bestselling *Necessità di stabilire una repubblica in Italia*. Better than any other, in fact, that text recapitulated and developed, in light of the new situation, the ideas and principles of the Enlightenment's patriotic and constitutional patriotism as expressed in the *Scienza della legislazione*. Galdi had been the youngest to attend Filangieri's Masonic funeral. In his 1796 pamphlet, which went through no less than four editions, Galdi reiterated the conception of fatherland as a political community of free and equal men to be constructed day by day with a republican pedagogy based on a 'democratic constitution,' focusing on the 'solemn proclamation of the rights of men and of citizens'[98] to be exercised through the mechanism of representation. In the context of the complex and still poorly studied Italian debate over the future republic's institutional structure, in which not all supporters of democracy, for example, insisted on the unitary hypothesis[99] – some in fact emphasized the strong relationship between direct democracy and federalism – he first of all clearly explained the patriotic position of the Enlightenment thinkers and their hostility to Italy's republican history; a history in which municipal particularism and self-interest always had prevailed. Consisting of many different peoples, the Italian nation had found a keystone for a possible unitary identity only in its common cultural, literary, religious, and philosophical roots. Galdi had no doubt that Verri, Beccaria, Genovesi, and Filangieri had, through the spread of their cosmopolitan reformism in Enlightenment Naples, Milan, Turin, and Florence, paved the way for a republican revolution in the entire peninsula. From a cultural community of great citizen elites it was now necessary to move on to the construction of a strong unitary, republican, and constitutional political community which finally also involved the people, promoting the birth of a modern 'patriotic spirit' made of 'love of justice and of liberty.' Always a land of liberty, the peninsula had seen the ancient pre-Roman republics die because they were too small, too divided, too torn apart by contrasts, between themselves and internally, to resist foreign invaders. The fate of the Roman republic had been different, but its 'long duration' and extraordinary success – Galdi specified, yet again confirming his idea of fatherland – 'let us comprehend what virtue and the power of well-directed democracy are capable of.'[100]

Galdi reconstructed the historical experience of Italian republicanism up to modern times, denouncing its persistently aristocratic preference for a municipalism made up of class interests, of constant and ruinous concessions to sectarianism, to the self-interest of groups and notables who weakened the republic from the outside with their partisanship and factiousness, undermining any possible glimmer of a true democratic and constitutional spirit. Dispassionately and sarcastically examining the 'evils which federalism could produce in Italy,' putting together many small republics of notables, hostile to every central power of a democratic or representative nature, the young patriot, acolyte of Filangieri, did not hold back from warning his readers that 'merely the names of Guelphs and Ghibbelines must fill us with dread; that the events suffered under the Sforza, the Visconti, the Medici, the Borgia, etc. make clear to us the fact that our liberty will be due to a single and indivisible republic.' In short, the moment had come to break once and for all with the republican experience of the past, renouncing the federation of so many small communities of nobles to instead build a large fatherland for all, Neapolitans, Piedmontese, Sicilians, and Lombards, in which to 'reunite with the tightest bonds of unity and of the democratic indivisibility of a single republic.'[101] Galdi believed that not only reactionaries wishing for a return to the Old Regime, but also the so-called 'moderate' patriots who looked, with increasing sympathy, towards a federalist solution as the lesser evil, resisted this project, which brought to maturity almost twenty years of late Enlightenment political theorizing. They 'would want that we let ourselves be scourged by tyrants'; in their eyes – and these words should be food for thought for those, and they are really too many, who still insist on applying the 'Jacobin paradigm' generically to the historical understanding of the convulsed events of the Triennial, supporting the comprehensible obsessions of contemporaries[102] – the Enlightenment patriots who fought to give life to the republican dream of the *Scienza della legislazione* were nothing but 'Jacobins' and traitors to the nation. '[T]hey consider he who passionately loves the fatherland, liberty and virtue a wicked Jacobin and terrorist; on the contrary, they consider he who scourges patriots, consumes the wealth of the republic, and conspires openly with its enemies to be a good and moderate citizen.'[103]

Galdi's entire text, which perhaps too schematically – it was, after all, a propaganda brochure – divided the republican front into moderate federalists and unitary patriots, militantly supporting the latter in their reasoning, rested, from the point of view of its proposed politics, on an appeal to the democratic circles of the French government, to the *Grande Nation* which with its armies could help bring about the birth of a democratic republic in Italy. Trust in Paris' good intentions was a common trope in the current affairs of the age. The 1797 Treaty of Campo Formio, with which Napoleon surrendered Venice to Austria, changed everything. Dreams and illusions vanished in a heartbeat. Italy was brutally divided among the great powers with the same logic by which Poland had been partitioned in the Old Regime. The gratuitous violence and pillaging of the *Armée d'Italie* and the flamboyant imperialist vocation of the French government appeared in all their crude and dramatic actuality, sowing discomfort and delusion in the lines of the patriotic and republican movement.[104] Despite the efforts of Italian and French republicans, the hard lessons of history seemed to lend credence to the theorists of political realism and moderation. It is hardly surprising that a growing number of texts at the time began to refer to the foundations of Italian national identity in terms of tradition, history, and ethnic community to contrast with a similarly defined French nation, sustained, however, by force of arms. Cuoco's denunciation of Neapolitan Enlightenment thinkers for erroneously and abstractly having separated the concept of fatherland from that of nation responded to a growing sentiment in public opinion.

After Campo Formio, and more strongly still in the wake of the 1799 tragedy in Naples, the constitutional and republican patriotism theorized by Filangieri was forced melancholically by circumstance to leave the scene, banished to the margins of the political struggle, entrusted to the testimony and courage of small conventicles. The behaviour, the politics of conquest and the crude republican propaganda of the commissaries of the *Armée d'Italie* had ended up degrading, to the level of tiresome rhetoric in the eyes of many Italians, the appeal to the rights of man and to the libertarian myths of the great heroes of classical republicanism. The Italian Enlightenment had precociously, even compared to France, criticized the economic system based on conquest rather than commerce and had come to realize the distance which separated the liberty of the ancients from that of the moderns. 'On top of this critical ferment,' Franco Venturi astutely emphasized,

> a very different layer superimposed itself with the revolution and the French invasion. It was an attempt to resurrect Brutuses and Camillos on Italian soil, where in reality they were long dead and buried. Jacobin propaganda, simultaneously monotonous and exalting, brought an ideal republicanism to Italy which aligned poorly with a country in which the republican experience was already deeply rooted. Classical forms thus became the weapon for breaking a tradition.[105]

In the years following the revolution of 1789, in the wake of episodes like the Terror and Campo Formio, even the great republican tragedies of Vittorio Alfieri soon ended up assuming a different tone and significance than what they started out with. It must in fact be stressed that when Pagano, Salfi, and Alfieri himself invoked, in their theatrical works of the 1780s, liberty, virtue, and the construction of a fatherland understood to mean a political community governed by laws, they addressed a participant, passionate public that was prepared to associate the emotions triggered by the authors' words immediately with the changing fortunes of the American colonists, which they could follow step by step in the gazettes. In that sense, the republicanism that vivified Alfieri's tragedies really represents something new and unusual compared to the old, glorious literary republicanism which nonetheless nobly had toured Italian theatres since the early eighteenth century, opposing absolutism and the doctrine of reason of state.[106] It was distinguished and characterized by a strong and profound political character born not only from the author's desire to communicate a specific message, but above all from new patterns of cultural consumption emerging in those years in the public, which was ready and willing to attribute the words liberty or fatherland a new valency and semantic content after the creation of the United States of America. Beyond his extraordinary poetic talent, Alfieri may have represented the political hopes and efforts of *fin-de-siècle* literati better than anyone. Almost paradigmatically, his personal and artistic experiences encapsulate the drama of Italian Enlightenment republicanism, carried away by events and, though a great project of emancipation and social transformation in Old Regime Italy, forgotten by historians.

There is no doubt that Alfieri rightly belonged to that late Enlightenment world of which Filangieri was a protagonist. An English Rite Freemason, he frequented milieus close to those of the Neapolitan jurist, read the same books and, importantly, cultivated the same passion for the *libertas Americana* and for the merciless fight against despotism which was mobilizing the lodges of Europe.[107] It is impressive to retrace the pages of *Della tirannide* or of *Del principe e delle lettere* after having read the *Scienza della legislazione*. The assonances of their language, commonalities of their principles and the similarities of their themes and solutions are numerous. Yet, it must immediately be qualified that this statement does not at all imply – though the issue cannot be philologically excluded, quite the opposite – that Alfieri relied on Filangieri's masterpiece wholeheartedly. If anything, the statement instead represents further confirmation of the historiographical thesis according to which those years were decisive in crystallizing a veritable style of thought common to many literati.

Like Filangieri, Alfieri too partook in those late Enlightenment circles which once and for all had abandoned, and began publicly to denounce, the politics of enlightened despotism in favour of republican and constitutional ideas. The *Panegirico di Plinio a Traiano* of 1785, in which Pliny exhorted the emperor to restore the liberty of the people of Rome, is a precious testimony of this. Alfieri wrote it to express publicly his frank dissent towards the Piedmontese scientists and literati who, in 1783, had established the Royal Academy of Sciences in the Turin of Victor Amadeus III, solemnly sanctioning an alliance between the crown and the Republic of Letters in the name of a profitable collaboration of *Veritas et Utilitas*, as the motto chosen by the academy reads. He found that project of enlightened despotic collaboration, which saw artillerymen, university professors, and literati united around the King of Sardinia, entirely unconvincing.[108] Already in 1777, in his first drafts of *Della tirannide* (which would appear, however, only in 1789, after continuous slight changes and adjustments), he had clearly explained that the monarchy was intrinsically a tyrannical institution if not accompanied by a constitution able to keep its abuses in check. Rather than supporting the logic of power of the so-called enlightened sovereigns, who really were nothing but 'virtuous tyrants,' philosophers had to vindicate the government of laws, civil liberties and the fatherland of citizens, specifying that one could in no way 'say fatherland where there is no liberty and security.' In contrast with Montesquieu's thesis whereby the European monarchies, resting on honour and their intermediary institutions, had guaranteed liberty to the moderns, and struck by readings of Rousseau and Helvétius, Alfieri instead saw fear, panic, and forms of domination and oppression spread everywhere. In that suggestive phenomenology of despotic and arbitrary power which is the *Della tirannide*, Alfieri turned to that great theme which was common to all of late Enlightenment culture, and that is *Delle tirannidi antiche paragonate colle moderne*, analyzing the psychological roots and historical and political causes of contemporary tyrannies, which were considered far more efficient, underhanded, and pervasive than the crudely ferocious ones of the ancients. The picture that emerged was terrible. At the origins of everything, one always found the domineering nature and violence of a man, the rejection of the government of laws and of the 'sacred and broken rights of man.' 'Every unlimited authority,' Alfieri specified, 'is thus either in its origin, or in its development, a manifest and extremely atrocious usurpation of everyone's natural rights.'[109]

Modern tyrannies rested on the tacit agreement and synergy of great institutions like the monarchy, the standing army, the Church, and the hereditary nobility. Like Filangieri and the English radical republicans, so Alfieri contested the strategic function which the great standing armies, the 'perpetual armies,' historically had always fulfilled in favouring the birth of absolute monarchies at the expense of republican governments, where instead the libertarian model of the citizen-soldier and the popular militia reigned. He expressed the same negative sentiments as Filangieri did of open rejection towards the brutal and authoritarian mentality of the military world, that 'infamous multitude of lazy soldiers, base in obeying, insolent and ferocious in following orders,' defining the profession of the soldier, which in those years was taking definite shape, as the 'most infamous of all occupations.'[110] On the basis of what he had gathered reading Machiavelli, Voltaire, Diderot, the Baron d'Holbach, and many libertine and materialist works of the Enlightenment, Alfieri did not spare the Church its share of his sarcasm and criticism for its bloody history of transgressions and offences to liberty: 'The Christian religion, which is that of almost all of Europe, is in itself not favourable to free living; but the Catholic religion is almost incompatible with free living.'[111] However it was to the nobility of birth, the feudal system, and the hereditary principle that Alfieri dedicated his clearest and most unequivocal words. They were the fundamental junctions targeted by that modern republicanism summed up in the *Scienza della legislazione* and in other famous texts of the late European Enlightenment. 'Hereditary primacy is always the origin of every tyranny,' the Piedmontese dramatist explained, almost disowning his own origins in the ancient nobility of Asti. The 'order of hereditary nobles' was really the 'bad seed,' the 'radical vice' that hindered the birth of a real republic of free and equal men distinguished only by talent and virtue. 'Aristocratic tyranny' generally accompanied that other great perverse institution of 'our modern tyrannies,' the feudal lords, the 'most corrupt' class 'and therefore the key ornament of the courts, the greatest threat of the servants, the right laughing stock of those few who think.'[112]

Alfieri passionately and impetuously carried out the job of historically and psychologically unmasking tyranny. He had little interest in developing the political and legislative foundations of a future 'republican theory,' also because he had no competence in the matter. This task was rightfully that of better equipped people like Filangieri or Pagano. If anything, his interest in expressing himself on the vexed question of the decisive function of the literati in the war on despotism was strong. In this delicate field, which risked the very identity of Italian writers, his positions were very similar to those espoused by the Neapolitan republicans. Compared to the generic and abstract politicization of French Enlightenment literature at the end of the century, on which Tocqueville's pages remain memorable,[113] the analogous phenomenon in Italy took concrete form in a precise political plan for a public and republican education system along the lines summarized in the famous book IV of the *Scienza della legislazione*. Though fearing the 'deplorable necessity' of recurring to violence and revolution to overcome the Old Regime, Alfieri was convinced that the key to 'remedy tyranny' lay in the gradual conquest of public opinion, of the sentiments and thoughts of the 'people,' understood as the middle class, 'the mass of citizens and peasants, more or less well off, in possession of personal funds or profession.'[114] 'The will or the opinion of all, or the majority, alone maintains tyranny; the will and the opinion of all, or the majority, can alone truly destroy it.'[115] It was up to philosophers, writers, and all literati to educate the masses and establish the republican and Enlightenment hegemony which, through all means of artistic and literary communication, gradually would sweep tyranny away without recourse to violence. 'Theatre, history, poetry, rhetorical eloquence, all aspects of culture, in other words, will become a lively school of virtue and liberty,' Alfieri hoped. 'It is true, these books will be prohibited, impeded, and persecuted; but when read, they will be meditated upon, and helpful. Everything penetrates in these times; and if all truths until now have not taken the required path, one must ascribe that to fear, or the insufficient genius of those who took it on themselves to reveal them.' Compared to the past, the literati finally had a new, powerful, and authoritative political institution upon which to call: public opinion. 'Opinion is the undeniable lord of the world. Opinion is originally always the daughter of such persuasion, and never of force.' That was why, in spite of the formidable standing armies, the battle for the conquest of public opinion could and had to be won by the men of Enlightenment. Alfieri also agreed with Filangieri on the need to proceed with theatrical reforms and the definite social re-evaluation of the protagonists of that world, which in the near past had always been denigrated and considered suspect. Observing 'the influence of excellent writers on opinion,' he too, with republican spirit, called for new honours and new tasks for the 'writing magistrates' and the 'writing-tribunals,' the new priests of patriotic and republican identity.[116] These were the final years in which Alfieri wrote and staged his extraordinary libertarian and republican tragedies like the *Congiura de' Pazzi*, the *Bruto secondo*, and his *Virginia*, which rhetorically questioned the fatherland's republican and constitutional nature with clear Enlightenment overtones: 'Does one have a fatherland, where only / one wants, and all obey?' (a. III, sc. II).

How different and distant is the *Misogallo*, repeatedly rewritten between 1793 and 1799, from these convictions! Alfieri seems like another man. In the meantime his context had changed radically around him. Enlightenment Europe no longer existed. Cultures, political designs, and different ideologies all came together in the great crucible of revolution; ancient, unresolved problems came to the fore, and sometimes solutions which had seemed forever trounced reappeared on the scene in new and blinding forms. In 1789, Alfieri had greeted the French Revolution with enthusiasm and great hope in the ode *Parigi sbastigliato*, just as previously he had dedicated another ode to the American colonists, *L'America libera*. In 1792, he escaped Paris in horror, frightened, as he would recount, of urban manhunts by 'unleashed slaves,' the same ones who became protagonists in the 'assassination of the king' and the assault on all 'those well off.'[117] The Terror, the invasion of Italy by Bonaparte's troops, and Campo Formio further confirmed, in his eyes, what had been a tragic illusion. In the *Misogallo*, Alfieri explained that the French, with their behaviour, had liquidated the very idea of liberty for the moderns, cloaking their actions with the hammering propaganda of a false and rhetorical republicanism: 'Although they don't have liberty, they still have Sparta / in all corners of Europe, every Galluzzo is Achilles; / and Athens, Rome, and Sparta are nothing.' With their 'paper republic' and their comical and magniloquent references to the liberties of the ancient world to justify their violence ('Semi-Athenians, the French are: who denies it? / hear their language and the Greek together'), the Jacobins risked killing off forever the republican spirit to which the great Piedmontese dramatist had dedicated his entire youth. Hence his wish, still in 1792, to distinguish the true republicanism of the Italians from the false and demagogic one of the French:

> Republic is the soil, where divine / laws are the basis and the shield of human laws; / where no man, with offensive impunity / can be enemy of another; / where I cannot be scared, or made to kneel; / where I am not robbed of my wealth; / where everybody's goal is the common good. / Republic is the soil, where pure / customs have force, and the right rules, / nor the wicked enjoy the weeping of others. / Are you a republic, Gallic herd, / which mute now serves armed, vagrant kings, / the vile dirt of which floats yours?[118]

Hatred towards the French was so strong as to drag with it all that remained of republican and constitutional patriotism in the late Italian Enlightenment. The *Satire* ridiculed human rights, stigmatized polemics against religion, derided 'barefooted philosophers and the rabble,'[119] and even saw the reappearance of previously repressed sympathies for the hereditary character of true nobility. But, most importantly, the angry primacy of nationalism began to overlap more and more with the cosmopolitan kind of republican patriotism. In the *Misogallo*, the word fatherland, *patria*, in the Enlightenment sense of political and constitutional community, forever left the stage in favour of the word 'nation,' identifying itself entirely with it. Like Cuoco, so Alfieri was unable to separate fatherland from nation, one people in arms against another. The French nation was in fact continuously described, in ferociously negative terms, as an historically and ethnically antagonistic community opposed to that of Italy: 'O Italy,' Alfieri declaimed, 'hatred of the French, under any stick and mask they present you with, becomes the fundamental and only base of your, whatever it is, political existence.'[120]

   With these words, prefiguring the future, implacable struggle between the nations of Europe, Alfieri took his leave from the great moment of Italian Enlightenment republicanism. An important chapter in the political and cultural events of the peninsula was closed forever. It is worth remembering, for all its symbolic and emblematic value, that in that same terrible year, 1799, in which Mario Pagano was executed and the Neapolitan republic smothered in blood, an unhesitant Alfieri himself rejoiced publicly at the arrival of Austrian and Russian troops in Florence to chase away the French and repress the patriots. Faced with these lacerating internal divisions in the patriotic movement as the new century dawned, a century which most importantly would witness the construction of nation states, the heirs of the great Italian tradition of Enlightenment prepared for a long and arduous roam across the desert. It would be a difficult crossing, which still awaits reconstruction, about which we know too little and which, for the past two centuries, profoundly has marred the origins of contemporary Italy.

Part Two

A DIFFICULT LEGACY

Chapter Eight

THE ORIGINAL CHARACTER OF ENLIGHTENMENT CONSTITUTIONALISM: FROM THE *SCIENZA DELLA LEGISLAZIONE* TO THE 1799 *PROGETTO DI COSTITUZIONE NAPOLETANA*

> There is a general constitution for all societies, which consists of the union of all their wills… [it] consists of two fundamental principles. First, the union of their wills aiming at the conservation of the natural rights of each; secondly, the way of reuniting those wills and strengths and of exercising them.
>
> F. M. Pagano, *Saggi politici*, II ed. (1792–93)

It is well known that the expression and concept of 'Enlightenment constitutionalism' does not exist in current historiography.[1] Given that the language of historiography until recently also lacked the concept of Old Regime constitutionalism, this should not be particularly surprising. Still, it seems very difficult not to employ it, or some similar term, if one really wishes to understand the deeper structures, nature, and true message of the *Scienza della legislazione*. The concept of Enlightenment constitutionalism of course has to be explained and its meaning specified beginning from its historical context, that is the crucial period between the two great revolutions, the American and the French, as well as the novel elements which characterized the most important parts of that grandiose project. This is what the previous chapters tried to do, examining decisive questions like the umpteenth metamorphosis of natural law brought about by Enlightenment thinkers who put the question of human rights at the core of the political debate of the late eighteenth century, and by exploring the unexpected consequences of that increasingly tangled nexus between rights to liberty and the principle of equality for ways of thinking about politics, morality, and religion. All these aspects, which had been treated in depth by Filangieri, were capable of explaining his proud claim of having bravely sought to rebuild traditional legislation from the foundations up.

> It is a strange thing: among so many writers which have devoted themselves to the study of the laws, some have treated this subject only as jurisconsults, or as philologists, some also as politicians, but never taking aim of more than a single part of this immense edifice; some, like Montesquieu, have reasoned more about what has been done, than what ought to be done; but nobody has yet given a complete and reasoned system of

legislation, nobody has yet reduced this subject to a safe and ordered science, uniting means to rules, theory to practice. This is what I intend to do with this work which bears the title *The Science of Legislation.* [I, 41][2]

As we saw earlier, the nature, function and tasks of the law were to be radically reconsidered, according to Filangieri, in light of the historical experience of peoples and above all in view of a universal and cosmopolitan project of comprehensively rationalizing the legal order, neglecting no aspect of social and political life. His ideas were far from the opinions of the medieval jurists, according to whom laws were to be found, tried, and decreed, rather than made or ordered into creation as a political expression of sovereignty. The *rex facit legem* of the theorists of absolutism had, in this sense, been a model for all the new supporters of popular sovereignty, and republicans like Rousseau and Filangieri had learned much from Bodin and Hobbes. Montesquieu's example of analyzing the spirit of the laws and their historical development like a cold and detached social scientist did not seem promising. It was no coincidence that this way of understanding legislation added fuel to the fire of Filangieri's first enemies, the supporters of the *interpretation*, the *sacerdotes juris* of the Old Regime, capable of transforming the law from an instrument of liberty and the happiness of all into a weapon to defend the privileged few, giving free reign to despotism and the conservation of all kinds of inequalities. Instead, contemporaries now had to be reintroduced to the Greek philosophers' preference for the so-called government of laws over that of men. Filangieri knew Plato's reflections in the *Statesman* on the advantages and disadvantages of similar options well. Against the demagogues, against the intemperance of the masses, and more generally against despotic and arbitrary power in all its forms, he had always shared Aristotle's conclusions regarding the law's importance as the only path through which constitutionalism could guarantee liberty.[3]

In the late eighteenth century, the decision of Enlightenment thinkers to turn mainly to rights and the law to limit government required, however, a mental revolution able to change many of the common tropes in traditional representations of reality. A clear realization of just how much the world of the moderns had changed compared to that of the ancients was necessary. Before rejecting outright, without possibility of appeal, what we today call modernity, it was, in fact, necessary to explore the possibility of uniting its effects with the rights of man and, more generally, with a possible project of emancipating the peoples of Europe. Filangieri's polemic with Rousseau, who opposed scientific progress as well as socio-economic modernity by reintroducing the ancient model of direct democracy and the omnipotence of the legislature, and his denunciation of the illegitimate and unjust character of the principle of hereditary nobility supported by Montesquieu, aimed precisely at this. Those two giants of eighteenth-century legal and political thought represented authoritative positions which, though politically opposed, both denied the future any room, as the first proposed an impossible return to the past, while the second legitimated what in fact existed. The new *Scienza della legislazione*, presented by Filangieri as an 'immense edifice' to be constructed brick by brick, instead raised itself self-consciously over the chaos and abuse of the different medieval legal systems, while at the same time questioning the limits and dangers of the ancient democratic assemblies. Filangieri believed he was creating 'a complete and reasoned system of legislation,' starting from a few interlocked principles and, in particular, from the theory of the rights of man, the true guiding light of the new legal order based on natural law. The system – rational, logical, and organic all at once – presented itself as a sort of gigantic pyramid, crowned by natural law. It was this law that gave legitimacy to those principles and rights which were destined to be consecrated as written norms, firstly in the so-called fundamental laws, collected in a 'small code apart' in accordance with the American constitutional model, only then to descend to all ordinary laws. The magistrature as 'censor of the laws' would have guaranteed 'harmony,' homogeneity and the 'absolute' and 'relative' 'goodwill' of all parts of legislation with respect to the 'universal principles of morality' and to that natural law which contained the 'immutable principles of what is just and fair in all cases.' The merciless critique of the British constitutional system, which Montesquieu had liked so much, was a classic example of this way of thinking about the legal order. How could one hope to really guarantee liberty without uniting it with the principle of equality, without respecting the principle of a single and indivisible popular sovereignty? How could one safeguard the natural right of all men to justice while accepting the idea that some people were born naturally to dominate others? How could one assure individual liberty without, on the legislative level, accounting for the equal right of all human beings to public and private happiness? Conditioned by the complex dialectic between princes and the respect for rights posed at the top of the pyramid, Filangieri's constitutional thought was, due to its immanent expansive logic, practically obligated to defend itself on every section of legislation, to bind and influence fundamental as well as ordinary laws, institutional questions and economic, political, and social choices, widening its field of action to include education, religion, and the market. By separating and elevating rights and principles onto a pedestal apart from positive law, understood as the political act of a legislator, the *Scienza della legislazione* ultimately ended up weaving an image quite similar to that of a modern constitutional state.[4]

The old English system, founded on mixed government and the hypothesis that the division of labour functioned as a guarantee, was too far away from such a representation of legislation for Filangieri's liking. Lucidly identifying its anachronisms and mystifications, he saw in it the total justification of the Old Regime, its class inequalities, the triumph of the hereditary principle and the attempt to crystallize the *status quo*, attributing to the king and the aristocracy a political power which was due them no longer. Filangieri explained to his readers clearly that mixed government, the theory of the *King in Parliament*, fractioning sovereignty between the monarch, the aristocracy, and the people, certainly did not produce the necessary balanced, but at the same time unitary repartition of powers needed to safeguard liberty, peace, and security. Indeed, it produced revolutions and conflict, sanctioning historical inequalities. One thing was power understood in a legal and institutional sense, which was never to be concentrated in the hands of a single individual, another was the sociological confusion that arose between an organ of the state and its dominant social groups in the divisionary system of mixed government.[5] His long-distance argument with William Blackstone, the greatest English constitutionalist, was not just about the very idea of a legal system which left excessive space to 'unwritten laws,' or about the dangerous 'inconsistency' of the British 'constitution,' which had never been moored to a clear and detailed document able to specify institutional tasks and functions. Above all, Filangieri criticized the limits of that constitutional thought in which too much room was reserved for traditions, customs and forces involved in the defence of liberty, trusting solely in the division of powers and their mutual opposition.[6] Even though the *Rights of Persons* occupied an important part of Blackstone's *Commentaries*, they did not, however, have that decisive function able to found a new and rational legal order allotted to them by the *Scienza della legislazione*, alongside the principles of justice and equality enounced in the American Declaration of Independence.[7]

In his foreword to the *Progetto di costituzione della Repubblica napoletana* of 1799, Mario Pagano, faithful disciple of Filangieri, summed up this decisive aspect well, writing that 'the most distinguished thing one finds among modern constitutions is the Declaration of the Rights of Man. The ancient constitutions lack this solid and immutable basis.'[8] According to the interpretation given to natural law by Enlightenment thinkers at the end of the eighteenth century, that book contained precise indication of veritable subjective rights and not simple philosophical and moral suggestions, as many moderate interpreters had begun to highlight in those stormy years following the Terror. The *Declaration* really constituted, Pagano argued, the beating heart and 'principal object of every regular constitution,' since it contained the solemn expression of those fundamental principles, anterior and superior to every legislation, which were to guide all aspects of life in modern political communities.

Insufficient thought has been focused on the fact that the 1799 Constitution developed by the Neapolitan jurist was not merely an extemporary product, an adaptation of analogous European experiences devoid of originality that was solely the fruit of the events and conditionings of its historical moment. It rested rather on a local intellectual tradition that was world-class. Substantial and decisive references to Antonio Genovesi's *Diceosina*, Filangieri's *Scienza della legislazione*, and to Pagano's own *Saggi politici* and the *Considerazioni sul processo criminale* abound between the lines of that document which arguably represents a masterpiece of political and legal thought in Enlightenment Italy, and certainly the highest and most solemn conclusion to the entire Enlightenment way of thinking about republicanism and constitutionalism on the peninsula. Even in more recent research, historians all too often forget the prestige and relevance which the Neapolitan school of jurisprudence enjoyed among contemporaries not only in Italy, but across Europe. As has already been said, Filangieri had been the friend and venerated mentor of authoritative members of the Convention and of the first *Société d'Auteuil* like Pastoret and Dupaty; his French translator, Gauvin Gallois, would become Benjamin Constant's colleague in the Tribunal. In the preface to the French edition of the 1787 *Considerazioni sul processo criminale*, published just two years later, the translator Antoine De Hillerin, member of the Paris parliament, specifically called for the use of the Neapolitan jurist's theories to reform 'our juridical system… it is in Italy that we long have found the examples to be followed in order to regenerate our juridical laws.'[9] Again in 1815, confirming a prestige which was not giving signs of decline, the principal voice of the '*Décade philosophique*,' Pierre-Louis Ginguené, wrote an ample and impassioned portrait of Filangieri for Michaud's *Biographie universelle*. Here he reiterated the image of Filangieri as an authoritative alternative to Montesquieu, presenting him as the exponent of a distinctive and famous scholarly tradition inspired by natural law, which merited the greatest attention. The 'last heir of this noble school' had been Mario Pagano, 'miserably deceased in the revolutions of his fatherland,' but author of works which destined him to remain an 'immortal name'[10] among the jurists of Europe.

In other words, when Pagano set about writing the constitution at the behest of the revolutionary government, during the tragic few months in which the Neapolitan Republic of 1799 existed, he was not just any jurist. His international fame was at its peak,[11] and his books, like those of Filangieri, were read and used all over Europe. It is therefore very difficult not to catch a hint of profound intellectual pride and awareness of his own scientific merits in the words Pagano was compelled to write to the *Consiglio degli Juniori* to protest against an improvident expulsion order which erroneously had been sent to him by the organs of government in the Cisalpine Republic upon his arrival in the city of Milan, after having escaped from Rome. This was how Pagano presented himself to the councillors in December of 1798:

> Twenty years as chair of civil law in Naples, during the course of which I sought to instil the theories and sentiments of liberty in the minds and hearts of the youth; the *Political Essays*, published sixteen years ago, in which I developed the principles of democracy and of the rights of man; the *Criminal Procedure*, translated into French and presented to the Constitutive Assembly, which ordered its honourable commendation in its minutes of August 1789 (old style); twenty-nine months suffered in gaol in Naples because of the liberty I expounded, my charge of magistrate and my considerable fortune sacrificed to this great cause; the escape to free soil as soon as I managed; my benevolent welcome in the Roman Republic; the invitation I received from the Ministry of the Interior to a chair in civil law which, renouncing the attached wage, I accepted; the escape from that Republic in the circumstances known seem to me titles enough not to be disturbed in the exile which I had sought on this soil.[12]

This was a man preparing himself to write a republican constitution to crown his life as a militant scholar and philosopher. Finally, the dream of Italian Enlightenment thinkers, and particularly of Filangieri, seemed set to become reality, and it was no coincidence that the latter, with the arrival of French troops, immediately was consecrated as the revolution's tutelary deity by his old acolytes. From the opening lines of his *Rapporto* to the members of government who were to examine the constitutional document, Pagano vindicated his autonomy as a legislator with respect to the French and American examples that had come before him. Certainly, the 'new science' of constitutions had begun to give its first concrete and extraordinary fruits in America. France had then produced important contributions to this field. Still, the Neapolitan constitution could and should follow its own distinct and specific path, respectful of the great Parthenopean tradition of natural law. According to Filangieri's teachings, one thing was the so-called 'absolute goodness' of the laws, another their 'relative goodness'; there was no ideal constitution valid in every aspect for all peoples and for all times. 'Differences of moral character, of political circumstances, and also the physical situation of nations necessarily require changes in the constitutions.'[13] Careful not to hurt the sensibilities of the French, on whose army the fate of the Neapolitan revolution depended, Pagano tactfully proposed a constitutional design that was very different in its theoretical and philosophical system from the more recent examples to come out of France, the 'mother republic.' While in the *Saggi politici* he had identified 'the great aim' of the constitution principally in the 'conservation and defence of the natural rights of man reduced in society,'[14] in the *Progetto* Pagano affirmed that 'society is formed by the union of the wills of men who want to live together for the mutual guarantee of their own rights,' crediting, with subtle patriotic spirit, this 'luminous principle, the basis of political law… later adopted by the celebrated French legal publicists Montesquieu and Rousseau,' to one of the fathers of modern Neapolitan jurisprudence, Gianvincenzo Gravina.[15]

Pagano had learned from the *Scienza della legislazione* that the constitution was to be a written code of extreme clarity and of the highest possible rigidity and constancy in time. Its comprehensive structure therefore had to be formulated in a rigorously reasoned manner through an exact and organic interlinking of rules and principles, always maintaining the rights of man as the ultimate horizon of reference. Instead, the Thermidorian constitution of 1795, offering the most obvious terms of comparison, seemed to him to confuse rights and principles, means and ends all too often, revealing frailties and logical imbalances which were absolutely to be avoided.[16] The question of equality, which had been debated for so long in eighteenth-century Naples, was, in this sense, exemplary. While all the Transalpine 'Declarations' thought of equality as a right, Pagano considered it a principle. The first and most important of all constitutional principles, it was born from reason and imbued with extraordinary moral force. 'We have benefited from the Declaration opening the French Constitution, but we have still advised that equality is not a right of man, according to the previously mentioned declaration, but solely the basis of all rights, and the principle on which they are established and founded. Equality is a relationship; rights are faculties.'[17] The importance of this distinction was clear in many cases, but above all when it came to justifying theoretically the presence, for the first time ever in a constitutional document, of duties alongside the enumeration of rights. For the Thermodorian constituents, the legitimacy and even the priority of duties over rights emerged from the necessity of guaranteeing, in every way possible, the 'preservation of society.'[18] There was nothing of the sort in Pagano. From the late 1760s, the question had been addressed and resolved theoretically by Antonio Genovesi, in a dense chapter of the *Diceosina*, who took as his starting point the very definition of equality as the fundamental principle of justice.[19] The Neapolitan constitution simply accepted the results of that extended long-distance debate between the Parthenopean school of jurisprudence and the greatest European theorists of natural law, affirming, in its characteristic language, that

the duties of man are obligations, that is moral necessities, which are born from the moral force of a principle of reason. That [principle] is the same from which we have derived rights, that is to say the similarity and equality of men… The fundamental duty of man is that of respecting the rights of others. Equality entails that our rights are worth as much as those of others.[20]

With analogous rigour and a general outlook in which principles and rights always interacted according to the methodological norms expounded in the *Scienza della legislazione*, Pagano claimed that in his constitutional project he had first 'derived all the rights of man from the unique and fundamental right to conserve oneself. Liberty, the faculty of opinion, of making use of one's own physical force, expressing one's thoughts and resisting oppression are all modifications of man's primitive right to preserve what nature has made of him, and to improve himself as it encourages him.'[21] It is evident that he found nothing similar in the farraginous theoretical scheme structuring the Constitution of the Year III, which, also stylistically, cannot have pleased him much. Pagani was, in fact, a demanding and refined jurist who, like Filangieri, sought to translate the cultures and principles of modern natural law into positive laws, into an ordered and consistent (above all in logical and rational terms) constitutional project.[22] Compared to members of the *Commission des Onze* who, in the *Déclaration*, had limited themselves to separating rights from duties, he preferred to develop a constitution that was simultaneously shorter and far more articulate. It separated the rights of man from those of the citizen and of the people, following a Lockian contractual scheme opposing natural man to man in civil society. He removed references to the people among the duties he listed, and introduced the absolute novelty of duties for public functionaries. In the history of Southern Italy, which had seen the dominion of the order of the *togati*, such a return to the obligation of a functionary to 'dedicate his talents, his fortune, and his life to the preservation and benefit of the republic' sounded like a sort of final reckoning between that class and the men of the Enlightenment. Closer to home, Filangieri seemed finally to have got the better of Montesquieu. Nevertheless, beyond the theoretical importance of these differences, which would merit their own analysis, there were other and far more decisive divergences from the Thermidorian constitution that are worth examining. For example, the strong focus on the republican spirit, understood as the widest possible participation in the government of the *res publica*, laboriously developed by Enlightenment thinkers in the 1780s, and in particular in book IV of the *Scienza della legislazione*, dedicated to public education.

The Neapolitan constitution is full of pointers in this direction. Pointers, however, that necessitate some further specification to avoid misunderstanding. We know that one of the principal motives for the vigorous opposition of Enlightenment thinkers to Rousseau's political theories lay in their frank aversion to his proposed return to the direct democracy of the ancients.[23] Fiery opinions were expressed on the matter by Carli, Delfico, Grimaldi, and truth be told, even by Filangieri, when he warned of the risks which a misguided form of ancient political liberty, by a dictatorship of the people disguised as a democratic general will ably manoeuvred by demagogues, posed to modern civil liberty. Moreover, opposition to interpreting popular sovereignty in terms of a plebiscite democracy was widespread in European Enlightenment circles in the second half of the eighteenth century.[24] In the second edition of his *Saggi politici*, Pagano emphasized the republican nature of 'representative government… in vast States,' almost as if to seal further the sad warning, of the 1783 first edition, against the dangers of 'pure democracies,' and of a despotic legislative power legitimately exercised, in the name of the sovereign people, against the rights of man.[25] The hard lessons of history had taught – as Francescantonio Grimaldi had constantly repeated in his works, citing episodes from the English Revolution to that of Masaniello – that the dangers of despotism could be manifested by a single person, by a group, but also by part of a multitude. In Naples, the *fin-de-siècle* debate over reforms to public education had quickly turned into considerations concerning the seemingly ever more necessary passage from civil liberty to political liberty, to popular emancipation in all its aspects.[26] The question whether it was best to educate the people or to deceive them, albeit with good intentions, had been fiercely discussed in lodges all over the continent. The solution to the dilemma seemed to have been found, in a republican spirit, in the option of supporting gradual popular emancipation through education. If, in fact, all were equally ready to enjoy civil liberty, all were not ready to assume the responsibilities of political liberty. One thing was the sacrosanct principle of popular sovereignty, its exercise another. In his *Saggi politici*, Pagano had drawn the outcomes of this eighteenth-century Italian debate, insisting on the Enlightenment dogma of human perfectibility, on that 'aptitude for becoming better,'[27] which with time was set to resolve the problem of full and conscious popular participation in the government of the *res publica*. In the *Rapporto*, he yet again questioned the real meaning of the word 'people,' disappointed by the fact that 'we lack, in modern languages, a word to express the notion we wish to designate' and that one therefore had to make do with generic approximations: 'When we say people we mean to speak of that people which is enlightened about its real interests, and not of plebs dull with ignorance and degraded in slavery, or the cankerous aristocratic part.'[28] This was, in other words, about the 'middle order' of which Antonio Genovesi incessantly had spoken about in earlier decades, identifying it as the political and social subject of reference for Enlightenment reforms.[29] Separating the rights of man from those of citizens and of peoples, Pagano sought only and finally to clarify the concrete, constitutional outcomes of this complex question. The principle of political equality, legitimate theoretically also, and above all, in representative governments, had to take the sad reality of the Old Regime into account, as 'In democracies, a man of the infamous plebs can arm himself with consular bundles when he has the courage of a Marius and the enlightenment of a Tullius. But an ignorant pedlar of hams, who is offered the government of Athens, will necessarily lose the republic.'[30] The right to vote could not be indiscriminately granted to all, just as not all could be elected. With the hereditary principle forever demolished, it was necessary to find realistic solutions, criteria aligned with the times, based first of all on the principle of merit, on property and on the census. The people Pagano had in mind consisted of an open class of ever-expanding boundaries, the public spirit of which was to be educated in republican customs. Where the bloody days of the Terror in Paris had taught Thermidorian jurists to quickly backtrack from the Jacobin constitution of 1793 by introducing suffrage based on the census, limiting citizenship, and excluding every dangerous and ambiguous reference to the sovereignty of the people,[31] in Naples the censorial choice and the circumscription of the active and passive electorate emerged almost naturally as a necessary development of the old political project of Italian Enlightenment thinkers, inspired by the idea that a just and fair society able to guarantee the rights of man could only emerge gradually. It is enough to analyze just a few elements of the Neapolitan constitution to prove, beyond any reasonable doubt, the existence of such a strategic design.

In his constitution, Pagano combined restrictions on political liberty with such a renewed and impassioned effort in the field of public education that it would certainly have alarmed the members of the *Commission des Onze*, ready as they were to see the Jacobin spectre everywhere. He accused the Thermidorians of having abandoned every pedagogical intent of educating the masses, circumscribing the few constitutional references in this field – considered so decisive for any future widening of the public sphere – only to 'instruction,' with more care for the 'intellectual than the moral part' of it. In a 'republican spirit,' which he explicitly invoked, the constitution ought instead to dedicate more space to laws encouraging education as well as the customs and practices of social virtues. As Filangieri had explained, the liberty of a people was to be defended by educating said people. 'It is our view,' Pagano commented, 'that the principles of all the laws, and particularly of those which regard education, should be incorporated fully into the constitution. It must contain the seeds of all legislation and must resemble the trunk of a tree, from which the branches marked in its knots sprout.' The establishment of republican theatres, and particularly of the *Collegio dei censori*, in 'imitation of the old republics,' with the task of overseeing customs and public morals (which were 'as cultivated by the ancients as they are neglected by the moderns'), aimed at progressively transforming the plebs into a self-conscious people, and generally overseeing the behaviour of citizens. It was up to the censors, the veritable 'clergy of the fatherland' and ministers of a renewed civil religion, to watch over customs and deprive 'those who did not live democratically of their active or passive civil rights.'[32] Only the people, aware of their rights, but also of their duties of citizenship, held the tremendous power connected with the right of insurrection which the Thermidorian constitution instead had cancelled definitively in fear of the Jacobin rage. Pagano in no way dared follow that road, because doing so would mean abjuring a decisive aspect of the teachings of Locke, of Filangieri, of natural law, and of the American Constitutions which had been subject to such scrutiny and discussion in the Neapolitan English Rite lodges, of which he was a venerable master. It would have signified disavowing his real points of reference, as clearly delineated in his earlier works.[33]

In no way did Pagano feel psychologically dependent on the French constitutions. Conscious of his own international fame as a great jurist, he did not hesitate to alter the tasks and functions which the *Commission des Onze* attributed the French bicameral system. He thus had no qualms, apart from the customary ones dictated by the necessity of not annoying valuable allies, in redefining the fundamental organization of justice provided for by the Thermidorians. This was a delicate sector in which he considered himself, quite rightly, superior to his Transalpine colleagues.[34] Ultimately, it was in the institution of the *Magistratura degli Efori* that his distance from the constitutional model of revolutionary Europe was clearest and most resounding. This was the definitive seal and true cipher of a completely different way of conceiving modern constitutionalism. The Ephors in fact represented the hinge of the 1799 Neapolitan constitution. That supreme tribunal, created for the 'custody of the constitution and of liberty,' really sanctioned the peculiar character of the Neapolitan school of natural law's way of understanding constitutionalism. An interpretation that, for its originality and theoretical robustness, put that school among the high points of Western constitutional history. According to Pagano, the 'addition we made to the French constitution' with the introduction of the Ephors was meant to address, finally, 'that healthy fear which we must have of despotism and of all arbitrary power' that had exhausted late Enlightenment political and legal thought. As Filangieri had explained, English constitutional practice, founded primarily on the automatic equilibrium of contrasting powers, which had so impressed

Montesquieu in the *Esprit des lois*, was deeply unconvincing, dangerous, and presented too many margins of error. Not that relying on the principle of separation to resolve the problem of constitutional guarantees against the usurpation of powers was misguided; quite the contrary. Modern written constitutions justifiably made the effort to specify forms of separation for every occasion. The principle had become an inalienable conquest of legal and political thought. Making it the keystone of a constitution, however, was not enough for Pagano to stop despotism and found a stable order. The largely negative results of the French constitutions would, with time, force jurists to reconsider the question and find other remedies. It was on this basis that he openly criticized the very philosophy of French revolutionary constitutionalism as being too dependent on the at times irreconcilable ideas of Montesquieu and Rousseau. In the Jacobin constitution of 1793, like the Thermidorian one of 1795, the principle of separation had been assumed to be the decisive and identity-defining point of reference, with results that were hardly reassuring. With the Rousseauan reading that prevailed in the 1793 constitution, the solemn proclamation of the division of powers had been unable to block the hegemony of the legislature and its manipulation at the hands of the Committee of Public Safety. In 1795, made wiser by the Terror, and despite the fact that Montesquieu's thesis on the division of powers had been further confirmed and reinforced, things seemed no better; indeed those powers would shortly produce a reciprocal deadlock.[35]

Pagano had first addressed the delicate question of constitutional guarantees in the 1792 second edition of his *Saggi politici*. Though aware that the argument, due to its importance, merited 'an entire book' on its own, he outlined briefly, but with extreme clarity, the essential terms of the problem, examining the different cases in which 'legislative power entirely destroyed executive and judicial power' and the less serious case where the excessive division and the inevitable 'contrast of forces produce[d] inaction.' The solution of engineering the constitution, provided so as to 'walk freely without colliding with the two extremes of the inertia of the social body and the immediate corruption of the established constitution,' was to be formalized in an impartial court:

> Another separate and temporary representative of tribunal power which has neither a legislative, nor judicial, nor executive function, which therefore is not moved by the interest of increasing any of those rights which it does not exercise, nor of executing that usurpation which on others it cannot perform; this tribunal power would be the bulwark of the constitution, the supreme tribunal of powers, the guardian of that line which those who exercise sovereign functions must not cross.[36]

The Tribunal in Rome and the Council of Ephors in Sparta had been vaguely similar institutions in the ancient world. In both cases – Pagano liked to underline[37] – those magistratures acted only against the usurpation of the executive. The idea of a division of powers, however, did not yet exist at the time, while the Tribunal proposed by Rousseau in his *Contrat Social* (which did not even accept the principle of the plurality of sovereign powers) was conceived solely with the objective of defending the primacy of the legislature against authoritarian attempts at government. The body of the Ephors in the Neapolitan constitution was, instead, shaped by very different theoretical considerations, and had very broad and decisive functions. Seven years later, in 1799 (never, as in this case, have dates had such a specific significance), the controversial and turbulent constitutional events in France seemed to have resoundingly vindicated Pagano's *Saggi politici*, which denounced the limitations of a simple division of powers devoid of further fetters. The time had come to dust off those old theories and to transform them into a concrete constitutional project. This is precisely what he did, delineating the rules and foundations of 'a supreme Tribunal which holds the balance of powers and encloses them within their proper boundaries; which, in short, has custody of the Constitution and of liberty. It will make the executive power retreat back into line if it should ever overstep it. It will operate a veto on the legislative body if it should usurp the executive.' One need only glance quickly through the *Progetto* to realize how culturally distant the beliefs of the Neapolitan philosopher were from those of the Parisian lawyers.[38] While the Constitution of the Year III dedicated an entire article, the 22nd of the *Déclaration*, to the principle of the division of powers, making it the true fulcrum of its system, in the Neapolitan constitution that principle seems taken for granted and, certainly not by chance, explicitly recalled in the context of the detailed discussion of the tasks of the Ephorate. A division of powers without a supreme court of constitutional justice capable of imposing abidance made no sense to Pagano whatsoever. The point becomes much clearer when we realize that many across the Alps were beginning to think the same. Today, we know that Sieyès, with his project for a *Jurie constitutionnaire* in Paris in 1795, was not the only one to propose something similar to a modern constitutional court.[39] Many began to recognize that it would not suffice simply to follow the indications of the two great fathers of French constitutionalism, Montesquieu and Rousseau. It was necessary to introduce new mechanisms and institutions to guarantee the constitution. Nevertheless, after a stormy debate, the decision to favour the traditional primacy of the legislature as the source of every legitimacy prevailed yet again. The strongman of the *Commission*, Antoine-Claire Thibaudeau, rejected the hypothesis of the *Jurie constitutionnaire*, peremptorily asking Sieyés who in the end would have controlled the controllers.[40]

It was another way, however, of thinking about politics and the law which was very different from what was emerging in the French revolution that hid behind the proposal for a constitutionalism based on the principle of a supreme court with tasks similar to the body of Ephors. A way of thinking which came from afar and which based itself essentially on the suggestions of natural law and, more specifically, on the unquestioned centrality of the rights of man and the ever clearer necessity of intervening in the potential conflict between the principles of the constitution and those of the nation's sovereignty. Indeed, that radical contraposition, which would mar the nineteenth and large parts of the twentieth century, between the transcendental and Enlightenment conception of law, which put the rights of man above history, and the historicist, romantic and immanent conception of law which instead tied rights to history, to context, and thus directly and without mediation to the legislative sovereignty of peoples and of nations, was beginning to take shape. As we often have stressed, the Neapolitan school was perhaps that which had meditated with greatest rigour on such philosophical and historical questions (just think of the works of Gravina and Vico), by analyzing, with the *Scienza della legislazione*, the nexus between law and politics in the modern world and developing an innovative

Enlightenment interpretation of constitutionalism on the basis of natural law. One of the key authors for the complex Southern-Italian debate was without a doubt John Locke. The ideas of the great English philosopher had been at the centre of passionate discussions since the arrival in Naples of the new *Cappellano maggiore del Regno*, Celestino Galiani, in the 1730s.[41] Antonio Genovesi had reproposed Locke's contractualism, and specifically the fundamental distinction between natural law and positive laws. The former, from which the rights of man drew their legitimacy, remained unchanged throughout time and acted in every place like an eternal rule, binding all legislators and all human beings: 'The Rules that they [the legislators] make for other Mens Actions,' Locke had written, 'must, as well as their own and other Mens Actions "be comfortable to the Law of Nature, i.e. to the Will of God, of which that is a Declaration."'[42] No legislative power could therefore ever go against natural law. Upholding the rights of man even came before the exercise of popular sovereignty. In jurisprudential terms, Filangieri reformulated this political philosophy in terms of positive laws, underscoring the need for all laws, in all fields, to draw always on the principles of natural law. In his *Saggi politici*, Pagano succinctly expressed this conviction, writing that 'the rights of man are chiselled in the hearts of all men; the idea of a moral order is felt by everyone before it is understood.'[43] The pages dedicated by the *Scienza della legislazione* to the magistracy of the *Censore delle leggi* and to the limits of English constitutionalism had finally explained the new role which constitutions were to take on for Enlightenment thinkers, in the form of a rigid written text, of few principles and fundamental laws, which by nature were superior to the ordinary laws of parliament. Pagano went even further in the 1783 first edition of the *Saggi*, where he explained that not all civil laws were legitimate and guarantees of liberty and of rights, and that the problem thus emerged of assuring the legislator's abidance by the principles of the constitution. The great eighteenth-century debate on the disquieting aspects of ancient direct democracy and the hidden dangers in the concept of the general will had, in this respect, been both instructive and greatly alarming.

In the 1799 *Progetto*, the different pieces of the mosaic finally fell into their logical and definitive legal and institutional place, probably owing also to the earlier American examples which had been discussed in newspapers all over Italy. To ensure compliance with the constitution and its consecrating norms and principles which were considered eternal, it was necessary to have a supreme tribunal and judges who were capable of exercising so-called judiciary control over the ordinary laws produced by the legislature. These were the elements (a constitution, a tribunal, and a judge) from which the Body of Ephors was shaped. Its tasks of constitutional justice were connected with the obligation to 'present the legislative body with the abrogation of those laws which are opposed to the principles of the constitution.' Pagano furthermore made the Ephors into watchful and intransigent guardians of the constitution. Theirs was the arduous task of ensuring that it was 'preserved in all its parts,' intervening with executive decrees to reject acts and laws deemed to conflict with constitutional rules and regulations.

Nothing of the kind had ever been pursued in France.[44] In 1795, when some jurists urgently had posed the delicate question of safeguarding the constitution from party passions, the solution had been found in a short and disconcerting phrase in Article 377, the last of the constitution, stating 'The French people entrusts the present constitution to the fidelity of the Legislative body, the Executive directory, the administrators, and the judges; to the vigilance of the fathers of families, to the wives and to the mothers, to the affection of young citizens, to the courage of all Frenchmen.'[45] A stupefyingly naïve formulation which compels us to reflect upon the profound differences between the constitutionalism of the Neapolitan school and that of the Parisian revolutionaries.

Pagano's Enlightenment constitutionalism appeared so rigorous and organic because the underlying political and philosophical vision *was* rigorous and organic. Where possible, the political culture of the Enlightenment should always be distinguished from that of the revolutionaries.[46] The 'great goal' of the constitution was above all, for the men of the Enlightenment, the 'preservation and defence of the natural rights of men reduced in society,' as the *Saggi politici* recited. That constant emphasis on the primacy of rights, as opposed to the Rousseauan emphasis on general will, the primacy of the legislature, and political liberty, and in contrast with the division of powers as a guarantee for civil liberty, made the constitutional politics of Enlightenment thinkers, and in particular of the Neapolitan school, something truly peculiar when compared to the precarious and oscillating constitutionalism of the French revolutionaries. It was in vain that they sought to find points of contact and synthesis between Rousseau and Montesquieu. The logic of rights, coherently applied in light of the principle of equality, had, as we will seek to demonstrate later, such subversive potential as to transform the future of European society radically. Behind the 'peaceful revolution' invoked by Filangieri in the *Scienza della legislazione*, there was more than just the harsh and merciless struggle against despotism, against the old hereditary hierarchies and against the injustices of the Old Regime. There was the concrete republican project for a new just and fair civil society, characterized by the moral and political effort to reduce all forms of inequality to a minimum, without recurring to an impossible return to the political liberty of the ancients or rejecting economic progress and modernity in the way of Rousseau and Mably's followers. Yet, despite the evident cultural differences between the 1799 Neapolitan constitution and the French constitutional tradition, as regards the most strictly juridical aspects of the pioneering works of a great master of legal philosophy like Gioele Solari,[47] Italian historiography has continued to accept Vincenzo Cuoco's tailor-made myth about the Francophile and anti-nationalistic nature of Pagano's work, and more generally of the entire legal and political culture of Enlightenment Italy. The defamatory and not too veiled accusation that this Enlightenment culture betrayed and distanced itself from a presumed national tradition, which was coldly and calculatingly formulated by the intellectuals of the new century, has weighted heavily on the history of modern Italy because it condemned an entire world of men and of ideas to marginality, oblivion, and fundamental contempt. Nonetheless, the accusation is worthy of further analysis, because paradoxically and in contrast, one would like to think, with the ruthless critiques of its most authoritative adversaries, it will allow us to identify the original character of Neapolitan Enlightenment constitutionalism more clearly.

Chapter Nine

VINCENZO CUOCO: THE NATIONAL CRITIQUE OF COSMOPOLITAN ENLIGHTENMENT CONSTITUTIONALISM

Durable constitutions are those which the people themselves form… One must take men as they are and as they forever will be, full of vices, full of errors… I do not believe that the constitution consists in a declaration of the rights of man and of the citizen… The more I reflect on these subjects, the more reasons I find for believing that founding the Neapolitan Republic is nothing but returning things to the old state.

Cuoco, Frammenti di lettere dirette a Vincenzo Russo (1801)

Cuoco has always occupied an important place in the history of Italian political thought over the past two centuries. Indeed, bitter battles have been fought around his *Saggio storico sulla Rivoluzione di Napoli*, contributing considerably to the formation of a historical consciousness for generations of Italians. Every now and then, that extraordinary text is read, appreciated or evaluated negatively, in its entirety or in its specific parts, by moderates and by radicals, by Catholics and by laymen, by democrats and liberals, by fascists and communists. Manzoni, Foscolo, Gioberti, Mazzini, Pisacane, and even Croce and Gentile engaged with, and were often willingly charmed by, Cuoco's critique of the 1799 republicans, which he presented as heroes which were generous but devoid of a real and realistic revolutionary culture. Through the *Saggio storico*, the Republic of 1799, with its terrible conclusion in the bloodbath brought about by the Bourbons and the *sanfedisti*, has in fact become a crucial and structuring event in the history of modern Italy.[1]

Born near Lucera, in Molise, in 1770, Cuoco has always been thought a moderate on the matter, who precociously denounced the myth of revolution from above and identified the first signs of the Italian nation's emerging patriotic spirit. An anti-Jacobin forerunner, he was the scourge of those dangerous dreamers who believed in social palingenesy, ever forgetful as they were of the reality and historical function of the masses. Some commentators have compared him to Burke and to de Maistre, others to Constant and Tocqueville. In the wake of World War II, Croce's epigones heralded Cuoco as the spiritual father of Italian liberal-democratic thought. Gramsci, who admired his genius and considered the *Saggio storico* an impressive document of the victory of the moderates in nineteenth-century Italy, made the concept of a passive revolution developed by Cuoco famous once again, applying it to the Risorgimento. It was, in other words, a fortunate concept which, to no surprise, the Bourbons also adopted with enthusiasm, since it unveiled the Neapolitan revolution's lack of popular support. Finally, Cuoco's continuous reference to the people, to their needs – which the intellectual elites neglected all too often – and to their historical function intrigued people on both the Right and the Left. On the Right, thinkers like Volpe and Gentile saw in it the prophetic call for a fascist nationalization of the masses. On the Left, it was precisely this obsessive and generic appeal to the people which, in the subsequent decades, led authoritative communist intellectuals to stress the concrete revolutionary nature of Cuoco's thought.[2] Serious historiographical reconstructions have appeared in recent years which see in the *Saggio storico* the proposal for a 'constitutional model of liberal monarchy,'[3] of a 'property-based and moderate constitutional liberalism,'[4] and the now debated and debatable hypothesis of a 'Jacobin Cuoco' in the unusual role of partisan of 'democratization'[5] on the peninsula. However, in spite of the proliferation of studies devoted to him, the enigma of Cuoco still remains largely unresolved. Furthermore, the elusive and problematic, not to mention downright contradictory nature of large parts of his thought invites different and antithetical interpretations which have seen him described alternatively as a moderate, a revolutionary, a liberal, democrat, or even a Jacobin. Perhaps what all this primarily and faithfully reflects is the difficulty of pinning down the historical context in which this thought took shape, the tortuous transition of Cuoco's era – an era in which new words and theories transformed themselves all too rapidly into tragically concrete facts, at times changing their original meanings entirely.

One must never forget that in 1800, when the *Saggio* saw its definite draft, Europe was everywhere aflame and history seemed, with its continuous frenetic proposal of new and unexpected scenarios, quite simply to have gone mad. Italians, who had lived in peace for almost a century, were dumbstricken to find themselves once again faced with old fears bound not only to wars and foreign invasions, but to something unexpected and disquieting, connected with the social breakdown of the Old Regime and the collapse of the old monarchies. The incredible, momentary end of the Pope's theocratic, centuries-old power, after he was chased from republican Rome, shook and alarmed all souls. The violent confrontation between patriots and insurgents, the horrible Bourbon and *Sanfedist* massacres in the *Mezzogiorno*, with their atrocious episodes of cannibalism, had opened deep wounds and lacerations destined to perpetuate themselves, taking on ideological significance and fuelling inextinguishable hatreds. Modern Italy, the Italy in which we still live today, was born in blood and the most incendiary conflict. The time was at hand for a reckoning and a first painful toll of the century of Enlightenment, which, opened in the intent of emancipating and laying the groundwork for public and private happiness, had instead ushered in a distressing age of endemic violence and civil war. The reformism which in effect had paved the way for revolution, that cosmopolitanism which had been proven wrong by the fermenting reality of national instincts, the solemn declaration of the rights of man, which was reduced to waste paper and proved incapable of holding back either the Jacobin terror or the war in the Vendée, that reason mocked by power, ever more accompanied by irrational concessions and by primitive forms of belonging, constituted the inevitable points of reference for the theoretical reflection of those who, like Vincenzo Cuoco, set out to reflect upon the bitter fate of his unfortunate generation. A young man in his thirties at the time he wrote the *Saggio storico*, he incarnated the new revolutionary culture that had taken shape after 1789. It was a complex and magmatic culture in continuous transformation, which brought together the results of the reformist influences of the Enlightenment and the traditions and the quotidian experiences of the Old Regime, apparently irreconcilable authors like Rousseau and Montesquieu, and mentor figures which had always been in profound disagreement such as Galanti and Filangieri, finally called to justice before the implacable tribunal of history. Written almost in one go, the *Saggio* is really a collection of many things: the political manifesto of a generation, the direct expression of a new culture, a subtle and ingenious historical analysis of an event, a dutiful testimony for posterity of a tragedy suffered by friends as well as military and political soulmates, but also a touching and lucid autobiographical document of a young man overcome by uncontrollable events. And it is precisely this last aspect that deserves special attention.

To this end, scarce use has always been made of the few of Cuoco's letters which remain from the period before the arrival of the French in Naples. They tell us about a young man who his teacher Galanti did not hesitate to define 'very slovenly and indolent and slothful,' above all receptive to female charms and not at all devoured by political passion or in any way interested in 'news from France.' The letters to his father reveal a daily attempt to insert himself, without trauma or criticism, in the traditional world of the 'lawyers' and the petty local nobility which always had been hostile to the capital. 'I have taken up the profession,' he wrote in November 1790, 'of being a *paglietta* [in the Neapolitan dialect, a lawyer of dubious morality and competence, astute and hair-splitting]… I am going around acquiring small shops everywhere.' The revolutionary 'whirlpool' had, effectively, taken him by surprise, changing his destiny in ways against which he could do nothing. In a letter by Cuoco dated December 1800, this sense of impotence in the face of events is described with words of great bitterness:

> If the King of Naples had not, without my knowing anything, declared war on the French; if the French had not prevailed over the King of Naples, and then had not abandoned that country which they had wanted to free; if I had not fallen into the error of believing that every good citizen should love his fatherland whatever its form of government; I would be in the bosom of my family, among my friends, occupied with the duties of my profession, enjoying the sweet warmth of the most delightful climate in Europe.[6]

The *Saggio storico* effectively reflected the consternation and fear of a man who, contrary to his own wishes, had found himself a protagonist in a revolution which was neither willed nor planned. The use of the concept of 'passive revolution' to describe the Neapolitan events was primarily shaped by personal experience – his own and those of thousands of young men forced to take sides. It is no coincidence that this idea had circulated in moderate circles of Italy for years during the republican triennial.[7] Never would Cuoco have shared in the heroic fury of his companion in misfortune and in exile, Francesco Lomonaco, who in those same years published the *Rapporto al cittadino Carnot*, an incendiary text which presented the Neapolitan events as an 'active revolution,' a great popular war against 'cannibal beast' kings.[8] Hence the need to clarify, without being overwhelmed by emotions, the logical causes of, and identify those responsible for, the tragedy of 1799.

The culprits were certainly not the so-called 'republican' patriots, but rather the Bourbon monarchy and the French.[9] The drama had begun with the first repercussions in Naples of the news arriving from France. Fearing contagion, the court, and in particular the prime minister John Acton and Queen Maria Carolina of Austria, had unleashed a veritable preventive counterrevolution, a ferocious repression of the Enlightenment clubs of 'philosophers' and the most lively forces of the nation. Any sign of sympathy for the events in France, any form of criticism that previously had been tolerated, was snuffed out by the omnipotent and ferocious *Giunta di Stato*, which was nothing but a secular form of 'State Inquisition.' In Naples they even prohibited periodicals. A tremendous spiral of trials and conspiracies had begun to poison and bloody public life in the Kingdom of Naples, fuelling a climate of reciprocal diffidence. 'One wanted blood and one got it… The nation was besieged by an infinite number of spies and informers. All the castles and all the gaols were full of miserable people.'[10] An incredible misunderstanding was at the origin of all these 'horrors,' a clamorous blunder (nonetheless bound to give life to an extremely popular interpretation even in subsequent centuries) committed by the court, but also by many intellectuals and authoritative contemporary observers, who seemed convinced that ideas, books, philosophers, and determined, self-conscious elites really could bring about a revolution from above. Such a hypothesis was stupefying and absurd for Cuoco, who attributed direct responsibility to the Parisian revolutionaries and to their propaganda, to the mystifying and misguiding ceremonies by which they consecrated people like Rousseau and Voltaire in the *Panthéon* as saints and fathers of the revolution. In reality, Cuoco explained, 'the French deluded themselves on the nature of their revolution and believed what was a consequence of the political circumstances of their nation to be the consequence of philosophy.'[11] In the language of modern-day historiography, he affirmed that it had not been the Enlightenment thinkers and philosophers to bring about the revolution; if anything such thinkers had been its greatest victims, according to an interpretative framework which would be elaborated on by many scholars in later years, and particularly by Madame de Staël in the 1800 volume *De la literature considerée dans ses rapports avec les institutions sociales.*[12]

Like many in Naples (just think of his master Galanti), Cuoco was absolutely convinced that people, not philosophers, brought about real revolutions, and people only acted to satisfy concrete, bodily needs – certainly not for ideals, let alone for 'rational reasons.'[13] Revolutions always had real institutional, social, and political causes. They were shaped from below, almost naturally, by long-term phenomena, by the deep and structural movements of communities and of nations, not by the hand of utopian men of letters. The French revolution, for example, was the classical outcome of the long-term struggles between 'the different estates of the kingdom.' Details like 'the imbecility of the king, the even more imbecile haughtiness of Antoinette and Artois, the ambition of the wicked and inept Orleans, the public debt, Necker, the assembly of notables and the Estates general' were nothing but superficial events, 'occasional causes.' The true 'revolutionary material, accumulated over many centuries,' was far more ancient and substantial.[14] France had looked much like a volcano ready to erupt for years, since by isolating itself without taking sides, the monarchy had left room for the ever more ferocious war between the ancient feudal nobility, the new nobles of talent and wealth, the Gallic clergy, which thought itself independent of both king and pope, and the increasingly more oppressed third estate. The failure of every kind of reform and the despotic sort of absolutism launched by Richelieu, and which Louis XIV, far from siding with the people against the barons, had transformed into a system of government, had inaugurated the revolutionary season by altering the delicate equilibriums established by the kingdom's ancient material constitution. Finally the *philosophes*, having become a powerful social group, had amplified and aggravated the situation, placing themselves in the service of the 'real interests of the classes.' Their responsibility lay in having transformed the 'principles of reform,' necessary in a France tormented by 'infinite abuses to be reformed,' into fantastic, 'abstract' projects, into utopias and social reveries worthy of the 'most abstruse metaphysics,' ending in the dis-education of entire generations. The vindication of the natural rights of the French had been distorted and presented as a universal question regarding humanity in its entirety. 'What was simply their own invention,' Cuoco ironized, 'they believed to be the rights and laws of all men. Anyone who compares the declaration of the rights of man made in America to that made in France will find that the first spoke to the senses, the second wanted to speak to reason; the French is the algebraic formula of the American.'[15]

The situation in Naples was different. Here, Enlightenment thinkers had never dreamt of hypothesizing something similar to a world turned upside down: 'Our philosophy was not incendiary, and procured, without pomp, the good of the fatherland.' Responsibility for the climate of tension and undeniable disquiet in *fin-de-siècle* political life, in the capital as well as in the provinces, was if anything due entirely to the monarchy and the disastrous politics of reform inaugurated by Maria Carolina and by Ferdinand IV in the 1780s. The Bourbon reforms of Charles III, in the first half of the eighteenth century, had aimed at healing ancient injustices resulting from the great power of the feudal barons, bringing to the fore the best forces of the Neapolitan nation, while always operating with caution, gradualness and with a realistic approach to the ancient equilibriums of power in the natural constitution of the Realm. The 'stupidly wicked' court of Ferdinand IV had, instead, distinguished itself by an impressive sequence of errors. Abruptly accelerating the centralizing and absolutist project of the monarchy, Acton, who knew 'neither the nation nor how things were,' had transformed reformism into despotism, a free nation of happy prospects into a sort of chaotic barracks in the hands of foreigners. The new politics of prestige and of power, and the need to find resources to compete with the other monarchies of Europe, had led to chaotic and irrational financial reforms, to the pretentious and extremely costly construction of a new navy and a national army, and to a debatable rethinking of the educational system. In achieving its plans, the government seemed designed on purpose to arouse 'the poisoning of the national spirit,' humiliating the autonomy of local forces and the prestige of ancient magistratures, directly fuelling corruption. 'The entire Kingdom of Naples tends towards despotism, that is to the concentration of all branches of administration in one hand. But this hand, not being able to do everything on its own, by necessity had to rely on servants that were not loyal, and the nation then fell into that deplorable state in which employment is not for the honour of the fatherland, but for the right to plunder it.'[16] According to Cuoco, the progressive political divestiture of the authority of local notables through the growing control of the provinces and the municipalities of the kingdom, which so greatly had annoyed important sectors of the legal profession directly affected, was certainly nothing but a classic example of metaphysical, abstract reformism, thought out in the salons of the capital – a dangerous politics come down from above, able to undermine social order and to deny those of majority age the very ethics of individual responsibility. This was a path down which the venerable constitutional equilibrium of the kingdom could not but emerge in pieces, thus laying the groundwork for the crisis at the end of the century and the tragedy of 1799.

Offended by a court thought to be in the hands of foreigners, Cuoco infused the pages of the *Saggio* with localistic biases and provincial patriotism, delineating a catastrophic image of the 1780s that would fuel the so-called 'black legend' of *fin-de-siècle* Bourbon reformism. This legend would quickly transform itself into a stainless, rock-hard historiographical paradigm which today remains hale and hearty also because, independently of the truth, or lack of it, in those virulent accusations (which are not always sustainable in light of modern research[17]), that paradigm faithfully reflects a vast and deeply grounded way of representing reality in large parts of Southern Italian public opinion. To give an idea, Niccolò Fraggianni, the head of the *togati*, would probably have subscribed willingly to it were he alive.

For Cuoco, the monarchy, insensitive to real national interests, had not hesitated for a moment in abandoning the cautious and valuable neutrality of Tanucci's era, bringing the Bourbon state into a European conflict for purely dynastic reasons. It had been a terrible error to wage war against France in a moment of grave economic and financial crisis. The French wanted peace and one had replied with war. The humiliating subsequent military defeat, the court's hasty escape from the capital upon the arrival of French troops, and the anarchic and bloody revolt of the Neapolitan *lazzaroni* unleashed by the court against the hated foreigners, had forced the most responsible part of the capital's population to establish the republic. It had been created almost by necessity to avoid worse things, to guarantee a modicum of legality, and to keep the social order under control. 'Some *republicans* (though at that time anyone in Naples who had property and tradition was a republican) prevented greater evils by mixing themselves with the people again and faking the same sentiments to direct them.'[18] The contradictions of this delicate situation, however, lay in wait just around the corner. It was not understood quickly enough – Cuoco explained, launching his impeccable reproach against the way in which republicans faced the revolutionary phase – that 'our revolution was a passive revolution in which the only means of success was that of winning over public opinion. But the views of the patriots and of the people were not the same. They had different ideas, different customs, and even two different languages.'[19] Instead of seeking popular consensus, of engaging in politics with moderation, realistically, respecting the exigencies, the customs, and the needs of the nation, moving from the bottom up, from the provinces and the municipalities, reactivating ancient institutions and traditional forms of organizing social accord, one had preferred the model of revolution and 'democratization' from above with the help of a foreign army.

Next came the mistaken reforms imposed by the centre on the provinces. The opportunity immediately to create a national republican army independent of the French was rejected. To mobilize the militants it was believed that the Enlightenment social models of patriotic societies would need to be adopted instead of taking to the streets ('a true patriot does not waste time chattering in salons'). These incredible errors were paid for in blood and with defeat. 'The mania of wanting to reform everything brings with it counter-revolution.'[20] 'The very excess of the enlightened thinkers, which surpassed the experience of the age, made them believe it to be easy what was actually impossible given the state in which the masses found themselves,'[21] declared Cuoco, adding 'Here is the secret of revolutions: to know what the people want and to do it; then they will follow.' 'We always return to the same principle: more was sought done than what the people wanted done, and a step back ought to have been taken.'[22] With the military defeat of the French and the destruction of the patriots by the *sanfedisti* and their allies, the drama of the Neapolitan Republic played itself out in just five months.

The revenge of those loyal to the Bourbon monarchy was terrible and inhuman. Large parts of the governing class, the best part of the nation, were exterminated. Summary trials, hangings, all kinds of violence and sentences to exile were legion. Neither women nor children were spared. 'The product of four centuries has been destroyed in a moment,' Cuoco wrote in the *Saggio*, dedicating pages and pages to the matter, which deservedly have become famous for their extraordinary civic passion, quivering with indignation and anger against the cynicism and hypocrisy of Cardinal Ruffo and the 'cowardice of Nelson,' who did not move a finger in the face of such atrocities. The Neapolitan intellectual world was left in pieces. By following the example of the French revolution, doors to tragedy had been thrown open and 'the false ideas which our men made of it have greatly contributed to our malaise.'[23] That revolution should never have been taken as an example, because it was entirely different from the Neapolitan one. It had 'a legal origin which was lacking in ours,' Cuoco thought; it was born from the convocation of the Estates General and had developed, maintaining its goal of 'remedying the ills of the nation,' until the Convention and the proclamation of the republic in 1792, legitimating itself, according to the concept of constitutional legality enunciated by Jean-Louis de Lolme in his celebrated *Constitution de L'Angleterre*, through an appeal to the ancient natural constitution of the kingdom. Only after the king's execution (a horrible gesture, but which still enjoyed 'wide popular consensus because the king deliberately had broken the oath which bound him constitutionally to the French people'), and then with Robespierre and the Terror, did every form of legality come to an end. From that moment on, 'ideas had reached their furthermost extreme and had to retreat. More had been reformed than what the people wanted.' 'In France, what had begun with *moderate maxims* had become *exaggerated*.' Against the 'beyond revolutionary [*oltrerivoluzionario*]' Jacobin model which aimed at the *ex novo* construction of a regime radically different from the past, Cuoco contrasted his personal conception of a legitimate revolution that, being moderate, was capable of restoring natural social equilibriums, traditional liberties and the legality of the Old Regime which had been violated by despotism. 'The system of the moderates,' for which he always showed his preference, 'brought things back to their natural state, and did not give them importance beyond what the people themselves did; thus its rigour and its sweetness were the rigour and sweetness of the people.'[24] Too little thought has been given to the fact that the concepts of Old and New Regime do not exist in Cuoco's political and constitutional language.[25] He held that, among the various ways of understanding the French Revolution during the Neapolitan Republic, the Jacobin model, *dirigiste*, centralizing, authoritarian in its pedagogical vocation, had won out over 'moderatism,' which instead supported the nation's real interests; the people were not satisfied, because they considered it the only source of legitimacy and guidance in the struggle. The feudal system, understood by everyone as unfair and oppressive, had not been dismantled in haste, while religious reforms had been imposed which were entirely extraneous to the traditions and customs of Southern Italians. The consequences were terrible. And it was all because of an old limitation and an original defect in the intellectual life of eighteenth-century Naples, which always had privileged the 'culture of the few,' of the elites, of salons and lodges, elaborating their own analyses 'on foreign models'[26] without ever caring to forge a national culture able to bridge the gap between high and low.

Examining the deep intellectual causes of the defeat, and even defending the good faith of the republicans, Cuoco ultimately vilified that patriotism, veined with cosmopolitan tensions, of Neapolitan Enlightenment thinkers who, like Genovesi, Filangieri, and Pagano, had always meditated on the problems of Southern Italy in light of natural law, of the modern theory of the rights of man and of all men whatever their nationality. Their generous universalist vision was, in this way, artfully banned and denounced as an equally banal and dangerous concession to foreign fashions. The cosmopolitanism of the Neapolitan Enlightenment tradition, which at first had been absolved of the terrible imputation of having caused the revolution, was now maliciously accused of not having been able to steer it, however extraneous it was to the spirit of the nation, in the people's real interest. To explain all this better, Cuoco addressed the issue directly in a piece written for the occasion, included at the end of his volume, in which he sharply criticized the intellectual roots, as well as the institutional and political conclusions, of what we have defined the end point of the Italian Enlightenment: Francesco Mario Pagano's 1799 project for a Neapolitan constitution.

The actual significance of the *Frammenti di lettere dirette a Vincenzio Russo*, the letters which contain these criticisms, has been discussed at length by Italian historians. It probably represents something other than a systematic and brilliant demolition of Enlightenment constitutionalism in the name of the new historicist and liberal constitutional thought emerging at the time. Included, certainly not by chance, by Cuoco as an appendix to the *Saggio storico sulla rivoluzione* in both editions, those of 1801 and 1806, the *Frammenti*, the absolute centrality of which can no longer be doubted for the book's general structure, acquired all their strength and fascination precisely by connecting themselves organically to the most original results of the dense previous pages, where the causes of the 1799 tragedy had been investigated, and direct and indirect responsibilities had been attributed. This rhetorical expositive structure, a well studied literary invention, vigorously affirms both its contingent nature as a document of political struggle in the context of the second *Republica Cisalpina* and the more general point of view of a text purposefully laid bare to decide the fate of what had become an inevitable generational and cultural confrontation.

By openly challenging the septuagenarian Pagano, it is important to note that Cuoco, then in his thirties, not only gave a voice to the youth,[27] whose education had largely taken place after 1789, in a convulsed and contradictory phase in the intellectual life of the *Mezzogiorno* dominated by the merciless rule of the revolutionary events, but also connected, ideally, and it could not be otherwise, with ancient masters and specific interpretations of 1780s Enlightenment reformism. Today, we know the important role played in Cuoco's development by Giuseppe Maria Galanti,[28] who, along with Francescantonio Grimaldi, had meditated on the necessity of re-launching the teachings of Machiavelli for the construction of a modern science of man, and on the political need to think realistically and empirically, privileging facts, the study of power relationships and the importance of customs, of history and of traditions; in short, to privilege the analysis of what *is* over what *ought to be*.

The moderate stream of the Enlightenment, which had conquered large parts of the legal order and the provincial notables who were hostile to the absolutist reformism of the Bourbon court, had always strongly criticized the utopian and abstract thinking of Pagano and Filangieri, deemed metaphysical and unrealistic. Cuoco was fully aware of this age-old struggle between moderates and radicals which prematurely had opened a rift in *fin-de-siècle* reformism. His *Frammenti* were, in this sense, configured also, and above all, as an irrevocable reckoning of those two spirits of the Neapolitan Enlightenment. The bloody revolutionary events and the crude lessons of history had probably convinced him of the absolute truth of Galanti's teachings. In his eyes, the eudemonism of the late eighteenth century seemed dead and buried in the war-torn Europe of those years. Besides, who in Italy could still long for the social dreams and utopias, however reasonable, proposed by the heirs of Antonio Genovesi in the face of the horrible events of the Terror, or when confronted with the agonizing sight of the gallows erected in Naples to execute Mario Pagano and an entire generation of republican and radical Enlightenment thinkers?

Nevertheless, precisely because of those heroic deaths and the myth of the patriotic and republican martyr to which it immediately gave rise, Cuoco was well aware of just how vigorous and prestigious the grip of that world was, with its late-Enlightenment reformist values and ideals, on the intellectual and political groups of the peninsula. During the so-called revolutionary triennial, from 1796 to 1799, the newborn Italian republics had almost competed against each other to republish new editions of the *Scienza della legislazione*. In Venice in 1796–7, in Genoa in 1798, in Leghorn in 1799, and finally in Milan, beginning in 1800, Filangieri's work had powerfully been brought back to life and diffused wherever possible. Research on these issues has only just begun. Sadly, we know practically nothing about these important editions, their circulation and their use in the numerous constitutional circles emerging across Italy.[29] Far from investigating the fates of Enlightenment reformers engaged in the revolutionary process launched by 'news from France,' Italian historians have, in wake of World War II, privileged a reconstruction of that crucial period in the country's history which is coloured by the blindingly ideological and teleological light of the French Revolution and by its interpretative categories, which artificially were applied beyond the Alps without any respect for the autonomous cultural identity of eighteenth-century Italy. Had things been done differently, we might now have known far more about these things. The political struggle in Milan, in the year IX of the republic, for example, which saw constitutional circles engaged with re-establishing the second Cisalpine Republic, and where Cuoco published his *Saggio storico*, would not seem to us like yet another French-styled conflict between so-called local Jacobins and the enemies of Robespierre and the Directory, but something more complex, which took account of the burdensome presence of Napoleonic troops and simultaneously made use of formulas and representations of the Transalpine debate to decide ancient cultural, social, and political diatribes of evidently national origins.[30] In short, rather than being interpreted as the umpteenth Italian chapter of the more general European history of the French Revolution, Cuoco's *Frammenti* is far more telling when read as an impressive document of the ruthless political struggles of a new generation. A generation which had brought to definitive fruition the initial forms of eighteenth-century political realism and moderation in the raw school of revolutionary culture, against the tradition of Enlightenment reformers represented by the likes of Genovesi, Pagano, Filangieri, Beccaria, and Verri.

Not by chance, in the contemporary views of exiled survivors on the outcomes of the Neapolitan Republic, the legacy of the past and the projects for future recovery were inevitably intertwined, giving birth to a debate destined profoundly to mark successive events in Italian political history. In the Milan of the second Cisalpine Republic, where many exiles had come together, the confrontation vigorously developed precisely around the contents of the new Milanese constitution until 1803, when a presumed anti-French conspiracy put an end to the frenetic activity of the patriots, definitively opening the way for the oppressive Napoleonic season.[31] The prestige and authority of the teachings of Pagano, Filangieri, Beccaria and more generally of the Enlightenment tradition had until that point been undisputed. The first of these, particularly after his cruel execution in Piazza Mercato in Naples, was then considered the venerated head of the republicans. And it was in Milan that his *Saggi politici* had been republished immediately and diffused. As a sign of respect and admiration for his real talent as a jurist, the Cisalpine government tasked Ludovico Valeriani in the first months of 1800 with editing the re-edition of the *Considerazioni sul processo criminale*, and with administering its widespread distribution to the judges of the departments.[32] In the *Rapporto al cittadino Carnot*, launching a clear signal about the future plans for political struggle of the patriotic and republican front, Lomonaco did not hesitate to define the constitutional project of Mario Pagano a 'masterpiece on politics.'[33] To accompany yet another reprinting of the *Scienza della legislazione*, the same Lomonaco published, in Milan in 1803, a short *Vita di Gaetano Filangieri* which concluded by affirming 'If this great man had continued to live, what services would he have rendered his fatherland during the past catastrophe? Perhaps the heads of so many virtuous men would not have dangled from the gallows because of English perfidy; perhaps now we would not taste all the bitterness of exile.'[34] The Enlightenment tradition's mortgage on future developments in Italy's political struggle were, in short, clearly delineated and present in the Milanese debates. That the constitutional philosophy of the Neapolitan school of natural law exercised such unquestionable appeal among contemporaries is testified to, for example, by Francesco Reina's 1801 *Progetto di costituzione per la Repubblica Cisalpina*. Reina, in fact, gave pride of place to the very same magistracy of Ephors so dear to Pagano.[35]

Cuoco's *Frammenti* are a decisive chapter in this political and constitutional confrontation. Those penetrating pages, purposefully inserted as an appendix to emphasize and delineate the content of the *Saggio storico*, represent the first important text of the modern counter-Enlightenment critique to appear on the peninsula; many others would follow in the course of the nineteenth century. Beyond the ceremonious respect Cuoco conspicuously and continuously displayed for his more famous adversary, purposefully selected to amplify the impact of his message, he was fully aware of participating in a great debate which could lionize him and give voice to the moderate wing of Italian patriotism, which had never looked upon the so-called reasonable utopias of Filangieri's followers with great sympathy. To that end, he armed himself with all the weapons of propaganda and of rhetoric to mercilessly demolish Enlightenment constitutionalism. He did not even hesitate, as we will see, to mystify blatantly and maliciously distort the thought of Mario Pagano. In any case the latter would neither be able to prove him wrong or to reply.[36]

Cuoco's constitutional philosophy was clearly delineated in the first *Frammento*. With pride, the author claimed its originality: 'I do not know what you will think of these ideas. They are not the ideas of everyday constitutionalists; perhaps they are nobody's ideas. What does it matter? They are mine, and I think they are confirmed by the experience of all centuries.'[37] In reality, though the ideas were indeed not very topical, they were not that original either. Their core dug its roots in the so-called constitutionalism of the Old Regime, revisited and reinterpreted in light of the American and French revolutions. If anything, their originality lay entirely in the brilliant way in which venerable questions, concepts, and terms were recombined in a modern language, accounting for changes that had occurred in the meantime. More or less self-consciously, and effectively taking a position in favour of the theses of the parliamentarians, Cuoco relaunched the debate begun in the 1770s in Paris between Le Paige and Mably, and which had then reappeared in the initial work of the National Assembly charged with '*fixer la constitution*,' with regards to the presence, or lack of it, of something similar to a constitution in France in the preceding centuries. Le Paige had responded affirmatively, and on that answer he created a solid theoretical base for vindicating the positive role of parliaments and intermediary bodies in safeguarding liberty in the face of monarchical despotism. Mably had instead denied the existence of a real constitution since the French people had never been able to express a constant political will to that purpose. That important debate had, among other things, marked the definitive abandonment, by a vast sector of the Enlightenment, of Montesquieu's theses in favour of the English model and his conception of a constitution as a historical product, a nation's and a people's political way of *being*. Montesquieu's teachings were replaced by the arguments of those, like Vattel, Rousseau, or the same Mably, who had instead underlined the voluntary and entirely political character of a constitutional text. The American Revolution had further deepened the divide between these two interpretations. In his *Rights of Men*, Paine even denied the existence of a constitution in Great Britain. A few years earlier, Filangieri had explicitly called for a profound review on the example set by the rigid American model. As we have seen, the *Scienza della legislazione* was conceived in Naples systematically to fight those lawyers who, headed by Niccolò Fraggianni, hid behind a mythical and secular 'fundamental constitution' of the kingdom to block the absolutist and centralizing reformism of the Bourbon monarchy. As an alternative to the constitutionalism of the Old Regime, respectful as it was of the *consensus gentium*, of the balance of power which naturally developed over time, Filangieri invoked the necessity of a new juridical science based on principles, on *demonstratio*, and on the *ought* of natural law theorized by Enlightenment thinkers. In his *Saggi politici*, Pagano had insisted strongly on the right of people to claim constituent power and adopt, as a concrete act of political will, a written constitution able to establish a modern government of laws and the primacy of the principle of legality. Cuoco found all of this wrongheaded. The *Contrat social*'s celebrated passages on the figure of the legislator, defined an 'extraordinary man,' seemed to him both dangerous and absurd. It was no coincidence that, following the indications of Rousseau and Mably, the French had already produced three constitutions, one worse than the other. Montesquieu, Le Paige, Fraggianni, and his own master Galanti, would never have dared to subordinate the historical and juridical nature of a constitution, built naturally over the centuries, in favour of an entirely political interpretation, as Filangieri and Pagano joined Rousseau and the Americans in doing. Opening the *Frammenti*, Cuoco had written tersely

> I have little faith in constitutions which have been dictated by force. Whether this force is that of a conqueror disposing of a hundred thousand bayonets, or of an assembly of philosophers, who with the help of a favourable prevention force upon a people a consensus which they do not understand, is of little importance. In the first case one does violence to the will, in the second to the intellect. Durable constitutions are those which the people themselves form. But this people, you say, do they not speak? It is true; but while they are silent, everything speaks for them: their ideas speak for them, their prejudices, their needs. Why have a people ever risen up in revolution? Well, the object for which a people have risen up must be the only one to be reformed. If you wish to touch the rest, you will offend the people unnecessarily.[38]

Moderation, in short, first of all meant respect for tradition and the refusal to take recourse to an artificial and omnipotent constituent power of the people, a people manipulated by 'philosophers' who were continually called into question and repeatedly mocked for their dangerous abstractness. Yet again, the legitimacy of political action in light of the classic reference to the *consensus gentium* returned to the forefront, masked, however, in this case by the continuous and obsessive recourse to the new keyword of post-revolutionary politics: people. In this way, the *consensus gentium* of seventeenth-century legal and political thought shed its skin principally to become a respect for popular will as expressed in the customs and long-term history of nations. The French Revolution had been legitimate up to the point where it restored ancient equilibriums disturbed by the king's despotism and by the abuses of some classes by others. Analogously, a constitution was such, and could be retained legitimate, only if respectful of the history, traditions, customs, and balance of power of a people, its very way of existing politically across the centuries. As Montesquieu, Bolingbroke, De Lolme, Blackstone, and Burke had explained, eulogizing the English constitutional model, laws fully revealed their effectiveness above all when they reflected the history and real needs of a nation. 'Constitutions are like clothes: it is necessary that every individual, that every age of an individual, has its own,' Cuoco wrote in agreement with those authors. The same Vico, the mentor of mentors which he held very dear, had recommended always respecting history rather than following Descartes in his polemic, in the name of the primacy of an abstract reason derived from the models of scientific research, against the *conensus gentium*: one should always follow 'nature rather than a system.' The people were not to be artificially educated and emancipated, like Enlightenment thinkers preached, but if anything listened to and respected as they *are* by nature and history. The cosmopolitanism and legal universalism of the *ought* advocated in the *Scienza della legislazione* claimed the impossible if it really thought to overthrow the logics of the Old Regime through constitutionalism and the despotism of the laws. 'Wanting to reform everything is the same as wanting to destroy everything. Wanting to imagine a constitution to serve wise men is the same as imagining a constitution for those who do not need it.' Constitutions must be made 'for men as they are and as they forever will be, full of vices, full of errors,'[39] Cuoco confirmed, highlighting his membership of that Neapolitan school of political realism which had found in Grimaldi its most recent interpreter and in Machiavelli the true founder of a bitter and negative political anthropology.

With the constant reference to principles and reason instead of customs and history, to the objective relations of power, Enlightenment constitutionalism had fuelled social dreams and given free rein to dramatic and uncontrollable situations like the Neapolitan Revolution of 1799. 'Our philosophers, dear friend, are often deluded by the idea of something excellent which is the worst enemy of the good…; the excellent is not made for man.' Sarcastically, Cuoco felled that idea of the perfectibility of man which Genovesi, Filangieri, and Pagano had placed at the foundations of the entire political and social edifice of Enlightenment thought: 'Oh! Forgive me. I did not remember that I was writing to he who, in the wake of the good memory of Condorcet, believes infinite perfectibility to be possible in a finite being like man. Forgive a wretched ignoramus of his ancient errors: work to make us angels, and then we will found Saint-Just's republic.'[40] Feigning to forget the peculiar natural law characteristics of Neapolitan constitutional thought which we have emphasized, as well as the cosmopolitan character of the *fin-de-siècle* republican patriotism developed by Enlightenment thinkers, Cuoco openly accused Pagano of having made a constitution which was 'too French and insufficiently Neapolitan,'[41] of having constructed a wrong-headed, abstract text that was profoundly alien to the history and public spirit of the southern Italian people; a text which mirrored and further confirmed the errors committed during the tragic five months of the Republic. Today, we know that Cuoco's accusations were more or less ungenerous, mystifying, imbued with broad, malicious concessions to the political propaganda of the moment. But then, in the climate of those years, which everywhere saw the growing resentment of Italians towards the imperialist politics of the *Grande Nation*, they were truly grave accusations, destined to weigh heavily on Italy's future history.[42]

Beyond their propagandistic mystifications, perhaps the true impact and fascination of the *Frammenti*, lay above all in their organic presentation as a radical alternative to Enlightenment constitutionalism. With respect to the crucial themes of sovereignty and representation, Cuoco fully demonstrated the efficiency of his constitutional philosophy based on the primacy of history and the realistic respect for the political reality of a people as they *are*, providing practical solutions compared to the rationalist *ought* of Enlightenment thinkers. 'We have in our nation,' he explained, 'the best basis for a republican government, an ancient basis, known and dear to the people, and raised on that basis the edifice of the sovereignty of the people would perhaps be organized better than elsewhere.'[43] This gave rise to the at once disconcerting and suggestive proposal of returning, through a Rousseauan direct democracy, to the venerable and glorious municipalism of the Old Regime, which for centuries had underpinned one of the pillars of the institutional and political system of the Neapolitan kingdom. Those same figures of Mably and Rousseau, who had brought to light the dangerous principles of Enlightenment constitutionalism, had now become a precious theoretical point of reference in the polemic with Pagano and the advocates of a centralized representative democracy. This should come as no surprise though. The political culture of the revolution, moulded primarily by practices rather than coherent political discourses, presented continually changing symbolic forms, representations, and languages, precisely through these unexpected and contradictory combinations of old and new, conservatism and innovation, passionate declarations of principle and realistic concessions to traditional interests and powers.[44]

In the preceding pages of the *Saggio storico sulla rivoluzione*, Cuoco had demonstrated the grave responsibilities of so-called enlightened absolutism, willed by the Bourbon monarchy in alliance with philosophers, in bringing about the serious crises at the end of the century. Beyond the momentary alliances, he astutely noted the substantial strategic continuity between the reformist programme of the Enlightenment thinkers, from the years of Ferdinand IV to the arrival of the French, and the five months of republican government administered by Filangieri's students. Since the 1780s, the equilibrium of the ancient natural constitution of the Kingdom of Naples had been violated by the centralizing politics of the crown; the provincial notables had been subjected to the reformist will of the infamous *Consiglio delle Finanze* animated by philosophers, determining that dangerous 'discouragement of the nation' and the birth of 'a frivolous mania for foreign fashions' which were to be counted among the principal causes of the revolution. In his constitutional project, Pagano had reproposed the very same form of centralized state which had served Acton to dismantle the system of local powers, though in a republican regime it was meant to democratize the provinces. That project, which combined representative democracy and a form of statehood so similar to absolutism, nonetheless definitively shed light on – in the eyes of large swathes of patriotic moderates – the authoritarian bonds and pedagogical intents of a constitutional philosophy which did not limit itself to guaranteeing individual liberty, but aspired to guide, from above, a process of emancipation from the subversive ends of the Old Regime. Cuoco gave voice to those who refused to accept such a way of thinking about the constitution. Its tasks were, rather, only to reflect the natural order of social equilibriums as they had been arrived at historically, and to guarantee liberty understood as an 'agreement' between the 'particular will' of individuals and the 'general will' expressed in the form of the nation's laws: 'The foundation of liberty is that every man is given permission to do what does not hurt another.'

It is at this point in his considerations on the nature of liberty that, on the trunk of Old Regime constitutionalism *à la* Montesquieu, Cuoco grafted his frank support for a reading of popular sovereignty in terms of Rousseau's direct democracy, adapted to the new historical phase of the Neapolitan nation: 'In a real democratic government, the people themselves should be the legislator.' Real liberty was, in fact, primarily that of the ancients, which permitted direct participation in public administration. 'The article which I would want to be fundamental in our constitution,' Cuoco explained, consisted in trying to identify, in every way, a form of state organization through which, 'while the population can still come together, representation is superfluous.'[45] In this way popular consensus was assured for institutions and the historical process of nations was endorsed from below. Cuoco was aware of how difficult it was to safeguard this ancient type of political and participatory liberty in the modern world. He was well-acquainted with the eighteenth-century debate on the matter and the more recent decisions of the Directory in favour of modern liberty and representative democracy. He agreed that the direct political participation of an entire people was technically impossible in large nations. The Jacobin experiment in France had given precise insight on the subject, as 'Robespierre's constitution conceded greater authority to the nation. It was, however, impossible to bring together the entire people in primary assemblies that often were tumultuous, and always terrible. Robespierre's constitution was neither a constitution of wisdom, nor of peace.'[46] The problem was to be faced differently. If the recourse to representation, in spite of Rousseau's sacrosanct criticisms ('a people which has representatives ceases to be represented, Rousseau says, and Rousseau is right'), had become inevitable, it was then necessary to agree on the concrete meaning of the term and verify the possibility of giving expression to forms of direct democracy wherever possible. Mario Pagano's virtual interpretation of representation ('each representative, Mario says, represents not the department which elects him, but the entire Neapolitan nation') seemed to him to confirm the elitist and pedagogical vocation of Enlightenment constitutionalism, systematically unable to apprehend the positive aspects of all those institutions allowing immediate political participation from below. 'Since it is then necessary to make use of representatives,' Cuoco explained, 'let us make sure they represent the people, and that their will is linked as far as possible to the will of the people,'[47] and thus to material interests, to the true needs of families, to real exigencies and not to generic and abstract appeals to the principles of the common good. Even on this burning question, in other words, Cuoco did not hesitate to give yet another lesson in political realism, explaining how the direct involvement of the masses could take place only by giving room to the representation of interests and not of utopian principles.

In the Kingdom of Naples, the old municipal system of local governments and the economic and subsistence administration of the so-called *universitates*[48] seemed to respond perfectly to this necessity. There was nothing similar in France, where absolutism long ago had begun to dismantle provincial powers. That 'surplus of sovereignty which our nation has always defended against the usurpations of barons and the tax collector,' properly reformed, constituted the future foundation of the new republican order for Cuoco. In those provincial institutions of distant, age-old origins – which he traced back, with fervid imagination, to the world of Republican Rome and even to the pre-Roman peoples of Italy – popular sovereignty finally could be exercised in modern terms of direct democracy: 'the entire people reunited [could have] discussed its interests, defended its rights, chosen the persons to whom to entrust their affairs.'[49]

Already in the course of the eighteenth century, a 'middle' class of authoritative notables, prepared and conscious of their roles, had emerged precisely in the provincial municipalities. Among them, there were many lawyers like Cuoco, who aspired to become the nation's future governors. Bourbon reformism under Ferdinand IV had in fact interrupted that process with iron absolutist determination. The time had come to obtain the 're-establishment of the municipal system.' 'The more I reflect upon these things the more reason I find for believing that the foundation of the Neapolitan republic would simply mean restoring things to their ancient state and removing the obstacles which historical events and human barbarism have erected against the natural liberty of peoples. While the reestablishment of the municipal system will procure us infinite advantages, at the same time it will save us from infinite evils.' The greatest of these evils was the dangerous reappearance, in Pagano's constitution, of the detested absolutist philosophy according to which a central state was able to suppress local energies and liberties in favour of simple functionaries sent from the capital. Cuoco passionately explained that only the Europe of the communes, of the powerful cities hailing from the Middle Ages, strong because politically autonomous, had guaranteed growth, civic development, and the diffusion of riches. Continuing to privilege the Neapolitan capital in the middle of a wasteland had been a grave error in the past, and could reveal itself an even graver error in the future. The centralization, standardization and imposition of laws from above would have stifled the provinces, hindered the development of the specific peculiarities and character of individual urban populations, and extinguished the right to the 'greatest individual liberty' in relation to the state. In contrast with the great debate over national politics launched in 1796 between those patriots who sought a unitary state in Italy and those who wanted a federation of sister republics, in the *Frammenti* Cuoco sought a new middle way with particular reference to the Kingdom of Naples:

> So you would like a federal republic?... No. I know the inconveniences brought about by a federation; but, since, on the other hand, it gives us infinite advantages, I would love to find a way to avoid the former without losing the latter. I would like to conserve, as far as possible, individual activities. Then the republic would be what it must be, the development of all the nation's activity towards the greatest good of the nation, which is nothing but the sum of private welfare. The activity of the nation develops on all points of the earth. If you restrict everything to the government, you ensure that a single eye, a single arm, from a single point, must see and do what a thousand eyes and a thousand arms in a thousand different points would see and do... everything will be misappropriated in the government, everything will be languorous in the nation.[50]

Against the centralized state provided by Pagano's constitution, in which legislative power was attributed solely to an assembly of 170 national representatives, ten for each department, divided into two Chambers with different tasks, Cuoco proposed two parliaments: 'a municipal one for every population of a canton' (which reserves to itself all important decisions in local politics, from public works to taxes, but also the very manner of the implementation of national laws); the other involved the election of a representative for every single canton with the imperative and binding mandate, as we would say today, to speak first and foremost for the particular interests of local communities. The rejection of pure representation thus translated, through limitations on the national parliament, into a veritable overturning of the institutional logic proposed by Pagano. Control of the political process moved irremediably from the centre to the provinces, from the representation of general interests to the unquestionable primacy of the representation of the specific interests of the small provincial communities; municipalities and cantons in effect took the place of the detested French-style departments and the national parliament.

Without considering the historical context of late eighteenth-century Naples, there is little point to discussing whether the form of government outlined by Cuoco was an expression of social conservatism and of a substantial political moderatism in favour of the local notability, or if the mechanisms provided by Pagano for elections and for granting the right of citizenship are to be considered more or less democratic than those of Cuoco. Both proposals, in line with the times and the analogous decisions taken by republican governments across the European continent, based themselves explicitly on the principle of property qualifications.[51] If anything, it would be worthwhile to reflect yet again on the fact that Pagano's conception of the 'people' was of a part of society to emancipate, open and dynamic, and not an objective body produced by nature and by history, simply to be accepted, as Cuoco would have it, thus inaugurating a sort of moderate and conservative populism destined to enjoy great fortune in Italian political history. The true, authentic character of the *Frammenti*'s constitutional philosophy is instead gauged by analyzing Cuoco's comprehensive reflections in their extraordinary and fascinating organicity. Nonetheless, there is no doubt that his declared objective was primarily the radical and systematic confutation of what we have defined Enlightenment constitutionalism. He found unbearable those 'constitutions which are too philosophical and thus without foundation because too distant from the sense and customs of a people.' Constructed at 'the drawing-board, neglecting men' and all their vice and their evil – on which his beloved Machiavelli instead had built his realistic conception of politics – those constitutional texts put too much trust in the 'solemnity of the law,' on the presumed efficiency of modern jurisprudence based on principles proclaimed in the *Scienza della legislazione*, in delineating a feasible, more just and fair socio-political order. 'I do not believe the constitution consists in a declaration of the rights of man and of the citizen. Who does not know his own rights?,' Cuoco wrote stingingly. 'Large parts of humanity give them up out of fear; very large parts sell them out of interest. The constitution is a way of ensuring that man is always in a state where he is neither induced to sell them, nor constrained to give them up.' A few pages later, continuing his tirade against Enlightenment thinkers like Pagano, he confirmed his crude realist approach by ironically adding: 'It is easy to return to the origins, to analyse the nature of the social contract, to declare the rights of man and the citizen; but to ensure that man, who is not always wise, and rarely just, does not abuse his rights, or that he uses them only when they produce common happiness, *hoc opus hic labor* [this is the difficulty].'[52] One thing was the proclamation of rights; another was their exercise. In short, Cuoco considered the *Declaration* little more than waste paper, an empty and useless rhetorical exercise by philosophers who loved to imagine a non-existent society. A serious constitution should instead have dealt with concrete individual liberties, with the separation of powers, the balance of powers and of interests and with taxes, always reflecting, however, the history, customs, traditions, and character of a nation. The myth, renewed by Enlightenment thinkers, of the 'government of laws,' set against the government of men, did not convince him at all. Sometimes, liberty was far better protected by the 'despotism of force' than by the omnipotent 'despotism of the law.' Linguet, the great enemy of the *philosophes*, had thoroughly explained that in Constantinople, by way of the customs and traditions of the 'barbaric' Turkish nation, one lived more freely than in the 'corrupt' Paris of Louis XIV, where modern legal society supposedly reigned. Laws alone did not guarantee anything. Even less so with laws that did not reflect the historical context, which were created arbitrarily on the basis of a few principles held to be eternal and universally valid for all the peoples of the earth, as the Neapolitan advocates of natural law of Filangieri's school claimed; they only produced dangerous illusions, separating the people from their natural élites.

The true object of Cuoco's diatribe was precisely the famous author of the *Scienza della legislazione*, lay patron saint of the Neapolitan Revolution of 1799 and silent presence in the imaginary long-distance dialogues produced in the *Frammenti*. Significantly, only once is Filangieri called from the shadows onto the stage, or into the dock, to face Edmund Burke's arguments on the primacy of tradition with respect to juridical rationalism. Polemically, Cuoco charges him with having propagated the new kind of universalistic and cosmopolitan jurisprudence, led by principles and rights, against the material and legal model of Roman jurisprudence held to be far more similar to that of the English.

> Filangieri accuses the Romans of an immoderate love of *particularizing* which they demonstrate in all their laws, and he does not see that their liberty was based on it. The Roman constitution was *sensible, alive, speaking*. A Roman treated every infraction of his rights like an Englishman treats infractions of the Magna Carta. Instead of this, imagine for a moment that the English had had the *declaration of the rights of man and of the citizen*; then they would not have had the compass which has guided them through all their revolutions… The sublimest of principles resemble the highest mountain peaks, from where one no longer recognizes the objects standing below.[53]

And again, depreciative of the fame his countryman had achieved in Europe, 'perhaps we have never been further from the real science of legislation than now that we think we have learned its most sublime principles.'[54]

Mario Pagano had faithfully followed the teachings of his master Filangieri, arriving as far as the absurdity – in Cuoco's eyes – of once again inserting that dangerous and abstract principle of the people's right to insurrection in a constitutional document. A principle which the constitution of year III, seeing in it an obvious invitation to permanent civil war, commendably had eliminated. Similarly, the institution of the magistracy of the censors introduced by Pagano in the *Progetto* to control the democratic and republican customs of a people further clarified how detached his philosophical and abstract way of thinking about the constitution was from reality. Who was to establish what virtue meant? On the legal level, 'how is one to prove, for instance,' Cuoco wrote, 'that a man does not live democratically?' 'Virtue is one of those ideas which presents itself to our intellect in many guises'; every historical epoch, every people had developed its own. As far as morals went, savages would certainly not have shared the teachings of the philosophers regarding the eternal value of the rights of man. Virtue responded to the logic of human passions and therefore to interests before timeless principles. The only way to avoid dangerous attacks on individual liberty by over-zealous republican censors was to recognize that the 'virtue of a citizen is nothing but the conformity of his manners with those of the nation.' 'When, speaking to men, we forget about all that is human; when, wanting to teach virtue, we do not know how to instil love for virtue; when, following our ideas, we want to overthrow the order of nature, I fear that instead of virtue we will teach fanaticism and instead of putting order in nations we will found sects.'[55]

The historical relativism and crude realism at the foundations of Cuoco's entire constitutional philosophy was even more evident in his treatment of executive power. Instead of following the teachings of Genovesi's *Diceosina* or Filangieri's *Scienza della legislazione* by searching for the mythical just government with the usual lamp of reason, was it not better to be content with identifying good government? 'Democratic government (you understand well that ours is not that) is always the most just, but cannot be regular if not where the people are wise.' Before being considered an institutional mechanism, democracy had, like all forms of government, to be understood in a Humean way, in other words primarily in terms of custom, mentality, tradition. More important than laws and institutions, it was men that stood at the centre of politics. Sometimes they were excellent, but more often than not they were evil and prey to passions and the will to dominate. The positive anthropology of Enlightenment thinkers thus had to be radically overturned. 'One should not hope for much from man, neither from his will to do good, nor from his impotence in doing evil. Whenever man can make a law to his advantage and can enforce it, one can be sure that he will disgrace the public good.'[56] In a serious constitutional project, these considerations had to become the lodestar of every decision that needed to be taken. It was not enough to separate powers on the legislative level and add some institutional mechanisms to break man's will to power. Instead, one had to analyze the forces at play, countervail interests, setting one against the other, the military against the *togati*, as a guarantee and to achieve equilibrium, while respecting the different national histories. If, in light of England's insular nature, it could permit itself to remove the control of the army from the executive, the same thing made no sense for France. The error of modern constitutionalists like Pagano was that of reducing, out of fear of abuse and despotism, the strength of governmental powers wherever possible. So doing, they did not realize that they sanctioned a despotism of laws, that is, a greater evil. It was far better to reinforce all the powers and balance them by playing on the countervailing interests of intermediary bodies. Cuoco for example resolved the question of whether to separate the police from the judiciary, which had been so intensively debated in the Cisalpine Republic, by calling for their unification and rejecting the fears, voiced by the first revolutionaries, of an increased accumulation of power in the hands of judges.

All the same, it is the analytical treatment of the Magistracy of the Ephors which most clearly demonstrates the theoretical difference between Filangieri and Pagano's Enlightenment constitutionalism, systematically conceived to embody the rights of man, and Cuoco's peculiar form of constitutionalism, influenced by the revolutionary dogma of popular sovereignty and the manner of its practice. Cuoco recognized that 'the institution of the Ephorate is the most beautiful part of Mario's project, but it is absolutely missing from the constitution of 1795.'[57] In examining its tasks, however, he ended up completely overthrowing its significance, its very logic, in effect reproposing Rousseau's old model of the Tribunal. As we saw in the previous chapter, Pagano conceived of the Ephorate as something very similar to today's supreme courts of constitutional justice, purposefully created for 'the caretaking of the constitution' in all its parts. The Ephors were entrusted with the delicate task of intervening in conflicts over the attribution of powers, but above all with 'presenting the legislative body with the abrogation of those laws which are opposed to the principles of the constitution' – principles solemnly declared in the declaration of rights and duties of the citizen. This was entirely inconceivable for Cuoco, who had dedicated pages and pages to ridiculing the idea that a constitutional text could be produced on the basis of abstract principles. In his eyes, the Ephorate could become a valuable magistracy only if understood as a 'senate to conserve popular sovereignty,' an organ to tutor legislative power along the classic lines proposed by Rousseau and loved by French constitutionalists.

Beyond his criticism of the number of Ephors and the length of their mandates, the real point of Cuoco's polemic was, in fact, his refusal to resolve any conflict between constitutional principles and popular sovereignty in favour of the former. 'In the face of legislative power, in the face of sovereignty,' he explained, 'there is no need for Ephors because sovereignty is inalienable. The tribunal in Rome opposed the senate; but as soon as the people had resolved the question, the tribunal was silent.' 'The *Ephorate* must not examine if the *general will* is right or wrong, but only if it is or is not the *general will*.'[58] One could not have summed up the rejection of the natural law matrix of Enlightenment constitutionalism, and the Ephorate's role as supreme court of justice, any better. In his frank and insuperable aversion to the political culture of rights formulated by the Neapolitan Enlightenment, Cuoco could not even conceive of the possibility of a conflict between the rights of man, the principles of the constitution, and popular sovereignty; so doing, he fully adopted the constitutional philosophy of the French revolutionaries, bending it and interpreting it in light of the demands of provincial moderatism in Southern Italy. The need to invent a new magistracy to oversee the rules of the constitution was, if anything, connected with doubts over democratic legitimacy raised by the sudden interruption of representative government and by the modern way of conceptualizing liberty itself, which undermined the very idea sovereignty. 'If the people cannot be a usurper, their procurators certainly can,' Cuoco replied,

usurp those powers which the people have not granted them. But I ask then, where is sovereignty? The people no longer have it because they have transferred it to their representatives; the representatives no longer have it because sovereignty is indivisible and they are subject to the Ephors. Who is thus sovereign? Either it is the Ephors, and that is how the Spartan nation fell; or there is no sovereign and that is how [all] nations fall.[59]

The technical solution to the problem lay not in the Thermidorian model of representation, or in that analogously proposed by Pagano, but rather in the municipalism invented by the 'Neapolitan nation.' Only with that peculiar federation of provincial communities could one guarantee a form of modern popular sovereignty and of direct democracy, all the while rendering valuable and efficient the institution of the Ephorate which Pagano had wanted. It would be up to this magistracy to guarantee the exercise of the general will, to organize elections for the government, to recognize the legality of municipal and cantonal parliaments after consultations, to verify the capacity and loyalty of public functionaries, but above all to cancel those acts of executive power which were contrary to specific articles of the constitution. 'Acts which are without indications of law, or contrary to the very law which is indicated,' Cuoco specified, 'are called anticonstitutional acts of the executive power. The English constitution offers a very clear idea of the unconstitutionality of an act.' It is needless to add that, by definition, the decisions of the legislature were never definable in terms of unconstitutionality in the general scheme of French revolutionary constitutionalism, or in that proposed by Cuoco.

One of the most interesting and significant functions which Cuoco attributed the Ephorate, in his systematic critique of Pagano's *Progetto*, was that of the public bestowal of citizenship following preliminary approval on behalf of the municipal parliaments. This is a central point of his political and cultural discourse which allows us yet again to underline just how far his ideas of *patria* and nations were from those developed by Neapolitan Enlightenment thinkers. Cuoco identified the nation as a *patria*, a fatherland, a community of men bound and strengthened by traditions, customs, history, and by deeply shared secular identities, whose political system was nothing more than a natural product of the people's evolution. In that sense, only the people as a whole could grant citizenship.

> In this regard, I will tell you that I find it very strange that the right to grant citizenship is entrusted to an assembly of representatives rather than to the people united in parliament, like it was done in all the ancient republics and also in our abolished constitution. I repeat, I greatly fear that the Neapolitan people will lose rather than gain by wanting to follow the institutions of other peoples. I have no love for that chimerical citizenship by which a man belongs to an entire nation, while he does not belong to any part of it: I would like that every man had a fatherland before having a nation. When a population solemnly has told a man: remain among us; you are worthy of being ours, then he shall present himself to the Ephorate, which shall announce to the nation as a whole that he is a citizen and that he has a fatherland.[60]

The idea of a national identity to which the hypothesis of a constitutionalism which respected history and traditions could be bound became, in 1806, one of the most interesting aspects of the second edition of the *Saggio storico*. This should come as no surprise if we bear in mind the analogous initiatives that emerged in other European countries battling the imperialism of France's armed forces, which were set on imposing their political, ideological, and cultural dominion by force.[61] In those same years, Cuoco had written three volumes of an equally bizarre and suggestive Masonic-initiatory novel, addressed to the ruling orders of the peninsula with the declared objective of promulgating among his compatriots the distant pre-Roman origins of the Italian nation, which he would have go back to the time of Pythagoras, when 'all Italians formed a single people,'[62] with an extraordinary philosophy, a wise and efficient political thought, and a language which was even 'far more ancient than the Greek.' Pythagoras and the mysterious Timaeus were the spiritual fathers of that 'Italian civilization more ancient than the Greek,'[63] which had sowed the seeds of the future West and for a long time had guaranteed Italy's primacy in the world. In the *Platone in Italia*, the miserable conditions of contemporary Napoleonic Italy, economically degraded and subjugated by foreigners, were explained between the lines by the thesis according to which 'the school of ancient knowledge is corrupted,' current philosophy and politics had forgotten the teachings and venerable truths which had been religiously respected by the first leaders of the Italian nation. 'In the language of these peoples,' Cuoco explained sibyllinely, '*truth* is nothing but *fact*; it has no other characteristic besides *being*; there is no demonstration of it but *doing*.'[64] Here he re-introduced Vico's philosophy and the entirely empirical and realistic reading of the *Scienza Nuova* given by an important part of Neapolitan Freemasonry headed by Francescantonio Grimaldi, in an open conflict with Filangieri's followers and the ideal of *ought to be* disseminated by the *Scienza della legislazione*.

In parallel, Cuoco further clarified, for those who were not Freemasons, his real thoughts concerning the necessity of finally empowering the Italian school of political realism as an antidote to the principles of the utopian revolutionaries.

> The Italian school of moral and political sciences followed other principles. Those whose minds were full of the ideas of Machiavelli, Gravina, and Vico could neither have faith in the promises nor applaud the actions of France's revolutionaries once they had abandoned the ideas of the constitutional monarchy. In the same way, the ancient French school, for example that of Montesquieu, would never have applauded the revolution. It resembled the Italian, because both resembled the Greek and the Latin.[65]

With these celebrated words, Cuoco literally invented the modern Italian political tradition, profoundly characterized by its so-called realist character. This tradition, which Croce and Gentile took upon themselves to develop further in the early twentieth century, emphasizing its conservative nature, was thus systematically invented to fight the purportedly reasonable utopias of Enlightenment constitutionalism, accused, for its abstractedness and for its cosmopolitanism, of being a dangerous outside influence on the public spirit of the nascent nation. Scornful and not content with merely having placed it at the margins of Italy's future *Panthéon*, Cuoco went so far, in the preface to the second edition, as defining Pagano as a sort of anarchist devoid of any real constitutional culture:

> Those same letters which I had written to my friend Russo on the constitutional project composed by the illustrious and unfortunate Pagano, even if they today are superfluous, yet I have saved them as a historical monument and a demonstration that all those orders which believed themselves to be constitutional were nothing but anarchic.

Before the 'great Napoleon,' with a hint of opportunism which only his personal genius can make us forget, Cuoco boasted of 'having desired many of those great things which he later did, and at a time when principles were exaggerated.'[66] Curiously, the need to defend a national identity challenged by foreign cultures resulted not only in Filangieri and Pagano being banished to oblivion, but in the complete liquidation of the Neapolitan and generally Italian tradition of natural law. After the publication of the *Saggio storico sulla rivoluzione di Napoli*, Italy turned a page. The age of Enlightenment and of the rights of man had come to an end. Had Pagano still been alive, he probably could easily have renewed his attacks on Cuoco and accused him in turn of having been culturally dependent on the French revolutionaries and on theorists like Rousseau, Mably and Montesquieu. Above all, if one assumes that there is any point in such reflections, Italy could perhaps have had a unique constitutional tradition, a tradition better able to withstand comparison with analogous experiences of democracy in Europe.

Chapter Ten

THE LIBERAL CONSTANT AGAINST THE ENLIGHTENED FILANGIERI: TWO INTERPRETATIONS OF MODERNITY

Closing the *Commentaire* [*sur l'ouvrage de Filangier*], at a distance, by then, of a hundred and forty years, we can no longer accept, as Constant's generation did, the validity of his verdicts and his critiques. How poorly Constant knew the world of eighteenth-century Naples! He did not understand that many of the contradictions he noted were nothing but attempts to understand the reality which surrounded Filangieri… And how can one not see that Constant did not fully understand that desire for justice and equality which so deeply underlies the eighteenth century, and which the nascent liberalism of the new century would evade in a thousand ways and perhaps hide with a thousand sophisms? Why not feel Filangieri's fear of war, rather than be overcome by Constant's optimism, which saw war excluded and impossible in modern economies and societies?

Franco Venturi, 'Gaetano Filangieri,' in *Illuministi italiani* (1962)

Between 1822 and 1824, a strong, unexpected attack on Filangieri appeared in Paris. It was a veritable public trial, masterfully studied and successfully concluded through the publication of two dense, caustic volumes, which culminated with the bitter banishment to oblivion of the entire Enlightenment school of natural law that had emerged in Naples in the second half of the eighteenth century.

In over four hundred printed pages entitled *Commentaire sur l'ouvrage de Filangieri*, Benjamin Constant, the spiritual father of European liberalism and author of this implacable condemnation, denounced the dangers, the anachronisms, and the possible misunderstandings hidden in the work of the Italian jurist and philosopher. The reasons for this singular work (produced in occasion of the third French edition of the *Scienza della legislazione* at the specific request of the publisher,[1] who wanted to combine it with a long and articulate eulogy of Filangieri written by Francesco Saverio Salfi, published as an introduction to the six expected volumes), have never been analyzed in depth. The question was finally addressed in recent decades, and scholars have begun to recognize the importance of this text and the need to clarify its multiple contents and meanings.[2] Indeed, the *Commentaire* did not only represent an authoritative political stance in the context of the European revolutionary movements of 1820–21, presenting itself as a mature and definitive overview of Constant's thought.[3] It was also a sort of reckoning within the progressive front, between the liberals of Coppet's group, ever more immersed in the burgeoning climate of Restoration Romanticism, and the heirs of that late Enlightenment culture which Filangieri had equipped with a powerful and organic political and constitutional theory. It is precisely to broaden our understanding of the deep structures of that theory and its more problematic aspects, in light of how those who had survived the revolution interpreted it, that it is essential to step back and focus on the *Commentaire*.

To do that, however, it is necessary, in a preliminary fashion, to reflect on the historical context in which it emerged. It was certainly no coincidence that this formidable final attack on one of the major figures of the late Enlightenment took place in the homeland of the phenomenon, in revolutionary France. After all, the success and European fame of the *Scienza della legislazione* had been ratified in Paris. On the banks of the Seine, and in salons like that of Madame Helvétius in Auteuil, Filangieri immediately had found friends and enthusiastic admirers of his resolute stance in favour of the American Revolution and for his punctilious critique of the British constitutional system and of Montesquieu's way of conceiving legislation. The first news of a possible translation appear as early as 1783, a few years after the appearance of the first volumes.[4] We have seen that Franklin personally took charge of acquiring and circulating several copies of Filangieri's openly pro-independence work among his 'friends of America.' His epistolary with the *Scienza*'s translator Jean-Antoine Gauvin Gallois, however, reveals the existence of a different path which is no less significant with respect to the American one and the political and constitutional debate in which Filangieri's French fame originated, which we have already discussed. It is a path which above all is connected to the controversy over penal law reform and the defence of the rights of man launched by the Masonic circles of the *Neuf Sœurs* lodge in the 1780s.[5] It is a chapter in the history of the crisis of the Old Regime which is as poorly known as it is relevant, and which saw many *philosophes* take a stand on the front lines, from Condorcet to Élie de Beaumont to Dupaty. The struggle for civil rights and the reform of the French criminal law, particularly ferocious and inhuman, occupied all the 'brothers' of the *Neuf Sœurs*, who set out – without much success – on influencing the work of the governing commission directed by the Minister of Justice Armand-Thomas Huet de Miromesnil, tasked with revising a new code and modifying the penal procedure to open the way for the accusatory process. The explosion of the so-called '*affaire des trois roués*,' in which three paupers unjustly were condemned to be broken on the wheel, between 1783 and 1789, and the controversy which followed, with the appeal to public opinion for justice in the face of the arbitrariness of the judges, imbued the old battles of the *philosophes* in favour of the Calas and Sirven families with legal, philosophical, and now also political meaning.[6] It suffices to read the *Mémoires* published by Condorcet on the occasion (*Réflexions d'un citoyen non gradué sur un procès tres connu*, 1786), or by Dupaty (*Lettres sur la procédure criminelle en France*, 1787) to make out the ever more decisive character of the struggle for civil rights compared to Voltaire's far calmer invitation in the 1765 *Question sur les miracles*: 'The more my compatriots will search for truth, the more they will love liberty. The same force of spirit which guides us towards truth makes us good citizens. What does it in effect mean to be free? It is to reason justly, recognize the rights of man; and when one knows them well, one defends them well.'[7] The blows of that battle on the eve of the great revolution echoed sharply in Gauvin Gallois' letters to Naples. Not only did he send Filangieri Transalpine texts on legal reform, but he also informed him, with growing enthusiasm, that his work was being diffused rapidly among the 'magistrates and literati' of the capital. All recognized, he wrote in 1784, that 'you have defended justice, *Monsieur*, with weapons worthy of it.'[8] Again, in the *Préface du traducteur* to the 1798 second edition of the *Science de la legislation*, he could not resist defining Italy, and particularly late Enlightenment Naples, as 'that country on earth in which the science of the rights and duties of man is cultivated with greatest ardour and, perhaps, even with the greatest success.' An idea reinforced, as we already have seen, by the translator of Mario Pagano's *Considérations sur la procedure criminelle*, which appeared in Paris during the first months of the Revolution.[9]

Gauvin Gallois was a young lawyer destined to play a significant role in the political life of revolutionary France.[10] A leading figure in the Auteuil salon and the *Neuf Sœurs* lodge, he was a friend of Condorcet, Cabanis, Ginguené, Volney, and above all Constant, with whom he joined the *Tribunat*, becoming its president in 1802. His career as high functionary in the service of Napoleon was no less important than that of Claude Pastoret, who alongside Charles Dupaty (both among the upper echelons of the *Neuf Sœurs* lodge) did much to introduce Filangieri's ideas in France. A prominent figure in the movement to reform the legal system, Dupaty wanted to meet the Neapolitan philosopher personally on his 1785 journey to Italy, both as a *Venerable*, or Master, of the Parisian lodge, and as a jurist who for a long time had been engaged in the Enlightenment battle for civil rights. In 1785, the court doctor Angelo Gatti announced Dupaty's visit to Filangieri, presenting him as 'the most eloquent and considerate magistrate in France, a great admirer of your work, of which he spoke much with Franklin, and himself personally occupied with writing on the same subject.'[11] The fruits of that encounter – set to attract the attention also of the Prime Minister John Acton, who quickly wrote a report on it for the queen – were immediately evident in the draft of some of the most celebrated pages of the *Lettres sur l'Italie*, in which the attorney general of the Bordeaux Parliament copied entire pages of the *Scienza della legislazione* to describe the tragic state endured by justice under the jurisdiction of feudal barons in the Kingdom of Naples.[12] More personal, though no less significant and conducive to an authentic and profound intellectual exchange, was Filangieri's encounter with the Marseille jurist Claude Pastoret. While Dupaty, as an exponent of the French parliamentary world, had remained ideologically close to Montesquieu's thesis, Pastoret instead embraced Filangieri's ideas with enthusiasm and conviction. His 1790 *Des lois pénales* was replete with references to and eulogies of the 'great work' of that 'distinguished philosopher the apologists of whom have called the Montesquieu of Italy.'[13] Pastoret publicly endorsed and drew on the *Scienza della legislazione* whenever he saw the opportunity – and opportunities were not lacking. From attorney general of Paris and member of the powerful Legislative Assembly, led by the party of the '*constitutionnels*,' to noble father of the legal reforms of the revolutionary period and professor of natural law at the Sorbonne in 1804, Pastoret managed, like many of his generation with some nonchalant pirouettes, to pass unharmed through the continuous change of regimes, concluding his spectacular career as member of the *Académie Française*, Justice Minister, and finally Chancellor of France in 1829.[14]

Though the history of Filangieri's fame in France still remains to be reconstructed, the evidence available clearly demonstrates that the repeated re-editions of the *Scienza della legislazione* responded to a vast demand in the book trade and in the learned community. The *Moniteur universel* often mentioned the Neapolitan jurist's name in its accounts of current political debates between 1791 and 1792.[15] As of December 1789, the Neapolitan ambassador to Paris, Luigi Pio, wrote enthusiastically to his Prime Minister Acton, reporting the revolutionaries' great interest in Filangieri. 'It is singular that all the principles of our famous Filangieri, who wrote with such energy on the public economy and deservedly merited the graces and recompenses of our Royal Court, are precisely the same as those adopted by the French National Assembly, and here the best and most impartial publicists converge.'[16] A few years later, in 1796, the notorious *Giunta di Stato* of the Bourbon government would unceremoniously change its opinion, suddenly denouncing the presence in the *Scienza della legislazione* of 'those mutinous principles of liberty which have produced the French Revolution.'[17] Yet, Filangieri's great prestige as a charismatic figure of the European Enlightenment – as Madame de Staël described him in 1800 in the two volumes of *De la littérature considérée dans ses rapports avec les institutions sociales* – was not enough to justify Constant's decision to make him the polemical target of his attack on the entire movement. Behind that demanding decision was something more immediate and contingent, something connected to the precise historical moment in which the *Commentaire* appeared. It was explained clearly in the over one hundred pages that comprised the *L'Éloge de Filangieri*, written by the Calabrian political exile Francesco Saverio Salfi[18] and included to open the first volume of the third French edition of the *Scienza*.

In that precious text, a veritable book within the book to be read alongside the *Science* and the *Commentaire*, Salfi depicted his great master and reinterpreted his work in light of the revolutionary movements of 1820–21 in Cadiz, in Turin, and in Naples, underlining its burning relevance and revealing its truly radical political and constitutional implications. Through the conspiratorial channels he was privy to as an exile and a Mason, Salfi probably knew that the *Scienza della legislazione* suddenly was returning to the fore in Spain and Italy, everywhere inspiring, directly or indirectly, the political actions of many leading revolutionaries aiming to obtain a written constitution from their sovereigns. New editions were published, appearing simultaneously in that crucial period in Madrid, Milan, Venice, Florence, and Leghorn.[19] The time had come to relaunch, with renewed vigour, the constitutional project of the Neapolitan Enlightenment on the European stage. The Parisian re-edition was an appetizing opportunity to realize this goal, and Salfi did not let it slip away. In the dense and passionate pages of the *Éloge*, he reproposed the myth of the young, unfortunate and precociously demised Neapolitan jurist, offering a very different interpretation of his theories from those of earlier biographers. First of all, he made it publicly known that Filangieri belonged to the world of eighteenth-century Freemasonry, sending a clear message to brothers infiltrating clandestine political organizations across the entire continent. 'It was there[in the lodges] that, learning to know better the rights of man, and at the same time contemplating the fate of the just and of the innocent, that I felt the need and conceived the design to, from then on, only serving the cause of humanity.'[20] Secondly, he proudly hailed Filangieri's republican and patriotic sentiments. A fervent admirer of the American insurgents (the so-called '*modernes républicains*') and an opponent of all forms of colonialism, Filangieri, according to Salfi, had always demonstrated his sincere republican and democratic sympathies between the lines of his *Scienza della legislazione*. He had preferred those 'governments in which the nation plays the greatest part.' A ferocious enemy of despotism in his work as '*législateur philosophique*,' the man everybody loved to call the '*Montesquieu d'Italie*' had actually been a proud and tenacious adversary of the great Frenchman ('*Il refute souvent les maxims de ce philosophe*'[21]), against whom he had developed almost all his principles and his conception of law, theorizing, finally, the possibility of creating a legal order which was radically different from that which had developed historically under the Old Regime. Dusting off a stereotype developed and diffused in France by Ginguené in his 1815 biography of Filangieri, Salfi maintained that the *Scienza della legislazione* represented the culmination of the political and philosophical thought of the *Mezzogiorno*, a centuries-old original tradition of study, derived from natural law, launched by Gravina's contractualist ideas, refined through the suggestive critique of natural law offered by Vico's '*histoire idéale*,' then enriched by Genovesi's analyses of the moral foundations of the modern theory of the rights of man. What Ginguené, however, had not said, was that this work also had united the youth of Naples into a veritable school of thought, a political movement which, though defeated in the bloody Bourbon and clerical reaction of 1799, courageously had continued the struggle to advance its ideals through the new secret societies of the time. 'Filangieri's school is widespread in Italy,' Salfi revealed, and 'what Filangieri prepared has since been executed by his followers. Hidden or stray, some in their own country, others abroad, they all took equal advantage from his teachings and from their own misfortunes; and as soon as they could, united in their homeland, they worked to make known the most important aspects of the *Scienza della legislazione*.'[22]

With the objective of relating the sudden upsurge in editions of the *Scienza della legislazione* to the revolutionary movements and the 'new political tendency of the Italians,' Salfi's *Éloge* took to the task of clarifying the deeply constitutional character of Filangieri's thought, explaining that what to many seemed a sort of singular 'silence' in Filangieri with regard to 'the constitution' was only an appearance. To realize this, it was enough to glance at the multiple footnotes where, wisely and for reasons of precaution to avoid drawing the attention of Bourbon authorities, the Neapolitan thinker had dedicated ample space to the subject of written constitutions on the rigid American model. What Filangieri instead systematically had refused to do was delineate a constitutional archetype, to upset the complex equilibrium of his immense book with a specific treatment of the argument. Salfi reminded Filangieri's superficial readers that above all he had felt the need to teach 'the method' of legislation in all its multiple dimensions, leaving it to others to speak '*ex professo* on the constitution.' 'One ought not to be surprised that Filangieri did not trace a political constitution in the comprehensive plan of his work.' His objectives had been different: 'he was content to merely give a glimpse of his own principles and intentions; and his disciples, like his fellow citizens, have good evidence on their side that they have not merely inherited his legacy, but worked further to realize it.'[23] Had not Bentham done the same in his *Traités de la législation civile et penal*, avoiding the formidable task of formulating an ideal constitutional model?

Salfi easily demonstrated how the *Scienza della legislazione*'s constitutional nature was clear to all those who really had read and understood the text's deeper meaning and true teachings. Pagano's constitution for the Neapolitan republic of 1799 was the decisive proof of this ('Mario Pagano had accredited and closely followed the spirit and school of Filangieri'), and nobody in Italy doubted the organic link between his work and the 'system' of the *Scienza della legislazione*:

> One cannot follow his entire system without everywhere feeling the need for a constitution that guarantees its execution. This is the great and only object that thenceforth attracted the attention and interest of the most enlightened Neapolitans. Ever since the fatal period of 1799, they had conceived the plan and hope to give themselves a constitution, and Filangieri's greatest friend, the unfortunate Mario Pagano, had occupied himself with presenting a project. This monument to his patriotic dreams outlived him, and served to fuel the desires of his colleagues.[24]

Salfi's statement was not accidental. Through his contacts with the secret societies of the *Mezzogiorno*, he probably knew that in Naples, precisely in the first months of 1820, the first republication of the *Progetto di Costituzione della repubblica Napoletana del 1799*[25] had appeared with the express purpose of supplying the rebels with a specific horizon of reference in their calls for a constitution. He had a blind and passionate faith in the fact that, no matter the defeats and the errors, 'the salutary impulse communicated to the public spirit of Naples and of Italy by Filangieri and his disciples' doctrine' would be victorious in the end. Yet, when he wrote the *Éloge* in 1822, Salfi knew full well that the Parisian reprint, besides sending a general message (which was not even that coded) to the revolutionaries of Europe fighting for a constitution, primarily addressed the French. In particular, it addressed the liberal opposition, which, after the 1820 assassination of the Duke of Berry, seemed definitely overrun by the violent reaction of ultra-royalists and by the ruinous effects of the irreconcilable differences between radicals and moderates, between the so-called independents, who mainly drew their inspiration from the Enlightenment, and the doctrinaires like Royer-Collard and Guizot, loyal to the legitimist spirit of the Charter of 1814 granted by Louis XVIII.[26]

Most likely speaking for all the new exiles who, deluded and bitter, had arrived from Italy in the wake of the decisive intervention of the English and French navies and the Austrian troops of the Holy Alliance, Salfi did not hesitate to denounce the betrayal by the moderate wing of the revolutionary movement as one of the causes of the latest dramatic defeat of the Neapolitan patriots in the spring of 1821. 'Under a false appearance of liberalism,' many exponents of the generation that had come to political maturity during the previous reign of the Neapolitan King Murat and had fought with the revolutionaries committed treason by, in effect, joining forces with the Bourbon monarchy and with noble privilege, thus weakening the cause of those promoting an Enlightenment constitutionalism more sensitive to democratic and republican needs. Hence his peremptory call on his French readers to ask themselves what the true significance of liberalism was, to re-read and meditate over the *Scienza della legislazione*, in essence to 'follow the method that Filangieri had proposed to make light rebound in the midst of darkness.'[27] Presented in these terms, the new Parisian edition inevitably became a resounding declaration of war. A systematic political manifesto which, in the heated climate of those years, must have seemed like a provocative challenge to the French theorists of the so-called liberal constitutionalism of the Restoration; to that moderate wing of the nascent liberal school which, from the opposition to the reactionary circles of the ultra-royalists, seemed to have found its most prestigious and authoritative representative in none other than Benjamin Constant, and its inalienable point of reference in the Charter of Louis XVIII.[28]

As is well known, Constant had punctiliously illustrated a form of monarchical constitutionalism in the recently published *Cours de politique constitutionelle*, which owed much to Montesquieu's theses on the mixed government of England and, more generally, to the traditional institutions of the Old Regime. After a republican phase of open sympathy towards the rationalist conceptions of the Enlightenment, which wavered with the advent of Napoleon and came to a definitive close with the return of the Bourbons to the throne, the great Swiss intellectual turned his thought to the necessity of preventing violations of the constitutional charter and conflicts between powers in light of the new historical situation. The idea dawned upon him of constitutionalizing the monarchy, making it a strong neutral power, the external guarantee of the entire system, of property arrangements and of individual liberties, which had been sought in vain by the Thermidorian jurists and particularly by Sieyès in his proposal for a *Jury constitutionnaire*. Constant ascribed the power to dissolve the Chambers and depose of the executive to the king, head of state, considered thus not by divine right but by the tacit consent of the nation. Accepting the hereditary and irresponsible nature of the sovereign on the political level, however, also implied a different approach to the great problem of legitimizing power which had so tormented European liberals through the clamorous and inevitable return to Montesquieu and the English system of mixed government.[29] 'No Englishman would believe in the stability of the monarchy for an instant if the House of Lords were to be suppressed,' wrote Constant, justifying his approval of the reappearance of hereditary nobility in France, and of an upper chamber next to the chamber of representatives of the people: 'This hereditary chamber is a body which the people do not have the right to elect, and which the government does not have the right to dissolve… The nobility needs, in our century, to latch onto determinate and constitutional prerogatives.'[30] Though rejecting the conservative theory of a pre-existing natural constitution in Old Regime France on the grounds that clear and stable modern principles had been lacking then, Constant's new brand of liberal constitutionalism nonetheless incorporated the earlier arguments of De Lolme, Blackstone and Burke. Thus, it too rejected the abstract egalitarian utopias clung to by so many Enlightenment thinkers, emphasizing the importance of history, customs, and traditions in formulating a modern written constitution respectful of social and political realities. There was, in other words, ample cause for a direct and personal confrontation with Filangieri and his followers.

Had the Neapolitan perhaps not denounced the illegitimate character of the House of Lords, calling for its closure or at least for profound reform to overcome its hereditary principle? Were there not, in the *Scienza della legislazione*, extraordinary pages written precisely against the contradictions of a mixed regime, against Montesquieu, and more generally against the hated and unjust hereditary principle of the nobility which violated the natural equality of all men? Finally, had it not been Mario Pagano's constitution which, following the natural law logic of Filangieri's work, proposed the magistracy of the Ephors as a possible solution to the conflict between powers and as a means of safeguarding the constitution, a problem which Constant instead had sought to overcome with the model of a neutral monarchy? Yet, in the *Commentaire*, there is no trace of these fundamental and specific questions which so clearly squared off the proponents of the Old and New Regimes, moderates and radicals, monarchists and republicans. To the probable disappointment of the expectations of contemporary public opinion, the attack evolved in unexpected ways, confronting complex as well as general theories of legal and political theory which readers of the *Scienza della legislazione* would certainly not expect to see brought to the fore with such force. In his disconcerting and implacable indictment, Constant seemed to avoid deliberately the major themes of the theoretical debates of the time, purposefully selecting phrases to incriminate and obfuscating important points in Filangieri's work with confident impertinence. He did so using a technique of argumentation repeatedly tested in his previous – as well as later – polemics against Rousseau, Mably, Bentham, and other political adversaries, in other words inventing, and not for the first time, an enemy to annihilate from start to finish.[31] In the case of the *Commentaire*, the complex result of this mystifying operation is so persuasive and penetrating as to induce a historian to put aside any search for falsifications and misrepresentations. Objectively, for the concepts it analyzes and the clarifications it supplies, that text in fact represents a moment in the history of European constitutionalism which is too important and has for too long been undervalued to be dismissingly considered the simple fruit of a particular political controversy shaped by particular historical circumstances. Rather it is a brilliant and efficient overview of Constant's constitutionalism, which revealed itself a sharp counterpoint to Filangieri's Enlightenment equivalent. The *Commentaire* really appears as something similar to a final reckoning between the new liberal political thought developed between Coppet and Paris and the legal and political tradition of the late Enlightenment, which had found its highest and clearest representative in Filangieri.

Constant made his intentions clear straight away in the opening pages, stating that in examining the work of the Neapolitan jurist 'we find a way of assuring ourselves of the advances of the human species with regards to legislation and politics this past half century, and of comparing the principles which at other times have been supposed by learned men with those which presently form the object of our analysis and of our daily arguments.'[32] After 1789; the Terror; the Napoleonic dictatorship; the final dramatic defeats of the revolutionaries in the movements of 1821–22 in Naples, Turin, and Cadiz; after the experiences and lessons of five decades, in short, the time had come for a definitive clarification as to the nature and aims of Enlightenment political thought. The skilled use of reason and of history finally would permit the wheat to be separated from the chaff. Like many Restoration intellectuals, he no longer hesitated to leave behind 'many maxims which today seem trivial,' anachronistic, abstract, and foolhardy to that glorious and far-away world, while saving those principles and values which remained eternally valid as time passed.[33] First and foremost, Western Civilization owed the disquieting, guiding idea that it was possible to force the hand of history and accelerate the course of human affairs to the Enlightenment: that the social and political order of the Old Regime could be transformed, thus rapidly bringing about a more just and fair society through reform, employing legislation and government successfully to this end.

'Novices in the science… of social organization,' the thinkers of the Enlightenment had delineated a naive and positive idea of power as an instrument through which reality could be transformed. 'Consequently, you see them call on the government to assist in all their proposed reforms; agriculture, industry, commerce, enlightenment, religion, education, morals, they subject them all to their points of view. Very few authors can be listed who have not fallen into this error.' In particular, Constant identified the greatest advocates of such an interventionist and reformist governmental strategy in 'Turgot, Mirabeau, and Condorcet in France, Dohm and Mauvillon in Germany, Thomas Paine and Bentham in England, Franklin in America.' Even the Physiocrats, though dedicated to theorizing '*laissez faire, laissez passer*'[34] and thus firmly condemning the mechanisms of public prohibitions, did not hesitate in calling for a princely politics encouraging the development of agriculture, thereby confirming the persuasive force of the idea of reform. The fact was that Enlightenment thinkers had lacked a correct analysis of the true nature of power, the perception of its negative presence in history as a necessary evil, a terrible force to be limited and circumscribed. What instead dominated Enlightenment sensitivities was a utopian and positive conception of man and of government which ignored the perennial conflicts of class and material interests that Restoration historiography was discovering and advancing – paving the way for Karl Marx – as a realistic foundation for political thought in the nineteenth century.

The 'gullible Filangieri,' wont to define himself 'a reformer,' had given an authoritative voice to, and a persuasive overview of, this utopian representation of history and of power as possible instruments of transformation. He had appealed to the morality of what *ought to be*, to the philanthropy of the nobility, to the reasonableness of princes, to the natural goodness of all human beings, beyond issues of rank, nationality, and interests. As Constant knew full well, Filangieri truly was the perfect adversary for his own Oedipal reckoning with the generation that had come before him. But we should not be fooled by his malevolent verdicts and his stylistic low-point of denigrating Filangieri's abilities and presumed naivety. One does not write two volumes totalling four hundred pages against someone if one does not consider the adversary an able opponent.[35] Had Filangieri perhaps not openly challenged the beloved Montesquieu, or proclaimed the imminent advent of the reign of reason, of a 'healthy revolution' which would see the conversion of princes and nobles to the cause of the common good? Instead, after decades of horror and bloodshed, the Restoration was in full swing. Where was 'that freedom of the press,' prophesized in the *Scienza della legislazione*; what had happened to the overcoming of 'superstition,' 'the defeat' of which had been celebrated by the 'Neapolitan publicist'? In that unhappy Paris of the 1820s, then in the hands of the ultra-royalists, Constant saw signs of a brusque return to the past everywhere, though in ways which differed from the 'now rancid axiom of divine right' or of the abuses of the reviled feudal regime.[36] The renewed despotism of the monarchy and the arrogant demands of the nobility and of the clergy were the poisoned fruit of the Enlightenment's emancipating project, the consequence of its abstract utopias and its theoretical errors, chief among them the faith in governmental reforms imposed on people from above. They had dramatically precipitated the final crisis of the Old Regime, launching the revolutionary process and paving the way for the Terror and then the Restoration. 'This retrograde movement,' wrote

Constant, 'was, as one can see, inevitable, and [yet] this same movement demonstrates a very important truth, which is that reforms from above are always deceptive.'[37] One must respect traditions and customs, and act with moderation. Re-launching the slow but relentless march of progress, in other words, necessitated the abandonment of utopian doctrines like those of Filangieri and of the Enlightenment thinkers. Their new form of liberal constitutionalism had to be united with Constant's realistic conception of politics and of history.

To criticize the foundations of a work like the *Scienza della legislazione* was, nonetheless, not an easy task. It in fact contained great and undeniable conquests of civilization that could not be renounced in the fields of individual rights and liberties, alongside conceptual errors in law and politics which were difficult to unveil. The confrontation involved two opposed ways of understanding modern constitutional politics, the concept itself of law and the governance of law, and the limits and nature of power and of political action. The 'difference between Filangieri's doctrine and my own,' Constant affirmed,

> applies itself to everything which in general concerns government. The Neapolitan philosopher seems to want always to entrust authority with the task of setting its own limits, but this task belongs to the representatives of nations. The time is long gone when one said it was useful to do everything for the people and nothing with the people.[38]

The irruption of the masses into political life and the history of the definitive triumph of the representative model in the past decades had demonstrated that government understood in the sense of legislative power, the power *par excellence* ('by the expression legislator one always intends government'), could end up in the wrong hands. Jacobins and ultra-royalists had, from different ends of the spectrum, shown how power could be seized and abused. Mixing the institutions and the tasks of the constitutional charter with the multiple possible functions of power had been the grave and dangerous theoretical error committed by the thinkers of the Enlightenment. The time had come to specify the boundaries, limits, and political nature of the Charter better, keeping the problem of power well separated from that of legislation. 'I want a constitution to prescribe power to favour liberty as much as Filangieri wants to obtain this directly from power itself. As I understand it, industry must conquer, through its independence, the advantages which he implores power to give it. The same goes for morality and education.'[39] The political tasks of such a liberal type of monarchical constitution were circumscribed and well defined, aimed only at guaranteeing individual liberties, while keeping legislative intervention in other fields to a bare minimum. It was something very different from 'Filangieri's system' invoked by Salfi when he affirmed that 'one cannot follow his entire system without everywhere feeling the necessity of a constitution which guarantees its execution.' This was a general system of legislation which, rigorously applied by Mario Pagano in 1799, conceived of constitutional politics, and thus the formulation of the constitutional charter itself, as an integral part of a new and larger set of legal rules inspired by natural law, of an 'immense edifice' to be purposefully constructed in time to promote the rights of man and to affirm principles favouring the emergence of a more just and fair society.

Nevertheless, a dark point remained in the background of Constant's invective, something unsaid which probably could have changed the final verdict. The reference here is to Constant's surprising silence on the evident importance of natural law in shaping the theoretical architecture of the *Scienza della legislazione*, a structure in which constitutionalism found space and legitimacy. Ginguené, on the other hand, had insisted on the importance of this in presenting the Neapolitan school of jurisprudence to a Parisian audience, and Salfi, in his *Éloge*, had repeatedly underlined the absolute centrality of the rights of man in Filangieri and in the republican constitution developed by Mario Pagano. The logical construction of that immense organic edifice privileged references to natural law and the consequent declaration of rights and principles above all else, in effect paving the way both for modern mechanisms of constitutional control and for the constitutional protection of rights against the exercise of sovereignty and of ordinary laws. But evidently, and much in line with the French constitutional tradition emerging in the wake of the Revolution, Constant was unable, or unwilling, to grasp the libertarian outcomes of that system which was so close to the American model.[40] Instead, he preferred to investigate, with an alarming tone, its negative and socially subversive potential, concentrating his attention purely on the disquieting aspects of Filangieri's way of understanding 'legislation,' consequently distorting it for posterity. Significantly, in this sense, Constant's criticism never took as its starting point an analysis of the centrality of rights in Filangieri's 'doctrine,' but rather it denounced the clamorous way in which Enlightenment thinkers had misunderstood the nexus between politics and jurisprudence. 'The seed of a great truth' was certainly enclosed in Filangieri's glorious claim of having been the first to reflect on the 'union of politics and legislation,' but it was also the true origin of an impressive sequence of errors. 'Filangieri's doctrine' was in fact the extreme consequence of the Enlightenment's take on the ancient myth of a government of laws, in its eyes achievable through a process of structural reform of the Old Regime. Under the rational empire of new legislation conforming to the existence of natural rights, the men of the late Enlightenment erroneously believed they had resolved what Marx would call the enigma of history once and for all, by uniting morality and politics, the rights of citizens with the logic of power, the material and spiritual needs of individuals with those of society. But that was not the way of laws. Constant was certain that even the best possible legal system and the best possible codes in no way could exhaust politics and its autonomy. The malicious nature of power had shown itself able to breach the sturdy walls of Filangieri's immense edifice with ease. Hence the necessity of a charter as a political machine, a simple institutional instrument to govern conflicts and guarantee individual liberties, resolutely posited outside of the great legislative framework theorized by the Neapolitan philosopher. 'The best legislation is nothing if not guaranteed by a good political organization,' affirmed Constant in defending his own model of a liberal constitution;

> we must distrust any attempt to draw our gaze away from politics to legislation… Without a constitution, the people would have no security in the observance of the laws. Without a constitution, not only does the authority make laws as it wishes, it observes them as it wishes too.[41]

The political myth of a government of laws, and thus of constitutionalism, woven by the Enlightenment only with strands of jurisprudence rested on a profoundly mistaken conception of the idea of law itself.

As we have seen in previous chapters, Filangieri had written significant passages against what was thought to be Montesquieu's conservative and traditional way of conceiving laws as objective and necessary relations derived from the nature of things. In line with the culture of the late Enlightenment, in which aspects of Locke's and Rousseau's theories merged, the Neapolitan philosopher instead emphasized the political and voluntaristic nature of laws as creators of new social and political orders on a contractual basis: 'the laws are formulas which express social contracts,' and thus acts of will between free and equal men. This definition, which made precise reference to individual and general wills, was considered 'completely false' and disquieting by Constant, who was an open supporter of the traditional and reassuring conception of the medieval and Old Regime *sacerdotes juris*, according to which the laws were not made but simply recognized. The laws, Constant insisted, were nothing but 'the declaration of relations between men'; they

> are the simple declaration of a fact; they do not create, they do not determine, they do not institute anything, if not some formalities to guarantee what existed before their institution. It follows that no man, no faction of society, nor society as a whole can, speaking properly and in an absolute sense… ascribe themselves the right to *make* laws… The law is thus not at the disposal of the legislator. It is not a spontaneous work. The legislator is for the moral universe what the physicist is for the material universe. Even Newton could do nothing but observe it and declare the laws which he recognized, or which he thought he recognized. He certainly did not think himself the creator of these laws.[42]

From these dry declarations, Constant moved on to demolish the Enlightenment myth of the great legislator as a true interpreter of the popular will with 'almost unlimited' power 'over human existence,' the creator of inexistent and utopian republics. In so doing, he denounced all those, and there were many on both sides of the Atlantic, who in the eighteenth century had dreamt of writing constitutions and compiling codes to mould a new social order. Although he conceded that Filangieri had explained well that the primary goal in the birth of a new society was the '*preservation* and *tranquillity* of its members' and that legislation served to guarantee these two objectives, Constant nonetheless held his subsequent efforts to define the exact 'jurisdiction of legislation' and its operational limits to be confused and imprecise. To affirm, as Filangieri had done, that the passage from the state of nature to that of civil society necessitated a public power, a union of all private powers gifted with a moral personality which, combined with a public cause, 'secured rights, regulated duties, prescribed the obligations of every individual to the whole of society by interpreting and developing the natural law… created and safeguarded an order apt to maintain the equilibrium between every citizen's needs and the means to satisfy them,' seemed to him to pave the way for a rather dangerous understanding of the legislator's real task. Purposefully forgetting the centrality of the rights of man and the inevitable limits it placed on the legislator in Filangieri's work, directly inspired by Locke's constitutionalism, not to mention the lively polemics of large parts of the Enlightenment, particularly in Italy, against the omnipotence of popular sovereignty and Rousseau's re-introduction of ancient direct democracy, Constant laconically denounced the despotic and tyrannical potential of what he considered an unlimited idea of legislation.

> If legislation is a moral person the will of which always represents all wills, then it follows that all the wills thus represented do not exist in any other particular way. If legislation is the interpreter of the law of nature, then man can no longer know nature itself but through this very legislation, which, finally, is a convention and an artefact. An eternal silence is imposed on that inner sense which nature itself had given him as a guide. If the legislator is he who determines the rights of all individuals, then individuals no longer have other rights but those which legislation wants to leave them. Conceived in this way, Filangieri's system does not differ in any way from that of Rousseau which I wage war on in another work and which I believe I have shown the terrible consequences and incalculable dangers of. Legislation according to Filangieri, and society according to Jean-Jacques, is a power without limits, to the advantage of which all individual beings would find themselves alienated.[43]

The *damnatio memoriae* of the *Scienza della legislazione* in the European liberal tradition was secured by this harsh and authoritative taking of position. By virtue of a rough and ready application of the theory of the heterogeneity of ends, Filangieri became a Jacobin and a Rousseauian *malgré lui*, a potential spiritual father of future subversives and terrorists in spite his asserted hatred of all forms of violence and the strong reservations which, as an advocate of natural law, he had always proclaimed against despotic and unlimited conceptions of sovereignty in his *Scienza*.[44] Enunciating a sort of dogma of modern liberal thought, Constant drastically delimited the tasks of legislation solely to that of guaranteeing internal public order, protecting against so-called attempts against life, property, and individual security, and defending society and the nation against external enemies: 'Punishing crimes and resisting aggression are the necessary limits of the sphere of legislation… what remains must be free.' 'To want, like Mably, Filangieri and so many others do, to extend the competence of the law to all issues is to organize tyranny.' Constant reacted with indignation to those Enlightenment thinkers who had believed they could use the majesty and power of the law to 'secure wealth in the State and distribute it fairly,' or to 'protect agriculture,' regulate trade, intervene in the processes of production and consumption, organize public education by subtracting it from the private prerogative of parents, interfering in the world of religion, the passions, and of honour. 'Liberty' rather than 'the laws,' Constant emphasized rhetorically, was 'the force which produces virtue.' There is a 'portion of human existence which necessarily remains isolated and independent and which by right lies outside of any social and legislative competence.' There 'reside individual rights, rights towards which legislation must never extend its hand, rights over which society has no jurisdiction.'[45]

Behind these categorical statements, the precise function of which was to furnish a solid historical and philosophical justification ('the ideas which are the basis of my doctrine'), were, first of all, the celebrated theoretical conclusions of his 1819 dissertation *De la liberté des anciens comparée avec celle des modernes*. Constant made continuous reference to its brief, persuasive conclusions, which contained the ultimate consummation of his thought, throughout the *Commentaire* to vigorously confirm the clean and irreversible break in human history between those two counterpoised worlds. It was no coincidence that attempts to turn back time, as some had sought to do in the revolutionary period, and in particular during the years of the Terror, had caused great tragedies, aroused horrors, and reawakened old ghosts. The ancients really represented an incommensurable reality with respect to the contemporary situation. The nature and mentality of those peoples reflected a historical phase of humanity which had ended once and for all, the material conditions of its existence inexorably having been changed. That distant world was made up of small republics, of numerous communities compelled to wage war incessantly to guarantee their survival in the face of reciprocal aggression. Modern western society, on the other hand, consisted of large territorial states endowed with social and political institutions favouring the trade, circulation and exchange of industrial and agricultural wealth. War was no longer man's essential horizon. The era of warrior nations had been replaced by the era of commercial nations dominated by the search for peace and that individual wellbeing which was so indispensible for trade.[46] This shift in scenario had changed the very idea of liberty. Organized socially and politically for war, the ancients knew nothing of representative government; their liberty essentially consisted in the 'active and constant participation in collective power' which they exercised by gathering in the public square. They were ignorant of individual rights and lacked a private life. The legislative power was exercised collectively and controlled all aspects of their existence, since social jurisdiction was unlimited and the laws regulated everything, from customs to the economy and religion. The era of commercial nations had replaced this with a new scale of values. The liberty of the moderns had been identified ultimately in the 'peaceful enjoyment of private independence'[47] guaranteed by laws; in the right to life, to security, and to the full enjoyment of property; in the free expression of personal opinion and the possibility of freely organizing one's own productive capacities, delegating political functions to others as necessary. In short, if happiness for the ancients was to be found in the public sphere, for the moderns it was located above all in the private sphere.

Constant let his readers believe that the works of the Enlightenment had been oriented towards the past, their gazes set on the virtues and liberties of the ancients. Though well aware of the furious polemics that had taken place throughout the eighteenth century between the followers of Rousseau and Mably and those, like Ferguson, Condorcet, and our Filangieri, who did not at all endorse the unquestionable favour found by all that which belonged to the ancient world, Constant did not hesitate for a second in placing the Neapolitan philosopher in the naive former group.[48] The *Scienza della legislazione*'s frank acceptance of the historical discontinuity between an old world of warriors and the commercial societies of the present did not keep it from seeking to reconcile the virtue and public spirit of the ancients with the progress and the wealth of the moderns. But Constant never analyzed, or took seriously, the complex and original theory which resulted. Yet again, the political struggle of the moment; the rigid application of the simplifying and demonizing scheme of the French Revolution, in which only friends and enemies of Jacobinism could be identified; and the necessity of rendering one's own propagandistic arguments more effective, all conspired to obscure the truth of the matter. That is a shame. The political utopia of the late Enlightenment, which had found its primary political laboratory in America, finally would have been able to confront the nascent liberal utopia, fully delineated in its every aspect by the *Commentaire*, on equal grounds. This might then have revealed quite plainly that the conflict between Enlightenment thinkers and liberals during the Restoration was a conflict between two different interpretations of what today we call modernity, the original aspects of modern civil society, the theory of progress and its consequences for human history. It would probably have shed light on an important moment in the history of western political thought – a moment which still resonates in modern debates.[49]

'An essential idea,' wrote Constant himself, flowed through the *Commentaire*, namely that the 'functions of government are *negative*; it must only repress evil and permit the good to emerge on its own… authority may well remain neutral, the laws keeping silent, *what is necessary will come about on its own.*'[50] To which he added his final exhortation to cancel forever from the dictionary of power the following words: 'compress, extirpate, and direct. With regards to education and to industry, the stance of government must be *laissez faire, laissez passer.*'[51] As we have seen, Constant explained why it was better to let do and let pass by invoking, above all, the tragic and irrevocable episodes of a history that repeated itself. There is no doubt that he conceived of modernity and its distinctive characteristics positively, considering it an objective fact quite divorced from the will of man. The economy, politics and customs had historically taken on forms in accordance with their own irrefutable internal logics, forms which could not be recaptured if not by recourse to violence and terror. It therefore sufficed to guarantee individual liberty above all, to create appropriate constitutional institutions to that end, and to let civil society unleash its extraordinary potential to obtain the inevitable progress of the entire human species. The expansive logic of the commercial spirit and the effects of scientific and technological innovations would in the end have eliminated conflicts and wars between peoples, diffusing the welfare and liberty of the moderns across the Earth. With a faith that already adumbrated the positivistic theory of progress and historical determinism – a faith permeated by propheticism and mysticism – Constant believed blindly in the self-regulating capacities of civil society. An invisible hand would guide economic and social processes, spreading wealth and welfare to ever larger parts of the population; private vices, as Mandeville put it, would become public virtues. Against the interventionist and reformist project of Enlightenment thinkers (the 'partisans of the intellectual supremacy and exclusive action of authority' which instead sought to construct a new, more just and fair society through a government of laws), he prophesized a 'government of opinion.' A kind of moderate government dear to liberals because it respected history, customs, traditions, and the social and political equilibriums of the moment, in which the intervention of authority followed rather than anticipated opinion. Thus, it would keep in step with the necessary unfolding of progress. 'The government of opinion,' Constant explained, reiterating themes close to those pursued by Vincenzo Cuoco in Italy, and before him by Edmund Burke in England, 'is the one which best safeguards a people from anarchy. Since opinion does not advance if not by degrees, everything which authority does under its influence is prepared, comes opportunely, finds antecedents in the souls of men, is connected to the past and linked with what is to come, corrects what is vicious, and grafts itself to what is good.'[52] It had nothing to do with reforms from above and with the attempts made by 'friend of power' to manipulate public opinion.

We now know, however, that the historical and philosophical culture of the late Enlightenment had a far more problematic and complex idea of history and of the very idea of progress than what, yet again tendentiously, Constant wanted his readers to believe. The exponents of the Scottish and Neapolitan Enlightenments, in particular, had arrived at important and original insights in meditating on the origins and character of modern civil society in the late eighteenth century, insights without which the emancipating project of the *Scienza della legislazione* would be meaningless. Developing Hume's, Robertson's and Ferguson's ideas about the stadial evolution of human societies, and the consequences of the division of labour in light of Vico's philosophy of history, authors like Grimaldi and Pagano (and Genovesi before them) had written fiery pages against Rousseau's hostility to scientific progress and modern civil society. They, and Pagano in particular, had put forth a cyclical representation of history in which human will was an unassailable fortress in the struggle against despotism, a force which lay in perpetual ambush.[53] Where modernity for Constant and the liberals coincided deterministically with progress and always produced positive consequences independently of human intervention, or, better still, in the absence of those feared interventions, that argument was far more complicated for the exponents of the late Enlightenment. Ferguson and Grimaldi, to name just two, had anxiously examined the extraordinarily advantageous effects of modernity in their writings, but without underestimating its disadvantages. In fact, they harboured no doubt that progress produced – and always would produce – new and more painful inequalities, iron hierarchies with novel configurations and unexpected forms of dominion which were no less ferocious than those of the past. This was written in the logic of how societies reacted to technological innovation, in the outcomes of the division of labour and the changing methods of production and ways of life. Rousseau had been right on this point. It was useless and dangerous to entertain illusions about man's future. Diderot and Voltaire, for example, in no way shared Condorcet's certainty over man's inevitably positive destiny. We have already mentioned that the *Scienza della legislazione* was designed systematically not to create a heavenly city where men all would become equal and happy, but rather to reduce in concrete terms the rapid, undisputed and predictable spread of present and future inequalities through the government of laws and the application of the principle of equal rights. Upon closer scrutiny, in contrast with the liberal Constant and far from nurturing a naive and entirely positive and deterministic vision of progress and the self-regulating capacities of civil society, Filangieri realistically noted that modernity was an ambiguous and indefinite historical process, the source of new and immense wealth and of great possibilities in view of a melioration of humanity's lot, but also of renewed inequalities and injustices. Only the constant political and reformist intervention of democratic governments, armed with the powerful new conception of a science of legislation based on the rights of man, could attempt to hold back the social evil waiting in ambush.

Unlike what in the end took place, the *Commentaire* could, in short, have presented a confrontation of two great philosophies of history and two interpretations of the development of modern civil society which were set to reappear again and again in the political history of the nineteenth century. On the one hand, the liberal utopia of the invisible hand and of the primacy of individual liberties, or negative liberties as Isaiah Berlin put it, which were held sufficient to guarantee mankind a better future; on the other the Enlightenment utopia of a democratic government of laws, where respect for the delicate constitutional equilibrium between the liberty of the ancients and that of moderns would pave the way for a more just and fair society. Instead, those pages witnessed a thorny and rather surreal debate between interlocutors who in effect were deaf. In his polemic against the culture of the Enlightenment, which he saw uniformly marred by Rousseau's thesis in favour of the ancients, Constant dedicated hundreds of pages to demonstrating Filangieri's presumed errors, and to propagandizing the merit of liberal thought for the burning questions of the day, constantly accusing Enlightenment thinkers of having preferred the political and social institutions of the ancient world. On the theme of war, for example, Filangieri's passionately pacifist critique of the military culture and values of Old Regime aristocrats, perhaps a bit rhetorical but certainly well argued, was dismissed in the name of the imminent and definite overcoming of endemic warfare by the modern order of commercial nations. The vexed question of the primacy of public over private education, theorized in the fundamental fourth volume of the *Scienza della legislazione*, also unleashed Constant's wrath, due to Filangieri's ceaseless argument for the necessity of somehow reproducing, in the modern world, the public spirit and civic virtues of the ancients, attributes without which no republican and emancipating project could succeed. Where Filangieri indicated that public education might be the best means of raising awareness of citizens' rights and duties and spreading modern knowledge to all social classes, Constant, on the contrary, primarily saw in it the dangers of manipulation and of ideological indoctrination by parts and factions upon attaining power. Filangieri's preoccupation with guaranteeing the democratic principle of equal rights in all fields through appropriate laws interested him little. Individual rights always trumped those of the collective, the liberty of the moderns always that of the ancients. The theory that comprehensive betterment rested on state actions in the delicate sector of education, which for centuries had been entrusted to the Church and private initiative, seemed dangerous and inacceptable to Constant. 'Public education must limit itself only to instruction,' he specified; 'society must respect individual rights, including those of fathers over their children.'[54] Only fathers could decide the kind of education to give their heirs. Yet again, the invisible hand governing civil society would have guided parents in making the right choices, severely limiting the actions of authority. As far as the poor and the excluded were considered, nothing kept them from bettering their own economic conditions in the new, free, and safe civil society theorized by liberals. Nothing, as such, kept them from accessing private education.

On the historical level, Constant doubted, as a myth to unravel, the existence of public forms of education in the Greek *poleis*, or city-states, much like he rejected Filangieri's conclusions regarding the necessity of promoting, through legislation, the birth of a modern civic religion inspired by the patriotism and civic ideals of the ancient world and of the Roman republic in particular. Indeed, Constant's opposition to Filangieri on this delicate and, to him, fascinating point was absolute. Educated under the severe culture of Protestant Geneva, and sensitive to the individualist influence of the nascent romanticism, he denounced the 'tendency towards irreligion,' towards libertinism and towards the materialism implicit in all the natural and historical reflections of the Enlightenment, and of Filangieri in particular. Constant was unconvinced by the arguments, inspired by Vico, that 'religion had no origin but in man's fears' and that theocracies and clerical power had always played a delicate civic and political role in the development of nations. In that sense, Filangieri was mistaken in attributing 'the bellicose disposition of the Roman people to the priesthood,'[55] along with the final foundation of its social and constitutional bonds. Religion had always been – and so it should remain among the moderns – a private and intimately free phenomenon of individual conscience, a profound and mysterious sentiment of communion between the individual and the eternal which was entirely unrelated to its hypothetical political and social utility for legislators. Paradoxically, in a curious turnabout with respect to his previous accusations of excessive utopianism, Constant now charged the idealistic Filangieri with Machiavellianism, of the ruthless and realist political exploitation of religion.

The *Commentaire*, which we cannot analyze in detail here, though it warrants a more extensive treatment, highlighted all the possible errors and misunderstandings of the *Scienza della legislazione* with regards to the specific Enlightenment interpretation of a government of laws, of the nexus between politics and law, and of the new reformist and interventionist constitutionalism which, in the name of the rights of man, aimed to unite the liberty of the ancients and that of the moderns, the principle of self-government and individual rights. The question of the 'slave trade,' for example, fully demonstrated the limits and dangers implicit in that 'system.' All thinkers of the late Enlightenment had made the slave trade a rallying cry in their battle against the Old Regime, and Filangieri had written fierce words against it. Constant took the promulgation in those years of laws against slavery in England to demonstrate that 'the abolition of the trade has, in the way in which it so far has been pursued, caused more harm than good.' A simple law, whatever its lofty principles, could not suffice to change the habits and mentalities of a nation. Instead of applying the liberal model of a 'government of opinion,' or in other words working, with the help of intellectuals, towards the creation of a new, modern public opinion hostile to the very idea of slavery, laws had been imposed from above which had only rendered the slave trade more ferocious and inhumane. The commanders of intercepted ships now preferred to rid themselves of their 'goods' at sea rather than end up in gaol. Completely untouched by the effects of the new legislation, the peoples of Europe adamantly kept their absurd and shameful convictions regarding the presumed inferiority of the black race, thus confirming the thesis that 'however just, reforms that anticipate [public] opinion are never effective, nor complete in their results.'[56] It would have been better, much better, to rely on the liberal 'government of opinion.'

Yet, beyond his polemical rage and his very low blows (only partially justified by the political struggle of the moment), Constant was often compelled to admit to sharing ideals and values with Filangieri. In spite of everything, there was something extremely familiar about the *Scienza della legislazione*. But of course one can contest one's parents, even hate and insult them, yet they nonetheless remain one's parents, and Constant could not deny his Enlightenment heritage. 'One will thus often find me disagreeing with Filangieri,' he was compelled to specify, 'not so much over his ends as over his means.'[57] The Neapolitan thinker's work certainly contained many errors, but also many truths and inalienable victories. The books dedicated to legal procedure, the critique of the inquisitorial system, the criteria for formulating punishments and to the defence of the individual's civic rights in any trial no doubt represented high points in Western legal tradition. The reforms of justice in France had utilized them widely and fruitfully. Constant knew this, and was not sparing in his praise when referring to these points in the *Scienza della legislazione*. With regards to norms for testimony, he exclaimed convinced, 'all the rules established by Filangieri in this chapter conform perfectly to the laws of humanity and of justice.'[58] With regards to the importance of transparency and the public nature of the legal process, he enthusiastically concurred 'this chapter is excellent from top to bottom.'[59] Nonetheless, even on this decisive point, on which they agreed out of a common liberal hatred of despotism in all its forms, Constant found a way to stress their differences of opinion. He did this in the context of a significant problem which was particularly important to Filangieri for the political and philosophical principles it implied, and namely the 'necessity of returning the right to accuse to the citizenry' in accordance with the classical scheme of the ancients, of Cicero's Republican Rome, where the individual's right to justice also was carried out – as an element of citizenship – through direct participation in all phases of the administration of justice. Constant held this request for popular participation to be manifestly utopian and devoid of sense. The experience of republicanism, he claimed, drawing from the teachings of his beloved Montesquieu, had been entirely overcome in the modern world. An ever more ardent proponent of a 'hereditary constitutional monarchy,' he yet again explained that the division and specialization of labour characterizing modern commercial societies entailed the sacrifice of direct participation in the exercise of many civic rights, without this jeopardizing the rights of individuals. If one wanted to guarantee justice, it sufficed to delegate 'a public person constituted by law to prosecute the guilty.'[60] But the thinkers of the Enlightenment, and Filangieri foremost among them, persisted in their refusal to accept that history had created a kind of hierarchy in the rights of man, and that individual liberties and securities came before participation in political life. One had to choose. Where the *Scienza della legislazione* argued vigorously and with passion that a compromise could be achieved between ancient virtue and modern wealth, Constant believed no such thing to be possible.

Albeit confusedly, and without ever confronting the question head on, Constant intuited the dangers inherent in Filangieri's republican interpretation of the rights of man. Above all, he harboured an understanding of the disquieting, expansive capacity inherent in that ethical principle of equal rights, a principle that immediately summoned the thorny question of how democratically to guarantee all human beings the exercise of their natural rights. The Neapolitan philosopher would, without difficulty, have subscribed to the liberal thesis according to which 'the sovereignty of the people is not unlimited; it is circumscribed to the limits given it by justice and the rights of individuals,' that is those of 'individual liberty, the liberty of religion, of opinion, the enjoyment of property.'[61] Constant, on the other hand, would hardly have done the same with the questions and attempts to find a solution to the problems delineated by Filangieri, not to mention by Jefferson or by Paine (to take only a few among the many who, towards the end of the eighteenth century, posed similar questions), with regards to the necessity of constitutionally guaranteeing all men equal rights to happiness and the exercise of liberty. That, however, was really the definitive theoretical nucleus of the *Scienza della legislazione*, a nucleus which never would be confronted directly in the *Commentaire*. Had he ventured down that difficult road, Constant, the father of liberalism, would perhaps have been forced to abandon the deforming lenses of the French Revolution, lenses which seemed to condemn the political experience of the last two decades of the eighteenth century once and for all. Perhaps he would also have engaged with the Enlightenment theory of the rights of man as it first encountered the emerging modern labour market, the persistence of great land tenures, and the privileges of the new aristocracy of wealth. In so doing, Constant might have lingered over, and refuted with greater efficiency, the progressive and democratic extension of the eighteenth-century theory of the rights of man from the civic rights of individual liberty towards those which we today call social rights, that is those *positive* rights whose protection requires the intervention of the legislative power in civil society.

Chapter Eleven

FILANGIERIAN HERESIES IN THE EUROPEAN DEMOCRATIC TRADITION: THE PRINCIPLE OF JUSTICE AND THE RIGHT TO HAPPINESS

We hold these truths to be self-evident, that all men are created equal, that they are endowed by their Creator with certain unalienable Rights, that among these are Life, Liberty and the pursuit of Happiness.

The Declaration of Independence of the United States of America (1776)

Art. 1. The scope of society is the common happiness.

Constitution of the French Republic (1793)

18. Every man must help others and push himself to preserve and better the existence of his similars… 19. Therefore, it is a sacred duty of man to feed the needy. 20. It is required of all men to enlighten and instruct others.

Progetto di costituzione della Repubblica napoletana (1799)

The full history of Filangieri's influence on the European democratic tradition in the opening decades of the nineteenth century remains to be written. Traces and circumstantial evidence are not lacking. The Russian Decembrists, who guided the 1825 revolt in St. Petersburg against the Czar calling for the birth of a modern constitutional regime, knew the *Scienza della legislazione* well and loved its incessant call to 'know our rights,' to 'know the rights of humanity.'[1] The Spanish insurgents, massacred by French troops in Trocadero in 1823, had learned much from those dense and passionate pages where Filangieri indissolubly tied the right to happiness of all men to a just and fair distribution of wealth, and particularly of land.[2] Finally, the *Scienza della legislazione* had a profound and well-documented presence in the writings on the so-called social revolution of Carlo Pisacane, one of the most radical heads of the Italian democratic movement.[3] The numerous republications, in various languages, of Benjamin Constant's *Commentaire*, which usually accompanied the nineteenth-century editions of the *Scienza della legislazione* with the publicly declared objective of neutralizing its democratic and republican virus, often had the opposite effect. It is therefore unsurprising, for example, that it was precisely by charting the diffusion of the *Commentaire* on the Italian peninsula that the police came to discover, among students at the University of Pisa suspected of holding subversive ideas, dangerous 'followers of Filangieri's constitutional ideas.'[4] Following the first Leghorn edition of 1826, Constant's book was republished in Italian no less than eight times in fifteen years![5] Elsewhere in Europe, as far as we know (though research is still continuing), the work was always accompanied by the *Scienza della legislazione*, and a new Parisian edition was released in 1840, preceded by an analogous Spanish edition of 1836, which would bring the results of the confrontation between the liberal Constant and the Enlightenment thinker Filangieri also to Latin America.[6] It is a curious question, what people found so singularly topical in the confrontation between the two to cause such a publishing phenomenon, certainly worthy of further inquiries to clarify finally, perhaps definitely, the real cipher of the *Scienza della legislazione* and its historical function in the development of democratic thought in Italy and Europe.

It should not be forgotten that when Constant wrote his harsh critique of Filangieri, the frightening spectre of social revolution seemed poised to reappear in all corners of the continent, everywhere riding on the back of the progressives' call for constitutional liberty. The anxious memory of the Reign of Terror and of the alarming questions posed by Babeuf and by the members of the Conspiracy of the Equals still lingered. The dramatic effects on the masses of the emergence of a modern market economy in England, the revolutionary demands for agrarian reforms to put an end to the concentration of land in the hands of the few in Russia, in Poland, in Spain and in Italy, are important themes which provide the backdrop for Constant's polemics. It was not only against Filangieri that he argued, but against Enlightenment thought in general regarding the existing relationship between politics and the economy, between the recognition of human rights and the intervention of a legislator to guarantee their free and concrete exercise. In some pages of the *Commentaire*, largely ignored by scholars of Constant, their author demonstrated his concern with these thorny questions, which strained his liberal thought and his economic liberalism, raised by the crude injustices characterizing the unregulated labour market in early forms of industrial capitalism in England.[7] Against the traditional eighteenth-century argument presented by Filangieri, by which an increasing population was an indicator of wealth and welfare, Constant took sides with Malthus and his fear of famine and the dearth of resources in the face of excessive and uncontrolled demographic expansion. It was, however, only a general leaning, troubled and full of doubt with the excessively bitter and punitive view of workers and the poor, which emerged from the Englishman's proposals. If, on the one hand, Constant attacked Filangieri for again having reproposed social principles in favour of demographic growth through legislation encouraging marriage on the model of the ancients, on the other hand he found the Poor Laws proposed by men ideologically close to him like Malthus and Sismondi to be dangerous and unjust. One could not stop 'the marriage of all those who have no property' as Sismondi had proposed. And it was 'neither good nor prudent' to stop English parishes by law, in the context of revising the *Poor Law*, from assisting the poor as Malthus mercilessly had suggested, only because their children added to social wretchedness and filled the lines of rebels and of mouths to feed.

Though ideologically opposed, in theoretical terms, to those who looked favourably upon 'public relief,' since individuals were to employ only their own resources to lead a life of dignity, Constant was not insensitive to the tragic and unjust situation of the

English working-class. 'Do not always pick on the poor to impose privations on him,' he implored,

> there is a certain harshness and severity in the arguments gathered by Mr. Malthus to prove that the poor do not have any right to the assistance of society... to declare from evangelical heights that from now on the children of parents who cannot feed them will be denied parochial assistance is too frank a declaration of a permanent state of war between those who own everything and those who own nothing.

Beware not to 'give life to a sort of servitude,' Constant warned alarmingly,

> because that would be to transform the workers into a body of pariahs, that would be to resurrect the tyrannical institutions of India and Egypt in Europe, in this Europe which promised to establish the highest level of individual liberty.[8]

The bitter class conflict which broke out in England in the opening decades of the nineteenth century concerned Constant greatly. From opposite fronts, what we today would call Left and Right, all invoked the recourse to legislative power as a weapon to impose their own convictions, without realizing that this raised obstacles in the way of the nation's natural civil and economic progress and opened the way to despotism. The homeland of liberalism seemed dangerously imprisoned by past political and institutional paradigms, and even set on a course towards a ruinous pre-revolutionary situation. It was, in fact, Constant's conviction that the indisputable primacy of the aristocratic principle in Britain's constitutional model no longer held up, and should be quickly abandoned in favour of a full and total establishment of that representative government adopted by the American and French revolutionaries; in other words, a government finally able to imbue new classes with a function and precise role in the modern political system. The decision, in short, was to be made to support economic and technological progress, and not resist it with government violence, thus favouring the irreversible political and social changes produced by modernity. England, however, needed to acquire an awareness of the dangers which ensued from an excessive polarization of wealth in the hands of the few, and widen the reach of political representation beyond past limits. 'It would be advisable,' Constant specified, 'that it renounce its concentration of property, which creates millions of proletarians, and its aristocracy, which having no clientele thus lacks utility.'[9] Radical reforms from above, like those proposed by Enlightenment thinkers, and then by the Jacobins, were not necessary to achieve all this; nor were the infamous agrarian laws discussed (or, rather, which he believed were discussed) in the *Scienza della legislazione*. The liberal solution to the problems of development in that sense remained rigidly based on the wholesale rejection of any sort of legislative intervention in economic or social affairs, on a deterministic philosophy of history, on the acceptance of the incommensurable discontinuity between the worlds of the ancients and the moderns, on an iron-willed respect for economic liberalism and, above all, on the recognition of the indisputable primacy of individual liberty and security with respect to all other rights.

The way in which the *Commentaire* treated the delicate questions of property and of free trade are exemplary in this regard. Though Filangieri had written 'very reasonable things' with which he could agree about the merits of small properties, which all liberal thinkers considered an important bulwark of liberty and civility, the Neapolitan thinker's philosophical and historical horizon was erroneous from beginning to end. Yet again, Constant denounced the Filangierian argument, common to many of the greatest exponents of the late Enlightenment, that some of the virtues and principles of the ancients were still useful, and even necessary to contemporaries if one wanted to construct a more just and fair society. According to the author of the *Commentaire*, the great land holdings, with their injustices and their abuses, would soon cease to constitute a real political and social problem. The growth of industry in Northern Europe had radically changed the terms of the question. In a modern industrial society, the wealthy entrepreneur was not only able to give life to ever new ways of creating wealth which were incomparable with those of the past, but he would directly influence the very destiny of large land-holdings, currently the depository of political power, through the natural alliance of interests between industrialists and the nascent and numerous class of workers. To maintain their influence, the great latifundists would have to divide themselves, widen their social base, and change their political attitudes. The liberal utopia of modernity guided Constant's visionary and prophetic gaze towards a future in which the figure of the powerful land-holder naturally would disappear, like a relic of the past, without traumas or bloody revolutions, leaving the stage to entrepreneurs, to workers, and to numerous small proprietors. 'The tendency of our century towards the division of property is so strong that our reasoning, which perhaps will be accused of having been paradoxical, will seem so commonplace in ten years' time as not to require proof.'[10] Germany, England, and France seemed to be the first to set out towards this luminous destiny of progress and peace. Sismondi was right, in his recent treatise on political economy, in stating that the great revolution of 1789 had forever transformed property ownership in France, 'prodigiously' widening 'the class of propertied peasants' and thus changing the grounds of successive political conflicts. 'This is the great cause of the differences between the revolution of 1813 and 1814 and that of 1789,'[11] Constant agreed.

Purposefully forgetting the situation in Poland, in Russia, in Spain and in Italy, where industrialization was still a mirage and the latifundia remained at the centre of the political struggle, Constant stigmatized Filangieri's solution of favouring the diffusion of small-scale land-holdings through agrarian laws and legislative intervention in the social and economic spheres. If one could agree with the latter's call to eliminate 'the right of primogeniture' and the feudal and ecclesiastical limits to the free trade of land, his calls for laws against the concentration of property in few hands seemed both dangerous and 'immoral' to Constant. Nothing could justify such measures. Constant had no doubts about the nefarious consequences of laws interrupting a natural process by which institutions like the latifundia would disappear by their own accord, melting like snow in the sun, since they were no longer 'in harmony with the needs of the century.' 'Since the division of property is free,' Constant reiterated, 'it tends to fragment itself; only laws could stop this.' One thing was Filangieri's call to prohibit fidei-commissa, which prevented the formation of a market in land. Another was his proposal that legislators should prohibit 'the right to bequeath' everything to a single heir: 'the right of primogeniture is a restriction, the right to bequeath is a liberty.'[12] No interference with the individual liberty to dispose of one's own estate could ever be legitimate.

The same argument against legislative intervention which was not 'negative' repeats itself in the long polemic over the freedom of the grain trade. Filangieri had reproposed the concerns of his fellow countryman Ferdinando Galiani over the need to guarantee both internal and external free trade and the minimum food supplies required to stave off dangerous revolts and insurrections. Constant replied in terms which would have been dear to Mandeville, theorist of private vices and public virtues, for private individual interest came before anything else: 'under the government of liberty, personal interest is the most prudent, the most solid, and the most useful ally of the general interest.' The question should never be approached from the point of view of consumers or the rights of consumers, as enemies of economic liberalism preferred to do, but from the point of view of production and of the indispensible preconditions for growth. Only this could, subsequently, increase the number of people able to benefit from economic development. 'Competition' was the magic solution to the economic problems of modern Western civilization. 'Laws do not protect one bit because they can be evaded; competition protects everything.'[13] With stupefying naivety, which would perhaps have brought a smile to the far more practical and sceptical protagonists of the late Enlightenment, Constant concluded his attacks with a bid to let nature operate freely. Its invisible hand would unfailingly resolve differences, remedy wrongs, and re-establish the just order of things, which had been derailed by human intervention: 'nature will establish equilibrium.'[14] Presented in these terms, the economic and political thought of Filangieri and the Enlightenment thinkers of the late eighteenth century was in effect condemned as an archaic way of thinking compared to the certainties of individualism and the granite dogmas on which the utopia of economic liberalism rested. It is worth reiterating once more that the *Commentaire*, conditioned as it was by an evidently teleological conception of the relationship between the Enlightenment and the French Revolution, presented an artificial, mystified, simplified, and generally trivial analysis of Filangieri's thought for clearly propagandistic purposes. Perhaps without Constant's full awareness, the *Scienza della legislazione* was the culmination of an important and original Italian and more specifically Neapolitan debate of the eighteenth century over how to understand the scientific autonomy of law and economics.

In the opening years of the eighteenth century, faced with the evident emergence of a modern market economy in nations like England and the United Provinces, the political and philosophical debate had become rapidly focused on identifying the foundations for a new rationalistic morality able to respond to the socially disruptive consequences of the neo-mercantilist and absolutist policies of the European states. Against the individualism of theorists such as Melon and Mandeville, in open polemic with the advocates of luxury, of selfishness, of the search for profit and of the primacy of the passions and of private interest as engines of economic development, reactions arose everywhere which highlighted the dangerous connections between wealth and corruption, between armed colonialism serving economic interests and the attack on individual rights. The debate was particularly intense in the England of the

Freethinkers, of Defoe, of *Cato's Letters*, and of Bolingbroke's alarming denunciation of Walpole and Whig politics.[15] It was there, after all, that the dramatic effects of the free market in labour were clear for all to see, as were the consequences of the definite overcoming of Tudor legislation safeguarding social equilibriums and of Old Regime forms of corporatist moral economy. In France, the vehement critiques of Louis XIV's continuous warfare and neo-mercantilist policies were woven ever tighter with the propaganda of what effectively has been defined the political and economic paradigm of *Christian agrarianism*,[16] profoundly hostile to individualism, to luxury, and to those who encouraged personal enrichment or the separation of private merchant interests from those of the community. In Naples, an analysis of the Anglo-Dutch economic model took shape in the opening decades of the eighteenth century, combining, in a way common to the European Republic of Letters at the time,[17] with the debate on Newtonian science and its inevitable consequences for civic and intellectual life.

Two camps soon faced each other mercilessly in the capital of the new Bourbon Kingdom. On one side stood the heirs of the Galilean tradition, the so-called *novatores* led by Bartolomeo Intieri and the *Cappellano Maggiore del Regno* Celestino Galiani, fighting in favour of the *libertas philosophandi* and of the diffusion of the Anglo-Dutch Newtonian worldview, where new ideas blended with those of Gassendi and of Locke, with the crude political realism of Machiavelli, the economic utilitarianism of Melon, and, above all, with the mathematical empiricism of Newton and Gravesande, who were considered the principal architects of a modern rational morality and an autonomous political and economic science in step with the times. The other camp was represented by the *veteres*, proponents of an internal renewal of the ancient humanist tradition of knowledge, fronted by Giambattista Vico, Paolo Mattia Doria, and Carlo Antonio Broggia, frankly hostile to the philosophical and epistemological consequences implicit in the mathematical empiricism of the Newtonian worldview, opposed to Descartes, to the scientific revolution, and to the growing dominion of that scientific method which seemed to have reached its definite triumph in the *Principia* and in the *Opticks*.[18] The division between the two groups was not only epistemological and philosophical, but also social and political. The first openly supported the absolutism of Charles III, his project for modernization and economic development through the encouragement of industry, his support for international trade, currency devaluation and the break-up of the old power arrangements privileging the *res publica* of the *togati*. The second group was more focused on defending society as an organic concept rather than as a sum of individuals and on stressing the primacy of civic life with respect to the creation of what they considered an increasingly unjust labour market. Paolo Mattia Doria was the real theorist of this second group of scholars who met in the *Accademia degli Oziosi* to discuss history and literature, but also politics and the economy. Acutely, he identified and denounced the connections between Newton's 'material and carnal science' and the 'Epicurean civil society' delineated in the works of Locke, Bayle, Mandeville, and Melon.

'Modern geometrists ruined geometry,' he repeatedly explained, 'and from that they came to destroy logic, philosophy, religion, morality, and politics; they have enslaved Europe and rendered it barbarian.'[19] Behind the English fleets, behind the protectionism which London guaranteed its manufactures in international trade, he could see the propaganda of the *Boyle Lectures* and the birth of a colonial empire able to draw legitimacy from the rigid mathematical laws of the new economic science. He did not like that Newtonian world, founded on individual utilitarianism and on sacred respect for the laws of profit, nor did he share Bartolomeo Intieri's idea, derived from modern political economy, that 'men run where there is profit.' Nurtured under the influence of the Second Scholasticism and on Christian agrarian persuasions, Doria's republican and anti-despotic spirit saw the damage done by luxury everywhere, and likewise the onset of corruption in the wake of the neo-mercantilist policies of the absolutist states. Doria was attached to the idea of a moral and Christian economics understood as an act of reciprocal love between men in which 'virtuous commerce' became 'an art of ensuring that men in civil society came to each other's *mutual assistance*, assisting one another with those goods which some lack and others have in abundance.' The primacy of the government of laws and of collective interests with respect to those of individual merchants was clearly beyond questioning in his way of understanding politics and civic life: 'civil law teaches this maxim, which is: *bonum publicum praefertur bono private.*'[20]

With the 1751 publication of Ferdinando Galiani's *Della moneta*, Bartolomeo Intieri's group, the followers of Locke and Newton, seemed to have won the battle. In that work of genius, the precocious nephew of Celestino Galiani had brought to conclusion half a century of Italian debate over the nature of money and, more generally, the autonomous identity of the new science of commerce, as it was called at the time, vindicating the scientific method and the decisive role of the passions in human action. Heir to a Galilean tradition which had always sought to develop a mathematical idea of economic laws and to construct solid rational bases for the study of monetary flows and their impact on the consumption and production of goods, Galiani no longer harboured any doubt – following the appearance of the *Principia* and the *Opticks* – that economic processes followed strict natural laws. 'Nothing,' he wrote, 'corresponds to the laws of gravity and of fluids like those of commerce. That which gravity is in physics, is the *desire to earn*, that is to live happily, in man; that said, all the physical laws of bodies can, by those who know how to meditate on it, be perfectly verified in the morals of our life.'[21] Nonetheless, his was a problematic and complex conception of the economy (suffice it to recall the subjective theory of value in his *Della moneta*), far from reductionist or abstract in its treatment of historical processes. Politics, morality and law could and always did interact with economic laws depending on context, historical circumstances, and priorities dictated by the exigencies of the moment.[22] The recognition of rational laws in economics was one thing; to subordinate the political sphere in its entirety to such laws was something else. His pointed and ironic polemic in the famous *Dialogues sur le commerce des bleds*, written against the Parisian *économistes* and their campaign in favour of unrestrained economic liberalism, was a mature return to the ideas he had expressed earlier regarding the continuous interaction of all aspects of civic life. In no way did it mark a new phase in his theoretical conceptions regarding what we today define as the autonomy of economic processes from politics and society. The same mixture of political realism, cynicism, and libertinism which had pushed him to argue in the 1750s – alone in Italy – for devaluation and for inflationary policies by the Bourbon government to encourage the economic development of the Kingdom of Naples, without concern for their social consequences, twenty years later had instead led him to warn governments of the terrible effects of abstractly libertarian economic policies on domestic order. Though he proudly proclaimed to be among the founding fathers of the new '*secte économique*' in Europe, Galiani was entirely convinced that the government of the economy should be in the hands of political power and not in the hands of the merchants.

In Naples, the key figure in this long and tormented debate was again Antonio Genovesi. Having been given one of the first chairs of political economy in Europe (willed so, and not without reason, by Intieri, who in 1754 financed the chair personally), he published a two-volume university textbook entitled *Delle lezioni di commercio o sia d'economia civile* between 1765 and 1767, which was destined to enjoy great success, also internationally. In it, Genovesi brought together nearly all the current conceptions of the 'economic sciences,' from the late mercantilists to the first English, French, and Spanish free-traders like Cary, Davenant, Uztáriz, Forbonnais, Plumard de Dangeul, and many others. In his transformation from philosopher to economist, or rather from 'metaphysicist' to 'merchant' as he liked to say, he had always dedicated great attention to the English economic model and to the great seventeenth and eighteenth-century debates which had followed the emergence of the first forms of market economies overseas. Translating the works of John Cary and Thomas Mun into Italian, discussing and diffusing the writings of Child, King, Petty, Misselden, and Malynes, he too had in some sense participated in the search for an interpretative paradigm able to comprehend the connections between commercial trade, monetary flows, financial mechanisms, production, consumption, devaluation, the values of goods and of labour and prices.[23] Although the abstract and modern concept of the market as an independent entity was still lacking at the time, Genovesi discussed Mun's classical theory of the balance of trade with his students, along with the psychological and utilitarian bases of economic processes and above all the first polemics over the autonomy or lack of it of economic activities with respect to political authority.[24] He was, however, not an economic theorist, nor was he particularly interested – like all the political economists of the Italian Enlightenment – in the formulation of any specific general theory of trade. If anything, he was attracted by the political and ideological struggle that accompanied those debates. His problem, particularly after the horrible Neapolitan famine of 1764, was to identify a science of man able to create a more just society in accordance with a common scheme among Enlightenment thinkers of the continent, giving man in his organic complexity centre stage in relation to the new sciences. Thus he was fascinated by a possible general vision of all modern forms of knowledge, among which he accentuated economics, as the Old Regime society rapidly changed. Appropriately, the *Lezioni di commercio* opened with a methodological approach indicating man and his rights, and the ethics and values of modern civil society, to be the ultimate goal of human understanding. Only later did he move onto the more specific questions of his discipline. The objective declared right from the start in the first pages was to teach students a moral and rational conception of the 'political science of commerce and the economy' in light of a rigorous respect for the rights of man. Against those who were transforming the presumed scientific autonomy and legality of economic laws into a free trade ideology, Genovesi clearly denounced those scholars and politicians who by 'liberty of commerce understand the absolute power of merchants to export and import every sort of good without any restriction, law or rule. But this liberty, or rather licence,' he exclaimed, 'cannot be found in any nation of Europe and is contrary to the very *spirit* of commerce.' Commerce 'must serve the State, rather than the State serving commerce.' There could be no doubt on the matter: 'commerce, as part of public order and of the body politic, must be entirely subjected to the law and serve the aggrandizement and preservation of civil society.'[25]

In substance, Filangieri shared these ideas. Nevertheless, he went further in his *Scienza della legislazione*. Particularly, he reflected on the juridical and political principles of a possible rational and cosmopolitan 'economic legislation' conditioned by the values of universal morality, of individual states and of international trade, all in the global historical context of the late eighteenth-century emergence of a modern market economy and the problems this entailed for ancient social equilibriums. To demonstrate the economic necessity of a 'government of laws,' he again took recourse to the cyclical philosophy of history developed in the Neapolitan Enlightenment, according to which modernity brought evident and extraordinary advantages but also new injustices, inequalities, conflicts, and unexpected forms of dominion which risked paving the way for a new stage of barbarism. It was a philosophy very different from the classical conception whereby the wars and conquering spirit of the ancients had been overcome thanks to the diffusion of modern commerce between nations, a theory developed throughout the eighteenth century by Melon, Montesquieu and Hume, and then rendered famous by Constant. Indeed, to Filangieri's eyes, which were used to weighing up in realistic terms even the most utopian of projects, many of those affirmations seemed to express a magnificent dream which had very little to do with historical reality. What have been defined 'arguments in favour of capitalism before its triumph'[26] convinced him only up to a certain point. Certainly, the spirit of commerce generally encouraged the necessity of peace between peoples, the spread of welfare, of civility and of good manners. Nobody could reasonably doubt this, and Rousseau had been mistaken in criticizing the progress of society and the common good brought about by economic growth. What was not self-evident was the deterministic idea that free trade automatically and inevitably bettered the conditions of modern societies. Filangieri had learned from Vico that history was made by men and not vice versa. It was wrongheaded to conceive of 'commerce' (a word which at the time simultaneously signified what we today call economics and the market) as an autonomous entity supported by its own laws, which were entirely independent of political power or moral duties to society or individual rights. Left to itself, without laws, that world propped up by the thirst for profits, made up of trade, of production and of consumption undoubtedly had the power to create great good, but also great harm: 'the legislator must protect it and direct it' [I, 271].

It sufficed to look around to find the bloody and terrible proof of this thesis which so irritated Constant. Everywhere, Filangieri argued at the end of the eighteenth century, armed struggles and 'wars triggered by commerce' raged. 'Commerce,' he continued, 'which by its nature should be a bond of peace [seems] to have transformed itself into a perennial cause of injustice, of war, and of discord.' Thus he loudly countered Jean-François Melon, who in 1734 resolutely had proclaimed that 'the spirits of conquest and of commerce are mutually exclusive in a nation.'[27] The reasons for this dramatic situation lay in the absence of a cosmopolitan and rational science of legislation finally able to shed light on such questions; a science of legislation accepted by all peoples, constructed on solid principles of justice, of liberty, and of equality, able to reconcile the 'universal interest,' the 'real interests of commerce' and the 'sacred rights of humanity.' Filangieri was not at all interested in discussing the specific merits of the most recent economic theories. He was probably acquainted with large extracts of Adam Smith's *Inquiry into the Nature and Causes of the Wealth of Nations*, which had been published in Italian journals, and he greatly valued, having read them directly, the Physiocrats, but he also appreciated Linguet's paradoxes and merciless critiques of the *économistes*. As a political and legal philosopher, he was far more interested in explaining that a truly free, just, and fair 'commerce' – today we would say a *market* – had never existed in nature, and nor could it exist without the intervention of men armed with the new principles of international law. Just as a social contract, a government of laws, had been necessary to guarantee individual rights in the state of nature, so regulated intervention, a sort of moral and political international government, was necessary to create a truly free and fair market; a market which prevented the subjection of the weak by the more powerful and was respectful of the equal rights of all nations. History, from the economic conflict between Rome and Carthage to the recent commercial wars between the French and the English, had always seen a naturalistic, leonine conception of international trade prevail. Nobody could envision the enrichment of their own nations without making it coincide with the impoverishment of others, with the economic annihilation of rival peoples. Neo-mercantilism, protectionism, monopolies, monetary policies, customs, and privileges of all kinds had done nothing but favour this antagonistic understanding of trade and thus increase the differences, inequalities, and natural forms of injustice and dominion between peoples, infinitely widening and promoting conflict. According to the *Scienza della Legislazione*, the market economy (and the painful birth of modernity in general) had to be understood as a way of favouring the development of humanity and the integration of individuals and nations; that is, as a way of combining the previously mentioned 'real interests of commerce' with the 'sacred rights of humanity.'

Legislative power would always have to avoid 'two opposed vices': the absolute disinterest fought for by liberalists and the 'excessive intervention of government' typical of Old Regime absolutism. Filangieri forcefully called for liberalization and for the confident opening of the gates of market economics, to the extent that his motto was 'intervening as little as possible, letting be as much as possible' [I, 229]. Yet, from his point of view, removing obstacles, privileging free trade and widening markets to include all did not only serve to secure the search for profit and the better circulation of goods, as argued by a chorus of Italian Enlightenment thinkers from Antonio Genovesi to Pietro Verri,[28] but also, and primarily, to brush aside privileges and guarantee the equal rights of all nations to participate, with a republican spirit, in international trade. As a political philosopher, Filangieri was careful to explain that an understanding of the market which was rational, cosmopolitan and respectful of rights was in the general interest. Rather than clashing to destroy one another, the European economies were to be coordinated and integrated, beginning with their specific natural wealth and the different types of production, considered not in light of the 'national' but rather of the 'universal interest.'

> In the physical world, as in the political one, all is dependence, all is relation, nothing is isolated… commerce wants that all nations consider themselves a single society, all the members of which have equal rights to participate in the good of all the others… persuade yourselves that if the nation with which you trade needs you, and if you need them as their prosperity increases, and their populations rise, you will find a greater number of buyers for your products and for your industry and a greater number supplying what you lack. [I, 289]

An analysis of the reasons for the war between England and the American colonists served to reveal the inexorable interconnection of politics and the economy. The British claim to forms of 'exclusive commerce,' to privileges and exemptions undermining the 'advantage of all members of the social confederacy' had, in fact, clearly shed light on the political links between the protection of the rights of man and mistaken economic legislation. Without a new cosmopolitan law based on the principles of justice, liberty and equality, respectful of the rights of people in the African, Asian, and American colonies, the future would only bring continuous war and tragedy. Filangieri's vision was therefore quite far from the self-regulating market of Constant's *Commentaire*, the clever invisible hand of which alone would bring an end to all wars. The armed conflict unfolding overseas was only the beginning of a long and tormented crisis of the old and unjust international order; a strong admonition of colonial policies, 'a terrible lesson to all the powers which divide the spoils of this vast continent' to stop in time [I, 302].

The same principles which would guide future international economic legislation also had to be valid for the internal politics of all states. Filangieri watched the progressive establishment of a free and modern market economy with sincere enthusiasm. Faced with the privileges and inequalities of the Old Regime, the rapidly changing social and economic order of Europe represented a great historical occasion, to be supported and guided politically with wisdom and long-term planning to prevent new and more dramatic forms of dominion. He called for the 'greatest liberty' in all sectors. Having forever repudiated the logic of privilege, blood, and heredity in the name of 'sacred property rights,' Filangieri did not hesitate to invoke the dismantling of all those bonds that in the Old Regime had prevented the formation of a free market in land – from feudal fetters, to the chains of primogeniture and of fidei-commissa, to the tithe and the ties of ecclesiastical property. Even on the debated issue of the English enclosures, he was resolutely in favour of those who occupied common lands to 'grow almost a third of the volume of annual production.' In the *Scienza della legislazione*, we find indignant pages against the 'barbaric right of hunting,' considered a veritable 'relic of feudalism,' harmful 'of property and the public interest.'[29] The same indignation was then directed against the odious survival of serfdom in Russia, Denmark, Poland, and large parts of Germany. After all the battles of the Enlightenment in favour of the 'rights of humanity,' it seemed incredible to him that 'this kind of slavery' still existed, in which property was concentrated in the hands of 'a few thousand nobles and priests' while 'the rest of the nation is made up of slaves bound to the soil' [I, 243].

His intervention in the struggle of Enlightenment thinkers against guilds in favour of a modern labour market in the second half of the eighteenth century represents a lone-standing chapter in his discussion of the subversive consequences of the market economy for the privileges and inequalities of the Old Regime.[30] Just as he had defended the demand for free trade internationally, eliminating monopolies and customs barriers, Filangieri did not hesitate in denouncing the 'pernicious system of the guilds and of the right to associate [*maestranza*]' as a systematic violation of every individual's right to dispose freely of their own labour and talent. As a jurist he considered that right to exercise labour freely an immediate expression of the '*personal* property of the citizen…, the most just, the most sacred of all properties, that which man acquires by birth' [I, 267]. His conviction that guilds 'destroy the liberty of the citizen,' limiting the potentials of artisans, workers, and writers, was therefore firm.[31] It was necessary to eliminate all forms of 'exclusive privileges' granted to social groups or individuals by governments, removing 'all those laws which tend to diminish competition between craftsmen' and impede 'emulation.' At the same time, Filangieri was also well-acquainted with the great debate triggered by the impressive growth of pauperism in late eighteenth-century Europe, a development which not only had taken place in spite of evident economic progress, but in fact in disconcerting parallel to it.[32] He had very much appreciated Linguet's furious denunciations, which signalled how, paradoxically, the lives of slaves in the ancient world had been far, far better than those of manufacturing workers in Paris and London. Owners had guaranteed the former food and their lives; the latter were left only with Christian charity or incarceration the moment they lost their jobs and became a threat to public order.[33] All Enlightenment thinkers realized that the nature of poverty had changed radically in the modern world. Montesquieu himself had written of it clearly in the *Esprit des lois*, affirming that 'a man is not poor because he has nothing, but because he does not work.'[34] The emergence of a market economy had redrawn Old Regime society implacably, eliminating all forms of protection. The inalienable right to life, which even Hobbes recognized as the only indisputable right of man, had inexorably acquired a very different significance in the recent past. In the hands of Enlightenment thinkers, it was, for example, no longer possible to interpret that right only in terms of security from violence in civil war or as a bulwark to appeal to as a defence against despotism. Rather, it was becoming the logical premise for the claim of a right to work and to a subsistence wage, beyond the right to exercise one's own talent.

If on the one hand the substitution of the guild system by a free labour market certainly opened the way for greater freedom of individual choice and an increase in production and in wealth, on the other hand it left salaried workers without any form of protection, in many cases condemning them to poverty. In short, leaving behind the Old Regime triggered social and political contradictions which were hard to resolve. Taking the bitter reality of the situation into account, Enlightenment thinkers only began to acquire full awareness of this towards the end of the century. In 1776, a Royal Edict finally abolished guild-membership for workers, something for which the *philosophes* had fought for years.

On the same occasion, Turgot for the first time officially proclaimed the birth of the right to work as a right of liberty, putting the following words in the mouth of Louis XVI:

> God, giving man certain needs, rendering the resource of work necessary for him, has made the right to work property of every man, and this property is the first and most sacred and most imprescriptible of all. We regard as an act most worthy of our charity to release our subjects from all attacks on this inalienable right of mankind.[35]

As we will see later on, the debate over the nature and significance of the modern right to work – to be interpreted as both a right of liberty (in the sense of overcoming the guilds) and as a social right (in the sense of legislative action to fight poverty) – could begin only after these celebrated declarations.

In the *Scienza della legislazione*, Filangieri dedicated ample space to these issues, discussing, with passion and originality, not only the principles, but also the concrete exercise of human rights in the face of the contradictions unveiled by the dismantling of the political, social, and economic order of the Old Regime. More than examining the question of the right to work directly, the keystone, or unifying thread of his thoughts on the relationship between rights and the political but also, and primarily, the social consequences of a modern market economy was the concept of the equal and universal human right to the pursuit of happiness. As is well known, *happiness* is omnipresent and polysemous in the vocabulary of the Enlightenment. Treatises, poetry, prose and reflections of all kinds were dedicated to it.[36] In the ancient world, happiness was always considered principally as a public thing, connected to the exercise of civic virtues, of just and honest individual action in favour of the community. It was no coincidence that Plato and Aristotle valued virtue as the indispensible premise of collective happiness in a political community. The primarily social and public rather than individual nature of happiness also became one of the strongholds of numerous Enlightenment treatments of the matter, from Rousseau, who held it impossible to speak of happiness without making reference to society, to Diderot, who in the entry *Société* in the *Encyclopédie* clearly wrote 'the entire economy of human society is based on this simple and general principle: I want to be happy, but I live with men who like me also want to be happy, every one of them for themselves; let us search for the means of procuring our happiness by procuring theirs, or at least without ever hurting them.' During the course of the eighteenth century, through the diffusion of a hedonistic and apologetic interpretation of luxury, then considered crucial for understanding economic processes, the analysis of the different facets of happiness shifted ever more towards the individual, the search for pleasure, the study of the body and its passions. These new observations too, however, kept the link between personal happiness and the horizon of 'social justice' and the rights and duties of the citizen centre stage, as Pietro Verri, the young follower of Locke, hastened to specify in his 1763 *Discorso sulla felicità*.[37] It would, in fact, be necessary to await Kant, Fichte, Humboldt, and the work of early nineteenth-century European liberals to find the concept of happiness definitely circumscribed to individual and private concerns without any reference to morality and the actions of the state. After that, this word, over which rivers of ink had been spilled, suddenly disappeared from the political vocabulary, dissolving itself like snow in the sun, above all after Kant authoritatively had stripped off its moral, political, and social connotations, favouring the irresistible ascent of a new key word destined to enjoy a great future: liberty. In his *Commentaire*, to make an example of this stupefying and sudden disappearance, Constant did not even notice the centrality of that ancient word for Filangieri's *Scienza della legislazione*. And to think that, by using it in a book dedicated to political and economic laws, the Neapolitan philosopher had brought the analysis of happiness to its apex in late Enlightenment political culture.

Like many in Europe, and particularly in Naples, Filangieri had been struck by the decision of the American revolutionaries to introduce, among the inalienable right of man in the 1776 *Declaration of Independence*, the right to the pursuit of happiness. The idea that happiness ever could be considered a fundamental right on the same level as life and liberty, to be guaranteed constitutionally, represented a real challenge for jurists and political philosophers. The question was no longer that of deepening the already worn out paths traced by treatises like the 1748 *Della pubblica felicità*, written by the pious Modenese priest Ludovico Antonio Muratori, which paternally entrusted the task of ensuring the happiness of his subjects to the prince, or that of the abbot François-André Pluquet, *De la sociabilité* of 1767, which yet again underlined the importance of being together for living happily. The time was now at hand to go well beyond even the humanitarian and moral Masonic utopias which had ascribed to philanthropy a strategic role in granting the right to happiness to the greatest number of people. The American provocation required new answers in keeping with the times.

Drawing on Locke's theories to compose the sacred text of the *Declaration*, Jefferson had exchanged the right of property with that to 'pursue happiness' without giving any further explanation in subsequent years of what he really had intended with this unexpected and disconcerting act. In vain, historians still debate the issue to this day, speculating on the presumed social interpretation of the right to happiness in connection to the suppressed natural right to property, or else on the entirely private and individual meaning hidden in the words 'the pursuit of happiness.'[38] In the *Scienza della legislazione*, Filangieri instead gave his clear interpretation. Considered an inalienable and natural right of man, the pursuit of happiness was, principally, a social and political fact with evident implications also for the economic realm. He explained in detail that happiness could in no way be tied down to the mere individual search for pleasure, but rather more generally to the satisfaction of the universal human need to live freely and with dignity in a modern civil society. The prevailing hedonist conception of the phenomenon, which had led many exponents of the Italian and European Enlightenments close to the principles of utilitarianism (such as Beccaria in his *Dei delitti e delle pene*) in indicating the goal of politics as achieving 'the greatest happiness divided among the greatest number' of individuals, was not Filangieri's cup of tea, since it created evident problems with respect to the fundamental ethical principle of modern natural law, namely the equality of rights. If happiness was connected only to the possibility of procuring the greatest amount of individual pleasure, the rich would be blissful by definition, while the weaker, less able, or unlucky part of society could end up systematically or even legitimately excluded from it. Inequality, also in the search for happiness, was counteracted by the facts of life, as Francescantonio Grimaldi polemically had argued in his *Riflessioni sopra l'ineguaglianza tra gli uomini*. 'No, it is not in pleasures,' Filangieri quickly specified,

> that the idle rich can find happiness. He will only savour it in those moments in which he satisfies the needs of life. In these moments all men are equally happy, [for] nature does not multiply the needs for food, for love, for sleep, etc. to favour the wealthy... At the time then, in which men satisfy their needs, they are all equally happy. The differences depend on the manner of occupying the intervals between the satisfaction of a need and its re-emergence. Now the idle rich which fill all this time with enjoyment and with the search for pleasure are just as unhappy as a poor man who must use it for excessive work. [I, 350]

Connecting the equal right to happiness to the satisfaction of needs, though different for all men, and vigorously specifying that the basic 'aim of politics and the law' is to create the necessary conditions for the exercise of the right to 'equality of happiness in all classes' [I, 350], Filangieri resolutely embarked – in accordance with the formulas and languages of the late Enlightenment – on the road towards what today we call social rights.[39] If the right to happiness was linked to the satisfaction of needs, 'how can one ensure,' the Neapolitan jurist asked himself, 'that all the citizens of a state can participate in this desirable happiness, which in a well ordered society should only be forbidden madmen and delinquents?' [I, 351].

In those same years, Adam Smith worried mostly about explaining the mechanisms for increasing the wealth of nations, mechanisms which Constant some decades later would give a rigidly deterministic interpretation which was entirely alien to the ethical preoccupations of the great Scotsman, entrusting the task of distributing wealth to the so-called invisible hand of the market. Filangieri, on the other hand, preferred to focus on the right to happiness as a social right with political, economic, and juridical implications, placing all his bets on the 'equal diffusion of the money and wealth of a state' and on the essential function of legislative power in mitigating those inequalities which history, at different times and in different forms, presented. As we have already highlighted, he was convinced that the market economy, with its formidable capacity for accumulation, represented a great historical opportunity to overcome the Old Regime from within. The panorama of unhappiness and severe injustices at the time was dramatic and discouraging, and certainly did not seem susceptible to immediate melioration. The total liberalization of the labour market in effect risked devastating the old social order, with grave consequences. In spite of this, Rousseau's condemnation of modernity was unacceptable, and so was Mably's idea that 'it would be better if all were equally poor.' 'If one observes the present state of European societies,' Filangieri argued,

> one will find almost all of them divided into two classes of citizens, one which lacks necessities, the other which abounds in superfluities. The first, which is the most numerous, cannot provide for its needs without recourse to excessive labour. As has

been demonstrated, it cannot know happiness. The other class lives in abundance, but, exposed to idleness and the anguishes of boredom, it is sometimes more unhappy than the first. [I, 351]

Filangieri wrote extraordinary pages, filled with great humanity and genuine moral outrage, to describe the terrible conditions of the so-called first class, that which suffered from growing pauperism, that 'people which have been downtrodden by a hundred despots.' In the following decades, many socialists would probably not have hesitated in subscribing to his vehement accusations against those who felt no shame in seeing the torment, the pain, and the unhappiness of the Southern Italian peasantry.[40] How could anyone hold back their tears and fury, Filangieri wondered, when faced with the exploitation of the humble peasant who 'picks up his hoe before break of dawn and does not put it down until night approaches, [he] is old at the age of forty and fifty. His days become shorter, his body curves, the violence done to nature is evident in him' [I, 352].

Masonic philanthropy no longer sufficed to placate the hunger and needs of the miserable masses crowding Europe's great cities. Nor was Christian charity enough, or the traditional forms of Old Regime government assistance. If, as Montesquieu had argued, poverty depended on the difficulty of finding work, the exercise of the right to happiness in the lowest classes of society now required some form of right to work and to a salary above subsistence. The economy had to take account of the rights of man and the principles announced in the *Scienza della legislazione*. Filangieri had no doubt that

> when every citizen in a State can, with *seven or eight hours of fair work a day*, comfortably take care of his needs and those of his family, this State will be the happiest on earth, it will be the model of a well-ordered society; in this State, wealth will be well distributed; finally, in this State, there will be no equality of faculties, which is a chimera, but the equality of happiness in all classes, in all orders, in all the families which comprise it, equality which must be the goal of politics and of the law.

To ensure this, however, one had to find a way to distribute the wealth produced by a nation, to assure the 'equal diffusion of money, which, by avoiding its gathering in a few hands, causes a certain common comfort, which is a necessary instrument for the happiness of men' [I, 349]. In the ancient world, the concentration of wealth had destroyed the liberty of the small republics. In modern states, after the dismantling of the guild system had begun, the accumulation of wealth in a few hands could, beyond undermining the political and individual rights of liberty, threaten social equilibriums and thus render the very exercise of the right of happiness of a nation impossible. Curtly, Filangieri went on,

> Public happiness is nothing but the aggregate of the private happiness of all individuals who make up society; when wealth is concentrated in a few hands; when few are rich and many are indigent, that private happiness of a few members will surely not make the happiness of the entire body. In fact, as I have said, it will ruin it. [I, 347]

But how to 'diminish the wealth of some and increase that of others without violating the sacred rights of property and without offending the decorum of justice?' Of course the time of the agrarian laws was over. On every occasion, Filangieri underlined the nexus between liberty and property, obsessively repeating that 'property is what creates the citizen' [I, 187], the very foundation of civil society. Though Constant would have him say the opposite in the *Commentaire*, Filangieri always pronounced himself clearly against the communist utopia of common property and against violent forms of expropriation. Referring to the ancient Germanic peoples who had liquidated the principle of individual property itself, 'to multiply the number of owners,' he admitted that in the modern world 'circumstances were different; thus remedies must be different' [I, 191]. If anything, the way forward once again lay in the government of laws, in a clever and targeted legislative and constitutional policy capable of favouring small property-owners. There was, in fact, no doubt that, as Paine, Jefferson and many other Enlightenment thinkers had thought,[11] he considered the diffusion of small properties to be the best way of guaranteeing the exercise of that right to the pursuit of happiness solemnly recalled in the Declaration of American Independence, in the 1789 French Declaration of the Rights of Man, and, in what was to be the last time in which the term appeared in an important published Western political document, in the Jacobin constitution of 1793. The creation of necessary legislative conditions for the emergence of numerous small property-holders would not only have favoured the birth of a modern form of rural democracy, longed for by Jefferson and many other radical thinkers of the late Enlightenment, but would also have strengthened the labour market for those peasants who had no 'property but that of their arms,' increasing consumption and encouraging trade and industrial production. All would benefit from a policy prohibiting the polarization of wealth and the concentration of boundless economic power in a few hands. In light of the 'principles' of redistributive justice expressed in the *Scienza della legislazione*, Filangieri listed an impressive series of legislative measures to promote in practice the fair distribution of wealth. It would not suffice simply to eliminate mortmain, majorat, feudal rights, and privileges and monopolies of all kinds. Direct intervention would be needed in family law, to prevent a father, for example, from bequeathing all his possessions to a single son, disinheriting the others. 'The immense ecclesiastical holdings' would have to be placed on a free market, even making a law which 'in the sale of lands, *coeteris paribus*, gave preference to non-owners' [I, 354].

The keystone, however, of the social and political programme Filangieri developed to guarantee the exercise of the right to happiness was his project for radical fiscal reform to set effective mechanisms of distributive justice in motion. During the course of the eighteenth century, Italian Enlightenment thinkers across the peninsula had often spoken up on this thorny question to ask for an end to the chaotic and unjust tributary system of the Old Regime.[12] Great attempts at renewing the land registries had been met with varying and generally disappointing results in many states. In Naples, Doria, Broggia and Genovesi had gone so far as to suggest the liquidation of all exceptions and privileges and to demand progressive forms of taxation to encourage greater fiscal equality. Filangieri was well-aware of this debate and of the numerous hindrances along the road to reform, but also of their increasing urgency in order to avoid the dramatic financial failure of the major nations of Europe, nations which were ever more threatened by the accumulation of unsustainable public debts. In his opinion, the first choice a government would have to make was that of focusing on direct taxation, eliminating every form of indirect levies. Taxes on the consumption and circulation of goods impinged on everyone indiscriminately, adding the injustice of their effects to their restraining consequences on the collective creation of wealth. Equally 'unjust' was the method of 'capitation,' which made everyone, rich and poor, pay the same sum. Instead, he proposed a single progressive tax on the net product of landed properties. The net product, he explained, was nothing but 'the surplus of income subtracted all the expenses of cultivation'; all lands were to be 'taxed in proportion to their net product' [I, 326]. In a polite polemic with Pietro Verri, who in his *Meditazioni sulla economia politica* had continued to uphold the importance of taxing manufactures as well, Filangieri resolutely opted for the argument of the Physiocrats, explaining that a single tax on land, properly calculated, would have facilitated the elimination of all forms of privilege, excluding private individuals from tax-collection, and finally bringing about a rationalization of the tax-system through a fair tax on all property-owners without exception due to class or the honours-system of the Old Regime. 'It takes little to know the value of lands,' Filangieri argued with a certain dose of optimism, forgetting the substantial failure of Neapolitan land-registry reforms in the first half of the century. Nevertheless, beyond technical and administrative discoveries and the not always convincing economic and psychological analyses in favour of a single tax on land, the principle of justice was the real underlying thread of Filangieri's strategic reforms. Whoever earned the most had to pay for the distribution of wealth and provide directly for the needs of the state, which was invested with the fundamental task of securing all citizens the right to the pursuit of happiness.

The eminently political character of the fiscal reforms suggested by the writers of the Neapolitan Enlightenment, and their immediate social consequences, was even more evident and explicit in a speech given by Filangieri's faithful disciple and companion in arms Mario Pagano, before the establishment of the Roman Republic in September 1798. Addressing the decisions to be made to assure the concrete exercise of the 'eternal truth of the rights of man,' the great constitutionalist posed the 'good patriots' in the audience a clear question: 'How can a democratic government guarantee the rights of man without taking property from its citizens?' Echoing what his mentors Genovesi and Filangieri had written in previous decades, he immediately rejected any reference to the myth of the agrarian laws or to the communist suggestions present in the works of Morelly and Mably, which had already been confuted, publicly and harshly, in eighteenth-century Naples. He gave the same treatment to those new followers of unrestrained economic liberalism against which Ferdinando Galiani had written with sarcasm and pointed irony. In order to 'reduce the gigantic possessions,' and make headway along the road towards the fair distribution of wealth, along the lines announced in the *Scienza della legislazione*, Pagano instead proposed introducing an effectively progressive tax on property. The Republic's decision to abolish majorat, requisition ecclesiastical properties, and proceed with the sale of so-called national goods would not suffice. One had to go beyond this to endow the state the necessary resources to satisfy the needs and rights of the collectivity. 'It would be useful,' Pagano wrote,

> to increase taxes ever more in accordance with the volume of possessions, so that when they surpass the value prescribed by the law, the tax doubles in proportion to property; so that, for example, whoever pays a tax of ten on a *rubbio* of land, if his property exceeds the limit set by law, he will contribute twenty for the same *rubbio* of land, and so on, progressively, the proportional series will always double.[43]

Pagano did not speak of the right to happiness in his writings or in his *Progetto di costituzione*. The term is not present in the constitutional document, and he had not given it any great space in his earlier writings. Nevertheless, the *Progetto* saw the juridical and political culture of the late Italian Enlightenment finally tackle what would be dubbed 'the social question' in the subsequent century. And it did so in rigorously legal terms and in light of the very rights of man which had been so dear to Filangieri. Fully exploring the expansive political and philosophical potential implicit in the logic of rights, Pagano based what today we call social rights not only on the concept of happiness, which in any case was implied, but on the inalienable right of existence of all human beings, a right which he connected organically to the principle of equality. The different approaches of the two thinkers are not surprising if one keeps in mind that, in the group of *fin-de-siècle* Enlightenment thinkers in Naples, Filangieri had taken on the hard task of tracing the general blueprint and philosophy of the new *Scienza della legislazione*, while it had been up to Pagano in practice to write a logically and legally consistent constitution for the Neapolitan Republic.[44]

On the basis of this requirement of consistency, and in open polemic with the French constitutionalists, Pagano – as we have seen – did not present equality as a right, but as a 'relationship,' 'merely the basis of all rights and the principle [of reason] on which they are founded and established.' From the universal principle of equal rights among all human beings, he in fact deduced the necessity of a social contract unifying the 'will of men who want to live together for the mutual guarantee of their own rights,' and above all the necessity of the *duties* of man. 'The duties of man are obligations,' he specified, 'or rather moral necessities born from the moral force of the principle of reason. This is the same principle from which we have derived rights, that is the similarity and equality of men.' In light of this principle of equality, in the *Dichiarazione dei diritti e doveri dell'uomo, del cittadino, del popolo e de' suoi rappresentanti* which opened the constitutional document, Pagano formulated the decisive articles of what we can define the Enlightenment conception of social rights, understood as man's duties to his similars.

> 17. The fundamental duty of man is to respect the rights of others. Equality means that our rights are worth as much as those of others. 18. Every man must help others and push himself to preserve and better the existence of his similar, since by natural similarity every man must have affection for others as for himself. 19. Therefore, it is a sacred duty of man to feed the needy. 20. It is required of all men to enlighten and instruct others.[45]

As is evident, Pagano's approach was quite far from that which the socialists and left-wing republicans sought to have passed against the liberals in the '*mémorable discussion*' of the Parisian parliament in September 1848, when they demanded the constitutionalization, in no less than the *Preamble*, of the 'right to work' of which Turgot first had spoken in 1776. That extraordinary debate, involving figures of the likes of Tocqueville, Thiers, Ledru-Rollin, Considérant and many others, definitively drew the curtains on a tormented period of history, inaugurated by the considerations, in frank polemic against the corporatist system of the Old Regime, of late Enlightenment thinkers with regards to the 'freedom of work.' The new period opened by the debates of 1848 would be entirely dominated by the social question and by the vindication of the social rights of workers, particularly in polemic with the right of property.

As is well known, a first Enlightenment response to the negative effects of abolishing the class-system of the Old Regime and its corporatist organization of labour, by which the individual would become even more isolated in his relationship to the state, was the concept and practice of philanthropy.[46] *Bienfaisance* and *humanité* were the passwords of Masonic associationism in the struggle against the growing phenomenon of pauperism. The invention of a new social structure appropriate for individuals who were formally free and, in terms of their rights, equal, and of new rules around the central right of assistance implicit in the demands of the late Enlightenment, found its moment of juridical and institutional realization primarily in the revolutionary period. In France, in 1790, shortly before the approval of the decrees of Allarde and the Le Chapelier law, which abolished the guilds, creating the conditions for a free labour market with all its social consequences, La Rochefoucauld-Liancourt bound the right to assistance to the right to work in the *Comité de mendicité*. The formulation was, however, strongly influenced by the ancient and authoritarian logics of Old Regime assistance. The right to work was in fact conceived of as a borderline right, that is as a duty and obligation to work in exchange for what was necessary to survive from the state: 'If he who exists has the right to say to society "make me live," society too has the right to answer "give me your labor."'[47] This scheme, which would lead to rapid growth in the social policies of the so-called *ateliers de charité*, launched by Turgot in 1780, was called into doubt by socialists and left-wing republicans precisely in the '*mémorable discussion*' of 1848. Theirs was the first attempt to put the expression 'right to work' in the preamble to the initial formulation of the constitution of the Second Republic, neatly separating it from the traditional right to assistance. 'The right to work,' the 7th article proposed for parliamentary approval solemnly affirmed, 'is that which every man has to live by working. Society must, with the productive and general means at its disposal, which will be further organized, procure work for valid men.'[48]

The electoral collapse of the Left and the bloody insurrection of a hundred thousand Parisian workers at the *ateliers nationaux* in June 1848 changed the situation radically. The liberal reaction in parliament against socialist proposals was extremely compact and above all victorious. Every attempt to introduce amendments which were favourable to the inclusion of a 'right to work' in the constitution was decisively outvoted. Assistance could only be conceived of as a free act of charity or solidarity. In his pamphlet *Justice et charité*, written for the occasion, Victor Cousin explained that 'the worker has no more a right to work than the poor has a right to assistance.'[49] In reality everyone had understood that the fiery discussion over the right to work had revolved around the right of property consecrated by the First Republic, which the Second Republic, 'social and democratic' as it was, now intended to debate publicly and limit drastically. But how could the right to work be guaranteed without transforming the state into an entrepreneur and heavily restricting private property? In his passionate address to parliament, Thiers openly warned that the right to work, as interpreted by the socialists, could lead to communism. Gualthier de Rumilly dryly repeated the argument that 'moral law, like Christian law, imposes the duty to help one's similar; but the unhappy cannot impose that obligation, he cannot force charity… the right to work implies a communist consequence.'[50]

The most persuasive and astute points would emerge, however, from Tocqueville's discourse. He defended the liberal and democratic nature of the 1789 revolution, accusing the socialists of reproposing, with the right to work, a veritable return to the Old Regime, to the art and craft guilds, to the omnipresence of the absolutist state in civil society. If the great conquest of the revolution had been above all the creation of a free market in private property (which had 'populated France with ten million property-owners'), the introduction of a right to work threatened to destroy all that. How could socialism claim to be the true heir of the revolution, and thus the 'legitimate development of democracy' by attacking the right of property? 'No gentlemen,' Tocqueville exclaimed, 'democracy and socialism are not in agreement with one another. They are not only different but opposite… Democracy extends the sphere of individual independence, socialism restricts it.'[51] From opposing fronts, many speeches on the concept of the 'freedom of labour' resounded with references to Turgot and the battles of the Enlightenment. They were almost always, however, imprecise and contrived interpretations compared to what really was said in the late eighteenth century, clearly demonstrating their detachment from that world which was so different and so irredeemably remote. If Constant, in the *Commentaire*, had highlighted the distance between the Enlightenment and modern liberalism, by then openly focused on all legislative impediments to economic and social liberalism, many socialist authors too, with their concentric attack on the right of property, began to feel and express an increasing sense of extraneousness to those ideas which nonetheless had brought the Old Regime to its knees and replaced the culture of heredity and the privileges of the few with the rights of the many. Some decades later, as class struggle became more and more accentuated and positions radicalized, and through a radical, caustic critique of the late eighteenth-century theory of the rights of man, Marx would mark the final break between the Enlightenment and that particular form of socialism represented by communism, which, on behalf of the new masses of workers, demanded the overcoming of private property and the emancipation of work and of man, rather than the reductive political emancipation of the bourgeois citizen hoped for by the men of the Enlightenment. Marx's authoritative argument contributed greatly to obscuring the innovations, in terms of social rights, present in the political and constitutional project of those late Enlightenment thinkers who were inspired more by natural rights than by utilitarianism. After Marx, in other words, the tradition represented by men like Condorcet, Jefferson, and Filangieri became the ideology of the 'selfish bourgeois individual' for large parts of the European Left.[52]

It is thus no coincidence that significant research has not been undertaken in this direction and that we know all too little about what the Neapolitan school of natural law theorized on the matter. As we have already suggested, the sphere of individual needs in the face of the emerging market economy and the social consequences of the so-called freedom of labour, interpreted – in accordance with Locke's teachings – as an aspect of the individual's right of property to his own labour, was primarily approached in light of the right to happiness in the *Scienza della legislazione*. In the political language of the late Enlightenment, which we find reaffirmed in the first French and American constitutional formulations, the horizon of reference for social rights was happiness rather than work. The interpretation of the right to work given by socialists in 1848, counterposing it to the right of property, made no concrete sense for the world of the Enlightenment, which always had considered the communist utopias of the ancient world with realist vexation. Filangieri could examine the question of the complex social nature taken on by labour in a market economy, and the need to guarantee everyone a subsistence wage, only through an analysis of the mechanisms of ensuring the universal right of all men to freely pursue happiness. Having reiterated, on every occasion, the 'sacred' nature of private property as a natural right,[53] the Neapolitan philosopher left it to the 'government of laws' and the instruments of constitutional politics to safeguard, albeit indirectly, the right to work as the socialists would have understood it. As we have seen, he proposed instruments of market regulation based on the principles of justice and fairness; the promulgation of laws favouring, over the long term, a greater distribution of wealth through progressive taxation, calling for intervention to promote, without revolutionary immoderation, the diffusion of small properties; and the elimination of monopolies and of excessive concentrations of wealth, encouraging, first of all, the creation of new production opportunities.

In the organic vision of a more just and fair future society sketched out in the volumes of the *Scienza della legislazione*, the loud appeal to respect the sacred rights to public education and to assistance was not made only as a function of the universal right to happiness, but also, and primarily, to safeguard the individual's right of liberty and to encourage direct participation in the public sphere in view of future political emancipation. The goal was to arrive, over time, at a sort of general class of producers and consumers, free and equal, capable of giving life to a republican civil society in which public happiness was not guaranteed merely by respect for individual liberties, but also by ongoing efforts to reduce the gravest and most intolerable inequalities produced by modernity, through the exercise of a new constitutional politics founded on rights and principles as delineated in the *Scienza della legislazione*. All this, however, demanded a complex redefinition of that principle of justice which was destined to represent the true keystone of late Enlightenment political thought in Naples, and the real foundation of the theory of the rights of man present in Filangieri's masterpiece.

The question had already been clearly posed in 1774, in the *Riflessioni politiche su l'ultima legge del sovrano che riguarda l'amministrazione della giustizia*, in which, polemicizing against the magistrates who arbitrarily deformed laws by recourse to the juridical and interpretative mechanism of 'fairness' in the formulation of sentences, Filangieri summarily had reconstructed the history of this concept (the 'inconsistency of its rules'), indicating its changing significance across the centuries and its particular nature as cultural horizon of reference for judges destined to condition the principle of justice itself as well as its application. He knew well that the concept of fairness among the Romans was something very different from what had been theorized and practiced by canonical and medieval jurists, who had never had any ethical qualms with applying (through the doctrines of the *jus singulare* and of the *privilegium*) a concept of fairness based on legal inequality.[54] It had all begun when Aristotle, in the *Nicomachean Ethics* (1129b–1130b5), in what would lay the foundations for the future power of magistrates, had affirmed that there were 'more forms of justice than one' and in particular that by 'just' one had to understand 'both the lawful and the equal or fair.' In the following centuries, the application of fairness to correct, by interpreting it, the abstract universalism of the laws had become an ever more important instrument in the hands of judges. With an acute sense of history, Filangieri polemically had unveiled the political and arbitrary use of it in Roman times to destroy republican liberty and impose imperial despotism, just like, more recently, it had been abused to give life to a 'body of despots,' the so-called *togati* who, usurping the role of other legitimate state powers, had rendered the words 'fairness, interpretation and arbitrariness' tragically synonymous. The time had come to change the conception of justice from the bottom up, beginning from the assumption – inspired by modern natural law – that it was always a grave 'error both in *morality* and in *politics* to distinguish fairness from justice. What is just is fair and what is unjust can never become fair.'[55] This required the development of an original conception of fairness which was finally in line with the values of the Enlightenment, as well as the definitive assumption of the principle of justice as the basis of every legitimate political community. Upon closer scrutiny, the *Scienza della legislazione* was probably written also to satisfy this urgent need. A new juridical, political, and cultural horizon of reference, different from that which for centuries had dominated the Old Regime, was in fact necessary for the magistrates and for the European élites alike. But the first in Naples to meditate at length on the necessity of formulating a new principle of justice to pose as the foundation of every aspect of civil society, in light of a re-evaluation of natural law, was not Filangieri but, yet again, his professor Antonio Genovesi.

In the 1766 *Diceosina*,[56] 'the idea of justice' was completely redefined, as a consequence of the modern 'science of natural law,' as respect for the rights of man on the basis of the principle that all men were born free and equal in rights.

> The first foundation of justice, as Lactantius astutely says, is the natural similarity, and with this the equality of rights, which all men possess from birth. For a *just* man, it is not possible to understand how one can escape this… Thus, in any nation where one believes that men are not of the same species, but that some men are gods, other men are beasts, others men, others half men, nothing can rule but injustice.[57]

If Aristotle had said a terrible and absurd thing in speaking of slavery as a fact of nature for some men, the more recent theorists of inequality seemed to want to turn to more scientifically pertinent arguments, without for that reason being convincing. Nobody, in fact, denied the physical differences between human beings, but could this statement suffice to solemnly affirm that 'the general equality of law was impossible, that is in the faculties of being, of living, and of pursuing liberty?' The theory of the 'rights of men' was examined by Genovesi in all its political, juridical, and above all moral implications not only in the *Diceosina*, but also in other important works, always drawing on the unquestionable assumption that 'one cannot live happily without justice' and that 'a right is always a faculty which is given us to be happy.' In the *Lezioni di commercio*, for example, the discussion of the possible spontaneous emergence of a 'conflict of rights' when reflecting upon how rights could be exercised paved the way for the vexed question of guaranteeing the sacred 'right to assistance' with respect to the right of property. Genovesi maintained that the former had to be located among the primitive and fundamental rights since society itself, upon closer scrutiny, rested on the 'reciprocal right to assistance.'[58] In a polemic with Mandeville, Hume, and the most famous exponents of utilitarianism, the father of the Neapolitan Enlightenment re-presented, on every occasion, the ideas which saturated Shaftesbury's *Enquiry concerning Virtue or Merit*, aimed at giving life to a new humanism, a Stoic conception of social harmony, respectful of all human rights and not just those of a fortunate few. The idea of justice developed by Genovesi was, in this sense, very different from that which slowly matured among the Enlightenment thinkers of Northern Italy in those same years. Where Beccaria's *Dei delitti e delle pene* had affirmed compendiously that 'for justice I mean nothing but the necessary limitations to unite particular interests without which they would dissolve into the ancient state of nature,'[59] Genovesi, Filangieri, and Pagano would never have subscribed to this definition, which conflicted directly with their faith in natural law.[60] Nor would they have accepted the utilitarian interpretation of the social contract between free and equal men as an instrument for attaining 'the greatest happiness divided among the greatest number.' Their way of understanding justice as a value and an ideal pushed them resolutely towards the reasonable utopia of the way things *ought to be*, towards a just and fair model of society consciously extended to embrace all; a model which foresaw subsequent choices in terms of the economy, society, and politics which were largely alien to Milanese Enlightenment thinkers. The crude utilitarian reading of happiness which, with time, affirmed itself in large parts of Enlightenment Europe, and not just in Italy, was, in the end, far from the Neapolitan way of reflecting upon the civil and social rights of modern man. The oblivion to which their ideas were condemned certainly rendered the Italian democratic tradition, which at that time was taking its first, uncertain steps, both weaker and more fragile.

NOTES

Foreword

1 J. W. von Goethe, *Italian Journey, 1786–1788*, London 1962, pp. 191, 202. For a biography of Filangieri see G. Ruggiero, *Gaetano Filangieri: Un uomo, una famiglia, un amore nella Napoli del Settecento*, Naples 1999. On Goethe's subsequent propagandation of Filangieri's work in Germany and its echoes, see P. Becchi, *Vico e Filangieri in Germania*, Naples 1986, pp. 93–150 as well as P. Becchi and K. Seelmann, *Gaetano Filangieri und die europäische Aufklärung*, Frankfurt am Main 2000.

2 See, on this, the extraordinary essays in A. Trampus, ed., *Diritti e costituzione: L'opera di Gaetano Filangieri e la sua fortuna europea*, Bologna 2005.

3 Benjamin Franklin to Gaetano Filangieri, 14 October 1787, in E. Lo Sardo, *Il mondo nuovo e le virtù civili: L'epistolario di Gaetano Filangieri*, Naples 1999, pp. 295–6; *A Catalogue of the Present Collection of Books, in the Manchester Circulating Library*, Manchester 1794, p. 39; Trampus, ed., *Diritti e costituzione; The Edinburgh Review*, or *Critical Journal: for Oct. 1806... Jan. 1807*, Edinburgh 1807, pp. 355–6. On the *Edinburgh Review* in the period, see B. Fontana, *Rethinking the Politics of Commercial Society: The Edinburgh Review 1802–1832*, Cambridge 1985.

4 F. Venturi, *Settecento riformatore*, 7 vols, Turin 1969–1990.

5 V. Ferrone, *La società giusta ed equa: Repubblicanesimo e diritti dell'uomo in Gaetano Filangieri*, Rome-Bari 2003, republished 2008; V. Ferrone, *La politique des Lumières: Constitutionnalisme, républicanisme, Droits de l'homme, le cas Filangieri*, translated by S. Pipari with T. Ménissier with a preface by T. Ménissier, Paris, 2008. For contributions to this debate in Italy, see C. Capra, 'Repubblicanesimo dei moderni e costituzionalismo illuministico: riflessioni sull'uso di nuove categorie storiografiche,' *Società e storia*, C/CI, 2003, pp. 355–407; V. Ferrone, 'Risposta a Carlo Capra,' *Società e storia*, CIV, 2004, pp. 401–7; E. Di Rienzo, 'Antichi e moderni: Filangieri e Constant,' *Nuova Rivista Storica*, LXXXVIII, 2004, pp. 365–9; G. Pecora, *Il pensiero politico di Gaetano Filangieri: Una analisi critica*, Soveria Mannelli, 2007, p. 21n; P. Costa, C. De Pascale, and M. Ricciardi, 'Gaetano Filangieri's The Science of Legislation, Edizioni della Laguna, 2003–2004,' *Iris*, I, 2009, pp. 253–76.

6 V. Ferrone, *Scienza natura religion: Mondo newtoniano e cultura italiana nel primo Settecento*, Naples 1982; English translation *The Intellectual Roots of the Italian Enlightenment: Newtonian Science, Religion, and Politics in the Early Eighteenth Century*, translated by Sue Brotherton with a foreword by M. C. Jacob, Atlantic Highlands, 1995. Among his other works it is worth mentioning *I profeti dell'illuminismo*, rev. ed., Rome-Bari, 2000; *L'illuminismo nella cultura contemporanea*, Rome-Bari 2002 (with D. Roche); *Una scienza per l'uomo: Illuminismo e rivoluzione scientifica nell'Europa del Settecento*, Turin 2007; *Lezioni illuministiche*, Rome-Bari 2010.

7 G. Filangieri, *La scienza della legislazione*, ed. Vincenzo Ferrone et al., 7 vols, Venice 2004.

8 F. Venturi, *Utopia and Reform in the Enlightenment*, Cambridge 1971.

9 For key works in this tradition see Q. Skinner, *Hobbes and Republican Liberty*, Cambridge 2008; P. Pettit, *Republicanism: A Theory of Freedom and Government*, Oxford 2000; E. Nelson, *The Greek Tradition in Republican Thought*, Cambridge 2004; J. G. A. Pocock, *The Machiavellian Moment: Florentine Political Thought and the Atlantic Republican Tradition*, Princeton 2003. On Genovesi's school in this context see N. Guasti, 'Antonio Genovesi's Diceosina: Source of the Neapolitan Enlightenment,' *History of European Ideas*, 32:4 (2006), pp. 385–405, who develops Ferrone's ideas.

10 On the idea that republics had to be small, see J. T. Levy, 'Beyond Publius: Montesquieu, Liberal Republicanism, and the Small-Republic Thesis,' *History of Political Thought*, vol. 27, no. 1 (2006), pp. 50–90. The locus classicus of the oppositional argument in the United States was Madison's Federalist #10, in A. Hamilton, J. Madison, and J. Jay, *The Federalist with The Letters of 'Brutus'*, ed. T. Ball, Cambridge 2003, pp. 40–46. The small-republic thesis was nonetheless extraordinary influential, for a layman reading of which see John, 2nd Lord Henniker, *A Northern Tour in the Years 1775 and 1776 through Copenhagen and Petersburgh to the River Swir joining the Lakes of Onega and Ladoga in a Series of Letters*, Cambridge University Library, Cambridge, UK, Add. MS 8720. On this manuscript see A. Cross, *By the Banks of the Neva: Chapters from the Lives and Careers of the British in Eighteenth-Century Russia*, Cambridge 1997, pp. 345–6.

11 For his library, which certainly did not exhaust his readings, see Lo Sardo, *Il mondo nuovo*, pp. 299–324. For his patronage of Neapolitan printers and booksellers as a means of procuring foreign works, see F. Luise, *Librai editori a Napoli nel XVIII secolo: Michele e Gabriele Stasi e il circolo filangieriano*, Naples 2001, p. 67.

12 M. C. Jacob, 'Foreword' to Ferrone, *Intellectual Roots*, vii–ix, p. ix.

Preface

1 On the international historiography of the Enlightenment, see V. Ferrone and D. Roche, eds, *L'Illuminismo. Dizionario storico*, Rome-Bari 1998.

2 I am, in particular, referring to the books *Scienza natura religione. Mondo newtoniano e cultura italiana nel primo Settecento*, Naples 1982; *I profeti dell'Illuminismo. Le metamorfosi della ragione nel tardo Settecento italiano*, Rome-Bari 2000.

3 On Filangieri's importance, see F. Venturi, 'Gaetano Filangieri. Nota introduttiva,' in *Illuministi italiani*, vol. V, *Riformatori napoletani*, Milan-Naples 1962, pp. 602–782. Though a monograph on Filangieri is lacking, many works of varying quality have been dedicated to him. See the excellent overview in P. Becchi, 'Gaetano Filangieri: profilo di un illuminista napoletano,' *Annali della Facoltà di giurisprudenza di Genova*, XXIX, 1999–2000, pp. 153–66. Among the more recent works to come out, see the proceedings of the conference held at Vico Equense in 1982, L. D'Alessandro, ed., *Gaetano Filangieri e l'Illuminismo europeo*, Naples 1991.

4 After the present volume first was published, I edited a critical edition of Filangieri's *Scienza della legislazione*, 7 vols, Mariano del Friuli 2004. Page references throughout this book are therefore to Pasquale Villari's 3-volume Florentine edition of 1864. References to this edition will henceforth appear in the body of the text, in brackets, indicating first the volume, then the relevant page number. The Florentine edition, which was preceded by a long and important introduction by Villari, contains, in the first volume, the *Libro primo, Delle leggi generali della scienza legislativa* and the *Libro secondo, Delle leggi politiche ed economiche* (Naples 1780); the second volume contains the *Libro terzo, Delle leggi criminali e Dei delitti e delle pene* (Naples 1783); the third volume contains the *Libro quarto, Delle leggi che riguardano l'educazione i costumi e l'istruzione pubblica* (Naples 1785–86) and the *Libro quinto, Delle leggi che riguardano la religione* which appeared posthumously (Naples 1791).

5 See Venturi, *Gaetano Filangieri*, pp. 648ff.

6 Currently, no less than 68 different editions of the *Scienza della legislazione* are known, of which 40 are in Italian and 28 are in other languages. The eighteenth- and nineteenth-century editions correspond to three main periods: the 1780s, immediately following the work's initial publication; from the Revolutionary period to the Restoration; and finally that of the constitutional revolutions preceding 1848. After these phases republications began to dwindle, until the total silence of the twentieth century. The principal Italian editions of the eighteenth and nineteenth centuries were: three in Naples (1780, 1782, 1784), three in Florence (1782, 1784, 1866), four in Milan (1784, 1804, 1817, 1858), three in Venice (1782, 1796, 1822), one in Catania (1789), one in Genoa (1798), five in Leghorn (1799, 1804, 1819, 1820, 1827), one in

Rome (1799). The most important foreign editions in the same period include: six in German (1784, 1788, 1794, 1808, 1848, 1849), five in French (1786, 1791, 1798, 1822, 1840), five in Spanish (1787, 1812, 1821, 1822, 1836), two in English (1792, 1806), one in Polish (1793), one in Russian (1804), one in Dutch (1804), one in Danish (1799), and one Swedish (1814). A catalogue of all editions is included in volume 7 of the 2004 Mariano del Friuli edition.

7 See 'Préface du traducteur' to G. Filangieri, *La science de la législation*, 7 vols, Paris 1786–91, vol. I, p. v.

8 See, on this theme, which deserves greater attention from European historians, for example the recent work of R. A. Primus, *The American Language of Rights*, Cambridge 2000.

9 See the introduction by Johann Christian Siebenkees to the German edition published with the title *System der Gesetzgebung. Aus dem Italienischen des Ritters Caietan Filangieri* (translation by Gottlieb Christian Karl Link), 8 vols, Anspach 1784–93, vol. I, pp. vii–viii.

10 On the German editions of the late eighteenth century, see A. Trampus, 'La traduzione settecentesca di testi politici: il case della Scienza della legislazione di Gaetano Filangieri,' *International Journal of Translation*, VI, 2002, pp. 20–44; P. Becchi, K. Seelmann, *Gaetano Filangieri un die europäische Aufklärung*, Frankfurt am Main-Berlin-Bern, 2000.

11 See C. Ugoni, *Della letteratura italiana nella seconda metà del secolo XVIII. Opera postuma*, Milan 1857, vol. IV, pp. 265ff.

12 See F. S. Salfi, 'Éloge de Filangieri,' in *Œuvres de Gaetano Filangieri. Nouvelle édition accompagnée d'un commentaire par M. Benjamin Constant*, 5 vols, Paris 1822, vol. I, p. 1.

13 See *The Science of Legislation of the Chevalier Filangieri Translated from the Italian by William Kendall*, London 1792, 'Advertisement.'

14 See the description of the ceremony of 26 February 1799, in the presence of the entire provisional government of the Neapolitan Republic, in the *Monitore napoletano*, ed. M. Battaglini, Naples 1974, pp. 178ff. The ceremony was repeated solemnly again in June 1799, 'there were speeched by the widow, the sister, and almost all of the family and the members of the Legislative Commission… with their well-known eloquence, the two legislators Pagano and Cirillo both paid their dead friend tribute, with lauds and affection, from the tribune' (ibid., p. 619).

15 On the centuries-old centrality of the Enlightenment-Revolution paradigm in international historiography, and on the need to overcome it, see V. Ferrone, D. Roche, *L'Illuminismo nella cultura contemporanea. Storia e storiografia*, Rome-Bari 2002, pp. 14ff. The book draws on, and modifies slightly, the 'Postfazione' to Ferrone, Roche, eds, *L'Illuminismo. Dizionario storico*.

16 See B. Croce, *La rivoluzione napoletana del 1799*, with an introduction by F. Tessitore, Naples 1998, 'Prefazione alla 2ª edizione' (1911), p. 12.

17 See G. Galasso, *Croce e lo spirito del suo tempo*, Milan 1990, pp. 236ff.

18 See P. Villari, 'Intorno ai tempi ed agli studi di Gaetano Filangieri,' introduction to the above cited Florentine edition of the *Scienza della legislazione*. The positivist Villarialso interpreted Filangieri's work in light of evolutionary schemes.

19 A good reconstruction of how idealist historiography has treated Filangieri can be found in S. Cotta, *Gaetano Filangieri e il problema della legge*, Turin 1954, pp. 10ff.

20 On the streams of pilgrims who reached Naples from every part of the continent to see him, see G. Ruggiero, *Gaetano Filangieri. Un uomo, una famiglia, un amore nella Napoli del Settecento*, Naples 1999, pp. 352ff.

21 See, on these themes, the recent reconstruction by A. De Francesco, 'L'ombra di Buonarotti, Giacobinismo e Rivoluzione francese nella storiografia italiana del dopoguerra,' *Storica*, XV, 1999, pp. 7–77. In the context of Marxist historiography, G. Berti's important *I democratici e l'iniziativa meridionale nel Risorgimento*, Milan 1962 would merit a critical revisitation. Though somewhat confused, in a text which is obscure and at times illegible, Berti was among the first to identify a fundamental component of nineteenth-century Italian democratic thought in the persistent heritage of the Enlightenment: 'Our democracy harboured two souls which in some coexisted and overlapped confusedly (Ferrari), in others determined themselves in a clear and insuperable antithesis (Mazzini on the one hand, Cattaneo and Pisacane on the other): the Enlightenment,

Jacobin (or Girondin) eighteenth-century soul and the mystical-romantic soul of the first half of the nineteenth century' (p. 30).

22 On this interpretation of these events, I must refer to my recent presentation at a conference held in Oxford, 24–26 September 1999, *Naples 1799. Enlightenment, Revolution, and Social Change*, now published as an appendix to the new edition of *I profeti dell'Illuminismo*, pp. 362ff. with the title 'L'Illuminismo italiano e la rivoluzione del '99. Un problema storico da ridefinire.'

23 On these issues see R. Pasta, *Editoria e cultura nel Settecento*, Florence 1997; L. Braida, *Il commercio delle idee. Editoria e commercio delle idee nella Torino del Settecento*, Florence 1995; M. Caffiero, *La politica della santità. Nascita di un culto nell'età dei Lumi*, Rome-Bari 1996; as well as the volume edited by A. M. Rao, *Editoria e cultura a Napoli nel XVIII secolo*, Naples 1998.

24 See F. Venturi, *Utopia e riforma nell'Illuminismo*, Turin 1970, p. 19. In this regard, Venturi's reflections in his celebrated 'La circolazione delle idee,' in *Atti del XXXII congresso di Storia del Risorgimento Italiano*, Rome 1954, pp. 203ff. remain fundamental: 'The subject which we propose to discuss this year is the history of ideas, of the circulation of political and social ideals, of the formation of mentalities and of public opinion. The chronological limit to political history is then less valid. We must observe not only the history of the emergence and affirmation of Italy's unity, in the framework of nineteenth-century Europe, but the history of all those ideas which at various times hindered, coloured, or bound themselves to a greater or lesser extent to the emergence of the unified state. These affirmed themselves in eighteenth-century Europe, and during the century of Enlightenment took on the form that would make them live on in the nineteenth century. It is there that we must look for them, not as precursors of something which did not yet exist, but as forces which have their own value and significance and which clarify the process of our *Risorgimento*, at the condition of distinguishing them from it historically.'

25 See the proceedings of the international conference held in Turin in December 1996, *Il coraggio della ragione. Franco Venturi intellettuale e storico cosmopolita*, ed. L. Guerci, G. Ricuperati, Turin 1998.

26 See, for example, the recent picture, delineated with clearly conservative political and cultural aims, offered by E. Galli della Loggia, *L'identità italiana*, Bologna 1998. Nor does one find any reference to the relevance of the Enlightenment experience in Italian history in the *Premessa* of the recent volume by A. Prosperi, *Tribunali della coscienza. Inquisitori, confessori, missionari*, Turin 1996. See in this regard the critical observations of M. Firpo, 'Tribunali della coscienza in età tridentina,' *Studi storici*, XXXVIII, 1997, p. 358.

27 The reference is to the volumes by F. Venturi, *Settecento riformatore*, 7 vols, Turin 1969–90.

1. The Enlightenment and the Political Critique of the *Scientia Juris*

1 Cf. V. Ferrone, 'Il problema dei selvaggi nell'illuminismo italiano,' *Studi storici*, XXVII, 1986, pp. 149–71.

2 In fact, the late Italian Enlightenment has been neglected by all historians. On the ideological reasons for this choice of always interpreting late Enlightenment culture in light of the French Revolution, see V. Ferrone, 'L'illuminismo italiano e la Rivoluzione napoletana del '99,' *Studi storici*, XL, 1999, pp. 993–1007, now in V. Ferrone, *I profeti dell'Illuminismo. Le metamorfosi della ragione nel tardo Settecento italiano*, Rome-Bari 2000, pp. 363–4.

3 The phrase, which speaks for itself, is by G. Astuti, *La formazione dello Stato moderno in Italia*, quoted and commented upon by Raffaele Ajello in *Arcana juris. Diritto e politica nel Settecento italiano*, Naples 1976, p. 284. 'As is well known,' Ajello writes, 'the Enlightenment critique of the system of common law was essentially directed at revealing its political presuppositions and conditionings. Similarly, it is not without reason that traditional juridical historiography has been brought to consider the Enlightenment conception to be intrinsically political, *ergo* not judicial and therefore negligible from the point of view of legal history' (p. 112).

4 Today, the traditional, obstinate, and inconsolable Counter-Enlightenment longing of a large number of Italian historians for the juridical pluralism in the age of common law and of particular rights blooms, for example, in the suggestive and debatable pages of P. Grossi, *L'ordine giuridico medievale*, Rome-Bari 1995. These, in fact, are pages dense with nostalgia for a lost world, where the efficiency of legal practice expressed itself best precisely in the absence of that state which was so exalted in the 'little Enlightenment fables' (p. 154) and in the abstract inventions of an 'obtuse modern legality' (p. 181). Along this road, which oozes of sincere nostalgia for the teachings of Aquinas and for the theorists of the Second Scholastic, see also B. Clavero, *Temas de historia del derecho. Derecho común*, Seville 1977, but above all Id. *La grâce du don. Anthropologie catholique de l'économie moderne*, Paris 1996 (I ed. Milan 1991). On the bullying return of Counter-Enlightenment thematics in recent legal historiography, see also the astute thoughts of R. Savelli, 'Tribunali, "decisiones" e giuristi: una proposta di ritorno alle fonti,' in *Origini dello Stato. Processi di formazione statale in Italia fra medievo ed età moderna*, ed. G. Chittolini, A. Molho, P. Schiera, Bologna 1994, pp. 397ff. On this subject see also G. D'Amelio, *Illuminismo e scienze del diritto in Italia*, Milan 1965; M. A. Cattaneo, *Illuminismo e legislazione*, Milan 1966; *L'illuminismo giuridico*, ed. P. Comanducci, Bologna 1978.

5 R. Ajello, *Arcana juris. Diritto e politica nel Settecento italiano*, Naples 1976, pp. 304, 311–12.

6 See, on this, the classic F. Diaz, *Filosofia e politica nel Settecento francese*, Turin 1962, pp. 465ff.

7 On the new aspects of the '*trionfo dei togati*' over the nobility beginning in the second half of the sixteenth century, and on their indisputable centrality in the history of the *Mezzogiorno*, see the important reflections of R. Ajello, *Una società anomala. Il programma e la sconfitta della nobiltà napoletana in due memoriali cinquecenteschi*, Naples 1996, pp. 166ff. See also P. L. Rovito, *La respublica dei togati, giuristi e società nella Napoli del Seicento*, Naples 1981; M. N. Miletti, *Tra equità e dottrina. Il Sacro Regio Consiglio e le 'decisiones' di V. de Franchis*, Naples 1995.

8 Quoted by R. Ajello in the critical introduction to the facsimile reprint of G. Filangieri, *Riflessioni politiche su l'ultima legge del sovrano che riguarda la riforma dell'amministrazione della giustizia*, Naples 1982. A clear sign of the difficulty of proceeding with reforms was the tough opposition of the *ceto togato*, against the Enlightenment principle of publishing all acts, to the institution of a public archive in the kingdom. See on this F. Cammisa, *La certificazione patrimoniale. I contrasti per l'istituzione degli archivi pubblici nel regno di Napoli*, Naples 1989, pp. 153ff., and particularly M. Tita, *Sentenze senza motivi. Documenti sull'opposizione delle magistrature napoletane ai dispacci del 1774*, Naples 2000. It is worth remembering that the motivation for sentences was adopted in France by the Lamoignon reform of May 1788, unleashing furious reactions, since sentences were considered by magistrates to be a priviledge *interna corporis* of sovereignty. See on this T. Sauvel, 'La motivazione delle sentenze in Francia. Lineamenti storici,' *Frontiere d'Europa*, I, 1995, pp. 69ff.

9 In R. Ajello, *Il problema della riforma giudiziaria e legislativa nel Regno di Napoli durante la prima metà del secolo XVIII*, Naples 1961, p. 274.

10 Ibid., p. 294.

11 See P. Verri, 'Sulla interpretazione delle leggi,' in *Scritti vari*, 12 vols, Florence, 1852–1854, vol. II, p. 165ff. On these interventions see M. A. Cattaneo, *Illuminismo e legislazione*, pp. 51ff.

12 On these matters see the ample bibliography and the arguments of M. G. Di Renzo Villata and M. R. Di Simone in *Cesare Beccaria. La pratica dei lumi, Atti del convegno 4 marzo 1997*, ed. V. Ferrone and G. Francioni, Florence 2000, pp. 29ff.

13 In F. Venturi, 'Gaetano Filangieri. Nota introduttiva,' in *Illuministi italiani*, vol. V, *Riformatori napoletani*, Milan-Naples 1962, p. 1042.

14 G. M. Galanti, *Testamento forense*, Venice 1806, I, p. 213.

15 G. Filangieri, *Riflessioni politiche*, p. 5

16 Ibid., p. 26. On the use of the term 'despotism' in the political debates of the second half of the eighteenth century see E. Di Rienzo, 'Per una storia del concetto di dispotismo nel '700 francese. Il manoscritto inedito dell'abbé Morellet: "Sur le despotisme légal et contre M. De La Rivière,"' in *Individualismo, assolutismo, democrazia*, ed. V. Dini and D. Taranto, Naples 1992,

pp. 321ff.; see also F. Venturi, 'Despotisme oriental,' in *Europe des lumières. Recherches sur le 18º siècle*, Paris 1971, pp. 130ff.

17 G. Filangieri, *Riflessioni politiche*, p. 42.

18 Ibid., p. 28.

19 Aristotle, *Nicomachean Ethics*, V (E), 2, 1130b–10: 'The unjust has been divided into the unlawful and the unfair, and the just into the lawful and the fair.'

20 G. Filangieri, *Riflessioni politiche*, p. 32.

21 Ibid., p. 29.

22 R. Ajello, *Arcana juris*, pp. 341ff. It must be remembered that Muratori, in *Dei difetti della giurisprudenza*, defined Ulpian's phrase a '*strepitosasparata.*'

23 See, on these events, D. Richet, 'Autour les origines lontaine de la Révolution française. Elites et Despotisme,' *Annales. E.S.C.*, XXIV, 1968, pp. 1–23, but, above all, the classic D. Richet, *Lo spirito delle istituzioni. Esperienze costituzionali nella Francia moderna*, Rome-Bari 1998, pp. 58ff.

24 D. Venturino, *Le ragioni della tradizione. Nobiltà e mondo moderno in Boulainvilliers (1658–1722)*, Turin 1993.

25 D. Richet, *Lo spirito delle istituzioni*, pp. 158ff. Large parts of the wonderful book by C. Maire, *De la cause de Dieu à la cause de la Nation. Le jansénisme au XVIIIᵉ siècle*, Paris 1998, pp. 378ff., are dedicated to the lawyer Le Paige.

26 On the importance of the doctirne of 'fundamental laws' in the seventeenth and eighteenth centuries as a constitutive element of monarchical absolutism, and thus as a premise for successive theories of a written constitution, see J. A. Maraval, *Stato moderno e mentalità sociale*, 2 vols, Bologna 1991, I, pp. 444ff. On the '*lois fondamentales*' in France see D. Richet, *Lo spirito delle istituzioni*, pp. 46ff.

27 In wake of the fundamental works on the political institutions of the Old Regime by O. Brunner and R. Mousnier, and of the great debate that followed among those who considered the term *constitution* an alternative to *absolutism*, and in any case meaningless before the French Revolution and the birth of the liberal and democratic written constitutions, the phrase 'Old Regime constitutionalism' has begun to circulate in international historiography, understood as practices and debates around a material but not formalized constitution. On this see the recent F. Di Donato, 'Constitutionnalisme et idéologie de robe. L'évolution de la théorie juridico-politique de Murard et Le Peige à Chaulaire et Mably,' *Annales E.S.C.*, LII, 1997, pp. 821–52, as well as the same author's introdcution to D. Richet, *Lo spirito delle istituzioni*, pp. viiff. See also M. Fioravanti, *Stato e Costituzione. Materiali per una storia delle dottrine costituzionali*, Turin 1993, pp. 107–18. On the use of the term constitutionalism in the context of the institutional and political history of Old Regime Southern Italy, see R. Ajello, 'Il viceré dimezzato. Parassitismo economico e costituzionalismo d'antico regime nelle lettere di M. F. Althann,' *Frontiere d'Europa*, I, 1995, pp. 193ff. Again on these issues, see I. Birocchi, *La carta autonomistica della Sardegna tra antico e moderno. Le 'leggi fondamentali' nel triennio rivoluzionario (1793–96)*, Turin 1992, in particular chapter V, *Leggi fondamentali e costituzionalismo moderno*.

28 N. Fraggianni, 'Dal "promptuarium excerptorum"' in the appendix to F. Di Donato, *Esperienza e ideologia nella crisi dell'Ancien Régime. Niccolò Fraggianni tra diritto, istituzioni e politica (1725–1763)*, 2 vols, Naples 1996, vol. II, p. 1013.

29 Ibid., p. 1011.

30 Ibid., p. 1015.

31 In this regard, the so-called 'scrutiny' of legality exercised over all the laws of the Kingdom by the Neapolitan courts were important, on which see M. N. Miletti, *Stylus judicandi. Le raccolte di 'Decisiones' del regno di Napoli in età moderna*, Naples 1998, pp. 146ff.

32 As Vico explained in the *Scienza Nuova Seconda*, it was no coincidence that in the great Neapolitan courts of justice one took the title of *Sacra Maiestas*. This was, in fact, the title suited the *Presidente del Sacro Regio Consiglio*, see R. Ajello, *Il viceré*, p. 181.

33 V. Ferrone and P. Rossi, *La nascita dello scienziato moderno*, Rome-Bari 1994.

34 On the transition from 'practical and erudite jurisprudence' to 'philosophical jurisprudence' in the second half of the eighteenth century, see the wonderful pages of G. Solari, *Studi su Francesco Mario Pagano*, Turin 1963, pp. 40ff.

35 C. A. Pilati, *L'esistenza della legge naturale impugnata e sostenuta*, Venice 1764, p. 10.

36 A. Genovesi, 'Discorso sopra il vero fine delle lettere e delle scienze,' in *Autobiografia e lettere*, ed. G. Savarese, Milan 1962, p. 231.

37 This way of thinking about the Enlightenment, generally attributed to Kant, was actually expressed by all the greatest thinkers of the European Enlightenment, on which see V. Ferrone and D. Roche, *Storia e storiografia dell'Illuminismo*, pp. 518ff.

38 On the social identity of the Enlightenment 'men of letters' of the Old Regime, see V. Ferrone, 'The Accademia Reale delle Scienze: Cultural Sociability and Men of Letters in Turin of the Enlightenment under Vittorio Amedeo III,' *Journal of Modern History* LXX, 1998, pp. 519ff.

39 A. Genovesi, *Della Diceosina o sia della filosofia del giusto e dell'onesto*, ed. F. Arata, Milan 1973, pp. 345–6.

40 G. Filangieri, *Riflessionipolitiche*, p. 1.

41 G. Filangieri, *La scienza della legislazione*, vol. I, p. 41.

42 G. Filangieri, *The Science of Legislation. Translated from the Italian of the Chevalier Filangieri, by William Kendall*, London [1791?], pp. 43–4.

43 On the extent of this conflict, in spite of the fact that many *togati* were open to the culture of the Enlightenment, see A. M. Rao, *L'amaro della feudalità'. La devoluzione di Arnone e la questione feudale a Napoli alla fine del '700*, Naples 1977; A. M. Rao, '"Delle virtù e de' premi": la fortuna di Beccaria nel Regno di Napoli,' in *Cesare Beccaria tra Milano e L'Europa*, Milan-Naples-Rome 1990, pp. 534–86; A. M. Rao, 'Dalle élites al popolo: cultura e politica a Napoli nell'età dei Lumi e della rivoluzione,' in *Napoli 1799*, ed. R. De Simone, Naples 2000, pp. 17–55; E. Chiosi, *Lo spirito del secolo. Politica e religione a Napoli nell'età dell'Illuminismo*, Naples 1992.

44 See R. Descimon, introduction to F. Di Donato, *Esperienza e ideologia*, p. xxiv.

45 Ibid., vol. II, p. 987.

46 Ibid., vol. I, p. 1.

2. The Critique of the British Constitutional Model and the Political Laboratory of the American Revolution

1 F. Venturi, *Settecento riformatore*, 7 vols, Turin, 1969–1990, vol. IV, book 1, *La caduta dell'antico regime (1777–1789)*, Turin 1984, p. 32. 'The American Revolution,' Venturi rightly noted, 'always retained a strong character of exemplarity for Filangieri.'

2 This letter can be found, along with all other known ones, in E. Lo Sard, *Il mondo nuovo e le virtù civili. L'epistolario di Gaetano Filangieri (1772–1788)*, Naples 1999, pp. 236–8.

3 See Franklin's letter of January 1783, ibid. pp. 238ff.

4 Ibid., p. 248, letter of 27 November 1783.

5 A precise reconstruction of the relationship between Filangieri and Franklin on the basis of their complete correspondence, there published for the first time, can be found in A. Pace, *Benjamin Franklin and Italy*, Philadelphia 1958. The regret is still strong for the loss of the copy of the American Constitution which Franklin sent Filangieri in 1787, and which Filangieri then sent back with his annotations. On this see Pace, ibid., pp. 153ff.

6 Through his friend William Hamilton, English envoy extraordinaire to the Neapolitan court, who gave him numerous books by British radicals, Filangieri probably had the opportunity to meditate on the celebrated 1784 book by R. Price, *Observations on the Importance of the American Revolution*, which presents America as a land of equality, austerity of customs, patriotic virtue, simplicity, and liberty in contrast to corrupt old Europe, eaten by the worms of mercantilism: 'with heart-felt satisfaction, I see the revolution in favour of universal liberty which has taken

place in *America*; – a revolution which opens a new prospect in human affairs, and begins a new era in the history of mankind… Perhaps, I do not go too far when I say that, next to the introduction of Christianity among mankind, the American revolution may prove the most important step in the progressive course of human improvement.' R. Price, *Observations on the Importance of the American Revolution*, London 1784, pp. 2, 5–6.

7 In this quotation, Filangieri drew heavily on his reading of Raynal's *Histoire des deux Indes*. See, on this, G. Goggi, 'Ancora su Diderot-Raynal e Filangieri e su altre fonti della "Scienza della legislazione,"' *Rassegna della letteratura italiana*, LXXXIV, 1980, pp. 112–160.

8 V. Ferrone, *I profeti dell'Illuminismo. Le metamorfosi della ragione nel tardo Settecento italiano*, Rome-Bari 2000, pp. 239ff.

9 F. Venturi, *Settecento riformatore*, vol. IV, book I, p. 32.

10 On the contradictions inherent in the problem of reconciling the rights of man proclaimed in the Declaration of Independence and the institution of slavery, which exploded in the very years that Filangieri was writing, see J. Appleby, *Inheriting the Revolution. The First generation of Americans*, Cambridge 2000, pp. 45ff. On these issues more generally see C. Biondi, *Ces esclaves sont des hommes. Lotta abolizionista e letteratura negrofila nella Francia del Settecento*, Pisa 1979.

11 See particularly F. Venturi, *Settecento riformatore*, vol. III,. *La prima crisi dell'antico regime (1768–76)*, Turin 1979, pp. 381ff., and vol. IV, book I, pp. 3ff.

12 G. Giarrizzo, *Massoneria e illuminismo nell'Europa del Settecento*, Venice 1994, pp. 155ff.

13 E. Chiosi, *Andrea Serrao. Apologia e crisi del regalismo nel Settecento napoletano*, Naples 1981, pp. 294ff.

14 A meticulous analysis of the great interest in the American Revolution shown by Italian journals can be found in volumes III and IV of Franco Venturi's above cited *Settecento riformatore*.

15 Ibid., vol. III, p. 406.

16 *Notizie del Mondo*, n. 71, 3 September 1776 and *Gazzetta universale*, n. 71, September 1776, p. 562. On the sacral character this document gradually took on in Americna history, see P. Maier, *American Scripture. Making the Declaration of Independence*, New York 1997.

17 On the European dimensions of this phenomenon see W. Schroeder, *The Trasformation of European Politics 1763–1849*, Oxford, 1993; *The Transformation of Political Culture: England and Germany in the Late Eighteenth Century*, ed. E. Hellmuth, Oxford, 1990.

18 See, for this constitution and for other important American documents, '*La costituzione la più convenevole*', ed. P. Del Negro, Milan 1987.

19 See, on this subject, G. S. Wood, *The Creation of the American Republic, 1776–1787*, Chapel Hill 1969, pp. 270ff.; J. Ph. Reid, *The Concept of Representation in the Age of American Revolution*, Chicago 1989. On the French context, see, D. Roche, 'Intellettuali e rappresentanza politica fra il tardo ancien regime e i primi anni della Rivoluzione,' in *La società francese dall'anciene règime alla Rivoluzione*, ed. C. Capra, Bologna 1982, pp. 231ff. As G. S. Wood emphasizes (in B. Bailyn, G. S. Wood, *Le origini degli Stati Uniti*, Bologna 1987, p. 297), one should always remember that the extension of the franchise to large parts of the population of the thirteen colonies resulted from the fact that 'the people of America are a people of property-owners, almost all of them are.'

20 Though seldom considered by historians of constitutional law, Peter Leopold's reflections, in the early 1780s, on the verification of constitutionality introduced in Pennsylvania's constitution are of great interest. See G. H. Davis, 'Observations of Leopold of Habsburg on the Pennsylvania constitution of 1776,' *Pennsylvania History*, XXIX, 1962, n. 4, pp. 373ff.; A. Wandruszka, *Pietro Leopoldo un grande riformatore*, Florence 1968, pp. 394ff.

21 In his *Rights of Man*, Paine clarified America's victories in terms of political theory. With regards to England's traditional constitutionalism, which confused the form of government and its constitution, he affirmed, 'A constitution is a thing antecedent to a government, and a government is only the creature of a constitution' (T. Paine, *The Rights of Man, Common Sense and other Political Writings*, Oxford-New York 1998, p.124). In England, there was no written constitution voted by the people, only the historical results of the ancient Norman conquest and the domineering claim of the victor's hereditary government. Entirely unknown in the ancient world, elective and representative governments – other great novelties – were

counterposed to the old hereditary government of the European monarchies, but it was above all the 'representative form' which finally resolved the 'defects of the simple democracy' of the ancients. From Paine's text it is clear that by representative government he intended that which we today call representative democracy. A classic case, in other words, of the same thing seemingly having two different names on the different sides of the Atlantic.

22 *The Federalist or, the New Constitution*, ed. W. R. Brock, London, 1996, p. 63. The same Madison had attacked popular governments based on the direct democracy of the ancients, writing that those small republics always had given 'spectacles of turbulence and contention; have ever been found incompatible with personal security or the rights of property' (p. 45).

23 It is anyway necessary to signal that it perhaps was precisely with Alexander Hamilton, in the United States, that the expression 'representative democracy' emerged in 1777, without, however, having a great and immediate following among other American intellectuals. See G. Stourzh, *Alexander Hamilton and the Idea of Republican Government*, Stanford 1970, pp. 48ff. In Europe, Kant was among those who followed the path, indicated in America, of defining the republic as a system of representative government, denying every reference to the word democracy, which they instead reserved only for the direct form of the ancients. See, on these themes, the fundamental work of L. Guerci, *Istruire nelle verità repubblicane. La lettura politica per il popolo nell'Italia in rivoluzione (1796–1799)*, Bologna 1999, pp. 177ff., which punctilliously has reconstructed the history of the expression 'representative democracy' up to its definite affirmation in Europe in the 1790s. See also F. Diaz, 'La rappresentanza dai precedenti americani al dibattito dell'89,' in *Mentalità e cultura politica nella svolta del 1789*, ed. P. Viola, Naples 1987, pp. 53ff.

24 Condorcet, 'Lettres d'un bourgeois de New-Heven à un citoyen de Virginie, sur l'inutilité de partager le pouvoir législatife entre plusieurs corps,' in *Œuvres de Condorcet*, ed. A. Condorcet O'Connor and M. F. Arago, vol. IX, Paris 1847, p. 84.

25 The debate has been reconstructed by F. Venturi, *Settecento riformatore*, vol. IV, book I, pp. 95–145. See also J. Appleby, *Liberalism and Republicanism in the Historical Imagination*, Cambridge 1992, and particularly the chapter *The American Model for the French Revolutionaries*.

26 E. Tortarolo, *Illuminismo e rivoluzioni. Biografia politica di Filippo Mazzei*, Turin 1986, pp. 104ff.

27 Ibid., pp. 152, 207. To confirm how strongly contemporaries felt there was a connection between Filangieri's work and the American experience it is worth noting that Masi's 1807 Leghorn edition of the *Scienza della legislazione* was dedicated to Jefferson, not coincidentally through Mazzei's direct intervention. The preceding edition of 1799 had instead been dedicated to Washington, with the following significant justification by the editor: 'when we now publish the immortal Filangieri's *Scienza della legislazione*, wishing to dedicate it to a subject the sentiments of which were analogous to those contained in said work, we choose the incomparable hero [Washington].'

28 On Jean-Antoine Gauvin Gallois and Filangieri's presence in the French debates, see chapter 9. Of particular interest with regards to the presence of Filangieri's work in the constitutional debate of those years see the notes of Condorcet, Du Pont de Nemours, and the previously mentioned Gauvin Gallois to the anonymous American piece, probably written by William Lingston, translated by Mazzei and published in France in 1789 under the title *Examen du gouvernement d'Angleterre comparé aux Constitutions des États-Unis. Où l'on refuse quelques assertions contenues dans l'ouvrage de M. Adams, intitulé: Apologie des Constitutions des États-Unis d'Amériques et dans celui de M. Delolme, intitulé: De la Constitution d'Angleterre, par un cultivateur de New-Jersey.* On this important work see N. Matteucci, 'Dal costituzionalismo al liberalismo,' in *Storia delle idee politiche economiche e sociali*, ed. Luigi Firpo, Turin 1975, IV, pp. 118–19.

29 *The Science of Legislation of the Chevalier Filangieri Translated from the Italian by William Kendall*, London 1792, 'Advertisement.'

30 Filangieri further specified his ideas on 'free and popular governments' such as those which were being delineated in the constitutions of the thirteen American republics (the reference was particularly to that of his beloved Pennsylvania, which also had the most democratically

advanced constitution), affirming that the first law was 'that which leaves to the whole people the choice of whom to confide some part of its authority in. The second is that which gives every citizen the right to achieve the highest charges of the State.' Only thus could one avoid destroying true 'equality, not that metaphysical equality longed for in the dreams of politicians, but that equality which is the soul of popular governments, which has rights rather than faculties as its object, and which, if altered, gives birth to the slave next to the hero' [I, 133]. Elsewhere, in a polemic with Polybius and indirectly with Rousseau, Filangieri also used the expression 'simple democracy,' meaning 'that government in which the people make the laws, create the magistrates, form a senate of the most respectable citizens,' something which anyway differed from a mythical direct conception of 'simple democracy' understood as 'that in which the people simultaneously are legislator, magistrate, senate, judge, commander of the army,' the existence of which he dryly defined a 'political impossibility [*un impossibile politico*]' [I, 110]. It is important to stress that the subject of representative democracy for the first time had been adumbrated in Italy, though always confusedly in relation to the mixed English model, through reviews of the celebrated work of Jean-Louis de Lolme, *Constitution de l'Angleterre ou Etat du gouvernement anglais, comparé avec la forme rèpublicaine et les autres monarchies de l'Europe*, Amsterdam 1771. In the *Gazzetta letteraria* of March 1772, pp. 89ff., the Piedmontese Enlightenment thinker Giambattista Vasco eulogized De Lolme's harsh criticisms of Rousseau's direct democracy, and shared his praise of the English constitutional model, underlining the importance of forms of representation in creating a free republic.

31 Like Paine, Filangieri too treated representative democracy without ever using that exact expression, which would affirm itself only in the subsequent decades. Differently from the Madison of the *Federalist*, however, he continued to count direct democracies and aristocratic governments among the republican forms of political community. For Filangieri, in fact, there were four forms of government: monarchy, aristocracy, democracy ('free and popular governments' exercising their sovereignty through 'pure' democracy or through 'representation'), and the mixed English government. Significantly, Gauvin Gallois' French translation did not use the locution 'representative democracy' either, neither in the first (1786–91) nor the second (1791–99) editions: 'une democratie parfaitene peut exister que dans un très-petit Etat. Si la République s'agrandit, si elle cesse d'être un simple cité, pour devenir une nation, alors il faut changer la forme du gouvernement, et recourir au droit de représentation.' Analogously, Kendall's English translation did not speak of representative democracy, but of 'recourse to representation.'

32 Filangieri defined mixed government as that in which 'the combination of the three moderate constitutions manifests itself,' that is monarchy, aristocracy, and democracy: 'I here call *mixed* government that in which sovereignty, that is the legislative faculty, is in the hands of the nation, represented by a congress divided in three bodies, the nobility, or patricians, the representatives of the people, and the king, who must exercise it in agreement' [I, 111]. On the eighteenth-century origins of the English debates over the mixed constitution, see C. C. Weston, *English Constitutional Theory and the House of Lords*, London 1965. The celebrated *His Majesty's Answer to the Nineteen Propositions of Both Houses of Parliament* of 1642, a fundamental text of mixed government, affirms 'In this Kingdom the laws are jointly made by a king, by a house of peers, and by a house of commons chosen by the people, all having free votes and particular privileges. The government according to these laws is trusted to the king'; quotation and comment in J. G. A. Pocock, *The Machiavellian Moment: Florentine Political Thought and the Atlantic Republican Tradition, with a New Afterword by the Author*, Princeton 2003, p. 363. On these issues see also L. D'Avack, *I nodi del potere. La teoria del governo misto nell'Inghilterra del Seicento*, Milan 1979; Id., *Costituzione e rivoluzione. La controversia sulla sovranità legale nell'Inghilterra del '600*, Milan 2000. On the theory of mixed government, Filangieri polemicized directly with Polybius, one of its founding fathers, for having confused, with regards to Sparta, democracy and mixed government (I, 110), and then with the Machiavelli of the *Discorsi*, who had contributed to the model's European fame. Mixed government had always enjoyed great currency in Italian

republican circles. Gravina, Doria, and Maffei had all fought for it. See, on this, G. Ghisalberti, *Dall'antico regime al 1848. Le origini costituzionali dell'Italia moderna*, Rome-Bari 1974.

33 F. Acomb, *Anglophobia in France, 1763–1789. Essays in the History of Constitutionalism and nationalism*, Durham 1950. On the fact that, in the eighteenth century, 'the idea spread that the English constitution represented the constitution *par excellance*,' see M. Fioravanti, *Costituzione*, Bologna 1999, p. 95.

34 On the political thought of Linguet see L. Guerci, *Libertà degli antichi e libertà dei moderni. Sparta, Atene e i 'philosophes' nella Francia del '700*, Naples 1979, pp. 142ff.

35 Montesquieu (*Spirit of the Laws*, ed. Anne M. Cohler, Basia C. Miller and Harold Stone, Cambridge 1989, p. 156) had defined Great Britain as the only 'nation in the world whose constitution has political liberty for its direct purpose.'

36 This is how Filangieri continued: 'to legitimate the act which removed James III's Anglican crown, did one perhaps not have to suppose that this prince had renounced the throne by fleeing the State, that he had deposed his crown willingly, and that no power legitimately could dethrone him in spite of his attacks on the constitution[?]' [I, 113]. As the source of his juridical analysis, Filangieri explicitly cited the French edition of W. Blackstone, *Commentaires sur les lois anglaises*, Brussels 1774, and particularly vol. I, chapter 7. On the widely discussed issue of the executive's independence of the legislature periodically claimed by monarchies, and more generally of the powers of the crown in a mixed system, which triggered popular tumults and revolts in the 1770s and 80s, see, in terms of the reception of London's political and constitutional struggle in Italian gazettes, F. Venturi, *Settecento riformatore* vol. IV, book I, pp. 191ff. as well as vol. III, p. 398. On these issues see also J. Brewer, *Party ideology and popular politics at the accession of George III*, Cambridge 1976; *Three British revolutions. 1641, 1688, 1776*, ed. J. G. A. Pocock, Princeton 1980. Like Montesquieu, so Filangieri probably underestimated, or, rather, did not fully understand, in his political and legal analyses, the innovative function of the prime minister in parliamentary life. Through the mechanism of cabinet government, the English constitution in fact seemed to have overcome the neat seperation of, and contraposition between, the executive and the legislature. See, on this, R. Shackleton, *Montesquieu. A critical biography*, Oxford 1961, p. 300.

37 Filangieri specified: 'Anglican legislation knew this remedy and implemented it. At the time in which its constitution was far more defective than what it is today, the king often wanted to decide on the controversies of citizens and judge their processes by himself. The use of this right immediately made known the inauspicious consequences which could result from it. It was thus established that the judicial power would always be exercised in the name of the king by his tribunals; and that these were immediate depositaries of the laws. Later, one also took away the king's right to capriciously depose of members of these tribunals... The 13th statute of William III, chapter 2, says that the incumbency of magistrates lasts as long as they conscientiously [*con esattezza*] perform their ministry *quamdiu bene se gesserint*; not as long as it pleases the king... This system, alongside the suppression of the *Camerastellata* [Star Chamber] assures, to a certain extent, the vigour and empire of the laws in England' [I, 120].

38 Filangieri used the expressions *separation* of powers and *distribution* of powers indifferently. In both cases he meant, like Montesquieu, to underline above all the necessity of balancing the three powers and distributing them in a way that never concentrated them in the same hands. Much has been written on the limits of, and errors in, Montesquieu's analysis of the English constitution. The same goes for the difference between *separation* and *distribution*. On these themes, see the rich bibliography discussed by Robert Derathé in Montesquieu, *Lo spirito delle leggi*, Milan 1989, pp. 569ff.

39 '[It is] too right,' Filangieri wrote, 'that he [the King] enjoys the negative faculty, that is the right of opposing himself to the decisions of the two other bodies. This is because, if this right did not belong to the king, the executive power could be destroyed by the legislative, which would find no resistance in the usurpation of his rights' [I, 114].

40 It worth noting the editor of the second English edition's harsh criticisms of the first two volumes of Filangieri's work (*The Science of Legislation*, Bristol 1806). A great defender of Blackstone and a refined scholar of Greece, Sir Richard Claydon wrote long polemical notes, which would merit closer study, attacking the work's first English editor, the radical Kendall, along with all 'over-zealous republicans' [I, 107] who like Filangieri criticized the British constitution. With horror, Clayton reminded Filangieri that the House of Lords had already been dissolved and the king decapitated in 1649, so that besides being provocative, his proposed reforms seemed 'to be an extravagant, unconstitutional and dangerous proposition. The King by the law of England is the fountain of honour, and to deprive him of this privilege would be an infrangement of constitution. The popular influence might acquire by such means a fatal preponderance and feeling its energy, other in roads might be made on the power of crow, till by repeated ancroachments the King's prerogative were reduced so much as to exist merely in name, and the balance of the constitution effectually destroyed' [I, 130]. On the political and constitutional struggle unleashed by radicals close to Filangieri's position, and in the very same Bristol, see A. Goodwin, *The Friends of Liberty; the English Democratic Movement in the Age of the French Revolution*, London, 1979; J. A. Hone, *For the cause of truth: radicalism in London 1796–1801*, Oxford 1982; *Biographical Dictionary of Modern British Radicals*, ed. J. O. Baylen and N. J. Gossman, 2 vols, Sussex 1979.

41 *La Scienza della legislazione* I, p. 123, n. 1. Filangieri's position was different and less restrictive on this issue in the case of American democracy [I, 132–3], where voting was nearly universal to the extent that the great majority of American citizens were property-owners.

42 These themes would be recovered and developed in France above all by Sieyes. Still, we know nothing of his possible awareness of the French translation of Filangieri's work. On Sieyes constitutional thought see P. Pasquino, *Sieyes et l'invention de la constitution en France*, Paris 1998.

43 Besides, Filangieri's criticisms found evident confirmation in the political debates which were developing in England in those very same years. See on this E. Gould, *The Persistence of Empire: British Political Culture in the Age of the American Revolution*, Chapel Hill 2000; I. Kramnick, *Republicanism and Bourgeois Radicalism. Political Ideology in Late Eighteenth Century England and America*, Ithaca 1990. Among the most important sources of Filangieri's thought one must mention the theory of mixed governments expounded by J. Locke, *Two Treatises of Government*, ed. Peter Laslett, Cambridge 1988, p. 108 and passim.

3. Against Montesquieu and Class Constitutionalism: The Denunciations of the 'Feudal Monster' and the 'Tempered Monarchy'

1 On the republican usage of Montesquieu's theories in the form of baronial resistance to royal absolutism in Europe, see *L'Europe de Montesquieu. Actes du colloque de Gênes (26–29 mai 1993)*, ed. A. Postigliola and M. G. Bottaro Palumbo, Naples 1995.

2 In R. Ajello, *Arcana juris.Diritto e politica nel Settecento italiano*, Naples 1976, p. 305.

3 These courageous attacks, which re-launched royal politics in Naples, resulted in Filangieri's denunciation to the Inquisition. See on this the 'Elogio storico del cavaliere Gaetano Filangieri scritto dall'avvocato Donato Tommasi,' in *La scienza della legislazione*, Philadelphia 1819, vol. I, pp. xlii–xliii. The I and II books of the *Scienza della legislazione* were condemned and put on the Index. See *Index librorum proibitorum… Pii sexti, Ponteficis maximi jussu editus*, Rome 1786, p. 322 (decree of 6 December 1784).

4 The literature on the feudal question in Southern Italy is vast. Among the most important works see A. Rao, *L'amaro della feudalità' La devoluzione di Arnone e la questione feudale a Napoli alla fine del '700*, Naples 1977 and P. Villani, 'Il dibattito sulla feudalità nel regno di Napoli dal Genovesi al Canosa,' in *Saggi e ricerche sul Settecento*, Napoli 1969, pp. 252ff.

5 G. Grippa, *Lettera al sig. Cavaliere D. Gaetano Filangieri sull'esame di alcuni suoi progetti politici*, Naples 1782, p. 5.On Grippa and those who intervened in the polemic, see P. Villani, 'Un oppositore di Filangieri: G. Grippa, professore nelle scuole di Salerno,' *Rassegna storica salernitana*, XXVII, 1966, pp. 33–8; P. Villani, *Il dibattito sulla feudalità*, pp. 269ff.

6 G. Grippa, *Lettera al sig. Cavaliere*, p. 21.

7 G. Giarrizzo, 'La coscienza storica del '700,' in *Il ruolo della storia e degli storici nelle civiltà, Atti del convegno di Macerata, 12–14 settembre 1979*, Messina 1982, p. 396.

8 E. Chiosi, 'Il Regno dal 1734 al 1799,' in *Storia del Mezzogiorno*, vol. IV, book II, Naples 1986, p. 440.

9 On the passage from the medieval origins of the concept of popular sovereignty to the natural law interpretation offered by thinkers like Locke and Filangieri, see O. von Gierke, *Johannes Althusius und die Entwicklung der naturrechtlichen Staatstheorien. Zugleich ein Beitrag zur Geschichte der Rechtssystematik*, Breslau 1880.

10 Filangieri probably used *Il governo civile di Mr. Locke tradotto nell'italiano idioma*, Amsterdam [but Venice] 1773, dedicated to Girolamo Durazzo. On Locke's reception in the Kingdom of Naples see P. Amodio, *La diffusione del pensiero di J. Locke a Napoli nell'età di Vico*, Naples 1990.

11 On this issue see M. Sbriccoli, *Crimen laesae maiestatis. Il problema del reato politico alle soglie della scienza penalistica moderna*, Milan 1974.

12 The Neapolitan prime minister Bernardo Tanucci demonstrated that he understood this well when, in a 1764 letter to Ferdinando Galiani commenting on the crisis of royal authority in the wake of Louis XV's collapse in the face of the parliamentary offensive, he wrote: by now 'everything shows that the administration and the force of justice, that is the government, the police, depend very little on the King, that the King is a commander in chief [*capitano generale*] or a stadtholder, that the government is an aristocracy inside.' In E. Chiosi, *Il Regno dal 1734 al 1799*, p. 444. Curiously, the attack on absolutism proceeded in parallel with the process of further sanctifying the figure of the monarch in the eighteenth century. See on this A. Boureau, *Le simple corps du roi. L'impossible sacralité des souverains français XV–XVIII siècles*, Paris 1988; M. Valensise, 'La dottrina giuridica della regalità nella Francia dell'Ancien Régime,' *Rivista storica italiana*, XCVI, 1984, pp. 622–36.

13 L. Salvatorelli, *Il pensiero politico italiano*, pp. 60ff.

14 G. Giarrizzo, 'L'Illuminismo e la società italiana. Note di discussione,' in *L'età dei Lumi. Studi storici sul Settecento europeo in onore di Franco Venturi*, 2 vols, Naples 1985, vol. I, pp. 181ff.

15 One must thus not confuse the 'tempered monarchy' of which Montesquieu spoke in the *Esprit des lois* with Filangieri's 'well constituted monarchy.' The former was entirely internal to the logic of the Old Regime, the latter went far beyond it. For Montesquieu, the monarchy could simply not exist without the nobility of the blood. 'In a way, the nobility is of the essence of monarchy… If you abolish the prerogatives of the lords, clergy, nobility, and towns in a monarchy, you will soon have a popular state or else a despotic state.' In that sense, beyond the prerogatives of the nobility of the sword, of the clergy, of the feudal lords, great attention was reserved for the nobility of the robe by magistrates and parliamentarians: 'there must also be a depository of laws. This depository can only be in the political bodies, which announce the laws when they are made and recall them when they are forgotten.' But if the nobility was indispensable in a 'tempered monarchy' then, Montesquieu specified, '[the law] must render it hereditary.' 'Noble lands, like noble persons, will have privileges. One cannot separate the dignity of the monarch from that of the kingdom; one can scarcely separate the dignity of the noble from that of his fief.' Montesquieu, *The Spirit of the Laws*, ed. Anne M. Cohler, Basia C. Miller and Harold Stone, Cambridge 1989, pp. 18–19, 55.

16 On the emergence of a modern culture of merit and talent also in noble circles at the end of the eighteenth century, see V. Ferrone, 'I meccanismi di formazione delle élites sabaude. Reclutamento e selezione nelle scuole militari del Piemonte nel Settecento,' in *L'Europa tra Illuminismo e Restaurazione. Scritti in onore di Furio Diaz*, ed. P. Alatri, Rome 1993, pp. 157–200.

17 'Stupid and vain men,' Filangieri wrote, addressing his own social class with his usual vigour, 'how long will the prejudices of your education resist the continuous push of the luminaries of this century?… Would the loss of this abusive authority, of which you are so jealous, not be a gain for you, when the prince, depriving you of every jurisdiction within your fiefs, renounced the right of *devolution*, and thus forced your serfs, with a forced ransom, to give you an indemnity for losing those very small emoluments to which you are entitled in the name of your absurd rights? Would not the full possession of the feudal lands, of which, as true owners, you could freely dispose, be preferable to an abominable satrapy which condemns you to great expenses and great risks? Would not the feudal lands which today are inalienable, thus put into the circulation of contracts, acquire a new value? This healthy operation, giving liberty to people and to things, would simultanously encourage industry, agriculture, and population growth' [II, 154].

18 Among the first to signal the possible republican interpretation of the *Scienza della legislazione*, and of the late Italian Enlightenment more generally, above all in its Masonic components, was G. Giarrizzo, *Massoneria e illuminismo*, pp. 281ff. For an informative critique of the historiographical concept of 'Enlightened Despotism,' see L. Guerci, *L'Europa del Settecento. Permanenze e mutamenti*, Turin 1988, pp. 501ff.

19 W. Goethe, *Italian Journey*, translated by W. H. Auden and Elizabeth Mayer, London 1992, pp. 191ff. See, on this meeting, also B. Croce, *Aneddoti di varia letteratura*, 3 vols, Bari 1953–4, III, pp. 21–35.

20 See, on this, note n. 6 of the *Introduction*.

21 This is how he was defined by the Parisian jurist and parliamentarian Antoine De Hillerin Écuyer, translator of Mario Pagano's *Considérations sur la procédure criminelle* (Paris 1789), who, describing the importance of the Italian Enlightenment for the reform of criminal legislastion, affirmed: 'Mais j'abrège ce tableau qu'on pourra voir tracé en grand et d'une main hardie et ferme, à la manière des grands maîtres, par le chevalier Filangieri, ce jeune Montesquieu d'Italie qu'une mort prématurée a moissonné l'année dernière. C'est dans son ouvrage (La science de la législation), qui mérite d'être lu, relu et médité, quoiqu'il n'ait pu le porter à la juste perfection de developpement et d'analyse de principe qu'il se proposait de lui donner; c'est dans son ouvrage qu'il fait voir avec quelle énergie, avec quelle courage, avec quelle force de raisonnement, de raison et de style, mais en même temps avec quelle décence, avec quelle justice l'homme sensible, l'écrivain patriote élève la voix contre les abus quand les droits sacrés de l'humanité et les intérêts de l'état l'exiget' (p. lix).

22 The work's success is testified to by the letters which arrived from all corners of Europe and are now conserved, among the few documents left to us, in the Museo Civico Filangieri di Napoli, Archivio Filangieri, Mazzo 28 (henceforth, M.C.F., m. 28). See F. Venturi, *Nota introduttiva a Gaetano Filangieri*, pp. 621ff., which examines many of these letters, as well as Pietro Verri, who wrote to his brother Alessandro describing the Neapolitan jurist as 'a great mind, he has great sentiments, he holds a great deal [*un ammasso*] of knowledge, and his work honours Italy.' To Filangieri himself, Pietro Verri then wrote enthusiastically, with reference to the *Scienza della legislazione*, 'I have listened to the voice of Hercules, echoing in my heart… May [your excellency] enjoy the applause of Europe and the admiration of its citizens for a long time! My grateful and sensible soul, moved by Italian patriotism, expresses this wish.'

23 Two important final volumes in fact remained to be written, which Filangieri would have dedicated fully to the right of property and the laws 'regarding the *patria potestà* [paternal authority] and the good order of families' [I, 60].

24 On the original aspects of the late Enlightenment in eighteenth-century Italy and Europe, see V. Ferrone, *I profeti dell'Illuminismo. Le metamorfosi della ragione nel tardo Settecento italiano*, Rome-Bari 2000, pp. 76ff.

25 Montesquieu, *The Spirit of the Laws*, p. 3.

26 On Montesquieu's political thought, and in particular for his distance from the modern natural law theories of the rights of man, see S. Rotta, *Il pensiero politico francese da Bayle a Montesquieu*, Pisa 1974, pp. 45ff.

27 F. Venturi, *Nota introduttiva* a *Gaetano Filangieri* , p. 615.

28 On Vico's importance for the Neapolitan school of natural law, and in particular for the definition of a 'science' in the field of law, see chapter 5.

29 The reference is to those who uncritically have accepted Benjamin Constant's polemical arguments against Filangieri, to which we will return later. On this interpretative current, see S. Cotta, *Gaetano Filangieri e il problema della legge*, Turin 1954, pp. 152ff.

4. Constructing a New Constitutionalism: Masonic Sociability and Equality

1 G. Stourzh, 'Constitution: Changing Meanings of the term from the Early Seventeenth to the Late Eighteenth Century,' in *Conceptual Change and Constitution*, ed. T. Ball and J. G. A. Pocock, Lawrence 1988, pp. 35–54. An important example of this Old Regime constitutionalism which, as we saw in the previous chapter, the Neapolitan magistrates had developed utilizing Montesquieu's theories, can be found in the works of N. Fraggianni (written around 1740). Referring to an ideal 'constitution,' he wrote 'The Kingdom has subsisted for two and a half centuries with these defective laws, with these unjust customs... we know, roughly, that its *Fundamental Constitution* and all its force lies in the civil arts, that is in the laws and in the forum. This is the foundation on which public tranquillity rests' (from the '*promptuarium excerptorum*,' in the appendix to F. Di Donato, *Esperienza e ideologia*, vol. II, p. 1013). For an up-to-date bibliography on the history of the term 'constitution' and its multiple meanings, see also M. Fioravanti, *Costituzione*, Bologna 1999.

2 See, for example, the *Statuti della laguna veneta dei secoli XIV–XVI*, ed. G. Ortalli, M. Pasqualetto and A. Rizzi, Rome 1989. The collection of Savoyard laws willed by Victor Amadeus II appeared in early eighteenth-century Piedmont with the title *Leggi e Costituzioni di S. M*. Cf. M. Viora, *Le costituzioni piemontesi (leggi e costituzioni di S. M. il re di Sardegna)*, Turin 1927.

3 G. Stourzh, *Constitution*, p. 43.

4 E. de Vattel, *Le droit des gens ou principes de la loi naturelle. Appliqué à la conduite et aux affaires des nations et des souverains*, Leyden 1758, p. 15. In chapter III, though contributing to specifying the difference between legislative power, form of government, and constitution, Vattel did not resolve doubts with regards to the latter's nature and form.

5 On Freemasonry, see the recent and excellent overview by A. Trampus, *La massoneria nell'età moderna*, Rome-Bari 2001. On the more than 250,000 brothers in the lodges of Europe, see Giarrizzo, *Massoneria e illuminismo nell'Europa del Settecento*, Venice 1994, p. 346.

6 L. N. de Luca, *I Santi Libri di Salomone*, Naples 1789, IV, p. 212.

7 See, on this point, the rightful emphasis made by M.C. Jacob, *Living the Enlightenment. Freemasonry and politics in Eighteenth-Century Europe*, Oxford 1991, chapter IV: *Creating Constitutional Societies*.

8 On the imporance of this translation of Locke for the history of European republicanism see M. C. Jacob, 'In the Aftermath of Revolution: Rousset de Missy, Freemasonry, and Locke's Two Treatises of Government,' in *L'età dei Lumi. Studi storici sul Settecento Europeo in onore di Franco Venturi*, 2 vols, Naples 1985, I, pp. 487ff. The republican reading of Locke based on Rousset de Missy's translation probably passed through Holland on its way to Naples. On the relations between Dutch and Neapolitan Freemasons see V. Ferrone, 'La massoneria settecentesca in Piemonte e nel Regno di Napoli,' in *La massoneria e le forme della sociabilità nell'Europa del Settecento*, ed. Z. Ciuffoletti, monographic issue of *Il Vieusseux*, IV, 1991, pp. 123ff.

9 N. Hans, 'Unesco of the Eighteenth Century. *La loge des Neuf Soeurs* and its Venerable master Benjamin Franklin,' *Proceeding of the American Philosophical Society*, vol. XCVII, 1953, p. 513ff.

10 G. Giarrizzo, *Massoneria e illuminismo*, p. 155.

11 T. Paine, *The Rights of Man, Common Sense and other Political Writings*, Oxford-New York 1998, pp. 22, 35.

12 In G. Giarrizzo, *Massoneria e illuminismo*, p. 186.

13 Cf. L. Amiable, *Une loge maçonnique d'avant 1789. La loge des neuf sœurs*, Paris 1989, pp. 132ff.

14 [H. T. Tschoudi], *L'Étoile flamboyant, ou la société des francs-maçons considéré sous tous les aspects*, quoted and subtly commented on in E. Chiosi, *Lo spirito del secolo. Politica e religione a Napoli nell'età dell'Illuminismo*, Naples 1992, p. 55.

15 Ibid., pp. 73ff. A broad selection of European documentation on this theme of equality in the lodges is presented and discussed by B. Fay, *La massoneria e la rivoluzione intellettuale del secolo XVIII*, Turin 1945, pp. 128ff.

16 An effective reconstruction of the history of the idea of equality through the centuries can be found in J.R. Pole, *The Pursuit of Equality in American History*, Berkeley 1993, pp. 43ff. A recent overview of the complex question, particularly in theoretical terms, can be found in N. Bobbio, *Eguaglianza e libertà*, Turin 1995. On the philosophical foundation of the concept of equality in the late Enlightenment, the reflections of an *Aufklärer* like Kant remain fundamental. See particularly his 1786 'Conjectures on the Beginning of Human History,' in *Political Writings*, ed. H.S. Reiss, Cambridge 1991, 221–34.

17 A. Genovesi, *Della diceosina o sia della filosofia del giusto e dell'onesto*, ed. F. Arata, Milan 1973, p. 197.

18 Ibid., p. 198. Aristotle had explained it well (*Politics*, book V), that, as dictated by historical context and the needs of the moment, it was necessary to rely on 'numerical [equality] in some cases, and proportionate in others.' If ever the problem arose from the contestation, developed in the *Nicomachean Ethics* (1131b–25–32), that 'all men agree that what is just in distribution must be according to merit in some sense, though they do not all specify the same sort of merit, but democrats identify it with the status of freeman, supporters of oligarchy with wealth (or with noble birth), and supporters of aristocracy with excellence. The just, then, is a species of the proportionate….' It is no coincidence that 'democratic justice is the application of numerical not proportionate equality; whence it follows that the majority must be supreme, and that whatever the majority approve must be the end and the just' (*Politics*, book VI).

19 M. C. Jacob, *Living the Enlightenment*, p. 9.

20 The theme of a nobility of birth which was virtuous at the same time was an established issue in the secular debate over the nature of nobility, see C. Donati, *L'idea di nobiltà in Italia. Secoli XIV–XVIII*, Rome-Bari 1988, pp. 30ff.

21 *Le Costituzioni della Società de' liberi muratori poste in ordine nuovo dal ex G.M.F.S.T. D.G.M.*, Cosmopoli, [s.d.], p. 12.

22 Voltaire to Rousseau, 30 August 1755, *Correspondance complete de Jean-Jacques Rousseau*, ed. R. A. Leigh, Oxford, Voltaire Foundation, 1984–, vol. III, pp. 156–7.

23 V. Ferrone, *I profeti dell'Illuminismo. Le metamorfosi della ragione nel tardo Settecento italiano*, Rome-Bari 2000, pp. 300ff.

24 G. M. Cazzaniga, *La religione dei moderni*, Pisa 2001.

25 See, on this theme, the marvellous book by G. Tocchini, *I fratelli d'orfeo. Gluck e il teatro musicale massonico tra Vienna e Parigi*, Florence 1988.

26 F. Grimaldi, *Riflessioni sopra l'ineguaglianza tra gli uomini*, 3 vols, Naples 1779, vol. I, p. xi.

27 J.-J. Rousseau, *'The Discourses' and Other Early Political Writings*, ed. V. Gourevitch, Cambridge 1997, p. 114.

28 Ibid., p. 159.

29 On the European polemic regarding the concept of 'state of nature,' see Landucci, *I filosofi e i selvaggi, 1580–1780*, Rome-Bari 1972, pp. 93ff.

30 F. Grimaldi, *Riflessioni*, vol. II, p. 22.

31 Ibid., vol. I, p. ix.

32 Ibid., vol. III, p. 17.

33 Ibid., p. 70.

34 Ibid., vol. I, p. x.

35 On Genovesi's polemic with Rousseau, see F. Venturi, *Settecento riformatore. I, Da Muratori a Beccaria*, I, pp. 603ff.

36 The problem of the rights of man in Rousseau is generally ignored by recent historiography, which prefers to insist on the centrality of the concept of the general will in his work. See, in any case, R. Derathé, *Jean-Jacques Rousseau et la science politique de son temps*, Paris 1974; P. Costa, *Civitas. Storia della cittadinanza in Europa 1. Dalla civiltà comunale al Settecento*, Rome-Bari 1999, pp. 497ff. On this subject, see also G. Del Vecchio, *Su la teoria del contratto sociale*, Bologna 1906, pp. 75ff.; G. del Vecchio, *La dichiarazione dei diritti dell'uomo e del cittadino*, Genoa 1903.

37 Modern scholars today know many of the thematics confronted by Filangieri mainly through the work of J. G. A. Pocock, *The Machiavellian Moment: Florentine Political Thought and the Atlantic Republican Tradition*, Princeton 2003. 'Rousseau was the Machiavelli of the eighteenth century' (p. 504), Pocock wrote, specifying that 'The "Machiavelliam moment" of the eighteenth century, like that of the sixteenth, confronted civic virtue with corruption, and saw the latter in terms of a chaos of appetites, productive of dependence and loss of personal autonomy' (p. 486).

38 Locke specified on this point: 'Though I have said above (2.) *That all Men by Nature are equal*; I cannot be supposed to understand all sorts of *Equality*: Age or Virtue may give Men a just Precedency: Excellency of Parts and Merit may place others above the Common Level: Birth may subject some, and Alliance or Benefits others to pay an Observance to those, to whom Nature, Gratitude or other Respects may have made it due; and yet all this consists with the Equality which all Men are in, in respect of Jurisdiction or Dominion one over another: which was the Equality I there spoke of, as proper to the Business in hand, being that equal Right that every Man hath to his Natural Freedom, without being subjected to the Will or Authority of any other Man,' *Two Treatises of Government*, London, printed for Awnsham Churchill, 1690, p. 273. Montesquieu, in his *Esprit des lois*, and Rousseau, in the *Contrat social*, had both written against an extreme conception of equality.

5. The Neapolitan School of Natural Law and the Historical Origins of the Rights of Man

1 With regards to this interpretative key, it must be highlighted that Filangieri's contemporaries were far more aware of it than later scholars have been, beginning with Franco Venturi's own fundamental contribution in his *Nota introduttiva a Gaetano Filangieri*, which I repeatedly have quoted and yet entirely ignores the question. That the *Scienza della legislazione* was based on the issue of rights was, for example, explicitly suggested to a French audience by its translator J. A. Gauvin Gallois when, in the preface to the 1786 first volume, he represented late eighteenth-century Italy as '*le pays de la terre où la science des droits et des devoirs de l'homme est cultivée avec le plus d'ardeur*' (*La sciencede la législation*, 7 vols, Paris 1786–91, I, p. ii). For an historical analysis of the rights of man, see R. Tuck, *Natural Rights Theories. Their Origin and Development*, Cambridge 1979. With regards to the central importance of the debate over rights in the constitutive phase of the French Revolution, see the fundamental work of M. Gauchet, *La révolution des droits de l'homme*, Paris 1989. See also the debatable, but nonetheless interesting works, as examples of a singular and traditional tendency in recent Catholic historiography to trace every form of modernity to medieval culture, to ecclesiastical institutions, and to canon law, B. Tierney, *The Idea of Natural Rights: Studies on Natural Rights, Natural Law and Church Law 1150–1625*, Atlanta 1997, and K. Pennington, *The Prince and the Law 1200–1600. Sovereignty and Rights in the Western Legal Tradition*, Berkeley 1993. On the presumed medieval origins of the 1789 declaration of rights and links between the Christian tradition of scholasticism and American constitutionalism, see the classic – for those with a preference for this kind of study – W. Ullmann, *The Individual and Society in Middle Ages*, Baltimore 1966. On the decisive influence of the second scholastic on modern natural law, see M. B. Crowe, *The Changing Profile of Natural Law*, The Hague 1970; on the allegedly omnipresent second scholastic, this time as nothing less than the source of the Enlightenment, see the somewhat less than cautious P. Prodi, *Una storia della giustizia. Dal pluralismo dei fori al moderno dualismo tra coscienza e diritto*, Bologna 2000: 'Sixteenth-century Spain,

with the great thought of the jurists and theologians of the so-called second scholastic, is the bridge across which the culture of Europe passed from the Middle Ages to modernity, transmitting and elaborating the great concepts of natural rights that later would be assimilated by modern natural law and by the Enlightenment' (p. 210).

2 Strangely, the central importance of the theory of the rights of man as the first foundation for a comprehensive and rigorous formulation of Enlightenment and republican criminal law, particularly in the case of Filangieri, seems never to have attracted the attention of historians. There is no reference to this even in the acute and valuable reflections of G. Tarello, 'Il problema penale nel secolo XVIII,' introductory essay to the monographic issue of *Materiali per una storia della cultura giuridica* on *Idee e atteggiamenti sulla repressione penale nell'età moderna*, Nr. 5, 1975 (where the three ideologies of reference for the eighteenth-century debate over the reform of criminal law are identified as the utilitarian, humanitarian, and proportionalist currents). For interesting thoughts on the conservative nature of absolutist natural law in the Tuscan penal debates of the eighteenth and nineteenth centuries, see P. Comanducci, *Settecento conservatore: Lampredi e il diritto naturale*, Milan 1981. Again on the absolutist and conservative reading of natural law offered by many Italian jurists of the eighteenth century, see also M. G. Di Renzo Villata, *Beccaria e gli altri tra ieri e oggi*, in *Cesare Beccaria. La pratica dei lumi, Atti del convegno 4 marzo 1997*, ed. V. Ferrone and G. Francioni, Florence 2000. For an overview of these issues see *La 'Leopoldina'. Criminalità e giustizia criminale nelle riforme del Settecento europeo*, 3 vols, Sienna 1986, and particularly the articles by M. Da Passano e P. Comanducci.

3 C. Beccaria, *Dei delitti e delle pene*, ed. F. Venturi, Turin 1965, p. 13. 'It was therefore necessity that compelled men to surrender a part of their liberty; he was sure that each man would not volunteer but the smallest possible portion to the public depository, that which would suffice to induce others to defend him. The aggregate of these smallest possible portions forms the right to punish.'

4 In this sense, Filangieri's reflections with regards to the function of the right to punish in the context of a cosmopolitan conception of international law is interesting: 'Without admitting the existence of this common right to punish in the state of nature, I do not know how one could justify the right of confederation of two or more nations, to allow them to make their rights respected, and for punishing the nation with the courage to violate them. Between them, nations are in the state of nature like men were before the formation of civil society. Now nobody has denied that all nations have the right to unite and bring war to that nation which has violated the right of peoples against one of them. It is not only the offended nation which has this right, but all the others can unite with her to avenge her; since every nation is custodian and avenger of the laws which depend on the rights of people. If one concedes this right to nations, one must concede it also to men in the state of nature, and if one denies men this right, one must deny nations this right [as well]' [II, 216].

5 Rivers of ink have been spilled on the sources of Beccaria's contractualism, and not always appropriately. The best account is that of G. Francioni, 'Beccaria filosofo utilitarista,' in *Cesare Beccaria tra Milano e l'Europa*, Rome-Bari 1990, pp. 69ff.

6 'What sort of right can it be, they say, which is attributed men to slaughter their own kind? Certainly not that from which sovereignty and the laws result. They are nothing but the sum of the minimum portions of everyone's private liberty; they represent the general will which is the aggregate of particular ones. Who has ever given others the right to kill him? How can the right to the greatest of all goods, life, be in the minimum sacrifice of everyone's liberty?' [II, 213]. Confuting Beccaria, who considered capital punishment to be both useless and unnecessary, Filangieri, an adherent of natural law, affirmed that 'man in the state of nature has the right to life; he cannot renounce this right, but he can lose it as a result of crime' [II, 218]. On the polemic between Beccaria and Filangieri see N. Bobbio, *L'età dei diritti*, Turin, pp. 184ff. It is worth underlining that, after having debated the ethical and utilitarian philosophical reasons for and against capital punishment (among the latter those of Aquinas, Kant, and Hegel), Bobbio argued that, in the final analysis, the argument against it had to take recourse to humanitarian reasons and to the Mosaic commandment not to kill one's own kind.

7 On the right to punish in Locke, see A. J. Simmons, *The Lockean Theory of Rights*, Princeton 1992.

8 On the great German criminologist Johann Anselm von Feuerbach's interest in Filangieri, see M. A. Cattaneo, 'Alcuni problemi nella dottrina della pena di Gaetano Filangieri,' in *Gaetano Filangieri*, in *Gaetano Filangieri e l'Illuminismo europeo*, ed. L. D'Alessandro, Naples 1991, pp. 262ff.; P. Becchi, *Vico e Filangieri in Germania*, Naples 1986; P. Becchi e K. Seelmann, *Gaetano Filangieri und die europäische Aufklärung*, Frankfurt am Main-Berlin-Bern 2000. Interesting points on Filangieri's theory of punishment are also found in the old 1925 book by U. Spirito, *Storia del diritto penale italiano da Cesare Beccaria ai nostri giorni*, Florence 1974, pp. 58ff. See also the many references to Filangieri in L. Ferrajoli, *Diritto e ragione. Teoria del garantismo penale*, Rome-Bari 1989.

9 See on this M. R. Di Simone, 'Riflessione sulle fonti e la fortuna di Beccaria,' in *Cesare Beccaria*, pp. 55ff.; M. R. Di Simone, *Aspetti della cultura austriaca nel Settecento*, Rome 1984; A. Trampus, 'L'Illuminismo e la "nuova politica" nel tardo Settecento italiano: "L'uomo libero" di Gianrinaldo Carli,' *Rivista storica italiana*, CVI, 1994, pp. 42ff.

10 It is no coincidence that Filangieri's ideas were interpreted in this way by Feuerbach, on which see M. A. Cattaneo, *Alcuni problemi*, p. 270.

11 The principle of equality before the law was defended by Filangieri also when examining the mechanisms of refusing a judge in cases of class differences. In his opinion, once feudal jurisdiction was abolished and a constitutional monarchy created, nothing could hinder any longer the effective juridical parity of all citizens, since 'the distinction between nobility and the people would [only be] a distinction of honour, not of empire' [II, 166].

12 This denunciation is, apart from this, one of the characteristic elements of the juridical Enlightenment. See J. M. Carbasse, *Introduction historique au droit pénal*, Paris 1990. The fundamental text which explicitly rivindicates the call to introduce the accusatorial process in the neo-republicanism of the late Neapolitan Enlightenment is that of F. M. Pagano, *Considerazioni sul processo criminale*, Naples 1787, which we will analyze in the successive chapters dedicated to the constitutional and republican patriotism of the Italian Enlightenment thinkers.

13 On the historical origins of the inquisitorial process in Western legal culture see the debatable interpretation of P. Prodi, *Una storia della giustizia*, pp. 92ff. See also C. Fantappiè, *Introduzione storica al diritto canonico*, Bologna 1999, and E. Brambilla, *Alle origini del Sant'Uffizio. Penitenza, confessione e giustizia dal medioevo al XVI secolo*, Bologna 2000, pp. 89ff.

14 See again, on this, A. Passerin D'Entrèves, *La dottrina del diritto naturale*, Milan 1962, p. 49, according to whom 'the real significance of natural law must be sought in its function rather than in the doctrine itself' in the face of its numerous historical manifestations. One cannot, in fact, confuse natural law according to the conception of the ancient Romans with the Christian one elaborated by the canonists. In cases of conflict, for example, the former always privileged positive laws, ignoring the very concept of 'rights of man.' Just like, in more recent times, the difference between the 'rights of the human person' vindicated by Thomistic philosophy and the 'rights of man' of which Enlightenment thinkers spoke was very clear. For the followers of Thomism, in fact, the point of departure was never 'the individual, but the cosmos, the notion of a well-ordered and hierarchical world of which natural law is the expression' (ibid., p. 68). One thing was, in other words, to constantly refer to an organic conception which privileged objective rights, to insist – like the thinkers of the Enlightenment did – on the subjective right of the individual, opposing the *facultas agendi* to the *norma agenda*, was something entirely different. A good and recent reconstruction of the different interpretations of natural law is provided by P. Costa, *Civitas. Storia della cittadinanza in Europa. 1. Dalla civiltà comunale al Settecento*, Rome-Bari 1999.

15 Particularly in Germany, where Filangieri's translators emphasized this particular aspect of the *Scienza della legislazione*. See P. Becchi, K. Seelmann, *Gaetano Filangieri und die europäische Aufklärung*.

16 On the rational and scientific pecularities unique to the modern concept of natural law developed by Northern European thinkers, see N. Bobbio, 'Il giusnaturalismo,' in *Storia delle idee politiche e sociali*, ed. L. Firpo, Turin 1975, vol. IV, pp. 502ff. See also F. Palladini, *Samuel Pufendorf discepolo di Hobbes. Per una reinterpretazione del giusnaturalismo moderno*, Bologna 1990.

17 On the extraordinary success of Cicero and of his ideal of *humanitas* in the European Enlightenment, see P. Gay, *The Enlightenment: An Interpretation, I, The Rise of Modern Paganism*, New York 1966, pp. 109ff. On the peculiar character of ancient concepts of natural law, in which inequality dominated as a fact of nature accepted by all, see L. Strauss, *Natural Right and History*, Chicago, 1999.

18 On the difference between seventeenth-century natural law and the political and legal culture of the Enlightenment, which reproposed the theories of rights in new forms, see the pioneering work of G. Solari, *La scuola del diritto naturale nelle dottrine etico-giuridiche dei secoli XVII e XVIII*, Turin 1904, pp. 214ff. Like many in the eighteenth century (it suffices to think of Genovesi, who in the *Diceosina* often spoke of the 'rights of humanity' like the Robespierre of the 8th Thermidor, who claimed that the French revolution had been 'the first revolution founded on the theory of the rights of humanity'), Filangieri used the expressions 'rights of humanity' and 'rights of man' indiscriminately. His radically universalist conception of rights, very far, for example, from Locke's more restrictive concept, is nonetheless evident in the above statements which connect the laws of nature to 'all individuals of our species,' affirming that they are 'by nature inseparable from thinking beings' [I, 76]. The expression 'human rights' already appeared during the French Revolution. It is very widespread today in the context of organicist Catholic natural law and in American political science, sensitive to the subject of minorities. It developed as an alternative to the traditional seventeenth and eighteenth-century expression 'rights of man,' which emphasized above all individual rights and seemed not to sufficiently take account of women and the debate over slavery. See L. Hunt, *The French Revolution and Human Rights. A Brief Documentary History*, Boston-New York 1996, pp. 4ff.

19 P. Costa, *Civitas*, p. 397.

20 Voltaire, *Political Writings*, ed. D. Williams, Cambridge 1994, p. 6.

21 See the profile of Filangieri prepared by Ginguené for Michaud's *Biographie universelle*, translated into Italian in *La Scienza della legislazione*, Milan 1817, vol. I, pp. 7–20. 'Since the beginning of the XVIII century,' Ginguené wrote, 'a great school of political philosophy has emerged in Naples. Giambattista Vico, a brave genius, wide-ranging and deep, but a bizarre and often obscure writer, planted the seeds in his *Principi di scienza nuova* which Genovesi, his student, a luminous and methodical mind [*spirito*], made fertile. The principles of natural law, of the laws of peoples, and of legislation were established in this school on different foundations than those of Grotius and Pufendorf.' Filangieri and Pagano were the last heirs of this school.

22 On Gravina, see C. Ghisalberti, *G. V. Gravina giurista e storico*, Milan 1962; A. Quondam, *Cultura e ideologia di G. V. Gravina*, Milan 1969.

23 See M. Capurso, *Accentramento e costituzionalismo. Il pensiero italiano del primo Settecento di fronte al problema dell'organizzazione dello Stato*, Naples 1959, pp. 180ff.

24 R. Shackleton, *Montesquieu. A Critical Biography*, Oxford, 1961, pp. 111ff. Again in Paris in 1766, Jean-Baptiste Requier published a translation of the great tract on Roman Law on the *Origines* with the title *De l'esprit des lois romaines*, to which he added the *De romano imperio* published in 1710. Polemically, Requier affirmed in the preface that 'the famous author of the *Spirit of the Laws* has drawn much from the parts in which the laws are examined from a philosophical point of view… He quoted it seldom, and could have made better use of it than he did.' In Montesquieu, *Lo spirito delle leggi*, Italian translation, Milan 1989, vol. I, 507.

25 M. Capurso, *Accentramento e costituzionalismo*, pp. 231ff. The author rightly reflects upon the evident similarities between Gravina's argument with regards to the legal limitation of government and the distinction between *gubernaculum* and *iurisdictio* introduced by the jurist Henry of Bracton, which is at the basis of medieval constitutionalism according to Ch. H. McIlwain. Very interesting, precisely for the central importance of Roman Law in the history of Neapolitan constitutionalism, are, additionally, McIlwain's considerations on Cicero's revolutionary definition of the State as a *vinculum iuris*, and above all on the decisive historical function of Roman Law, not in the construction of absolutism, as many historians argue wrongly, but in the creation of modern Western constitutionalism. See Ch. H. McIlwain, *Constitutionalism*, Ithaca 1940.

26 G. Fasso, *I quattro autori del Vico, saggio sulla genesi della Scienza nuova*, Milan 1949, pp. 59–63; S. Mazzarino, *Vico l'annalistica e il diritto*, Naples 1971.

27 G. Capograssi, 'Dominio, libertà e tutela nel De Uno,' in *Per il secondo centenario della 'Scienza nuova' di G.B. Vico*, Rome 1931, as well as the recent F. Piro, 'I presupposti teologici del giusnaturalismo moderno nella percezione di Vico,' in *Bollettino del centro di Studi Vichiani*, XXX, 2000, pp. 125–49.

28 See, on the historical foundation of natural law in Vico, in frank contrast with Grotius' rationalism, T. J. Hochstrasser, *Natural Law Theories in the Early Enlightenment*, Cambridge 2000, pp. 33ff.

29 On the theme of natural law in Naples, and in particular on Vico's critique of Grotius and Pufendorf, see G. Solari, *La scuola del diritto naturale*, pp. 158ff. According to Solari (p. 172), in the *De uno universi iuris principio et fine uno* of 1720, investigating the relationship between historical law and eternal ideal law, Vico sought to arrive, on the basis of a 'concept of natural fairness developed by practical [jurists], with the assistance of Roman Law as restored by the erudite, at that eternal idea of justice which Grotius essentially had derived from human reason.' Using the principle of identity between truth and certainty as a gnosiological model, Vico thought philology and the study of *auctoritas* to be the source of *certum*, while the *ratio*, or philosophical reflection, to be the source of *verum*.

30 G. Vico, *Autobiografia, poesie, Scienza nuova*, ed. P. Soccio, Milan 1983, p. 58. The quotation is from the *Autobiografia*.

31 Ibid., p. 274. Vico largely considered his *Scienza nuova prima* to be the understanding of a universal right of absolute validity which also became historical, because it was considered to begin with the concrete history of nations.

32 A. Genovesi, *Delle lezioni di commercio*, 2 vols, Naples 1765, p. 7. On the importance of Vico's thought for Genovesi see P. Zambelli, *La formazione filosofica di Antonio Genovesi*, Naples 1972, pp. 239ff.

33 F. M. Pagano, *Saggi politici. De' principii, progressi e decadenza delle società*, II ed. 1791–92, p. 10. From this point onwards, references to this text will be to the edition edited by L. Firpo e L. Salvetti Firpo, Naples 1993.

34 Ibid., p. 11.

35 Cf. Ibid., p. 14. Pagano credited Filangieri with having developed the 'maxims of sound morals and true politics' in Italy.

36 Goethe's testimony is fundamental in this regard. He referred to their encounter of 4 March 1787 in this way: 'Soon after we met, he introduced me to the work of an older writer, whose profound wisdom is so refresing and edifying to all Italians of this generation who are friends of justice. His name is Giambattista Vico, and they rank him above Montesquieu. From a cursory reading of the book, which was presented to me as if it were sacred writ, it seems to me to contain sibylline visions of the Good and the Just which will or should come true in the future, prophecies based on a profound study of life and tradition It is wonderful for a people to have such a spiritual patriarch...' (J. W. von Goethe, *Italian Journey, 1786–1788*, London 1962, p. 192).

37 It suffices to think that still, in the course of the twentieth century, Italian historicism and idealism above all underlined the absolute philosophical inconsistency of natural law. In 1949, Benedetto Croce commented on the new Universal Declaration of Human Rights promulgated by the United Nations the year before, and answered the precise questions of Jacques Maritain regarding 'the search for the foundations and philosophical meaning of the rights of man' (*Dei diritti dell'uomo. Testi raccolti dall'UNESCO*, Milan 1952, p. 19). He disparagingly wrote that the theory of natural law, once and for all confuted by nineteenth-century historicism, was 'philosophically and historically... unsustainable.' 'Since those rights vary *historically*, it confines them to those of *historical man*, that is, it considers them as those of a man at a certain time. They are therefore not eternal exigencies but historical facts, expressions of the needs of specific epochs.' Even if he expresses himself in more modern terms, N. Bobbio's interpretation is

analogous to that of Croce, even in his terminology, in *L'età dei diritti*, Turin 1990. For Bobbio, who even uses Croce's same words, it is in fact a 'misplaced problem' (p. xiii) to question the philosophical foundations of rights: 'That study is the task of social and historical sciences. The philosophical problem of the rights of man cannot be disjoined from the study of the historical, social, and economic problems related to their implementation' (p. 16). On the bitter polemic triggered in the Italian scientific community (always hostile to natural law) by the juridical, historical, and philosophical interpretation of Article 2 of the Italian Constitution, where reference is made to the 'inviolable rights of man,' see the acute introduction of Guido Alpa to L. Strauss, *Diritto naturale e Storia*, Italian translation, Genoa 1999. See also Hans Welzel's very interesting 1927 effort to give a philosophical foundation to rights in the sense of an 'existentialist natural law' in *La dottrina giusnaturalistica di Samuel Pufendorf. Un contributo alla storia delle idee dei secoli XVII e XVIII*, Turin 1993. Recently, P. Grossi violently attacked the 'strategy of natural law' of the rights of man based on the 'intensification of politics' which is extraneous to the juridical tradition in 'Modernità politica e ordine giuridico,' *Quaderni fiorentini*, XXVII, 1998, pp. 13ff. and *Scienza giuridica italiana. Un profile storico 1860–1950*, Milan 2000. In denouncing the 'convincing linear fables of natural law' (ibid., p. 123), which would pave the way for the juridical absolutism of legal positivists, Grossi does not hesitate to thunder against the 'dogmas and mythologies of the Enlightenment and Post-Enlightenment conception of right, so hard to extinguish even in the twentieth century' (ibid., p. 218).

6. Beyond 'Reason of State': The Moral and Religious Foundations of the New Politics *Ex Parte Civium*

1 The total number of soldiers in service around Europe in 1710 has been estimated at 1.3 million men. See G. Parker, *The Military Revolution: Military Innovation and the Rise of the West, 1500–1800*, Cambridge 1996, p. 46.

2 On the recent Renaissance of studies on reason of state, see the volumes edited by A. E. Baldini, *La Ragion di Stato dopo Meinecke e Croce. Dibattito su recenti pubblicazioni*, Genoa 1999; and *Aristotelismo politico e Ragion di Stato, Atti del convegno internazionale di Torino 11–13 febbraio 1993*, Florence 1990.

3 See G. Botero, *Della Ragion di Stato*, Turin 1948, p. 55. On the Jesuit Botero, see now *Botero e la 'ragion di Stato'. Atti del convegno Torino 8–10 1990*, ed. A. E. Baldini, Florence 1992.

4 N. Machiavelli, *The Prince*, ed. Q. Skinner and R. Price, Cambridge 1988, pp. 54–5.

5 Under the entry 'politics' in the *Encyclopédie*, Machiavelli was accused as usual of having 'masked the bad faith of princes behind the name "politics."' Cf. *Enciclopedia*, Italian translation, Rome-Bari 1968, p. 817.

6 In reality, knowledge of Machiavelli's works had never ceased to spread in eighteenth-century Italy. See G. Procacci, *Machiavelli nella cultura europea dell'età moderna*, Bari-Rome 1995, pp. 338ff.

7 F. Grimaldi, *Riflessioni sopra l'eguaglianza tra gli uomini*, 3 vols, Naples 1979, vol. III, p. 75.

8 Ibid., p. 179.

9 Cf. M. Perna, 'Giuseppe Maria Galanti editore,' in *Miscellanea Walter Maturi*, Turin 1966, pp. 221ff.

10 For an overview of ancient and recent theories of political realism, see P. Portinaro, *Il realismo politico*, Rome-Bari 1999.

11 *Elogio di Niccolò Machiavelli cittadino e segretario fiorentino con un discorso intorno alla costituzione della società e al governo politico*, s.l., [Naples] 1779, p. 26.

12 Ibid., p. 58. Galanti harboured no love for Filangieri or for his work. In the *Testamento forense*, Venice, 1806, vol. I, p. 252, he wrote this on the matter: 'Filangieri has tried to develop civil science in its full extension. He was too young to succeed, and thus his work was imperfect and superficial. His early death did not permit him to perfect it and unless one is fifty years

old, one cannot be a good writer on politics.' In the *Descrizione geografica e politica delle Sicilie*, ed. F. Assante and D. Demarco, 2 vols, Naples 1969, vol. I, p. 256, Filangieri was openly accused of being 'animated by metaphysical principles.'

13 L. A. Muratori, *Della pubblica felicità oggetto de' buoni principi*, ed. B. Brunello, Bologna 1941, p. 8.

14 See, for the Italian case, the dated but still useful L. Salvatorelli, *Il pensiero politico italiano dal 1700 al 1800*, Turin 1975.

15 See V. Sellin, *Politica*, Venice 1993, p. 68. On the Renaissance origins of this counterposition see M. Viroli, *From Politics to Reason of State: The Acquisition and Transformation of the Language of Politics, 1350–1600*, Cambridge 1992.

16 See V. Ferrone, 'Seneca e Cristo; la "Respubblica christiana" di Paolo Mattia Doria,' *Rivista storica italiana*, XCVI, 1984, pp. 5–68.

17 P. Mattia Doria, *La vita civile*, Augusta 1710, p. 6.

18 Ibid., p. 7.

19 R. Tuck, *Natural Rights Theories. Their Origins and Development*, Cambridge 1979, pp. 174ff; K. Haakonssen, *Natural Law and Moral Philosophy. From Grotius to the Scottisch Enlightenment*, Cambridge 1996. On Genovesi's natural law, see E. Pii, *Antonio Genovesi. Dalla politica economica alla 'politica civile'*, Florence 1984. Alongside the works of Grotius, Pufendorf, Locke, Wolff, and Thomasius, Genovesi intelligently retraced the Stoic thesis of the natural equality of men, commenting on the famous pages of Cicero's *De Legibus* on natural equality, and reread the juridical conception of ancient Roman republicanism in light of the rights, but also of the duties of modern citizens in a political community born from a fair and free social pact in accordance with Locke's schemes. Particularly, Genovesi commented on the celebrated passage of *De Legibus* thus: 'There is really nothing which is so similar to something else, as every one of us is with others. That if the corruption of customs, and the vanities of opinion had not been wrong and tempted weak souls to capriciousness, nobody would be as similar to himself as we are with everyone' (I, X, 29, XXII, 32). Actually, this celebrated passage could also be interpreted as a confirmation of the inegalitarian character of the classical natural rights of the ancients. See on this L. Strauss, *Natural Right and History*, Chicago 1999.

20 The quotation is taken from Barbeyrac's preface to the French translation of this work, published in Amsterdam in 1712, p. c. In the *Encyclopédie*, Diderot did not hesitate to collocate the entry 'natural law' in the field of morality.

21 A. Genovesi, *Della Diceosinao sia della filosofia del giusto e dell'onesto*, ed. F. Arata, Milan 1973, p. 58.

22 Ibid., p. 164.

23 J.-J. Rousseau, *'The Social Contract' and Other Later Political Writings*, ed. V. Gourevitch, Cambridge 1997, p. 53.

24 R. Koselleck, *Critique and Crisis: Enlightenment and the Pathogenesis of Modern Society*, Cambridge 1988, p. 79.

25 *The Constitutions of the Free-masons. Containing the History, Charges, Regulations, etc. of that most Ancient and Right Worshipful Fraternity*, London 1723, p. 50; analogously, the French version, *Constitutions, histoires, lois…, traduit par Jean Kuenen*, La Haye 1736, p. 52, stated '*Un maçon est obligé, selon son ordre, d'obeir à la loï morale.*' The same thing was repeated in Italian catechisms.

26 See the discussion in J. Palou, *La franc-maçonerie*, Paris 1964, pp. 317ff. See also the comments of F. Venturi, *Le origini dell'Enciclopedia*, Turin 1963, pp. 17ff.

27 See *Istituto o sia Ordine de' Liberi Muratori. Traduzione germana dal Idioma francese nell'italiano fatta da un curioso dilettante…*, a 1765 manuscript held by the Biblioteca di Storia Patria di Napoli, c.160.

28 Exemplary, in this regard, is the study of the tensions existing in the lodges between the cosmopolitanism theorized in their constitutions and official discourses on the one hand, and the spontaneous diffidence towards the *other*, in relation to the birth of the first forms of national identities, on the other. See P.-Y. Beaurepaire, *L'Autre et le Frère. L'Étranger et la Franc-Maçonnerie en France au XVIIIᵉ siècle*, Paris, 1998.

29 See V. Ferrone, 'La massoneria settecentesca in Piemonte e nel Regno di Napoli,' in *La massoneria e le forme della sociabilità nell'Europa del Settecento*, ed. Z. Ciuffoletti, monographic issue of

the journal *Il Vieusseux*, IV., pp. 103ff. Scholars have long beenaware that Freemasonry from the beginning was, rather than a new, peculiar, and important structure of socialization, a sort of informal coccoon, an empty bottle, capable of containing, at different times, different political projects, cultural strategies of consensus and opposition to power, disparate philosophical and religious ideologies, radical or moderate, dreams of refounding the new noble elites, or brave attempts at instead laying the foundations for an egalitarian co-existence between classes and orders. For a precise articulation of this research-hypothesis which always privileges the analysis of the historical contexts and cultural experiences of individual Masons, in contrast with the history of Masonry written by Masons, sometimes also philologically valuable, but openly apologetic and self-referential, above all open to the internal confrontation of the different rites, let me refer to V. Ferrone, *I profeti dell'Illuminismo. Le metamorfosi della ragione nel tardo Settecento italiano*, Rome-Bari 2000, pp. 214ff. Furthermore, it seems to me that the best work on the topic produced in Italy reached analogous conclusions, see G. Giarrizzo, *Massoneria e illuminismo*. Referring to the final confrontation between *Aufklärung* and *Schwärmerei* in the central European lodges after 1785, the author in fact writes 'Freemasonry returned to being an empty box in which to place new themes and new projects' (p. 339).

30 On the politicization of Masonry in the Italian context, after the reflection on its identity and future fuction launched by European Masons at Wilhelmsbad in 1782, see V. Ferrone, 'The Accademia Reale delle Scienze: Cultural Sociability and Men of Letters in Turin of the Enlightenment under Vittorio Amedeo III,' *Journal of Modern History*, LXX, 1998, pp. 553ff.

31 See the valuable information on the topic gathered by E. Stolper, 'Massoneria settecentesca nel Regno di Napoli,' *Rivista massonica*, LXVI, 1975, pp. 395–432.

32 An in-depth study of this important thinker of the Italian Enlightenment is still missing. Among the few available things, see the still significant entry by F. Venturi, 'Bianchi Isidoro,' in *Dizionario Biografico degli Italiani*, vol. 10, pp. 129–39.

33 *Dell'Instituto de' veri liberi muratori*, Ravenna 1989, p. 24.

34 Ibid., p. 27.

35 Ibid., p. 28. In effect, the first Masonic constitutions seemed fully to accept the logic of reason of state, virtually separating morality from politics. An interesting difference also existed between Anderson's first *Constitutions* and their translations into different European languages. In both cases, brothers were discouraged from taking up politics and above all from plotting against governments. In England, however, a hypothetical rebel brother could absolutely not be expelled from the lodge, and fully maintained the protection of the brotherhood; on the continent, where the logic of absolutism ruled instead, this part of the constitution had been significantly suppressed. See *The Constitutions*, p. 50. Referring to the relationship between Masonry and *The Civil Magistrate Supreme and Subordinate*, we find the following affirmations: 'A mason is a peaceable subject to the civil powers, wherever he resides or works, and is never to be concern'd plots and conspiracies against the peace and welfare of the nations... If a brother should be a rebel against the State he is not to be countenanc'd in his rebellion, however he may be pitied as an unhappy man; and if convicted of no other crime, though the loyal brotherhood must and ought to disown his rebellion, and give no umbrage or ground of political jealousy to the government for the time being; they cannot expel him from the lodge, and his from the lodge and his relation to it remain indefeasible.' In the French edition of 1736, *Constitutions, histoires, lois..., traduit par Jean Kuenen*, p. 53, the last phrase was deleted. On the other hand, the ban on politics, religion, and any other argument which in some way could trigger divisions between brothers was translated literally, see p. 59 of the French edition: 'C'est pourquoi il faut se defaire de toutes les querelles et des toutes les brouilleries avant que d'entrer dans la loge; d'autant plus si elles sont des disputes sur la Religion ou sur le mérite des Nations et des Gouvernements, parceque étant seulement maçon de la Religion Catholique mentionnée çi-dessus [in the sense of a universal religion], nous sommes aussi de toutes les Nations, de toutes les langues et parentées; et nous sommes resolus contre tous les maximes de la Politique

de ne point embrasser des partis, qui n'ont jamais fait ni ne feront jamais prosperer la loge. Ce devoir à toujours été fort recommandé et exactement rempli: mais particulierment depuis la Reformation faite en Angleterre, ou depuis la separation de ces Nations que s'opposerent aux sentiments de ceux de la Communion Romaine.' On this issue see B. Fay, *La massoneria e la rivoluzione intellettuale del secolo XVIII*, Italian translation, Turin 1945, p. 279.

36 On the Illuminati see the ample bibliography in A. Trampus, *La massoneria nell'età moderna*, Rome-Bari 2000, p. 138.

37 J. de Maistre, *La franc-maçonnerie, mémoire au Duc de Brunswick*, Paris 1925, p. 122.

38 *Dell'Instituto*, p. 32.

39 Ibid., p. 48.

40 Isidoro Bianchi referred to Paolo who, in *Colossians* 3:11, affirmed the equality of all Christians: 'Here there is no Greek or Jew, circumcised or uncircumcised, barbarian, Scythian, slave or free, but Christ is all, and is in all.' Always in the context of Masonry, the broche Thomas Paine indicated, without hesitation, the absolute foundation of the rights of man and of their equality in god, see *Rights of Man, Common Sense and Other Political Writings*, Oxford-New York 1998, p. 117.

41 Ibid., p. 49.

42 An in-depth study of the questions of when and how the language of rights was introduced to the circuit of European lodges is still missing. For a first exploration of the problem see V. Ferrone, 'Il nuovo repubblicanesimo dei diritti dell'uomo nelle leggi italiane alla fine del XVIII secolo,' *Rivista Storica Italiana*, CXIII, 2001, pp. 843–58.

43 In this direction, a reference to the Jesuit A. Barruel, *Mémoires pour servir à l'histoire du jacobinisme*, which appeared for the first time in 1797–98, is obligatory.

44 See the description of this ceremony in L. Amiable, *Une loge maçonnique d'avant 1789. La loge des Neuf Sœurs*, Paris 1989, pp. 66ff.

45 R. Koselleck, *Critique and Crisis*, p. 147. On the denunciation of the Enlightenment as an essential factor of the permanent crisis of modern society, as formulated by Koselleck, see V. Ferrone and D. Roche, *Storia e storiografia dell'Illuminismo*, pp. 560ff. In this sense, the original title of his work is clearer and more reflective of its contents: *Kritik und Krise. Ein Beitrag zur Pathogenese der bürgerlichen Welt*.

46 R. Koselleck, *Critique and Crisis*, p. 85.

47 See F. Venturi, *Giovinezza di Diderot*, Palermo 1988, p. 11. In this extraordinary book of 1937, Venturi highlighted the essentially political nature of the phenomenon of Enlightenment, inaugurating an avenue of interpretation which still today is extremely valid.

48 I. Kant, *Toward Perpetual Peace and Other Writing on Politics, Peace, and History*, translated by David L. Colclasure, New Haven 2006, p. 100.

49 The example of Kant is exemplary in this case. 'Morality,' for Kant (*Groundwork for the Metaphysics of Morals*, translated by Allen W. Wood, New Haven 2002, p. 57), presents itself as 'the relation of actions to the autonomy of the will, that is, to the possible universal legislation through its maxims.' 'The categorical imperative is thus only a single one,' Kant wrote, 'and specifically this: *Act only in accordance with that maxim through which you can at the same time will that it become a universal law*' (ibid., p. 37). Differently from Kant, who drew his conclusions regarding these difficult issues above all from the universality of human reason and the principle of equality, inspired by contractarianism and Rousseau's theories of the general will, Filangieri preferred to insist primarily on the discourse of rights.

50 A first reply to these questions can be found in V. Ferrone, *I profeti dell'Illuminismo*, and above all in G. Giarrizzo, *Massoneria e illuminismo*.

51 See F. Trentafonte, *Giurisdizionalismo, illuminismo e massoneria nel tramonto della Repubblica veneta*, Venice 1984, pp. 76ff. Analogous attempts were made by Frederick II, Gustav III, Victor Amadeus III, and other European sovereigns.

52 See A. Trampus, *I gesuiti e l'Illuminismo. Politica e religione in Austria e nell'Europa centrale (1773–1789)*, Turin 2000, pp. 145ff.

53 G. Giarrizzo, *Massoneria e illuminismo*, pp. 168ff.

54 Shaftesbury had sojourned in Naples for several years in the early eighteenth century, leaving a deep mark. See on this B. Croce, 'Shaftesbury in Italia,' in *Uomini e cose della vecchia Italia*, Bari 1927, pp. 274–311; and the recent work of F. Crispini, *L'etica dei moderni. Shaftesbury e le ragioni della virtù*, Rome 2000. On Shaftesbury's importance to Filangieri, see. F. Venturi, *Nota introduttiva*, p. 605.

55 On the change of course in Enlightenment thoughts on religion triggered by the appearence of Boulanger's 1761 *Recherches sur les origines du despotisme oriental*, which shed light on the important nexus between politics and religion and the opportunity of constructing a sort of Enlightenment religion for the masses, see F. Venturi, *L'antichità svelata e l'idea di progresso in N. A. Boulanger (1722–1759)*, Bari 1947; V. Ferrone, *I profeti dell'Illuminismo*, pp. 349ff.

56 The social study of M. Agulhon, *Pénitents et Francs-maçons de l'ancienne Provence. Essai sur la sociabilité méridionale*, Paris 1968, remains fundamental in this regard.

57 On the sharp confrontation between Masonry and the Church in Italy in those years, see G. Giarrizzo, 'L'Illuminismo e la società italiana,' in *L'età dei Lumi. Studi storici sul Settecento europeo in onore di Franco Venturi*, 2 vols, Naples 1985, pp. 165ff. It was certainly no coincidence that Giannone's *Triregno* was reintroduced again by Neapolitan Masons, and in particular by Longano, in view of constructing a modern civil religion at the end of the eighteenth century; see E. Chiosi, *Lo spirito del secolo. Politica e religione a Napoli nell'età dell'Illuminismo*, Naples 1992, pp. 197ff.

58 See Nicola's opinion among the papers held in the Archivio della Congregazione per la dottrina della fede, Vatican City State, fondo *S. C. Indicis*, Protocolli, 1781–84, N. 17, cc. 9ff. Nicola, prefect of studies at the *Collegio di Propaganda fide* and professor of canon law, affirmed that Filangieri had established, employing the materialist theses of the *Militaire philosophe*, that 'Revelation' was 'superfluous, since only natural law is necessary for proper and wise action [*operare*],' and the 'inexistence of original sin'; and finally he had increased 'hatred towards the professors of celibacy,' one of the fixations of the 'reforming philosophers.' The *Scienza della legislazione* was the object of distinct censorial by Rome's press censors. The work was first prohibited, in fact, by the Congregation of the Index on 7 December 1784 following an examination of the first two volumes of the 1781 Neapolitan edition. The measure was subsequently ratified by decree on 17 June 1826, aimed at the third, fourth, and fifth volumes of Filangieri's work (read in a Roman edition dating from the republican period which, to date, it has been impossible to find a copy of). Finally, on 11 June 1827, the Italian translation of Benjamin Constant's *Commentaire* published the previous year was put on the Index. The entire documentation relative to this is still held by the Archivio della Congregazione per la dottrina della fede, fondo S. C. *Indicis*, Protocolli, 1781–84, 491r–495r, passim; ibid., Protocolli, 1784, nn. 16 e 17; ibid., Protocolli, 1826, 51r–52r and Protocolli, 1827, 136v–137r. I would like to thank Franco Motta for bringing this information to my attention.

59 See on these themes P. Prodi, *Una storia della giustizia. Dal pluralismo dei fori al moderno dualismo tra coscienza e diritto*, Bologna 2000.

60 See on this C. Ginzburg, *Il nicodemismo. Simulazione e dissimulazione religiosa nell'Europa del '500*, Turin 1970.

61 See R. Koselleck, *Critique and Crisis*, p. 3. On the openly counter-Enlightenment nature of great parts of this critique, see J. Habermas, *Der philosophische Diskurs der Moderne: zwölf Vorlesungen*, Frankfurt am Main 1993.

62 See V. Ferrone and D. Roche, *Storia e storiografia dell'Illuminismo*, pp. 537ff.

63 See *La déclaration des droits de l'homme et du citoyen*, ed. S. Rials, Paris 1988, p. 24.

64 An example of the Enlightenment contribution to the creation of the modern public political sphere can be found in Filangieri's own correspondence, where one finds letters documenting the readings made of the *Scienza della legislazione* in provicial literary societies. See, for example, the letters from Mola in the province of Bari, from Domenico Pepe, who refers to the 'periodic public reading' of passages from the first two volumes with interesting comments on Filangieri's ability

to 'speak to the heart,' in G. Ruggiero, *Gaetano Filangieri. Un uomo, una famiglia, un amore nella Napoli del Settecento*, Naples 1991, pp. 181ff. On the decisive function of the Enlightenment thinkers in the birth of the modern public political sphere, see J. Habermas, *The Structural Transformation of the Public Sphere: An Inquiry into a Category of Bourgeois Society*, Cambridge, MA 1991.

7. Nation or Fatherland? The Republican and Constitutional Patriotism of Italian Enlightenment Thinkers

1 Among the best studies, see J.-M. Goulemot, 'Sul repubblicanesimo e sull'idea di repubblica nel XVIII secolo,' in *L'idea di repubblica nell'Europa moderna*, ed. F. Furet and M. Ozouf, Rome-Bari 1993, pp. 5–43; J. K. Wright, *A Classical Republican in Eighteenth-Century France: The Political Thought of Mably*, Stanford 1997; *Republicanism, Liberty and Commercial Society 1649–1776*, ed. David Wootton, Stanford 1994; K. M. Baker, 'Transformations of Classical Republicanism in Eighteenth-Century France,' *Journal of Modern History*, LXXIII, 2001, pp. 32–53.

2 The reference is, respectively, to *The Machiavellian Moment* of 1975 and *The Foundations of Modern Political Thought* of 1978, which have triggered a lively and highly interesting debate, primarily in the English-speaking world, over the possible implications of the European republican tradition for the intellectual origins of the American Revolution. See particularly, on these themes, the critical reflections of I. Kramnick, 'Republican Revisionism Revisited,' *American Historical Review*, LXXXVII, 1982, pp. 629–64; J. Appleby, *Liberalism and Republicanism in the Historical Imagination*, Cambridge 1992, pp. 1–33. For a first, largely endorsable attempt to take stock of the historiography, see M. Geuna, 'La tradizione repubblicana e i suoi interpreti: famiglie teoriche e discontinuità concettuali,' *Filosofia politica*, XII, 1998, pp. 101–32.

3 Montesquieu, *Spirit of the Laws*, ed. A. M. Cohler, B. C. Miller and H. Stone, Cambridge 1989, p. 155.

4 Ibid., p. 168. As is known, after having discussed the different ways in which the word liberty had been interpreted historically, Montesquieu enunciated that polysemic word's connection above all with the principle of legality: 'liberty is the right to do everything the laws permit.' It is in any case only 'moderate government,' with its distribution of powers, which historically reflected the real forces at play, which really could guarantee individual liberty understood as security and absence of domination according to an expression which Machiavelli would have liked: 'Political liberty in a citizen is that tranquillity of spirit which comes from the opinion each one has of his security, and in order for him to have this liberty the government must be such that one citizen cannot fear another citizen' (p. 157). Montesquieu clearly understood political liberty as that which, over the course of the eighteenth century, would be defined as civil liberty by many Enlightenment authors. One must in fact specify that only later in that century – it suffices to think of the *Saggi politici* (II ed. Naples, 1791–92, cap. XV, *Saggio V*, pp. 340ff.) – did the distinction become clear between natural liberty, civil liberty, and political liberty, redefined in light of the modern theory of the rights of man. Pagano, for example, explained political liberty as the 'geometrical equality of rights… according to which no citizen is more than the other,' a liberty which could be achieved fully, from all points of view, only in the 'pure democracies' of the ancients.

5 Montesquieu, *Spirit of the Laws*, p. 157. Montesquieu did not hesitate to define the Italian republics of the eighteenth century as 'miserable aristocracies which subsist only by the mercy accorded them and in which the nobles, without any sentiment of greatness or of glory, have no ambition but that of maintaining their idleness and their prerogatives,' quoted in G. Cambiano, *Polis. Un modello per la cultura europea*, Rome-Bari 2000, p. 293.

6 Montesquieu, *Spirit of the Laws*, pp. 25–6.

7 See the recent and acute reflections on Montesquieu's republicanism in G. Cambiano, *Polis*, pp. 260ff. This is an issue which does not seem to move English and American historians of republicanism.

8 See Q. Skinner, *Liberty Before Liberalism*, Cambridge 1998. If the centrality that this author gives the texts of the classical Roman tradition seems convincing and historically documented, his thesis of a specific republican theory of liberty of Roman and Machiavellian origins, entirely different both from the positive conception of liberty and the negative one which would emerge in the subsequent liberal tradition, seems exclusively suggested by the contemporary debate among political scientists. In this regard, it should be underscored that, in the republican arsenal elaborated in England in those years, different spirits, strategies of approaching liberty, and in particular the ways of its political and institutional application coexisted confusedly. Perhaps a careful re-reading of Montesquieu on the subject of liberty in the ancient republics and in the modern monarchies could help to clarify these problems.

9 F. Venturi, *Utopia e riforma nell'Illuminismo*, Turin 1970, p. 76.

10 See G. Cambiano, *Polis*, pp. 266ff. In Turin, Italy, in 1750 the Barnabite Giacinto Sigismondo Gerdil wrote a controversial book in defence of monarchy entitled *Virtutempoliticam ad optimum statum non minus regno, quam reipublicae necessariam esse oratio*.

11 F. Venturi, *Utopia e riforma*, p. 95.

12 J. Locke, *Two Treatises of Government*, ed. P. Laslett, Cambridge 1988, p. 355. Locke defined political power as that power which 'every Man, having in the state of Nature, has given up into the hands of the Society... And this Power has its Original only from Compact and Agreement, and the mutual Consent of those who make up the Community' (pp. 381–2), adding that no 'polities' could be 'founded on anything but the consent of the people' (pp. 384–5).

13 See J. G. Pocock and R. Ashcraft, *John Locke. Papers read at a Clark Library Seminar 10 December 1977*, Los Angeles 1980, p. 17.

14 See M. P. Zuckert, *Natural Rights and New Repubblicanism*, Princeton 1994, particularly pp. 305ff. *Cato's Letters* had previously been read by Pocock and Wood as a traditional expression of civic humanism and of classical republicanism without any specific reference to Locke and more generally to natural law, the great absence in all recent interpretations of seventeenth and eighteenth-century English and continental European republicanism. However, in his *Introduzione all'edizione italiana* of the *Machiavellian Moment* (Bologna 1980, I, p. 20), referring to the works of Skinner, Pocock himself affirmed 'None of us thus (though for different reasons) pushed himself to ask if (and, if so, why) the typical language of republican virtue arrived at combining that of individual rights. Such a question must be engaged with by those who study the political thought of the late seventeenth and eighteenth centuries.'

15 Rousseau, *'The Social Contract' and Other Later Political Writings*, ed. V. Gourevitch, Cambridge 1997, p. 53. The 'transition from the state of nature to the civil state,' Rousseau specified on this subject, 'produces a most remarkable change in man by substituting justice for instinct in his conduct, and endowing his actions with the morality they previously lacked.'

16 Ibid., p. 67. 'What, then, is Government?,' Rousseau asked himself, 'An intermediary body established between subjects and Sovereign so that they might conform to one another, and charged with the execution of the laws and the maintenance of freedom, both civil and political. The members of this body are called magistrates or *Kings*, that is to say Governors, and the body as a whole bears the name *Prince*' (p. 83).

17 See H. Rosemblatt, *Rousseau and Geneva. From the 'First Discourse' to 'The Social Contract', 1749–1762*, Cambridge 2000.

18 This is the thesis of Franco Venturi, *Utopia e riforma*, p. 117, according to which, in relation to the American Revolution, 'the importance of the European Enlightenment is proven against all hasty rebuttals.' J. G. A. Pocock remains of a different opinion, (*Machiavellian Moment*, p. 462), instead considering the Revolution to be the 'last act of the civic Renaissance.'

19 T. Jefferson, *Political Writings*, ed. J. Appleby and T. Ball, Cambridge, 1999, p. 207. Also John Adams, in 1806, wrote alarmed 'There is not a more unintelligible word in the English language than republicanism,' quoted in D. Wootton, *Republicanism, Liberty and Commercial Society*, p. 1.

20 See K. M. Baker, *Trasformations of Classical Republicanism*, p. 32.

21 T. Paine, *The Rights of Man, Common Sense and Other Political Writings*, Oxford-New York 1998, pp. 230ff.

22 F. Venturi, 'L'Italia fuori d'Italia,' in *Storia d'Italia*, vol. III, Turin 1973, p. 1137.

23 See G. Giarrizzo, 'Alle origini della medievistica moderna,' in *Vico e la politica e la storia*, Naples 1981, pp. 13ff.

24 J.-C.-L. Simonde Sismondi, *Histoire des républiques italiennes du moyen âge*, Paris 1809, I, p. 415.

25 See F. Venturi, *L'Italia fuori d'Italia*, pp. 1135ff. 'That which the French conquest instead had unleashed in Italy,' Venturi specified in his reconstruction of the revolutionary triennial, 'was primarily a popular, communal rebellion, a resumption of the centuries-long struggle between municipalities, which, underneath the structures of the principates, rediscovered an ancient will to reaffirm the self-government of their own cities. Alba and Asti against the King of Sardinia, Reggio against the Duke of Modena, Bologna and Ferrara against the Papal States, Bergamo, Brescia and Padua against Venice, the cities of The Marche against each other, etc. And quickly, in every one of these centres, the struggle immediately became social, between town-dwellers and peasants, nobles and bourgeois, patricians and plebeians,' a struggle which was accompanied by the ruinous explosion of 'an endemic peasant rebellion in the hilly and mountainous zones.'

26 The centrality of Roman Law, and particularly of the works of Cicero, is, in this sense, fundamental in Antonio Genovesi. See the very definition of republic given by the Neapolitan reformer in *Della Diceosina o sia della filosofia del giusto e dell'onesto*, ed. F. Arata, Milan 1973, p. 296, referring to the Roman tradition. By 'republic,' one had to understand 'a body composed of many families, which by a primitive social pact, either expressive or tacit, became a confederation to assure their mutual security and happiness, subjecting themselves to a common law and to a common empire which one must believe divinely established. The social pact from which republics are born contains three essential parts: 1) that the general aim of all the families and persons must be the public health, *salus publica summa lex*; 2) that they be subject to the same law...; 3) the form of the empire, or fundamental law which makes of it a kingdom, an aristocracy, or a democracy. Where one of these parts is lacking, the unity of the body is impossible... Formed in this way, a republic or political body consequently gains all the rights which people naturally have, and is subject to the same duties by nature.'

27 See N. Machiavelli, *Il Principe e i Discorsi sopra la prima deca di Tito Livio*, ed. S. Bertelli, Milan 1977, particularly pp. 256 and 139, where Machiavelli, referring to the cases of Sparta, Rome, and Venice, clearly draws up the primary objective of his republicanism, identifying it in the creation of institutions ('constitute a guardian of liberty') able to guarantee the free and positive deployment of the social and political conflict through which to avoid unilateral forms of dominion, counterpoising power against power, ambition to dominate against ambition to dominate: 'E sanza dubbio, se si considerrà il fine de' nobili e degli ignobili, si vedrà in quelli desiderio grande di dominare ed in questi solo desiderio di non essere dominati, e per conseguente maggiore volontà di vivere liberi, potendo meno sperare di usurparla che non possono i grandi.' One must never forget that, for Machiavelli, 'public liberty' was born in Republican Rome only though the conflict between the plebeians and the nobility (p. 137).

28 E. Garin, *L'educazione in Europa 1400/1600*, Rome-Bari 1976, pp. 19ff.

29 Montesquieu, *Spirit of the Laws*, p. 35.

30 See, on these themes, C. Bitossi, *'La repubblica è vecchia'. Patriziato e governo a Genova nel secondo Settecento*, Rome 1995, pp. 188ff.

31 For a first comprehensive synthesis of these themes, see *Passioni, interessi convenzioni. Discussioni settecentesche su virtù e civiltà*, ed. M. Geuna and M. L. Pesante, Milan 1992.

32 See the analysis of these themes in P. Costa, *Civitas. Storia della cittadinanza in Europa 1. Dalla civiltà comunale al Settecento*, Rome-Bari 1999, pp. 469ff.

33 On Helvétius' sympathies for the model of the Roman Republic and more generally for small 'poor and warlike republics' like Sparta, see ibid., pp. 463ff.

34 See Y. Séité, 'Romanzo,' in *L'illuminismo.Dizionario storico*, ed. V. Ferrone and D. Roche, Rome-Bari 1998, pp. 301ff.

35 Much work remains to be done on Filangieri's pedagogical thought, but see in any case P. Romano, *Il piano di educazione di Filangieri*, Pompei 1968. See also the dated, but insightful U. Spirito, *Il pensiero pedagogico di Gaetano Filangieri*, Florence 1924.

36 See, on this theme, A. Andreatta, 'Gaetano Filangieri: legge, costume e legislazione sui costumi,' in *Gaetano Filangieri e l'Illuminismo europeo*, ed. L. D'Alessandro, Naples 1991, pp. 165ff.

37 The literature on patriotism has grown considerably in the past few years. On patriotism as a formula of political struggle in Walpole's England, see C. Gerrard, *Walpole and the Patriots. Politics, Poetry and Myth, 1707–1742*, Oxford 1995. More generally, see L. Colley, *Britons. Forging the Nation, 1707–1837*, London 1992. A key text of English patriotic ideology was certainly written by Bolingbroke in 1738, *The idea of a Patriot King*, recently edited by G. Abbattista, Rome 1995, with an ample and rich introduction entitled 'Il "Re patriota" nel discorso politico-ideologico inglese del Settecento.' Again on English patriotism, see also E. H. Gould, *The Persistence of Empire. British Culture in The Age of The American Revolution*, London 2000. In France, a specific and politically important form of 'patriot ideology' was, for example, developed for the first time during the crisis of Maupeou (1771–73) by the parliamentarians who vindicated the representation of the 'nation' against the absolutism of the monarchy, see S. Maza, *Private Lives and Public Affairs. The Causes Célèbres of Prerevolutionary France*, Berkeley 1993, pp. 107ff. On these themes see D. Van Kley, *The Religious Origins of the French Revolution. From Calvin to the Civil Constitution 1560–1791*, New Haven 1996.

38 On patriotism in eighteenth-century Italy, see F. Venturi, *Settecento riformatore*, 7 vols, Turin 1969–90, vol. V*, *L'Italia dei Lumi*, Turin 1987, pp. 600ff.; F. Venturi, *La rivolta greca del 1770 e il patriottismo dell'età dei Lumi*, Rome 1986.See also *Identità territoriali e cultura politica nella prima età moderna*, Bologna 1998.

39 On Roberti's text, and more generally on the patriotic critique of Enlightenment, see V. Ferrone, *I profeti dell'Illuminismo. Le metamorfosi della ragione nel tardo Settecento italiano*, Rome-Bari 2000, pp. 168ff.

40 F. Venturi, *Settecento riformatore*, vol. V*, pp. 659ff.

41 See the *Vocabolario degli accademici della Crusca*, Venice 1612, p. 601.

42 Though very dated and debatable, see, on the process of sopraposition of the terms fatherland and nation during the nineteenth century, for example in Mazzini, F. Chabod, *L'idea di nazione*, Rome-Bari 1997, pp. 80ff.

43 A good reconstruction of this debate can be found in D. Bianchi and G. Rutto, *Idee e concezioni di patria nell'Europa del Settecento*, Turin 1989; M. Viroli, *Per amore della patria*, Rome-Bari 1995. It must, anyway, be noted that Viroli, for that matter like Pocock and Skinner, favours a reading of republican patriotism which always highlights, attributing it a paradigmatic significance which truly is excessive, Machiavelli's experience and the matrix of civic humanism at the expense of Enlightenment natural law and the centrality of the theory of the rights of man in the republicanism of the moderns.

44 One must, nonetheless, not forget that an explicit link between republic and fatherland already had been introduced in Neapolitan political culture during the revolution of 1647. See R. Villari, *Per il re o per la patria. La fedeltà nel Seicento*, Rome-Bari 1994, pp. 85ff.

45 F. Venturi, *Utopia e riforma nell'Illuminismo*, Turin 1970, p. 91.

46 V. Ferrone, 'Seneca e Cristo; la "Respubblica christiana" di Paolo Mattia Doria,' *Rivista storica italiana*, XCVI, 1984, pp. 32ff.

47 Referring to the 'generation of the heroic kingdoms' in the first period of the lives of nations, with a language which would have made Filmer happy, Vico wrote: 'Now, the fathers were already the sovereign kings of their own families; and their equality in that state, combined with their Cyclopean ferocity, meant that none of them would naturally yield to another. Instead, there spontaneously emerged ruling senates, composed of as many kings as there

were families. These rulers found that, even without any human insight or planning, they had united their private interests in a common concern. They called their *patria*, which is shortened from *patria res*, meaning "the concern of the fathers." The nobles were accordingly called patricians, *patricii*, and must have been the only citizens of the first *patriae*, fatherlands,' G. Vico, *The New Science*, translated by D. Marsh, ed. A. Grafton, London 1999, p. 254. For an interpretation of Vico's conception of archaic Roman history analyzed in light of a dualistic scheme of sacred and profane history, see A. Momigliano, '"Bestioni" ed "eroi" romani nella Scienza nuova di Vico,' in *Sui fondamenti della storia antica*, Turin 1984, pp. 204ff. On Vico's sympathy for absolutism, see M. Capurso, *Accentramento e costituzionalismo*, pp. 26ff.

48 A. Genovesi, *Della diceosina*, p. 338.

49 Ibid., p. 335.

50 In his *Viaggio per la capitanata*, Naples 1790, p. 41, with ill-concealed irony, Francesco Longano wrote 'today no book is written that does not characterize a nation, not only one million, but eight million times the inhabitants of Spain, or fifteen times those of Italy…'

51 When speaking of national identity in the Old Regime, one must never forget the fundamental role assumed, above all in the seventeenth century, by the great monarchies and by the logic of the absolutist states. See, on this, in terms of the function of national troops in modern standing armies as a decisive moment in the formation of Old Regime nation-states around the figures of kings, S. E. Finer, 'State- and Nation-Building in Europe: The Role of the Military,' in C. Tilly, ed., *The Formation of National States in Western Europe*, Princeton 1975, pp. 84–163. A good discussion of these themes and a rich bibliography on the argument can be found in I. Hont, 'The Permanent Crisis of a Divided Mankind: "Nation-State" and "Nationalism" in Historical Perspective,' in *Political Studies*, XLII, 1994, pp. 166–231, now in I. Hont, *Jealousy of Trade: International Competition and the Nation-State in Historical Perspective*, Cambridge, MA 2005, pp. 447–528. It is no coincidence that, during the course of the eighteenth-century, a new meaning of the word nation affirmed itself in the common language, which was closely connected to the territory of the state, which was added to the old and traditional meaning of ethnic, cultural, religious, or historical and linguistic community which had always been in circulation. See for example the *Encyclopèdie* (ed. Neuschâtel, 1765, vol. XI, p. 230), in which the nation was presented as 'une mot collectif dont on fait usage pour exprimer une quantité considérable de peuple qui abite une certaine ètendue de pays, renfermée dans certaine limites et qui obéit au même gouvernement,' and thus independent of the nature and form of government (an aspect which, instead, as we have seen, deeply marked the term *patria* in the classical tradition loved and reproposed by the thinkers of the Enlightenment), and by the fact that 'chaque nation a son caractère particulier: c'est une espèce de proverbe que de dire leger comme un françois, jaloux comme un italien, grave comme un espagnol, méchant comme un anglois.'

52 A. M. Rao, 'Esercito e società a Napoli nelle riforme del secondo Settecento,' in *Eserciti e carriere militari nell'Italia moderna militari nell'Italia moderna*, ed. C. Donati, Milan 1998, pp. 183ff.

53 L. Radogna, *Storia della marina militare delle Due Sicilie (1734–1860)*, Milan 1978.

54 E. Chiosi, 'Il Regno dal 1734 al 1799,' in *Storia del Mezzogiorno*, vol. IV, book II, Naples 1986, pp. 414ff.

55 A. M. Rao, *Esercito e società a Napoli*, pp. 202ff. Again on the theme of the nationalization of the Neapolitan armed forces, the theoretical debate following the first phase of Tanucci's military reforms is of extraordinary interest. In 1760, the Duke of S. Arpino, Alonso Sanchez de Luna, published an important volume in Naples entitled *Lo spirito della guerra o sia l'arte da formare, mantenere e disciplinare la soldatesca*, which vigorously relaunched the thesis of nationalization as an unavoidable necessity for the Neapolitan army. That would, in fact not only 'diminish the weight of the public treasury [*erario*],' but also discipline the people and nobility, strenghten the loyalty of all orders to the monarchy, and finally make 'the people kneel to the profession of arms.' De Luna explicitly used the term 'armed nation,' and, in particular, he always referred to the word 'nation,' as construed in the eighteenth century and succinctly stated in the *Encyclopèdie* (in a previous footnote), which defined it as a specific

community of subjects of the same territorial state, though without forgetting the traditional ethnic and naturalistic connotations of the term. With regards to the *vexata quaestio* of how many officers were necessary to direct a battalion of Frenchmen, Prussians, or Piedmontese, the Duke of S. Arpino, for example, brought into the discussion also 'the natural inclination of the nation' to arrive at the conclusion that one certainly needed more officers in Naples than in Prussia. In their works, though with different political perspectives – one favouring Enlightened absolutism and the other a more republican interpretation, Giuseppe Palmieri and Gaetano Filangieri insisted much on the national component, on the necessity of arming a people in defence of the fatherland and of the liberty of the kingdom. On Filangieri's republican position in the Italian debate at the end of the century, see V. Ferrone, 'Un re, un esercito, una nazione. Il riarmo italiano nel '700 tra innovazioni tecnologiche, assolutismo e identità nazionali d'antico regime,' in *Storia d'Italia, Annali,* vol. XIIX, *Guerra e pace,* Turin 2003, pp. 383–414.

56 A. M. Rao, *Esercito e società a Napoli,* p. 203.

57 One must not forget that the *togati*'s strategy for laying claim to power in Naples in the name of the ancient 'Constitutions of the Kingdom' certainly did not wait for Paris to show the way. See, on this, the documents which circulated during the 1647 revolution studied by R. Villari, *Per il re o per la patria,* pp. 42ff.

58 V. Cuoco, *Saggio storico sulla rivoluzione di Napoli,* ed. A. De Francesco, Manduria-Bari-Rome 1998, p. 327. See also the whole of chapter XVI, *Stato della nazione napoletana.*

59 On these very interesting matters, if nothing else but to contrast the points of contact and the differences in the solutions which matured in the Italian context with respect to the cases of France, America, or England, see the recent monographic issue of the *American Historical Review,* vol. 106, October 2001, *Creating National Identities in a Revolutionary Era,* and particularly the articles by D. A. Bell, 'The Unbearable Lightness of Being French: Law, Republicanism and National Identity at the End of the Old Regime' and B. Anderson, 'To What Can Late Eighteenth-Century French, British, and American Anxieties Be Compared? Comment on three Papers.'

60 The historiography of the metamorphosis of the concept of nation is immense, but see A. D. Smith, *The Nation in History: Historiographical Debates about Ethnicity and Nationalism,* Hanover 2000. On Italy, though not sufficiently documented and reliable with regards to the eighteenth century, see A. M. Banti, *La nazione del Risorgimento. Parentela, santità e onore alle origini dell'Italia unita,* Turin 2000, who discusses the famous theses sustained by Federico Chabod in *L'idea di nazione* with regards to a presumed substantial difference between the Italian national movement, which insists on the nexus between liberty and will, and the German one which is ethnic and naturalistic. As we have sought to demonstrate though, the risk of slipping towards a solely historical and ethnic conception of nation was clear already in the late eighteenth-century debate over patriotism, and then in the progressive assimilation of the terms fatherland and nation made by parts of the revolutionary tradition. The truth is that the history of the creation of modern national identities should always be written reflecting on the dissolving effects on the ancient social structures of order and corporations which resulted from the crisis of the Old Regime and developments in the logic of an absolutist state around the crown. It is against the background of this epochal crisis that the new and original forms of social bonds developed by the culture of the late Enlightenment were born and, later, in the revolutionary years, the centrality of the concept of nation as a synonym for fatherland affirmed itself.

61 V. Cuoco, *Saggio storico,* p. 439.

62 F. M. Pagano, *De' saggi politici. Ristampa anastatica della prima edizione (1783–1785),* ed. F. Lomonaco, Naples 2000, p. 656.

63 The literature on the birth of public opinion is today vast, but see the efficient overview in E. Tortarolo, 'Opinione pubblica,' in *L'Illuminismo. Dizionario storico,* pp. 283ff. On an understanding of changes in the 'political culture' of the eighteenth century in relation to the

appearance of the phenomenon of public opinion, see K. M. Baker, *Au tribunal de l'opinion. Essais sur l'imaginaire politique au XVIIIᵉ siècle*, Paris 1993, pp. 13ff.

64 J. Habermas, *The Structural Transformation of the Public Sphere: An Inquiry into a Category of Bourgeois Society*, Cambridge, MA 1991.

65 The quotations are from K. M. Baker, *Au tribunal de l'opinion*, pp. 225ff.

66 On the conception of democracy as the government of public opinion diffused in the late Enlightenment, see E. Tortarolo, '"Opinionepubblica" e illuminismo italiano. Qualche appunto di lettura,' in *Cesare Beccaria. La pratica dei Lumi*, pp. 127ff. Tortarolo rightly underlines the assonance between the ideas of Filangieri and of Diderot as expressed in Raynal's *Histoire philosophique et politique*, where the *philosophe* wrote: 'L'opinion publique, chez une nation qui pense et qui parle, est la règle du gouvernement: jamais il ne la doit heurter sans des raisons publiques, ni la contrarier, sans l'avoir désabusée. C'est d'après cette opinion que le gouvernemet doit modifier toutes ses formes... La réclamation publique est constamment le cri de l'opinion; et l'opinion générale est la règle du gouvernement: c'est parce qu'elle est la reine du monde, que le rois sont les maître des hommes.'

67 See the letter in G. Tarde, *L'opinion et la foule*, Paris 1901, p. 83. Among the many works to appear on the subject of public opinion, it is worth returning to this extremely acute text in which Tarde, polemicizing with the neo-positivists, who attributed a sort of autonomous life to public opinion independent of the will of individuals, relaunched his theory of imitation as the mechanism at the basis of all social formations, insisting on the fact that public opinion must be considered and studied as the simple transformation of an individual opinion into social opinion.

68 Filangieri, for example, would probably have subscribed to Mercier's claims that public opinion had been created directly by the works of literati, or the words of Jacques Peuchet, who, in the *Encyclopédie méthodique* in 1789, defined public opinion as an historical and social product of enlightened men able to interpret and communicate popular will. See K. M. Baker, *Au tribunal de l'opinion*, pp. 259. More generally on the French debate, see A. W. Gunn, *Queen of the World. Opinion in the Public Life of France from the Renaissance to the Revolution*, Oxford 1995.

69 See S. Maza, *Private Lives and Public Affairs*, pp. 107ff, but above all C. Maire, *De la cause de Dieu à la cause de la Nation. Le jansénisme au XVIIIᵉ siècle*, Paris 1998, pp. 563ff.

70 See A. Trampus, *I gesuiti e l'Illuminismo. Politica e religione in Austria e nell'Europa centrale (1773– 1789)*, Turin 2000, pp. 252ff. On these issues see also M. Rosa, *Settecento religioso. Politica della ragione e religione del cuore*, Venice 1999; M. Caffiero, *La politica della santità. Nascita di un culto nell'età dei lumi*, Rome-Bari 1996.

71 G. Tarde, *L'opinion et la foule*, p. 8.

72 See K. Marx, 'La questione ebraica,' in *Opere complete*, Italian translation, Rome 1976, vol. III, pp. 182ff.

73 It is no coincidence that a scholar sensitive to the ideological construction of cultural hegemonies in the modern world like Antonio Gramsci did not hesitate to define the emancipatory project of the *philosophes* as a 'magnificent revolution.' Referring to the strategic role effectively assumed by the Enlightenment in preparing the revolutionary masses, he wrote in the newsletter of the Turinese socialists *Il Grido del Popolo* in January 1916 that 'The latest example, the closest to us in time and thus the least alien to us, is the French Revolution. The preceding period in culture, known as the Enlightenment, a period which has been so slandered by facile critics of theoretical reason, was in fact not – or at least not entirely – a featherweight gathering of superficial, dilettante intellectuals, discoursing about anything and everything with complacent indifference, believing themselves to be men of their time only when they had read d'Alembert and Diderot's *Encyclopùèdie*. It was not, that is to say, simply a phenomenon of pedantic, arid intellectualism, like the one we see before our eyes now, exhibited in its full glory in the low-grade popular Universities. The Enlightenment was a magnificent revolution in itself; and, as De Sanctis acutely observed in his *History of Italian Literature* it created a kind of pan-European unified consciousness, a bourgeois and spiritual

international, with each part sensitive to the tribulations and misfortunes of the whole, which was the best preparation for the bloody revolution which would subsequently take place in France... The same phenomenon is occurring again today, with socialism.' 'Socialism and Culture,' in A. Gramsci, *Pre-Prison Writings*, ed. R. Bellamy, Cambridge 1994, pp. 10–11.

74 On the entire debate before the revolution, see the overview of E. J. Mannucci, *Il patriota e il Vaudeville. Teatro, pubblico e potere nella Parigi della Rivoluzione*, Naples 1998, pp. 2–63.

75 Generally on these topics, in which the phenomenon of the politicization of the literati, innovations in social and artistic communication, and the birth of the first signs of the public sphere of modern politics intertwine, see G. Tocchini, *La politica della rappresentazione. Comunicazione sociale e consumo culturale nella Francia di antico regime (1669–1752)*, Turin 2001; C. Jouhaud, *Les pouvoirs de la littérature. Histoire d'un paradoxe*, Paris 2000; *Policing the Public Sphere: Political Criticism and the Administration of Aesthetics*, ed. R. Burt, Minneapolis 1994.

76 On the influence of Filangieri's ideas on this point, above all through the reflections and work of his faithful follower Matteo Galdi during the republican triennial, see P. Themelly, *Il teatro patriottico tra rivoluzione e impero*, Rome 1991.

77 On Salfi's activities, see B. Alfonzetti, *Teatro e tremuoto. Gli anni napoletani di Francesco Saverio Salfi*, Milan 1994, and G. Tocchini, 'Dall'antico regime alla Cisalpina. Morale e politica nel teatro per musica di F. S. Salfi,' in *Salfi librettista*, ed. F. P. Russo, Vibo Valentia 2001.

78 On this intense debate over the educational and political function of tragedy in the early eighteenth century, see the works of B. Alfonzetti, *Teatro*, pp. 47ff.; B. Alfonzetti, *Il corpo di Cesare. Percorsi di una catastrofe nella tragedia del Settecento*, Modena 1989; B. Alfonzetti, *Congiure. Dal poeta della botte all'eloquente giacobino (1701–1801)*, Rome 2001.

79 F. M. Pagano, 'Saggio del gusto e delle belle arti,' in *Opere filosofiche, politiche ed estetiche*, Brussels 1841, pp. 413–14.

80 Cf. F. M. Pagano, *Corradino. Tragedia*, Naples 1789, p. 3. In his preface, Pagano encouraged the creation of a national political theatre according to schemes aimed increasingly at combining republican and constitutional patriotism with respect for cultural and national traditions. On Pagano's theatre, see R. Sirri, 'La cultura a Napoli nel Settecento,' in *Storia di Napoli*, Naples 1971, vol. VIII, pp. 242ff.

81 F. M. Pagano, *Gli esuli tebani. Tragedia*, Naples 1782, p. 12.

82 F. M. Pagano, *L'Emilia*, Naples 1792, p. 21.

83 See the 'Progetto di costituzione della Repubblica napoletana presentato al governo provvisorio dal Comitato di legislazione,' in M. Battaglini, *Mario Pagano e il progetto di costituzione della repubblica napoletana*, Rome 1994, p. 38. It is worth underlining the remoteness and originality of Neapolitan Enlightenment constitutionalism, deeply marked by the spirit of republicanism, compared to the French constitution of year III, which said nothing with regards to the educational function of theatres. R. Ajello rightly insists that Pagano's republicanism was already present largely in the first edition of the *Saggi politici*, on which see 'I saggi politici di Mario Pagano e il loro tempo,' *Il pensiero politico*, XXVIII, 1995, p. 57, and A. Pagden, 'Francesco Mario Pagano's "Republic of Virtue": Naples 1799,' in *The Invention of the Modern Republic*, ed. B. Fontana, Cambridge 1994, pp. 139–53.

84 F. M. Pagano, 'Considerazioni sul processo criminale,' in *Biblioteca scelta del foro criminale italiano*, Milan 1858, vol. XI, p. 514. On the fortunes of this little, repeatedly re-published volume, see G. Solari, *Studi*, pp. 391ff. On Pagano as a student of penal law, see E. Palombi, *Mario Pagano alle origini della scienza penalistica del secolo XIX*, Naples 1979. One must underline the fact that Pagano was a great lawyer and a master of generations of valorous lawyers of penal law as the holder, from 1785 to 1786, of the chair of penal law at the University of Naples. Besides some of his defence briefs as counsel in celebrated trials, we have two small volumes dating from his life as a penal lawyer, *I principii del codice penale* (published posthumously by his students in two different editions, Milan 1803, and Naples 1806) and the *Logica de' probabili applicata a' giudizi criminali*.

85 F. M. Pagano, *Considerazioni*, p. 488.

86 Ibid., p. 536.

87 In that republic, Pagano wrote, where 'legislative power remained with the people which had already become sovereign, the consuls retained executive power and that of judgement passed to the praetorians,' the 'ancient Roman system presents us the image of a war executed with every solemnity.' 'The prosecution,' he specified, finally, 'among the Romans, was a public office, and the prosecutor was considered a public person, that is as a magistrate of the fatherland' who had nothing to do with the judge charged with presiding over the debate. 'The prosecutor and the accused conducted the inquisition, that is [the] search for the evidence that made his case' (ibid., pp. 493–4).

88 Ibid., p. 522.

89 Ibid., p. 505.

90 Ibid., p. 512.

91 Ibid., p. 521.

92 On this important character and the events of those years, see L. de' Medici, *Memorie dei miei tempi*, ed. Ileana Del Bagno, Naples 1988.

93 Ibid., p. 554.

94 G. Solari, in *Studi su Francesco Mario Pagano*, pp. 327ff., has noted quite rightly that when one evaluates the legal reforms sought by the republicans, and by Pagano in particular, reference should not only be made to the constitution of 1799, but also to the law of 14 May voted by the revolutionary government. The legislative activity of that government was incredibly wide-ranging and deep for such a short period of time. See M. Battaglini, *Atti, leggi, proclami ed altre carte della Repubblica napoletana 1798–1799*, Chiaravalle 1983.

95 On this important trial, through which the situation got out of hand, and the *Difesa* written by Pagano on the occasion, see G. Solari, *Studi su Francesco Mario Pagano*, pp. 105ff.

96 On this interpretative hypothesis formulated – as we have seen – primarily by Franco Venturi, see the recent studies in *Folle controrivoluzionarie. Le insorgenze popolari nell'Italia giacobina e napoleonica*, ed. A. M. Rao, Rome 1999.

97 Venturi (*L'Italia fuori d'Italia*, p.1141) rightly defined it 'the most important debate on Italy for centuries. The roots of the modern idea of an Italian nation must be sought in the contrasts and hopes of those years between 1796 and 1797.' On these matters, see G. Vaccarino, *I patrioti 'anarchistes' e l'idea dell'unità italiana (1795–1799)*, Turin 1955.

98 [Matteo Galdi], *Necessità di stabilire una repubblica in Italia*, Vicenza 1797, p. 77. The first edition appeared in 1796.

99 It suffices to think of Fantoni and Ranza. But on this complex debate, see A. M. Rao, 'Unité et fédéralisme chez les jacobins italiens de 1794 à 1800,' in *Les Fédéralismes. Réalités et représentations, 1789–1874*, Aix-en-Provence 1995, pp. 381ff., and the historiographical overview of E. Di Rienzo, 'Neogiacobinismo e movimento democratico nelle rivoluzioni d'Italia (1796–1815),' *Studi storici*, XL, 2000, pp. 403ff.

100 [Matteo Galdi], *Necessità*, p. 6.

101 Ibid., p. 66.

102 In this sense, one can fully agree with L. Guerci's call (*Istruire* cir. p. 13) to abandon once and for all the term 'Jacobin Triennial' which has caused and still causes so much confusion. The so-called Italian Jacobins who espoused radical positions, Guerci argues, were a 'clear minority on the republican front.' On the political and ideological nature of the birth of the Jacobin paradigm in Italian historiography in the 1950s and 60s at the hands of Cantimori and Saitta, see A. De Francesco, 'L'ombra di Buonarotti, Giacobinismo e Rivoluzione francese nella storiografia italiana del dopoguerra,' *Storica*, XV, 1999, pp. 7ff.

103 [Matteo Galdi], *Necessità*, p. 75. See also the entire chapter entitled *Anti-Moderantismo*.

104 See G. Candeloro, *Storia dell'Italia moderna*, vol. I, *Le origini del Risorgimento 1700–1815*, Milan 1978, pp. 287ff. Some patriots, like Fantoni, even offered to stab Napoleon, guilty of betraying the cause. On the negative effects of the Treaty of Campo Formio on public opinion across

Europe, see M. Vovelle, 'La fine della Repubblica di Venezia nella storiografia francese,' in *Il triennio rivoluzionario italiano visto dalla Francia 1796–1799*, Naples 1999, pp. 107ff.

105 F. Venturi, *Utopia e riforma*, p. 31.

106 See, on this topic, the always valuable work of M. Rosa, *Dispotismo e libertà nel Settecento. Interpretazioni 'repubblicane' di Machiavelli*, Bari 1964, particularly the second chapter entitled *'repubblicanesimo' politico e teatro 'repubblicano'*, pp. 17ff. See also F. Diaz, 'L'idea repubblicana nel Settecento italiano fino alla rivoluzione francese,' in *Per una storia illuministica*, Naples 1973, pp. 423ff.

107 On Alfieri the Mason and republican, who frequented the same milieus and engaged with the same problems which agitated Neapolitan and European Masons in those years, dominated by the events in America and by neo-republicanism, see G. Giarrizzo, *Massoneria e illuminismo nell'Europa del Settecento*, Venice 1994, pp. 226ff.

108 See G. Ricuperati, 'Il Settecento,' in *Il Piemonte sabaudo. Stato e territori in età moderna*, Turin 1994, p. 670.

109 C. Alfieri, 'Della tirannide,' in *Opere*, I, Asti 1951, p. 24.

110 Ibid., p. 43.

111 Ibid., p. 44.

112 Alfieri concluded the violent harangue against the hereditary principle using analogous expressions to those of Filangieri: 'The hereditary nobles are thus an integral part of tyranny, because true liberty cannot flourish for long where a class rules for reasons but virtue and election' (p. 64). For self-consistency, as is well known, in 1778, Alfieri renounced his feudal lands and embarked on his *'spiemontesizzazione,'* his de-Piedmontification, to the extent that he could not be 'both *a subject* of his majesty of Sardinia and *an author*. I chose the latter, and being an enemy of all chicane and subterfuge, I took the most direct road to disfranchise myself, by resigning the whole of my property to my sister Julia' (Alfieri, *Memoirs of the Life and Writings of Victor Alfieri*, translated by H. Colburn, London 1810, vol. II, p. 70).

113 A. de Tocqueville, *The Old Regime and the Revolution*, translated by J. Bonner, New York 1856, particularly p. 170ff, in the chapter entitled 'How, toward the middle of the Eighteenth Century, literary Men became the leading Politicians of the Country, and the Effects thereof.'

114 C. Alfieri, *Della tirannide*, p. 41.

115 Ibid., p. 98.

116 Ibid., pp. 247–8.

117 C. Alfieri, 'Il Misogallo,' in *Scritti politici e morali*, vol. III, Asti 1984, pp. 217ff.

118 Ibid., sonnet XVI, pp. 261–2: 'È Repubblica il suolo, ove divine / leggi son base a umane leggi e scudo; / ove null'uomo impunemente crudo / all'uom può farsi, e ogniuno ha il suo confine; / ove non è chi mi sgomenti, o inchine; / ov'io di ricco non son fatto ignudo; / ove a ciascuno il ben di tutti è fine. / È repubblica il suolo, ove illibati / costumi han forza, e il giusto sol primeggia, / né i tristi van del pianto altrui beati. / Sei repubblica tu, gallica greggia, / che muta or servi a rei pezzenti armati, / la cui vil feccia in su la tua galleggia?'

119 See V. Masiello, 'Ragioni e senso di un libello controrivoluzionario il Misogallo,' in *Vittorio Alfieri e la cultura piemontese fra illuminismo e rivoluzione*, San Salvatore Monferrato 1983, p. 270. In 1802, on occasion of the republication of his political works, which took place without his consultation, he did not hesitate to affirm, in a letter to Caluso, that 'the spring of these books was the impetus of youth, the hatred of oppression, the love of truth, or of what I believed that to be. The aim was the glory of saying the truth, of saying it with force and novelty, of saying it thinking to do good. The reasoning of these books seems to me chained [*incatenato*] and deduced, and the more I have thought about it later, the more have they seemed to me real, well founded, and if questioned on these points I would always return to say the same thing, or rather I would be quiet. But, this said, was this to be done, should one have printed these works, should one have published these writings? I am the first to say no; I disapprove of who has done it… the damage can be greater than the usefulness.' The times, in short, had changed (ibid., p. 271).

120 V. Alfieri, *Il Misogallo*, p. 199. With the intention of defending the positions adopted by Alfieri, Ginguené, on the occasion of the death of the great Piedmontese dramatist, wrote : 'il déteste les français pour le mal qu'ils lui ont fait, et sourtout pour celui que les français ont fait à la liberté.' Alfieri had attacked the revolution, 'non pas parce qu'on établit la république, mais par les horreurs insensés dont on ensanglanta son berceau' (see F. Venturi, *l'Italia fuori d'Italia*, p. 1183).

8. The Original Character of Enlightenment Constitutionalism: From the *Scienza della legislazione* to the 1799 *Progetto di costituzione napoletana*

1 See, for example, the recent overview *Le basi filosofiche del costituzionalismo*, ed. A. Barbera, Rome-Bari 1997. On the appearance of the term *Constitutionalism* in the United States in the late eighteenth century, see *Constitution and Revolution aux État-Unis d'Amérique et en Europe (1776–1815)*, ed. R. Martucci, Macerata, 1995, pp. 3ff. In Italy, though the term appears late, the concept was already clearly delineated in the inaugural lecture delivered by Giuseppe Compagnoni in Ferrara in May 1797 for the new chair of democratic constitutional law. Written for the occasion, the textbook entitled *Elementi di diritto costituzionale democratico ossia principi di giuspolitico universale*, Venice 1797, was publically burned with the fall of the Cisalpine Republic. See, on this, *Giuseppe Compagnoni. Un intellettuale tra giacobinismo e restaurazione*, ed. S. Medri, Bologna 1993. As we will see later on, Mario Pagano, referring to the competences necessary to develop the constitutional texts in his project for the constitution of the Neapolitan Republic of 1799, spoke explicitly of a veritable '*new science*.' 'America had already taken great steps in this, we will say, *new science*, forming the constitutions of its free States.' See the *Rapporto del Comitato di legislazione al governo provvisorio*, prefaced to *Progetto di costituzione della Repubblica napoletana* (in M. Battaglini, *Pagano e il progetto di costituzione della repubblicana napoletana*, Rome 1994).

2 A similar book had been attempted by an author Filangieri was familiar with, Georges-Louis Schmid d'Avenstein, with *Les principes de la législation universelle*, Amsterdam 1776. It was, though, a far less ambitious and original work compared to that of the Neapolitan philosopher. See on this F. Venturi, *Europe des Lumières. Recherches sur le XVIIIe siècle*, Paris 1971, pp. 203ff.

3 Aristotle, *Politics*, 1292a, 'where the laws do not govern there is no constitution.' Yet, on the particular meaning of the doctrine of the *politeia* in the ancient world, understood generally as a legitimate political constitution founded on the common good and on the government of laws, see M. Fioravanti, *Costituzione*, Bologna 1999, pp. 25ff.

4 On the difference between the nineteenth-century state of law, in which the guarantee of rights was reduced to the 'reserve of the law' and the modern forms of a constitutional state, the Enlightenment roots of which seem to me evident above all in virtue of the subjective and unviolable nature of the rights of man resolutely placed above the law, see the clear considerations in G. Zagrebelsky, *Il diritto mite. Legge diritti giustizia*, Turin 1992, pp. 21ff. In any case to specify the differences, in the modern constitutional state, the constitution is charged with the 'task of creating the conditions for the possibility of common life, not the task of directly creating a pre-determined project of common life' like the *Scienza della legislazione* clearly delineated.

5 On these two ways of understanding the separation of powers, see N. Bobbio, *La libertà politica*, ed. A. Passerin d'Entrèves, Milan 1974, pp. 86–6.

6 On the different historical forms assumed by modern constitutionalism and in particular on the model of the division of powers and mixed government as an alternative to constitutionalism in providing a government limited by laws and by rights, the centuries-long tradition to which Filangieri clearly made reference in his *Scienza della legislazione*, see N. Matteucci, *Organizzazione del potere e libertà. Storia del costituzionalismo moderno*, Turin 1988; *Constitutionalism*, ed. J. W. Chapman, New York 1979; L. Compagna, *Gli opposti sentieri del costituzionalismo*,

Bologna 1998. An important and debatable interpretation of modern constitutionalism as the limitation of government through the law and the work of judges (which intentionally ignores the specific influence of natural law, emphasizing instead the historical function of the medieval tradition of laws legitimizing the sovereign, *Lex facit regem*), see the works of H. McIlwain, and particularly *The American Revolution: A Constitutional Interpretation*, New York 1923.

7 It suffices to observe the structure of the *Commentaries* themselves to realize this. The book dedicated entirely to the *Rights of Persons* was only one of the many books of written laws and simple sentences provided by English law. See. W. Blackstone, *Commentaries on the Laws of England*, facsimile of the 1765–1769 edition, 4 vols, Chicago-London 1979, vol. I, pp. 119ff.

8 See the *Rapporto del Comitato di legislazione*, p. iii.

9 See the *Considerations sur la procedure criminelle*, Strasbourg 1789, p. lxviii.

10 See Ginguené's profile translated into Italian in the 1807 Milanese edition of the *Scienza della legislazione*, vol. I, pp. 7–20.

11 See, on this, G. Solari, *Studi su Francesco Mario Pagano*, Turin, 1963, pp. 380ff. Particularly regarding the interest for the German edition of the *Saggi politici*, published in Leipzig in 1796 by Johann Gottfried Müller. In France, Amaury Duval, one of the most important editors of the *Décade philosophique* and loyal friend of Pagano, began, and then abandoned, because of linguistic difficulties, the French translation of the *Saggi politici*. See F. Venturi, 'L'Italia fuori d'Italia,' in *Storia d'Italia*, vol. 3, Turin 1973, p. 1142.

12 See N. Ferorelli, 'Mario Pagano esule a Milano,' *Archiviostoricolombardo*, XLIV, 1917, pp. 15–16.

13 See the *Rapporto del Comitato di legislazione*, p. iii. Among his contemporaries, Pagano's dear friend Amaury Duval immediately noted the profound differences between the Neapolitan constitution and that developed in Paris in 1795. In the *Décade philosophique* of 28 June 1799, he wrote: 'Le plan de la nouvelle constitution est fait et même été publié. Elle est entièrement démocratique et différente en beaucoup de points essentiels de celles qui existent; ce qui ne pas un mal. La même constitution ne saurait convenir à tous les peuples. Le dernier Directoire français semblait n'être pas dans ces principes, supposé qu'il eut des principes…,' quoted in F. Venturi, *L'Italia fuori d'Italia*, p. 1163.

14 F. M. Pagano, *Saggi politici. De' principii, progressi e decadenza delle società*, II ed. 1791–92 , p. 350. 'Every regular government must safeguard a fundamental law made in this way,' Pagano specified. See also p. 336, where he affirms 'all societies thus have a general constitution, which is placed in the will of all, the object of which isto conserve the rights and properties of everyone.' In the *Progetto*, Pagano attributed this idea of a constitution to Gianvincenzo Gravina.

15 *Rapporto del Comitato di legislazione*, p. vi. Pagano hailed Gravina (known throughout Europe for his fundamental work on the history of Roman Law, *Originum juris civilis libri tres*, 1708) a sort of father of modern constitutionalism, a precursor of Locke's contractarian ideas.

16 A punctilious analysis of the debate which accompanied the birth of that 'bizarre [*cervellotico*]' constitution (an 'aberrant *pastiche*' as many contemporaries defined it), the fruit of extenuating mediations, of contingent pressures, of political exigencies dictated by tragic events such as the Prairial revolt more than by an organic constitutional doctrine, can be found in S. Luzzatto, *L'autunno della rivoluzione. Lotta e cultura politica nella Francia del Termidoro*, Turin 1994, pp. 296ff.

17 *Rapporto del Comitato di legislazione*, p. vi.

18 'Art. 1 Dei doveri,' in 'Costituzione della repubblica francese del 5 fruttidoro anno III,' in *Costituenti e costituzioni della Francia rivoluzionaria e liberale (1789–1875)*, ed. A. Saitta, Milan 1975, p. 467.

19 A. Genovesi, *Della Diceosina o sia della filosofia del giusto e dell'onesto*, ed. F. Arata, Milan 1973, pp. 81ff., chapter V, 'Dei doveri.' Filangieri too, in line with Pufendorf's thesis, conceived of rights only in relation to the respective duties they entailed.

20 *Rapporto del Comitato di legislazione*, p. xviii. See, for what has been written on this, G. Solari, *Studi*, p. 303, according to whom, in Pagano, 'the rigid logic of the rights of man found its natural limit in the notion of duties.'

21 Ibid., p. vi.

22 The 'laws in the period of cultured society should be written in unchanging codes and not simply included in uncertain, and arbitrarily interpreted, uses and customs. Furthermore, the laws should be clear, general, short, precise, and not subject to the interpretation of quibbling lawyers' (F. M. Pagano, *Saggi politici*, II ed., p. 358).

23 See V. Ferrone, *I profeti dell'Illuminismo. Le metamorfosi della ragione nel tardo Settecento italiano*, Rome-Bari 2000, pp. 304ff.

24 See L. Guerci, *Libertà degli antichi e libertà dei moderni. Sparta, Atene e i 'philosophes' nella Francia del '700*, Naples 1979, pp. 109ff.

25 See F. M. Pagano, *De' saggi politici. Ristampa anastatica della prima edizione (1783–1785)*, ed. F. Lomonaco, Naples 2000, pp. 544ff, vol. V, chapter XV, *Come la legge civile possa nuocere alla libertà inducendo la servitù*. On representative government, see the second edition of the *Saggi politici*, p. 354. It must be noted that the Pagano of the first edition tends to be less egalitarian than Filangieri.

26 See E. Chiosi, *Lo spirito del secolo. Politica e religione a Napoli nell'età dell'Illuminismo*, Naples, 1992, pp. 80ff; G. Giarrizzo, 'l'Illuminismo e la società italiana,' in *L'età dei Lumi. Studi storici sul Settecento europeo in onore di Franco Venturi*, 2 vols, Naples 1985, pp. 180ff.

27 See F. M. Pagano, *De' saggi politici*, vol. II, 6. It was certainly no coincidence that Francescantonio Grimaldi, in his *Riflessioni*, threw himself against the principle of perfectionability enunciated by Helvétius.

28 See the *Rapporto del Comitato di legislazione*, p. vi. Pagano had already treated the problem in the 1783 first edition of his *Saggi politici*, writing the *Generale prospetto della storia del Regno*. The people seemed to him different, 'divided into the powerful body of feudal lords, the ecclesiastics, the lawyers, and the poor and degraded plebeians.' Already then, however, he indicated the birth of a 'third order' of small proprietors as the social class which in the future would be able to guarantee the development of southern society.

29 On the social forces to which Italian Enlightenment thinkers, and particularly Genovesi, counted on making reference to, see R. Villari, 'Antonio Genovesi e la ricerca delle forze motrici dello sviluppo sociale,' *Studi storici*, XI, 1970, pp. 26–52.

30 *Rapporto del Comitato di legislazione*, p. xii. Rousseau too had said analogous things in the *Contrat social*.

31 Article 7 of the 1793 constitution recited that '*Le peuple souverain est l'universalité des citoyens français*,' whereas Article II of the constitution of year III instead affirmed '*L'universalité des citoyens français est le souverain*.' The great difference between them is analyzed deservedly by G. Luzzatto, *L'autunno della rivoluzione*, p. 301.

32 *Rapporto del Comitato di legislazione*, p. xi.

33 Nor was it, however, a reiteration of Article 31 of the Jacobin constitution of 1793, which referred to a right to resistance to be attributed to 'all men united in society' (see *Costituenti e costituzioni della Francia rivoluzionaria*, p. 313). Instead, though firmly maintaining such a right in his constitutional text, Pagano attributed it to the 'people,' aware of their own rights, and not to men in general, explaining that it was above all the citizen who had the 'invariable right to rise up against hereditary, perpetual, and tyrannical authorities.' This would avoid the danger of that 'anarchic insurgency' of plebs unleashed.

34 For a careful analysis of the important legal and functional differences between the two chambers, see G. Solari, *Studi*, pp. 322ff.

35 Pagano dryly affirmed, criticizing his French colleagues, 'if the executive power is too dependent on the legislative body, as it was in the French constitution of 1793, in that case the Assembly will absorb the executive power and, with all the powers concentrated in it, it will become despotic. If then [as was the case with the Thermidorian constitution], one is independent from the other, two disorders can arise: either inaction, and the languor of the political machine due to the dullness of the rival bodies; or the usurpation of other powers by one body because of that natural tendency of every power to increase' (*Rapporto del Comitato di legislazione*, pp. xiii–xiv).

36 F. M. Pagano, *Saggi politici*, II ed., p. 356.

37 See *Rapporto del Comitato di legislazione*, p. xiv.

38 See *Titolo XIII. Custodia della Costituzione*, pp. 47–8. Pagano listed the prerogatives of the Ephors, which were directly nominated by the electoral body, one for every department of the Republic. 'It appertains exclusively to the Ephors to examine. 1. Whether the constitution has been conserved in all its parts. 2. Whether the powers have observed their constitutional limits, overstepping, or ignoring what the constitution establishes. 3. To return all powers to their respective limits and duties, impeding and annulling the acts of that power which has exercised them beyond the functions attributed it by the Constitution. 4. To propose to the senate the review of an article of the constitution if, by experience, it has not been found convenient. 5. To present the legislative body with the abrogation of those laws which are opposed to the principles of the constitution.' Other important points, which characterized the work of the Ephors well, followed: '360. This body has the power to have presented to it all the papers and all the registers which will be necessary. 361. The decrees of the Body of Ephors shall be printed, read, and published in all the Cantons of the Republic, and the following year they are to be re-read to the primary and electoral assemblies in the period of their usual sessions. 362. From the day of their publication, these decrees shall have full effect. 363. The preface to the same [decrees] shall state the date of the session of the Body of Ephors and the articles of the Constitution which have been transgressed. 364. The annulment of an act against the Constitution expresses itself with this formula, signed by at least two thirds of the Ephors who intervened in the session: *The Constitution retries and annuls the act of the power etc.* 365. On the same day, the Body of the Ephors shall send its decree to the legislative body and to the Archonship, which must conform to it. 366. The act annulled by the Ephors' decree shall no longer have the force to compel any citizen, who shall no longer be obligated to obey it.' Finally, it must be mentioned that the court would act 'both at the request of the powers to end their controversies and *ex officio.*' For a valuable analysis of the Ephorate, see the classic work of G. Solari, *Studi* pp. 312ff.; M. Battaglini, *Mario Pagano e il progetto di costituzione*, pp. 179ff.; J. Luther, *Idee e storia di giustizia costituzionale nell'Ottocento*, Turin 1990, pp. 31ff.

39 See G. Luzzatto, *L'autunno della rivoluzione*, pp. 310ff. On the *Jury constitutionnaire*, see P. Bastid, *Discours de Sieyès dans les débats constitutionnels de l'an III*, Paris 1939.

40 See G. Solari, *Studi*, p. 312.

41 It would be worth finally publishing the unreleased *Scienza morale* written in those years by Celestino Galiani; on the importance of this work, see V. Ferrone, *Scienza natura religione. Mondo newtonianoe cultura italiana nel primo Settecento*, Naples 1982, pp. 359ff.

42 J. Locke, *Two Treatises of Government*, p. 358. On this quote, and the following considerations, which convincingly explain the natural law roots of American constitutionalism, see M. Einaudi, *Le origini dottrinali e storiche del controllo giudiziario sulla costituzionalità delle leggi negli Stati Uniti d'America*, Turin 1931, p. 20. See also, by the same author, 'Interpretazioni europee della dottrina americana del sindacato di costituzionalità della leggi,' *Studiurbinati*, VI, 1932, pp. 7–30 and *The Physiocratic Doctrine of Judical Control*, Cambridge 1938.

43 F. M. Pagano, *Saggi politici*, II ed., p. 17.

44 France never wanted to admit the principle of judicial control. The constitutions of 1791 and of 1795 expressly prohibited it. On this legal and political aspect of the revolutionary constitutional doctrine, rightly defined '*un des paradoxes les plus célèbre de l'histoire costitutionelle française,*' see P. Raynaud, 'La déclaration des droits de l'homme,' in *The French Revolution and the Creation of Modern Political Culture*, ed. C. Lucas, Oxford 1990, vol. II, pp. 139ff. On the original character of French revolutionary constitutionalism, see also G. Zagrebelsky, *Il diritto mite*, pp. 65ff, who stresses how the decision not to introduce the mechanism of constitutional justice, through a supreme court, left the way open for the primacy of the legislature, understood as the expression of the general will over rights: 'In the end, whatever the intentions of the Constituents of 1789–91 could have been, the very taxing theoretical conception of the law as a codification of rights could not but reveal itself an enemy of the juridical value of the

Déclaration, rejected in the Hyperuranium of general political proclamations, itself devoid of legal impact and not susceptible to direct application to social relations. In this way, what may appear a paradox came true in the Country in which the salient contribution to the development of constitutional conceptions is no doubt represented by human rights, what was affirmed was not the centrality of rights but what has been called *"légicentrisme"*… Thus, the laws were not subject to the control of rights, but, to the contrary, control was taken of the legality of rights, the true legally operative "constitution" of which was not the *Déclaration* but the *Code civil*, not without reason often called the "constitution of the liberal bourgeoisie." As we will see, the way chosen by the Americans and – autonomously, we might add – by the Neapolitans in their constitutional blueprints was very different.'

45 *Costituenti e costituzioni della Francia rivoluzionaria*, p. 502.

46 See the important, yet undervalued analyses of S. Moravia, *Il tramonto dell'Illuminismo. Filosofia e politica nella società francese (1770–1810)*, Roma-Bari 1986, pp. 205ff. with regards to the ferocious conflict between Robespierre and Condorcet, between the last heirs of the *philosophes* and the different spirits of the revolutionary movement.

47 After having underlined the importance, in Pagano's project, of the American and French constitutions, and particularly that of 1795 constitution, Solari summed up his long, punctilious, and generally neglected analysis thus: 'If one looks well at the nature and reach of the innovations, they are enough to modify profoundly the spirit of the mother constitution [the 1795 French constitution] in accordance with Pagano's personal views. It was neither more nor less than the spirit of the *Saggi politici* which penetrated the Neapolitan Constitution and which gave it that unique colour and significance which Pagano's critics, beginning with Cuoco, could not explain if not as arbitrary additions by Pagano' (*Studi su Francesco Mario Pagano*, pp. 128–9). 'In the Constitution,' Solari reiterated again, 'everything is the author of the *Saggi*, with his defects and with his illusions, with his obstinate faith in progress, in liberty, with his hatred of despotism, and with his enthusiasm for the common good. Man must be what the writer and the legislator was, who with his life paid for all the errors, if that indeed is what they were, of his time' (p. 133). On this, see also the valuable analysis of M. Battaglini, *Mario Pagano*.

9. Vincenzo Cuoco: The National Critique of Cosmopolitan Enlightenment Constitutionalism

1 Benedetto Croce's celebrated words in the preface to the second edition of his *La rivoluzione napoletana del 1799* remain fundamental, stating that the revolution, 'finally, gave the modern Italian liberals the first rudiments of political wisdom, teaching them not to trust the words of foreign governments, when there is no way to render them serious by converting them into interests of advantage and of security. Thus, as a consequence of the sacrifice and the illusions of the patriots, the Republic of Ninety-nine, which by itself would have been nothing but an anecdote, arose to the solemn dignity of a historical event.And it is to that which we now turn our gaze, almost as if to search in it for the sacred origins of the new Italy' (Naples 1998, p. 12).

2 See A. De Francesco, 'Il *Saggio storico* e la cultura politica italiana fra Otto e Novecento,' in *Saggio storico della rivoluzione di Napoli*, ed. A. De Francesco, Manduria-Bari-Rome 1998, pp. 75ff., but the entire essay is worth reading.

3 See F. Tessitore's 'Presentazione' to the facsimile edition of the first, 1801 edition of the *Saggio storico*, Naples 1988, p. xvi.

4 See P. Villani, 'Introduzione' to V. Cuoco, *Saggio storico sulla rivoluzione di Napoli*, Milan 1999, p. 15.

5 See A. De Francesco, 'Il *Saggio storico* e la cultura politica italiana,' p. 93. 'Vincenzo Cuoco, Jacobin, then: the association is not at all intended to be provocative. Though it is immediately worth underlining how this reading which accompanies the reproposal of the *Saggio storico* has been made possible by the recent recovery of interest in the democratic movement during

the years of the French Revolution – a return of interest which, now established principally on the French side, has nonetheless begun to bring repercussions also in Italy.' In the very complicated ideological struggle over the significance of the word Jacobin in the Italian context, which has created such confusion and which continues to generate it, De Francesco belongs to those who do not accept employing the word Jacobin only to the followers of Robespierre and the cherishers of the Terror. See A. De Francesco, 'L'ombra di Buonarotti, Giacobinismo e Rivoluzione francese nella storiografia italiana del dopoguerra,' *Storica*, XV, 1999, pp. 8ff.

6 See the letters in V. Cuoco, *Scritti vari*, ed. N. Cortese and F. Nicolini, 2 vols, Bari 1924, vol. II, pp. 289ff. See also the letter to his brother Michele of 1802, in which Cuoco defines himself 'a man who was condemned only because he was carried away into a whirlpool which he hated, but which was impossible to resist; a man for which love of the fatherland, love of peace, and love of virtue are not mere words' (p. 304).

7 See M. A. Visceglia, 'Genesi e fortuna di una interpretazione storiografica: la rivoluzione napoletana del 1799 come "rivoluzione passiva,"' in *Annali della Facoltà di Magistero dell'Università degli studi di Lecce*, I, 1972, pp. 3–47. See also L. Guerci, *Istruirenelle verità repubblicane. La lettura politica per il popolo nell'Italia in rivoluzione (1796–1799)*, Bologna 1999, p. 55.

8 F. Lomonaco, *Rapporto al cittadino Carnot*, in V. Cuoco, *Saggio storico sulla Rivoluzione napoletana del 1799*, ed. F. Nicolini, Bari 1913, p. 288. See, on the *Rapporto*, A. M. Rao, *Esuli. L'emigrazione politica italiana in Francia (1792–1802)*, Naples 1992, pp. 431ff. The concept of a passive revolution has recently been contested efficiently by A. M. Rao in *La repubblica napoletana del '99*, Rome 1997, pp. 8ff.

9 On Cuoco's hatred of the French see the letter to Diodato Corbo of 1802: 'Here I thus am a citizen of the Cisalpine Republic, because I am in Milan, a hater of the Gauls, as I was in '93, in '94, in '95, in '96, in '97, in '98, and finally at Capua in '99. My sentiments are eternal,' V. Cuoco, *Scritti vari*, vol. II, p. 300.

10 V. Cuoco, *Saggio storico*, p. 245.

11 Ibid., p. 254.

12 The work of Madame de Staël seems to have been written purposefully to respond to the paradoxical conclusions of those (R. Chartier, *The Cultural Origins of the French Revolution*, Durham 1991) who more recently have argued that the Enlightenment was an invention of the Revolution. On these issues, see V. Ferrone, D. Roche, *L'Illuminismo nella cultura contemporanea. Storia e storiografia*, Rome-Bari 2002, pp. 521ff.

13 In the 1806 second edition of the *Saggio storico* (p. 586), Cuoco introduced a variation to reaffirm that it was the people, not the philosophers, who were 'the great and only agent of revolutions and counterrevolutions.'

14 Ibid., p. 255.

15 Ibid., p. 258. Though destined to become commonplace in Italian thought on the French Revolution, Cuoco's interpretive grid is not particularly original. See the valuable reconstruction of the issue in A. M. Rao, 'Napoli e la rivoluzione,' *Prospettivesettanta*, III–IV, 1985, pp. 405ff. Furthermore, on the sources of this analysis, it must be remembered that the works of Vincenzo Ugo and Saverio Scrofani, which appear to have influenced Cuoco greatly, had been in circulation around Italy for some time. In particular, attention should be brought to the debate on the revolution fuelled by Giovan Leonardo Marugi's journal entitled *Analisi ragionata de' libri nuovi*, which had, for example, discussed the Venetian translation of Burke's *Reflections on the Revolution in France* and the latter's polemics with Paine ever since 1791. On the wide circulation of Burke's and Paine's works in Italy, see also R. Zapperi, 'BurkeinItalia,' *Cahiers Vilfredo Pareto*, VII–VIII, 1965, pp. 5–62 and above all M. Cuaz, '"Le nuove strepitose di Francia". L'immagine della Rivoluzione francese nella stampa periodica italiana,' *Rivista storica italiana*, C, 1988, pp. 457–527, and L. E. Funaro, '"Un governo avaro e mercantile". Tre edizioni italiane di un'opera di Tom Paine,' *Studi storici*, XXXI, 1990, pp. 481ff.

16 V. Cuoco, *Saggio storico*, p. 279.

17 See the debate on the issue in G. Nuzzo, *A Napoli nel tardo Settecento. La parabola della neutralità*, Naples 1980, pp. 12ff. For a return to the issues developed by Cuoco, see instead R. Ajello, 'I filosofi e la regina. Il governo delle Due Sicilie da Tanucci a Caracciolo (1776–1786),' *Rivista storica italiana*, CIII, 1991, pp. 398–454, and 657–738.

18 V. Cuoco, *Saggio storico*, p. 314.

19 Ibid., pp. 326–7.

20 Ibid., p. 334.

21 Ibid., p. 586.

22 Ibid., p. 383.

23 Ibid., p. 335.

24 Ibid., p. 340.

25 On the emergence of these concepts in those very years, see D. Venturino, 'La naissance de l' "Ancien Régime,"' in *The French Revolution and the Creation of Modern Political Culture*, pp. 11ff.

26 V. Cuoco, *Saggio storico*, p. 326. 'The Neapolitan nation,' Cuoco wrote, 'could be considered divided into two different nations, by two centuries of time, and by two degrees of climate. Since the cultivated part had formed itself on foreign models, so its culture was different from that needed by our nation, and which one could only hope for from the development of our faculties. A few had become French and English, and those who had remained Neapolitans were still savages. Thus, the culture of the few did not benefit the nation, and thus the rest of the nation almost despised a culture which was not useful to it and which it did not understand.'

27 The generational problem has been emphasized by G. Galasso, 'I giacobini meridionali,' in *Rivista storica italiana*, XCVI, 1984, pp. 69ff.

28 See F. Tessitore, 'Cuoco e Galanti,' in *Contributi alla storia e alla teoria dello storicismo*, vol. I, Rome, 1995, pp. 303–32. To understand the cultural universe in which Cuoco formed himself and, more generally, from where he might have drawn many of his verdicts on the 1799 revolution, one must read that extraordinary document which is the memoirs of G. M. Galanti, *Memorie storiche del mio tempo*, ed. A. Placanica, Cava de' Tirreni, 1996, with an astute introduction by the editor. In Galanti – but they were evidently commoplace in moderate Neapolitan circles – one finds, for example, the entire debate against the imperialist politics of the Directory and of France; against the republican system of an arbitrary division into Departments; against the system of 'democratization of the villages in the provinces'; against the arbitrary reform of municipalities, as well as an appreciation for moderate monarchies against the abstract constitutionalism of philosophers like Pagano. Having become an enemy of the revolution and of the 1799 Republic, Galanti contemptuously considered the latter a veritable 'republican possession' (see G. Solari, *Studi su Francesco Mario Pagano*, Turin 1963, p. 286).

29 Among the few works of importance, see *Il Gran Circolo Costituzionale e il 'Genio democratico' (Bologna, 1797–1798)*, ed. U. Marcelli, 3 vols, Bologna 1986 and the numerous references in R. De Felice, *Il triennio giacobino in Italia*, Rome 1990 and in L. Guerci, *Istruire*, pp. 74ff. On the Roman constitutional circles in which Filangieri constantly was recalled, see D. Cantimori, 'Vincenzio Russo,' *Annali della Scuola normale superiore di Pisa*, XI, 1942, p 179. See also the treasure-trove of information which is S. Pivano, *Albori costituzionali d'Italia (1736)*, Turin 1913.

30 See, on this, an eloquent article which appeared in a 1797 volume of the *Giornale de' patrioti d'Italia*, (*Giornale de' patrioti d'Italia*, ed. P. Zanoli, vol. III, Rome 1990, p. 318) in relation to the prestige of the Italian constitutional tradition at the time:, which wrote that 'In the French journal *La Sentinelle*, n. 892, one reads the following article. It is constantly said that Bonaparte has asked for legal publicists for Italy, but that they are no longer partial to going, because the Conquerer has abandoned the theatre of his glory. We do not believe that such a request has been made. It would be an injury to the new republics to believe that they are in need of our luminaries to form law. Has not Italy been fertile, in this era, with famous men of merit? The fatherland of Beccaria and of Filangieri has no need for foreign help.'

31 On the history of the second Cisalpine Republic, and in particular on its constitutional debate, see C. Zaghi, *L'Italia di Napoleone dalla Cisalpina al Regno*, Turin 1986, pp. 259ff.

32 Pagano's work had already appeared in two editions in Naples during the 1799 Republic, and two other editions appeared in Milan (among these the one edited by Valeriani) the following year at the precise encouragement of Neapolitan exiles, see G. Solari, *Studi*, p. 394.

33 F. Lomonaco, *Rapporto al cittadino Carnot*, p. 337.

34 The quotation is taken from the second edition which appeared in the *Vite degli eccellenti italiani composte per Francesco Lomonaco*, vol. II, Lugano 1836, p.154.

35 See the text in A. Saitta, *Alle origini del Risorgimento: i testi di un 'celebre' concorso (1796)*, 3 vols, Rome 1964, vol. III. In the *Titolo III. Dell'Eforato*, Reina wrote, with evident reference to Pagano's constitution, 'The Ephorate decides if the acts which are denounced by the Legislative body, by the Archonate, and by the censors are in keeping with the Constitution, and it overturns them, when they are contrary to it' (p. 418). A short note on the subject can be found in M. Battaglini, *Mario Pagano*, pp. 45–6, who documents the presence of Pagano's constitutional ideas in the project approved on 27 August 1800 by the *Consulta legislativa* willed by Napoleon for the Costitution of the second Cisalpine Republic.

36 Probably, the sixty-year-old Mario Pagano had not even met the young Cuoco, who had never written anything of significance before the *Saggio storico* apart from his marginal participation in the denunciation of Baccher's conspiracy against the Republic (but definitive evidence is lacking on this point too). Cuoco's affirmations, which presented the *Frammenti* as a precise response to Pagano, who supposedly sent him a copy of the Constitution through Vincenzio Russo to have his comments, is nothing but a rhetorical fiction which has now been amply recognized as such by scholars. Writing to Russo, he spoke directly to Pagano. By a theatrical act, Cuoco (then still an illustrious unknown among the many who animated the so-called low-brow literature of the Neapolitan Kingdom) thus proclaimed himself the privileged interlocutor of Italy's greatest constitutionalist. Similarly, one never puts enough emphasis on the fact that the contents of the Neapolitan constitution of 1799 became known in the nineteenth century primarily though the adulterated caricature proposed in the *Saggio storico*. On the very rare editions of the Constitution (the first to appear with a reasonable print-run, through with many imperfections, dates from 1820), see M. Battiglini, *Mario Pagano*, pp. 25ff.

37 V. Cuoco, *Saggio storico*, p. 529.

38 Ibid., p. 514. The fact that Cuoco shared the ideas of Le Paige with regards to the existence of material constitutions in the Old Regime which were to be compared to the modern, rigid, and written constitutions so dear to Enlightenment thinkers like Filangieri, is demonstrated by the fact that, on numerous occasions in the *Frammenti*, he explicitly spoke of 'our abolished constitution' (p. 556 and p. 574) and of the 'ancient constitution of the Kingdom of Naples' (p. 447). Elsewhere, finally, specifying his opinion against the modern constitutionalism of Enlightenment thinkers, he writes 'do you want proof of what I say? Take one of the many constitutions which men have made until now and show me a single one which our *philosophers* do not say is evil? Meanwhile the nations which had them were happy, and they have been happy and great precisely because of those constitutions which we blame so. I fear greatly that, wanting to create a constitution to the *philosophers'* liking, it will form the people's desolation' (p. 556).

39 Ibid., p. 516.

40 Ibid., p. 517.

41 Ibid., p. 518.

42 Cuoco accused Pagano of not realizing the singular specificity of the Southern Italian people: 'We speak of the constitution to be given to the lazy *lazzaroni* of Naples, to the *ferocious* Calabrians, the *light-headed* people of Lecce, the *spurious* Samnites, and other people of that kind.' An argument which is false,as can be seen simply by reading Pagano's celebrated pages in the first edition of the *Saggi politici* on the *Generale prospetto della storia del regno* where he affirms that Naples is a country with 'as much diversity of climate and of temperament as all the rest of Europe. An inhabitant of the mountains of the Abruzzo differs from an Apulian like a German from a Sicilian. Thus the prodigious variety of moral characters and the very

physiognomies of the kingdom's inhabitants' (I ed. *Saggi politici*, vol. V, p. 250). Even more false, finally, was Pagano's allegedly pro-French attitude. To corroborate the thesis that this was a common opinion among contemporaries, the verdict of Flaminio Massa, author of the *Elogio storico di Francesco Mario Pagano* (in *Saggi politici*, Milan 1800) was constantly quoted. In reality, a careful reading of that text brings to light a surprising fact: as the source of this verdict, Massa simply noted the opinion of his friend Cuoco (p. xxxi), a fact which alone is enough to confirm, if ever, the emergence of a powerful interpretative paradigm which still dominates Italian historiography today and which, regardless of all the studies made of the Enlightenment, continues uncritically to accept Cuoco's opinions without searching for possible confirmations in Pagano's works. Let us not forget that Pagano wrote a caustic and impertinent comedy in 1792, the *Emilia*, precisely to ridicule the modern followers of French fashions in the field of education, who suddenly seemed to dominate Neapolitan intellectual life after 1789. The truth is that Pagano's patriotism, through politically close to Filangieri's constitutional stance, owed much, above all in the 1790s, also to Genovesi's ideas on the multiple meanings of the word *patria*. In the *Saggi politici*, Pagano for example invoked 'a theatre, an institution of study, a national code'; 'if I only could inspire [my fellow citizens] with my enthusiasm for the glory of our nation, and for the arts and sciences, hereditary daughters of this favoured soil of nature. Generous fellow citizens, magnanimous Italians, think once of yourself and your native soil… remember that you are the descendants of the same people that dictated laws to the world and spread culture throughout the entire West… So, let us ensure that one cannot only say *we were*, but, on the contrary, *we still are*.' See the quotation, with an ample comment on Cuoco's falsification of this issue, in G. Solari, *Studi*, p. 160.

43 V. Cuoco, *Saggio storico*, p. 520.

44 On the revolutionary culture, see L. Hunt, *Politics, Culture, and Class in the French Revolution*, Berkeley 1984.

45 V. Cuoco, *Saggio storico*, p. 538.

46 Ibid., p. 522. On the first constitutional debates in France, see P. Pasquino, *Sieyés*.

47 V. Cuoco, *Saggio storico*, p. 521.

48 On this fundamental point for understanding the history of southern Italy, see. A. De Martino, *La nascita delle intendenze. Problemi dell'amministrazione periferica nel regno di Napoli 1806–1815*, Naples 1984, in particular pp. 20ff. which illustrate how the ideas of the *fin-de-siècle* Enlightenment reformers were re-launched during the Napoleonic period. c See also (ibid., pp. i–xvii) the precious reconstruction of the debate and eighteenth-century contributions to it in R. Ajello, *Presentazione. Il governo delle provincie: un problema costituzionale*, which explains the logic behind the centuries-old Neapolitan government founded on the 'discordant accord between the *togati* in the capital and the fuedal lords of the provinces,' and the Enlightenment's views on it. On the same theme, see M. G. Maiorini's studies of Tanucci's failed attempts to regain control of the provinces in M. G. Maiorini, 'Tanucci e il problema della riforma amministrativa durante la reggenza,' in *Bernardo Tanucci. Statista letterato giurista*, ed. R. Ajello and M. d'Addio, 2 vols., Naples 1986, pp. 204–36.

49 V. Cuoco, *Saggio storico*, p. 522.

50 Ibid., pp. 531–2. In 1806, in occasion of the publication of the second edition of the *Saggio storico*, and of the consolidation of the Napoleonic regime, Cuoco yet again gave an efficient lesson in *political realism*, one could say, to those unfortunate philosophers like Mario Pagano who conceived of politics as the unwavering moral adhesion to principles, by repeatedly changing ideas in favour of a strengthening of the executive with respect to the legislative and of the central power incarnated in the Neapolitan prefects with respect to the peripheral notables. The quotation in the text above is, in fact, purposefully integrated by an opportune reference to the fact that the 'government must see everything, direct everything,' p. 532.

51 I am not convinced by the analytic approach and the conclusions arrived at by the recent work of A. De Francesco (*Il Saggio storico e la cultura politica italiana*). Erroneously considering Cuoco 'fully inserted in the only frame of reference of the political culture of the French Revolution' (p. 154),

De Francesco examines his pro-municipal constitutional theories in light of a presumed interest in a Parisian political campaign to 'subtract the work of Rousseau and Mably from the field of egalitarianism to bring it instead into a field in which they could found the new post-Robespierrian order.' In light of this approach, which yet again is obsessively dependent on the French Revolution and not on the real dynamics of the Italian historical context, Pagano becames a follower of the Thermidor, and Cuoco, instead, a Jacobin. 'Cuoco, in brief,' De Francesco writes, 'contested Pagano's constitutional project, which seemed to him to focus on an elective assembly composed only of members of the property-owning elite, from a rigorously Jacobin position' (p. 126). De Francesco insists on the allegedly more democratic suffrage mechanisms suggested by Cuoco, though these were always rigorously property-dependent. I share the punctilious critique of De Francesco's analysis developed in P. Villani, *Introduzione*, pp. 26ff. As Cuoco himself admitted, neither of the two constitutional proposals were to be considered entirely democratic, since they only privileged one part of the population: property owners.

52 V. Cuoco, *Saggio storico*, p. 546.

53 Ibid., pp. 553–4.

54 Ibid., p. 546.

55 Ibid., p. 578.

56 Ibid., p. 547.

57 Ibid., p. 565.

58 Ibid., p. 566.

59 Ibid., p. 567.

60 Ibid., pp. 568–9. Confirming his support for Old Regime constitutionalism, it is worth again underlining Cuoco's expression 'in our abolished constitution.'

61 See, for example, R. Koselleck, *La Prussia tra riforma e rivoluzione (1791–1848)*, Bologna 1988, pp. 30ff.

62 V. Cuoco, *Platone in Italia*, vol. I, Milan 1806, p. 106.

63 Ibid., p. 223.

64 Ibid., p. 162. A recent analysis of Cuoco's novel can be found in P. Casini, *L'antica sapienza italica. Cronistoria di un mito*, Bologna, 1998.

65 *Saggio storico*, p. 259. See, in the context of the definition of an Italian political tradition, Cuoco's important articles in the *Giornale Italiano*, and particularly his writings dedicated to Machiavelli (V. Cuoco, *Scritti vari*, pp. 313ff.) and his reflections in the 1804 'Scrittori politici italiani,' which appeared in the same journal. After having sung the hymns of Machiavelli, Gravina, and Vico, he brushed aside the thinkers of the Enlightenment, affirming that 'I will not speak of Filangieri, nor Beccaria, nor Pagano, nor the many others who in some way have cultivated the science of legislation, for there would be an infinite number of them' (ibid., p. 124).

66 V. Cuoco, *Saggio storico*, p. 590.

10. The Liberal Constant against the Enlightened Filangieri: Two Interpretations of Modernity

1 As we have seen, the first French edition of these seven volumes had been published by Cuchet in 1786–1791; the second '*revue et corrigée*' was published by Dufart in 1798, again in seven volumes with a new and significant preface by the translator J. A. Gauvin Gallois. The third edition, again published by Dufart with the title *Œuvres de G. Filangieri traduites de l'italien. Nouvelle édition accompagnée d'un commentaire par M. Benjamin Constant et de l'éloge de Filangieri par M. Salfi*, Paris 1822–1824, consisted of six volumes. The *Commentaire* appeared in two volumes, the first in 1822 and the second in 1824.

2 See E. Passerin d'Entrèves, 'Gaetano Filangieri e Benjamin Constant,' *Humanitas*, VII, 1952, pp. 1110–22; L. Neppi Modona, 'Quelques réflexions sur le Commentaire de B. Constant,' in *Benjamin Constant. Actes du Congrès de Lausanne*, Geneva 1968, pp. 57–63; P. Bastid, *Benjamin*

Constant et sa doctrine, Paris 1966, pp. 367ff. The most precise work on the subject nonetheless remains P. Cordey, 'Benjamin Constant, Gaetano Filangieri et la "Science de la législation,"' *Revue européenne des sciences sociales*, XVIII, 1980, pp. 55–79. See also G. Galasso, 'Filangieri tra Montesquieu e Constant,' in *La filosofia in soccorso de' governi. La cultura napoletana del Settecento*, Naples 1989, pp. 453ff.

3 See M. Gauchet, *Préface* to B. Constant, *Écrits politiques*, Paris 1997, pp. 71ff. See also M. Barberis, *Benjamin Constant. Rivoluzione, costituzione, progresso*, Bologna 1988, pp. 290–300.

4 See the letters, conserved in Naples (AMF ms. 28, f. 30), of two French literati that have not been properly identified, Lafisse and Orgie, who began negotiations to produce a French translation. Gallois' letters between 1784 and 1787 (AMF ms. 28, ff. 19ff.) are extremely interesting. Not only did he produce the translation, but he circulated the work among *plusieurs magistrats et gens des lettres*' in Paris, accurately referring the enthusiastic reactions to Filangieri.

5 See L. Amiable, *Une loge maçonnique d'avant 1789. La loge des neuf sœurs*, Paris 1989, pp. 205ff.; L. Amiable, *La Franc-Maçonnerie et la Magistrature en France à la veille de la Rèvolution*, Aix 1894.

6 See A. Wattinne, *L'affaire des trois roués: études sur la justice criminelle à la fin de l'Ancien Regime*, Macon 1921; and above all W. Doyle, 'Dupaty (1746–1788): A career in the late Enlightenment,' *Studies on Voltaire*, CCXXX, 1985, pp.102ff. On the importance of the *Mémoires judiciaires* in the political struggle at the end of the century, see S. Maza, *Private Lives and Public Affairs. The Causes Célèbres of prerevolutionary France*, Berkeley 1993.

7 In L. Amiable, *Un loge maçonnique*, p. 56.

8 See in particular the letter of 18 October 1785, which recounted the details of the encounter and listed the books which had appeared in France on the argument; AMF, ms. 28, ff. 20ff.

9 M. Pagano, *Considerations sur la procedure criminelle*, Paris, 1789, p. lxix: 'La science des lois va devenir l'affaire de tous… C'est dans l'Italie que nous trouvons depuis longtemps les exemples qu'il faut suivre pour la régénération des lois judiciarires.' On the importance of the Italian jurists, and in particular of Filangieri, in late eighteenth-century France, see also D. Roche, *France in the Enlightenment*, Cambridge, MA 1998, p. 316.

10 See, on him, A. Guillois, *Le salon de madame Helvétius Cabanis et les idéologues*, Paris 1984, pp. 3ff.

11 See F. Venturi, 'Gaetano Filangieri. Nota introduttiva,' in *Illuministi italiani*, vol. V, *Riformatori napoletani*, Milan-Naples 1962, p. 647.

12 [C.-M. Mercier Dupaty], *Lettres sur l'Italie en 1785*, Paris 1792, pp. 403ff. Acton's report is quoted in G. Ruggiero, 'Gaetano Filangieri e l'ordinanza sulle milizie provinciali del 1782,' *Frontiere d'Europa*, II, 1999, p. 191.

13 See *De lois pénales*, 2 vols, Paris 1790, vol. I, p. 7. See Pastoret's very interesting use of Filangieri against Mably on the issue of the death penalty. Pastoret's letters to Filangieri between 1787 and 1788 are full of information regarding French penal reforms; AMF, ms. 28, ff. 2ff.

14 On Pastoret's decisive role in the reform of criminal law during the revolutionary period, see E. Saliman, *La justice en France pendant la Révolution 1789–1792*, Paris 1913, pp. 114ff.

15 Still, on the 26 Fructidor of the year VI (12 August 1798), the *Moniteur* signalled that the interior minister of the Republic considered the *Scienza della legislazione* '*comme indispensable à tous ceux qui se vouent à la législation*,' see F. Venturi, 'L'Italia fuori d'Italia,' in *Storia d'Italia*, vol. III, Turin 1973, p. 1100.

16 See A. Simioni, *Le origini del Risorgimento politico dell'Italia meridionale*, vol. I, Naples 1995, p. 361.

17 See G. Ruggiero, *Gaetano Filangieri. Un uomo, una famiglia, un amore nella Napoli del Settecento*, Naples 1999, p. 409.

18 Valuable information on Salfi and his political activities can be found in M. A. Renzi, *Vie politique et littéraire de F. Salfi*, Paris 1834; C. Nardi, *La vita e le opere di Francesco Saverio Salfi (1759–1832)*, Genoa 1925; *Francesco Saverio Salfi, un calabrese per l'Europa*, ed. A. De Lisio, Naples 1981; and the recent work by G. Tocchini, 'Dall'Antico Regime alla Cisalpina. Morale e politica nel teatro per musica di F. S. Salfi,' in *Salfi librettista*, ed. F. P. Russo, Vibo Valentia 2001.

19 Two editions appeared in Spain. The first was published under the title the *Ciencia de la legislation. Obra scrita en italiano por el cabalero Cayetano Filangieri. Nuovamente traducida por Don Juan Ribera*,

Madrid 1821–1822, 6 vols. The second was translated by Jaime Rubio and also appeared in Madrid, 1822, 10 vols. On these editions, as well as on the preceding ones of 1787 and 1815, much remains to be written, particularly in terms of their relation to politically subversive currents in contempoary Europe, which were dominated by secret societies like the *Carboneria* and the Masons. For a first overview, see F. G. Ayuda, 'La scienza della legislazione en el nacimiento del liberalismo espagñol,' in *Gaetano Filangieri e l'illuminismo europeo*, ed. L D'Alessandro, Naples 1991, pp. 375ff; J. L. Abadìa, 'El echo de Gaetano Filangieri en España,' ibid., pp. 453ff; S. Scotellari, 'Alcune note sull'influenza di Filangieri nella codificazione penale spagnola del 1822,' ibid., pp. 519ff. Interesting notes on the Spanish translations can also be found in J. Astigarraga, 'Victorián de Villava traduttor de Gaetano Filangieri,' *Cuadernos aragoneses de economia*, 1997, vol. 7, pp. 171–86. In Italy, the new season of editions began with that published by Silvestri in Milan, in 6 volumes between 1817 and 1818, followed by another edition published by the Freemasons of Leghorn (Filadelfia, Nella Stamperia della Provincie Unite, 1819, 5 vols), and then by another Milanese edition of 1822. In Florence, it was published by Niccolò Conti in 5 volumes in 1820–1821, immediately followed by a Venetian edition, published a year later, which contained Ginguené's eulogy of Filangieri.

20 See F. S. Salfi, 'Éloge de Filangieri' in *Œuvres de G. Filangieri*, p. xx.

21 Ibid., p. xxxii.

22 Ibid., p. xci. Salfi did not lie with regards to the strong Enlightenment component, directly inspired by the works of Pagano and of Filangieri, in the ranks of the *Carboneria* and of the democratic and republican secret societies in Southern Italy, see G. Berti, *I democratici*, pp. 154ff.

23 Ibid., p. cxxvii.

24 Ibid., p. xcii.

25 On this re-edition by Angelo Lanzellotti, see M. Battaglini, *Mario Pagano il progetto di costituzione della repubblica napoletana*, Rome 1994, pp. 26ff. Lanzellotti is listed among the members of the *Carbonari* in G. Berti, *I democratici*, p. 181.

26 On these themes, see the dated but always interested A. Omodeo, *Studi sull'età della Restaurazione*, Turin 1970, pp. 62ff.

27 F. S. Salfi, *Élogede Filangieri*, p. xcii. It must be noted that Constant, in addition to having collaborated with the Neapolitan King Murat, agreeing with his initiatives in favour of a monarchical constitutionalism, was no fan of the *carbonara* and republican nature of the 1821 Italian revolutionary mobvement. 'Tout est terminé. Il valait mieux ne pas commencer,' he wrote in a letter of April 1821, adding that 'les napolitaines se sont conduits avec une lâcheté insigne… L'on obtient des nations que ce pour quoi elles sont mûres' (see P. Cordey, Benjamin Constant, p. 76).

28 On the constitutional texts and the origins of liberal thought in France, see P. Rosanvallon, *La Monarchie impossible. Les Chartes de 1814 et de 1830*, Paris 1994; L. Jaume, *L'individu effacé ou le paradoxe du libéralisme française*, Paris 1997. A good analysis of the rich literature on Constant can be found in S. de Luca, *Il pensiero politico di Constant*, Bari-Rome 1993.

29 See M. Barberis, *Bejamin Constant*, pp. 195ff.

30 See B. Constant, *Corso di politica costituzionale*, 1st Italian ed., Naples 1848, pp. 43ff.

31 On Constant's *modus operandi* see M. Barberis, *Benjamin Constant*, pp. 261ff.

32 See B. Constant, *Comento [sic] sulla scienza della legislazione di G. Filangieri*, Italy 1828, p. 8. Successive references will say *Commento*. The first Italian edition of this book had been published in Leghorn two years earlier with this title, see *Commentario alla scienza della legislazione di G. Filangieri*, Italy 1826.

33 On the critical reflection, begun by the group which gathered in the castle at Coppet, against the '*utopiens*' and the '*politiques moralistes*,' as Madame de Staël called them, see J. Roussel, 'L'ambiguité des Lumières à Coppet,' in *Le groupe de Coppet. Actes du 2ᵉ colloque de Coppet*, Geneva 1977, pp. 171–84.

34 B. Consant, *Commento*, pp. 15–16.

35 In his 'manuscripts de 1810' of the *Principes de politiques*, Constant still wrote of Filangieri with great admiration: 'J'ai beaucoup cité dans mon ouvrage et principalement des auteurs

vivents ou morts depuis peu d'année, ou des hommes dont le nom seul fait autorité, comme Adam Smith, Montesquieu, Filangieri' (see P. Thompson, *La religion de Bejamin Constant*, Pisa 1978, p. 576). Constant had probably begun reading and annotating Filangieri with great interest already in 1795–6, to then return to the Italian philospher later at Goethe's suggestion, P. Cordey, *Benjamin Constant*, p. 69.

36 B. Constant, *Commento*, p. 28.

37 Ibid., p. 29.

38 Ibid., p. 6.

39 Ibid., p. 7.

40 On Constant's profound extraneousness to the concept of constitutional justice and the method of legal contraposition of rights to sovereignty, see M. Fioravanti, *Costituzione*, Bologna 1999, pp. 126–7 and M. Barberis, 'Divisione dei poteri e libertà da Montesquieu a Constant,' *Materiali per una storia della cultura giuridica*, XXXI, 2001, p. 105. The question would perhaps merit reconsideration in light of this confrontation with Filangieri's system to better understand the reasons for his rejection.

41 B. Constant, *Commento*, p. 33.

42 Ibid., pp. 51–2.

43 B. Constant, *Commento*, pp. 49–50.

44 The long reach of this disconcerting interpretation of Filangieri's work can be found even in O. Gierke, *Johannes Althusius und die Entwicklung der naturrechtlichen Staatstheorien. Zugleich ein Beitrag zur Geschichte der Rechtssystematik*, Breslau 1880.

45 B. Constant, *Commento*, p. 50.

46 See ibid., p. 12. 'We have arrived at the era of commerce,' Constant wrote, 'the era which must *necessarily* suceed that of war.'

47 B. Constant, 'Della libertà degli antichi paragonata ai moderni,' in *Principi di politica*, ed. U. Cerroni, Rome 1970, pp. 226–7. Another text repeatedly quoted in the *Commentaire* was the 1814 *De l'esprit de conquête et de l'usurpation*.

48 Constant actually had some doubts, but the direct polemic with the Enlightenment was too important to indulge in subtleties. He specified this with reference to Filangieri: 'I see well, through the vagueness of his phrases, that he is no more eager than I am to transform the moderns into Athenians, and even less to change them into Spartans, but nonetheless falls into the grave error of considering the customs of people as derivates of the will of the legislators' (B. Constant, *Commento*, p. 380). On these issues see G. Cambiano, *Polis. Un modello per la cultura europea*, Rome-Bari 2000, p. 122, from whom one learns that, ever since the sixteenth century, many held that real political liberty consisted in having guarantees protecting life and property, not in participating in political life.

49 On these issues, mandatory reference should be made to the classic I. Berlin, *Four Essays on Liberty*, Oxford 1969, which takes a contemporary look at that ancient diatribe, exploring the concepts of negative and positive liberty. There is, however, no reference to Constant's polemic with the thinkers of the Enlightenment in that work. Today, such themes are of central interest to scholars. See, for example, Q. Skinner, 'A Third Concept of Liberty,' *London Review of Books*, 4 April 2002, pp. 16ff.

50 B. Constant, *Commento*, p. 380.

51 Ibid., p. 403.

52 Ibid., p. 391–2.

53 On these issues see V. Ferrone, *I profeti dell'Illuminismo. Le metamorfosi della ragione nel tardo Settecento italiano*, Rome-Bari 2000, pp. 279ff.

54 Ibid., p. 343.

55 Ibid., p. 371.

56 Ibid., p. 116.

57 Ibid., p. 5.

58 Ibid., p. 309.

59 Ibid., p. 272.

60 Ibid., p. 262.

61 B. Constant, *Principi di politica*, p. 60.

11. Filangierian Heresies in the European Democratic Tradition: The Principle of Justice and the Right to Happiness

1   See F. Venturi, 'Gaetano Filangieri. Nota introduttiva,' in *Illuministi italiani*, vol. V, *Riformatori napoletani*, Milan-Naples 1962, p. 643. As Venturi has documented, the fourth volume of the *Scienza della legislazione* was translated and published in St. Petersburg in 1803, and republished in 1807, attracting great interest in revolutionary circles.

2   Cf. J. Lalinde, 'El echo de Filangieri en España,' *Anuario de historia del derecho español*, LIV, 1984, pp. 477–522.

3   Cf. G. Berti, *I democratici e l'iniziativa meridionale nel Risorgimento*, Milan 1962, pp. 392–8.

4   J. Godechot, *Histoire de l'Italie moderne. Le Risorgimento*, Paris 1971, p. 360.

5   P. Cordey, 'Benjamin Constant, Gaetano Filangieri et "la Science de la législation,"' *Revue européenne des sciences sociales*, XVIII, 1980, pp. 76–7, and above all E. Passerin d'Entreves, 'Gaetano Filangierie Benjamin Constant,' *Humanitas*, VII, 1952, pp. 1113ff, who underlines Manzoni's, Rosmini's, and Tommaseo's interest in the *Commentaire* and thus, by reflection, in Filangieri and the Neapolitan Shool of natural law.

6   Cf. J. C. Chiaramonte, 'Gli illuministi napoletani nel Rio de la Plata,' *Rivistastoricaitaliana*, LXXVI, 1964, pp. 114ff.

7   See on this the classic E. P. Thompson, *The Making of the English Working Class*, New York 1966; K. Polanyi, *The Great Transformation: The Political and Economic Origins of Our Time*, Boston 2001.

8   B. Constant, *Commento sulla scienza della legislazione di G. Filangieri*, Italy 1828, p. 158.

9   Ibid., p. 103.

10 Ibid., p. 175.

11 Ibid., p. 180.

12 Ibid., p.189.

13 Ibid., p. 202.

14 Ibid., p. 206.

15 See, on these themes, J. Pocock, *Virtue, Commerce and History*, Cambridge 1985; I. Kramnick, *Bolingbroke and His Circle. The Politics of Nostalgia in the Age of Walpole*, Ithaca-London 1968.

16 On this theme, see the still valuable L. Rothkrug, *Opposition to Louis XIV. The Political and Social Origins of French Enlightenment*, Princeton 1965, pp. 10–85.

17 See, on this, J. Israel, *Radical Enlightenment. Philosophy and the Making of Modernity 1650–1750*, Oxford, 2001.

18 See, on the entire debate, V. Ferrone, *Scienza natura religione. Mondo newtoniano e cultura italiano nel primo Settecento*, Naples 1982, pp. 590ff.

19 P. M. Doria, *Narrazione di un libro inedito*, Naples 1745, p. 57.

20 P. M. Doria, 'Del commercio del Regno di Napoli,' in *Manoscritti napoletani di Paolo Mattia Doria*, ed. G. Belgioioso, Galatina 1981, I, p. 148. To evaluate the scholastic component in the economic thought of Doria and Broggia fully, the work of B. Clavero, *La grâce du don. Anthropologie catholique de l'économie moderne*. Paris 1996, is valuable.

21 F. Galiani, *Opere*, ed. F. Diaz and L. Guerci, Milan-Naples 1975, p. 59.

22 On these themes, the work of F. Venturi, *Settecento riformatore*, 7 vols, Turin 1969–1990, vol. I, *Da Muratori a Beccaria*, pp. 514ff., remains fundamental.

23 See A. Genovesi, *Scritti economici*, ed. M. L. Perna, Naples 1984. Acute reflections on these problems can be found in J. Robertson, 'The Enlightenment above National Context: Political Economy in Eighteenth-Century Scotland and Naples,' *The Historical Journal*, XL, 1997, pp. 667–97.

24 On these issues, which attracted Genovesi's attention, one must refer to the great book by J. O. Appleby, *Economic Thought and Ideology in Seventeenth-Century England*, Princeton 1978.

25 A. Genovesi, *Delle lezioni di commercio*, 2 vols, Naples 1765, vol. I, pp. 269–70.

26 See A. O. Hirschman, *The Passiones and the Interests: Political Arguments for Capitalism before Its Triumph*, Princeton 1977.

27 Ibid., p. 62. It is no coincidence that Melon's book was republished in 1778 in Naples, and bitterly criticized for its liberalist arguments by Longano, another student of Genovesi's. See V. Ferrone, 'La fondazione panteistica dell'eguaglianza. Contributo al pensiero politico di Francesco Longano,' *Rassegna iberistica*, LVI, 1996, pp. 193–202.

28 On Verri's economic thought, see the important book by C. Capra, *I progressi della ragione. Vita di Pietro Verri*, Bologna 2002, and particularly chapter VIII, *Dall'economia politica all'economia morale*.

29 The political importance of this theme in the eighteenth century is explained well by E. P. Thompson, *Whigs and Hunters. The Origins of the Black Act*, New York 1975.

30 See J. Revel, 'Les corps et communautés,' in *The Political Culture of the Old Regime*, 4 vols, Oxford-New York, 1987–94, vol. I, pp. 225–42. For the Italian debate see F. Venturi, 'Il concorso veronese sulle corporazioni (1789–1792),' *Rivista storica italiana*, C, 1988, pp. 528ff.

31 These were decisive years also for the birth of the modern rights of authors. See on this E. Di Rienzo, *Il principe il mercante le lettere*, Rome 1979, pp. 80ff. Still to this day, we lack a legal reconstruction of the foundations of this right as both a right to intellectual property and a subjective right of liberty.

32 On pauperism see L. Guerci, *L'Europa del Settecento. Permanenze e mutamenti*, Turin 1988, pp. 117ff.

33 See, on this, the fundamental D. Roche, *Il popolo di Parigi. Cultura popolare e civiltà materiale alla vigilia della Rivoluzione*, Bologna 1986.

34 See the quotation and an ample analysis of the eighteenth-century debate on the differences between the economies of the ancients and the moderns, for which the issue of labour had become a point of reference, in G. Cambiano, *Polis. Un modello per la cultura europea*, Rome-Bari 2000, pp. 339ff.

35 In G. Zagrebelsky, *Il diritto mite. Legge diritti giustizia*, Turin 1992, p. 101. The author rightly underlines that 'contrary to current opinion, the primacy in proclaiming labour a right is neither Christian nor socialist, but belongs to the Enlightenment.' It must still be specified, as we will see more clearly later on, that Turgot considered it a subjective right of individual liberty, to be guaranteed by dismantling the limitations to the exercise of the right to ownership of one's own labour established by the corporations, and not as a social right as we would say today.

36 See, on this, the monumental overview by R. Mauzi, *L'idée du bonheur dans la littérature et la pensée françaises au XVIII siècle*, Paris 1994, and the recent contribution by P. Roger, 'Felicità,' in *L'Illuminismo. Dizionario storico*, ed. V. Ferrone and D. Roche, Rome-Bari 1998, pp. 40ff.

37 See P. Verri, *Discorsi sull'indole del piacere e del dolore, sulla felicità e sulla economia politica*, Milan 1781, pp. 146ff.

38 See P. Maier, *American Scripture. Making the Declaration of Independence*, New York 1997, pp. 270; as well as W. B. Scott, *In Pursuit of Happiness: American Conceptions of Property from the Seventeenth to the Twentieth Century*, Bloomington 1977; and C. Redenius, *The American Ideal of Equality. From Jefferson's Declaration to Burger Court*, London 1981, pp. 13ff.

39 On the linguistic and legal levels, Filangieri used the expression '*social rights*' differently from us. We prefer, in the wake of Constant, to neatly distinguish between first-generation rights of liberty and second-generation social rights which need to be safeguarded by the state. In the *Scienza della legislazione*, all rights connected to citizenship were social: 'As a man,' Filangieri specified, 'I have certain rights, as a citizen I have others. Society assures my enjoyment of the former and gives me the latter. Both become social rights when society gives them or defends them' [II, 211].

40 Carlo Pisacane, for example, who loved these passages of Filangieri deeply, did so. See G. Berti, *I democratici*, p. 396. Filangieri's denunciation of the concentration of landed property always remained pertinent. See M. Grillo, *L'isola al bivio. Cultura e politica nella Sicilia borbonica (1820–1840)*, Catania 2000, p. 52.

41 See on this, T. Jefferson, *Political Writings*, ed. J. Appleby and T. Ball, Cambridge 1999, p. 323, and particularly the project of T. Paine, 'Agrarian Justice, Opposed to Agrarian Law and the Agrarian Monopoly. Being a Plan for Meliorating the Condition of Man, etc.,' in *The Rights of Man, Common Sense and Other Political Writings*, Oxford-New York 1998, pp. 416ff.

42 The fundamental work on this remains the great F. Venturi, *Settecento riformatore* vol. I *Da Muratori a Beccaria*.

43 See F. M. Pagano, 'Discorso recitato nella società di agricoltura arti e commercio di Roma,' in *Opere filosofiche-politiche ed estetiche*, vol. I, Capolago (Canton Ticino) 1873, pp. 576ff.

44 On the division of labour in the late Neapolitan Enlightenment, see. V. Ferrone, *I profeti dell'Illuminismo. Le metamorfosi della ragione nel tardo Settecento italiano*, Rome-Bari 2000, pp. 339ff.

45 F. M. Pagano, 'Progetto di costituzionedella Repubblica napoletana presentato al governo provvisorio dal Comitato di legislazione,' in M. Battaglini, *Mario Pagano e il progetto di costituzione della repubblica napoletana*, Rome 1994, p. xviii.

46 See C. Duprat, *'Pour l'amour de l'humanité': le temps des philantropes. La philantropie parisienne des Lumières à la monarchie de Juillet*, Paris 1993.

47 In P. Rosanvallon, *L'État en France de 1783 a nos jours*, Paris 1999; on these issues see also P. Rosanvallon, *Le capitalisme utopique. Critique de l'idéologie économique*, Paris 1979.

48 See the important collection of texts *Il diritto al lavoro. Un grande dibattito parlamentare nella Francia del 1848*, ed. G. Longhitano, Catania 2001, p. lxv.

49 Ibid., p. lxxii.

50 Ibid., p. 62.

51 Ibid., p. 81.

52 See the salient points of the Marxian requisitory in F. Engels and K. Marx, *La sacra famiglia, ovvero critica della critica critica contro Bruno Bauer e soci*, Rome 1986, pp. 105ff. More generally on Marx and the Enlightenment see V. Ferrone and D. Roche, *L'Illuminismo nella cultura contemporanea. Storia e storiografia*, Rome-Bari 2002, pp. 540ff.

53 On how the right to property was conceived by thinkers of the Italian Enlightenment, see A. Trampus, 'l'Illuminismo e la "nuova politica" nel tardo Settecento italiano: "L'uomo libero" di Gianrinaldo Carli,' *Rivista storica italiana*, CVI, 1994, pp. 42–114.

54 On the subject of *aequitas* in the doctrines of the glossators and then in those of the canonists, as far as to its egalitarian denunciation by Enlightenment thinkers, who clearly highlighted the political nature of the different way of understanding the word equity in the different eras, see the beautiful pages by V. Piano Mortari, *Dogmatica e interpretazione. I giuristi medievali*, Naples 1976, pp. 352ff. See also A. M. Hespanha, *Introduzione alla storia del diritto europeo*, Bologna 1999, pp. 80ff, who rightly underlines how 'classical Roman equity, inspired by Aristotelian or Stoic philosophy, was not that of Christianized rights, post-classical medieval or modern, nor that of the individualist and lay right of our days.' Actually, the theme of the political nature of fairness was well known in the Neapolitan legal culture, see G. Giarrizzo, 'Aequitas e prudentia. Storia di un topos vichiano,' in *Vico e la politica e la storia*, Naples 1981, pp. 145ff.

55 G. Filangieri, *Riflessioni politiche su l'ultima legge del sovrano che riguarda la riforma dell'amministrazione della giustizia*, Naples 1982, p. 32. On the subject of justice as fairness, formulated in important sectors of eighteenth-century natural law, and revisited in modern liberal and democratic analytical philosophy, see J. Rawls, *A Theory of Justice*, Cambridge, MA 1971; J. Rawls, *La giustizia come equità. Saggi 1951–1969*, Naples 1995. One must anyway underline that in Rawls' works, *fairness* has no connection to the historical nature of the concept developed by European jurists, but refers primarily to the original position of parties in a contract, who together develop rational ideas of justice from a fair initial condition.

56 In deciding on the title of his course in ethics at the University of Naples, Genovesi had invented the neologism *Diceosina* inspired by the Greek word διχαιοσύνη, meaning justice.

57 A. Genovesi, *Della Diceosina o sia della filosofia del giusto e dell'onesto*, ed. F. Arata, Milan 1973, p. 374.

58 Ibid., p. 141. In general terms, specific historical works on the theoretical foundations of social rights in the eighteenth and nineteenth centuries are lacking. See nonetheless, on the history of Catholic natural law, the great book by E. Troeltsch, *Die Soziallehren der christlichen Kirchen und Gruppen*, Tübingen, 1912. Brief historical references can also be found in G. Gurvith, *La dichiarazione dei diritti sociali*, Milan 1949, pp. 60ff, who considered the problem of social rights, not from the point of view of the individual, like the thinkers of the Enlightenment did, but from the concept of society as an organic and autonomous entity imbued with its own rights.

59 C. Beccaria, 'Dei delitti e delle pene,' ed. G. Francioni, in *Opere*, national edition directed by Luigi Firpo, vol. I, p. 32. The editor's rich annotations with regards to Beccaria's sources for defining justice are particularly interesting. See also, more generally on the different theories of justice in history, and with a highly critical take on natural law, H. Kelsen, *Das Problem der Gerechtigkeit*, appendix to *Reine Rechtslehre*, Vienna 1960.

60 See, on this, the different theoretical frame of reference delineated by M. Pagano in his posthumously published 'Principi di diritto penale,' in *Biblioteca scelta del foro criminale italiano*, Milan 1858, pp. 401ff. On these differences, which have been ignored for too long by Italian historians, see *Storia del diritto penale italiano da Cesare Beccaria ai nostri giorni*, Florence 1974, pp. 47ff. See also S. Armellini, 'Le due anime dell'Illuminismo giuridico e politico italiano,' *Rivista Internazionale di Filosofia del Diritto*, LV, 1978, pp. 253–93. In the *Saggi politici*, II ed., pp. 18ff., Pagano insisted on the fact that the idea of justice was innate in man: 'nature calls on justice every hour… Force forms states, force often changes them, but only justice preserves them… Even a society of thieves (Plato says) cannot preserve itself without a shadow of justice.' The same savages who seem not to know the idea through reason, nonetheless have a clear 'sentiment' of it.

INDEX